Witnessing Stalin's Justice

Witnessing Stalin's Justice

The United States and the Moscow Show Trials

Kelly J. Evans and Jeanie M. Welch

BLOOMSBURY ACADEMIC
LONDON • NEW YORK • OXFORD • NEW DELHI • SYDNEY

BLOOMSBURY ACADEMIC
Bloomsbury Publishing Plc
50 Bedford Square, London, WC1B 3DP, UK
1385 Broadway, New York, NY 10018, USA
29 Earlsfort Terrace, Dublin 2, Ireland

BLOOMSBURY, BLOOMSBURY ACADEMIC and the Diana logo are trademarks of
Bloomsbury Publishing Plc

First published in Great Britain 2023
This paperback edition published in 2025

Copyright © Kelly J. Evans and Jeanie M. Welch, 2023

Kelly J. Evans and Jeanie M. Welch have asserted their right under the Copyright, Designs and Patents Act, 1988, to be identified as Authors of this work.

For legal purposes the Acknowledgments on p. x constitute an extension of this copyright page.

Cover image © The Trial of the Twenty-One, Moscow, USSR, 1938.
Heritage Image Partnership Ltd / Alamy Stock Photo

All rights reserved. No part of this publication may be reproduced or transmitted in any form or by any means, electronic or mechanical, including photocopying, recording, or any information storage or retrieval system, without prior permission in writing from the publishers.

Bloomsbury Publishing Plc does not have any control over, or responsibility for, any third-party websites referred to or in this book. All internet addresses given in this book were correct at the time of going to press. The author and publisher regret any inconvenience caused if addresses have changed or sites have ceased to exist, but can accept no responsibility for any such changes.

A catalogue record for this book is available from the British Library.

A catalog record for this book is available from the Library of Congress.

ISBN: HB: 978-1-3503-3818-0
PB: 978-1-3503-3831-9
ePDF: 978-1-3503-3819-7
eBook: 978-1-3503-3820-3

Typeset by Deanta Global Publishing Services, Chennai, India

To find out more about our authors and books visit www.bloomsbury.com and sign up for our newsletters.

To our mothers

Contents

List of Plates	viii
Preface and Acknowledgments	x
Timeline of Events	xi
Introduction	1
1 The United States and the Soviet Union (1917–33)	7
2 Prelude to the Moscow Show Trials (1917–35)	21
3 The First Moscow Show Trial: The Case of the Trotskyite-Zinovievite Terrorist Centre (1936)	35
4 The Second Moscow Show Trial: The Case of the Anti-Soviet Trotskyite Centre (1937)	49
5 Other American Reactions to the Second Trial (1937)	69
6 The Army Trial: The Case of the Trotskyist Anti-Soviet Military Organization (1937), the Navy Purges (1937–8), and the Anti-Foreigner Campaign (1937–8)	83
7 The Third Moscow Show Trial: The Bloc of Rightists and Trotskyites (1938) and The Moscow Trials: A Statement by American Progressives (1938)	109
8 The Aftermath of the Moscow Show Trials: Part I—1939–55	131
9 The Aftermath of the Moscow Show Trials: Part II—1956 to the Present	149
Notes	185
Selected Bibliography	258
Index	263

Plates

1.1 Anti-Bolshevik advertisement, *Birmingham (AL) Age-Herald*, November 23, 1919   6

Chapter 2   20
2.1 Vladimir Lenin, the first Bolshevik head of state
2.2 Joseph Stalin. "Stalin before 1929"
2.3 Leon Trotsky in exile
2.4 Sergei Kirov, assassinated leader of the Leningrad Communist Party

Chapter 3   34
3.1 Lev Kamenev, defendant in the first Moscow show trial
3.2 Arrest photograph of Grigori Zinoviev, defendant in the first Moscow show trial
3.3 Andrey Vyshinsky, state prosecutor for all three Moscow show trials
3.4 Loy W. Henderson, the only American diplomat to attend the first Moscow show trial

Chapter 4   48
4.1 Karl Radek, defendant in the second Moscow show trial
4.2 US ambassador Joseph E. Davies, an American diplomat who attended the second and third Moscow show trials
4.3 George F. Kennan, an American diplomat who attended the second Moscow show trial
5.1 John Dewey, American philosopher and educator, the chair of the Dewey Commission   68

Chapter 6   82
6.1 Five Soviet marshals, 1935
6.2 People's Commissar for Foreign Affairs Maxim Litvinov (ousted in 1939, survived)

Chapter 7   108
7.1 Nikolai Bukharin. "N. Bucharin"
7.2 Charles Bohlen, American diplomat who attended the third Moscow show trial

Chapter 8   130
8.1 A photograph of Leon Trotsky and American followers in Mexico in 1940
8.2 The March 4, 1953 issue of *Pravda* announcing Stalin's ill health (3 days after his stroke)

Chapter 9   148
9.1 Nikita Khrushchev and Joseph Stalin in 1936 when Khrushchev was a rising star in the Communist Party
9.2 The Twentieth Party Congress of the Communist Party of the Soviet Union, 1956, where Nikita Khrushchev denounced Joseph Stalin

Preface and Acknowledgments

Witnessing Stalin's Justice is based on contemporaneous American sources from the time surrounding the Moscow show trials from 1936 through 1938 and their aftermath. Comments by the present authors within these documents or after direct quotations are enclosed in brackets. One of the challenges of writing about Russia is the transliteration of Russian names. Throughout the manuscript the authors have endeavored to use uniform spelling of Russian names, including the English transliteration of the names of the trial defendants as stated in the official Soviet translations of the trial transcripts. However, direct quotations containing variant spellings (e.g., Trotski and Kiroff) are left in the original transliterations within the quoted documents.

The authors would like to acknowledge the institutions that have provided digital access to original documents, including the University of Wisconsin's Digital Library which has uploaded over 100 years of *Foreign Relations of the United States*. The Marxist Internet Archive (www.marxists.org) was a very useful resource for American Communist and Trotskyist publications. Unz.org was a valuable source of popular periodicals of the time.

The authors would like to acknowledge the invaluable assistance of the Interlibrary Loan Service at Eastern Washington University, the Hoover Institution (Stanford University), the University of Wisconsin—LaCrosse and Davidson College.

Timeline of Events

1917	Overthrow of the tsarist regime
	Bolshevik Revolution with Vladimir Lenin as leader
	United States severs diplomatic ties with the Bolshevik government
1918	Peace with Germany
	Cheka (secret police) established
1918–20	Allied Expeditionary Forces sent to aid Whites in the Civil War
1918–21	Russian Civil War
1919	Communist Party USA established
	Comintern established
1919–20	"Red Scare" in the United States
1922	Lenin has first stroke
1922–33	Earlier show trials
1924	Lenin dies
	Joseph Stalin becomes General Secretary of the Communist Party
1924–58	*Daily Worker* published in New York City
1925	Leon Trotsky ousted as People's Commissar for War
1926	Trotsky, Lev Kamenev, and Grigori Zinoviev expelled from the Politburo
1927	Trotsky expelled from the Communist Party of the Soviet Union
1928	Trotsky sent into internal exile
1928–32	First Five Year Plan
1929	Trotsky exiled from the Soviet Union
1932–3	Famine in Ukraine
1933	US official recognition of the Soviet Union; American diplomats sent
1934	Assassination of Sergei Kirov
	Passage of revised Article 58 of the Russian Criminal Code, used to justify the Moscow show trials
1934–5	Trials of accused conspirators in Kirov's death, including Zinoviev and Kamenev
1936	First Moscow show trial

	Gengrikh Yagoda purged from NKVD; Nikolai Yezhov replaces him;
	American Committee for the Defense of Leon Trotsky formed
	New Soviet constitution
	Leon Trotsky expelled from Norway; continues exile in Mexico
1937	Second Moscow show trial
	"Open Letter to American Liberals" published
	Dewey Commission investigates charges against Trotsky
	Trial and execution of Soviet Army leaders
1937–8	Purge of the Soviet Navy
	Intensified anti-foreigner campaign
	"Yezhovshchina"—Intensified NKVD campaign of arrests
1938	Trotskyist Socialist Workers Party founded in the United States
	Third Moscow show trial
	"Statement of Progressives" published
	Nikolai Yezhov ousted as head of NKVD; Lavrenti Beria replaces him
1939	Soviet-Nazi anti-aggression pact
	"Official" end to the purges
1939–40	"Winter War" with Finland
1940	Nikolai Yezhov executed
	Trotsky assassinated
1941	Publication of *Mission to Moscow* and *Darkness at Noon* in the United States
1941–5	"Great Patriotic War" against Germany and Italy
1941	Soviet defector Walter Krivitsky dies under mysterious circumstances
1943	Passage of the Smith Act; used to prosecute US radicals
	Comintern disbanded
1945	Soviet Union declares war on Japan
1946	Beginning of intensified anticommunist campaign in the United States
1953	Doctors' Plot announced (later disavowed)
	Death of Stalin
	Collective leadership in the Soviet Union
	Purge and execution of Lavrenti Beria
1956	Nikita Khrushchev's "secret speech" and the beginning of destalinization
	Dissension within the Communist Party USA ranks

1964	Nikita Khrushchev ousted from power
1971	Publication of Nikita Khrushchev's memoirs
1988	Khrushchev's "secret speech" published in the Soviet Union
1991	End of the Soviet Union and the opening of government and Communist Party archives
1999	Vladimir Putin appointed president of the Russian Federation (later elected)
2022	Russia invades Ukraine

Introduction

From 1936 through 1938 the Soviet government held three major show trials in Moscow to purge veteran Communist Party members known as the Old Bolsheviks. The defendants in these trials were charged with being counter-revolutionaries, plotting assassinations and a *coup d'état* in order to restore capitalism, being agents and sympathizers of the exiled Leon Trotsky, spying for fascist powers (usually Nazi Germany), plotting to cede land and to give economic concessions to foreign governments and for being saboteurs (called "wreckers") of the Soviet economy, agriculture, and infrastructure. Previously, some defendants had endured *samokritika* (public self-criticism) and had been sentenced to internal exile.[1] All were found guilty, most were shot, and a few were sent to prison from which none survived. Their families were also persecuted.

These show trials were part of the purges that affected millions of Soviet citizens and foreigners residing in the Soviet Union. According to J. Arch Getty and Oleg V. Naumov, between 1935 and 1938 over 1.8 million people were arrested and convicted for "counter-revolutionary crimes" and "anti-Soviet agitation."[2]

To say that the United States had mixed feelings about the Soviet government would be an understatement. The United States ceased direct, formal diplomatic relations with Russia on December 6, 1917. The US government opposed the Bolshevik government's unilateral peace treaty with Germany, the confiscation of private property (including the property of US-owned businesses), the repudiation of the tsarist government's war debts and the Bolsheviks' persecution of organized religion. The fact that the Bolshevik government referred to the United States and other Western nations as imperialists and oppressors did not improve matters.

In spite of no direct diplomatic relations, journalists for US newspapers and news magazines reported from the Soviet Union, American radicals and intellectuals visited there, and American companies did business there. Before diplomatic recognition, the US government used its diplomatic missions in surrounding countries as listening posts to monitor events and conditions and would informally contact their Soviet counterparts in countries where both had diplomatic relations (e.g., Germany).

The United States was the last major power to recognize the Soviet government when President Franklin D. Roosevelt finally restored diplomatic relations in 1933. Thus, US diplomats were eyewitnesses to the show trials, saw the effects of widespread arrests on the Soviet citizenry, and witnessed the climate of fear that pervaded the Soviet Union. American diplomats recorded and analyzed these events as they unfolded, as did Moscow-based journalists. At home, US radicals waged a battle of words either for or against Stalin, the Soviet government, and the Moscow show trials.

Witnessing Stalin's Justice provides an account of an overlooked aspect of standard works on the subject—contemporaneous American reactions to the purges and the show trials. These include diplomatic cables with US Embassy employees' eyewitness accounts of the trials and their reactions to other trials, to the fears of Soviet citizens, and to the hostility toward foreigners. Three of the Embassy secretaries—Charles E. "Chip" Bohlen, Loy W. Henderson, and George F. Kennan (all Russian speakers)—served in Moscow during the trials and went on to lengthy careers in diplomacy. In spite of their lack of access to the hidden aspects of these trials, they had greater insights into the false nature of the charges and the defendants' self-condemning confessions than other eyewitnesses. These communiqués were compiled in the Department of State's *Foreign Relations of the United States* (*FRUS*).[3] These Embassy secretaries and US ambassador Joseph E. Davies later published their accounts of the trials in their memoirs.[4]

Even before the restoration of diplomatic relations, US news media had reporters in the Soviet Union who had to deal with Glavlit, the Soviet censorship agency. The *New York Times* ran extensive front-page articles on events in the Soviet Union, on all of the show trials, and on Leon Trotsky's exile, including lengthy articles by Trotsky himself. Other mainstream news magazines and wire services and scholarly journals and the leading liberal weekly magazines *The Nation* and *New Republic* also reported and editorialized on the trials.

The Moscow show trials had a tremendous impact on the radical left in the United States, sharpening the differences between American Communists and Trotskyists. The Communist Party USA's leadership closely followed the directives of the Comintern (Communist (Third) International), supported the Stalinist line, defended the show trials, and vilified Trotsky and his supporters. Relying heavily on *Pravda*, the Party published eyewitness accounts of the trials, held rallies and gave speeches of condemnation of the trial defendants and of Trotsky and his followers, and extolled Stalin and the defendants' persecutors.

The exiled Trotsky, the special object of Stalin's wrath, was constantly cited in the trials as the mastermind of counter-revolutionary plots, all in collusion with his exiled son Lev Sedov and with his alleged fascist allies, chiefly Nazi Germany. Trotsky's American followers had formed the Socialist Workers Party, and while far fewer than the Communists, American Trotskyists tirelessly defended their leader in print and at rallies. The show trials led to the Communist Party USA and American Trotskyists denunciations of each other.

Some left-wing American intellectuals had become fascinated with the Soviet Union as the world's first socialist workers' state. The Moscow show trials caused a split among them. Some joined the American Committee for the Defense of Leon Trotsky and supported the Commission of Inquiry (the Dewey Commission) that interviewed Trotsky in Mexico about the charges made against him in the first two public show trials. In contrast, a number of prominent left-wing intellectuals voiced their support for the Soviet state as a bulwark against fascism. Their statements of support, the "Open Letter to American Liberals" and the "The Moscow Trials: Statement of Progressives," are among the most well-known defenses of the Soviet Union by American intellectuals. These statements came back to haunt them during the anticommunist investigations of the postwar era as the US Congress held hearings on Communist influence in Hollywood and on the pro-Soviet stance of the signers of the Open Letter and the Statement to Progressives.

Nikita Khrushchev, First Secretary of the Communist Party, delivered his famous "secret speech" ("On the Cult of Personality and Its Consequences") in 1956 to a closed session of the Twentieth Communist Party Congress. Khrushchev denounced Stalin and cataloged the injustices of the trials and the purges. The secret speech stunned both the Soviet populace and Western nations and began the period of destalinization. American diplomats were astonished by the secret speech and labored to develop strategies to use it for the benefit of US foreign policy during the Cold War. American Communists and leftist intellectuals who supported the show trials had to disavow their adherence to the Stalinist line.

For years the leading sources on the Moscow show trials and the purges were Robert Conquest's *The Great Terror* and Roy Medvedev's *Let History Judge*, both of which were critical of the trials. Conquest termed Joseph Stalin to be the "architect of terror" and that the "effect of terror is produced . . . when a given proportion of a group has been seized and shot. The remainder will be cowed into uncomplaining obedience."⁵ Medvedev concluded that "The Soviet Union passed through a serious disease and lost many of its finest sons."⁶ Concerning Stalin, his biographer Stephen Kotkin cited a quote that claimed that "few knew the depth" of Stalin's "malice."⁷

Through access to the Soviet and Comintern archives after the fall of the Soviet government, the extent of the purges has been more fully chronicled. Historian J. Arch Getty published comprehensive works on the purges and the show trials. In his earlier work *Origins of the Great Purges* Getty was of the opinion that too much emphasis has been placed on Stalin's personality in discussing the purges.⁸ In his later work *The Road to Terror*, he and co-author Oleg V. Naumov continued this theme by concluding that members of the Central Committee supported the purges, writing: "There was a joint project of a power-hungry Stalin and an insecure elite to centralize power, protect the regime, and clean up the Party."⁹ In 1990 Robert C. Tucker in his massive work *Stalin in Power*, wrote this about Stalin concerning the third trial: "The courtroom drama was nothing less than Soviet history as he would have wished it to occur, with all credit redounding to him and all evil and unhappy events . . . attributed to camoflaged enemies of the revolution."¹⁰

The American Communist Party leadership's obedience to the Stalinist line has been chronicled by historian Harvey Klehr and his co-authors through compilations of Comintern communications. According to Klehr: "The trials were frauds and the confessions false, extorted by a combination of torture, threats of execution and promises of clemency for the defendants and their families."¹¹ Other comprehensive works on American radicalism in the 1930s have analyzed the American Party's following the Stalinist line. Former *Daily Worker* reporter Theodore Draper published *The Roots of American Communism* in 1957. In 2003 he published an updated edition in which he wrote: "The 'Old Bolsheviks' were condemned in the 'show trials' and liquidated. Stalinism in all its brutality and vindictiveness showed itself at its worst."¹²

For the first time, *Witnessing Stalin's Justice* brings together contemporaneous American reactions to the Moscow show trials and analyzes their impact on the United States and Soviet-American relations. Most comprehensive works on the purges and the show trials barely mentioned contemporaneous American reactions. The eyewitness accounts of American diplomats were rarely cited, even though they have been available to the public since 1952 when Stalin was still alive.

The Moscow show trials sharpened the various American attitudes toward the Soviet Union and toward Stalin and his government. Concerns about these trials reached the highest level of the Department of State and were an ongoing preoccupation with US diplomats as they dealt with reporting on the trials and living with the adverse effects of the Soviets' anti-foreigner campaign. In the mainstream press, those who opposed Stalin's rule considered these trials to be the fruits of communism and to be gross examples of Stalin's dictatorial nature and personal vindictiveness. The trials also showed the lack of protection of individual rights in the Soviet justice system and showed the harsh nature of the Stalinist regime.

American trial supporters ranged from the obedient Communist Party USA leaders to leftists who held that criticizing the Soviet Union strengthened the fascist cause during the rise of Nazi Germany. Differing opinions on the trials further split the very active radical left of the 1930s and provided fodder for the anticommunist, postwar investigations of liberals and left-wing intellectuals. Khrushchev's denunciations of the Moscow show trials were pondered upon by American diplomats as to their usefulness in the Cold War and further weakened an already battered Communist Party USA as it split between pro-Stalinist and pro-Khrushchev factions.

The chapters on the three major show trials are arranged as follows: summaries of the conduct of the trial, the official reactions of US diplomats and their later recollections, the reporting of Moscow-based journalists, US news magazines and opinion journals, and the reactions of American radicals and left-wing intellectuals.

Plate 1.1 Anti-Bolshevik advertisement, *Birmingham (AL) Age-Herald*, November 23, 1919. Chronicling America: Historic American Newspapers. Library of Congress, public domain. <https://chroniclingamerica.loc.gov/lccn/sn85038485/1919-11-23/ed-1/seq-48/>

1

The United States and the Soviet Union (1917–33)

Introduction

According to a New York City police inspector, in 1917 Leon Trotsky made the following statement as he was leaving his exile in the United States to return to Russia: "I want you people here to organize and keep on organizing until you are able to overthrow this damned, rotten, capitalistic Government of this country."[1] Secretary of State Robert Lansing wrote the following to the American ambassador to Great Britain in 1920: "The Government of the United States is convinced that Lenin and his immediate disciples will never permanently forego the dream of world revolution or enter loyally into amicable relations with non-Bolshevik governments."[2]

These two quotations epitomized the strained relationship between the United States and the Soviet Union during the 1920s and the early 1930s. While the United States had no direct, formal diplomatic relations with the Soviet government after the October Revolution, Americans had an interest in developments there. US companies were allowed to do business with the Soviets, and thousands of Americans visited there. This chapter is a brief summary of US–Soviet contacts during this time, including the establishment of diplomatic relations in 1933.

The End of Diplomatic Relations

Leon Trotsky, then People's Commissar for Foreign Affairs, sent a formal communiqué to US ambassador David Francis on November 7, 1917, stating that there was a new government in Russia with Vladimir Lenin as its head. The note included a request for an immediate armistice to end the First World War.[3]

On President Woodrow Wilson's orders, the United States did not respond to the note and discontinued direct, official contact with the Bolshevik government on December 6, 1917. According to the Office of the Historian of the Department of State:

> The new Bolshevik government had refused to honor prior debts to the United States incurred by the Tsarist government, ignored pre-existing treaty agreements with other nations, and seized American property in Russia following the October Revolution. The Bolsheviks had also concluded a separate peace with Germany at Brest-Litovsk in March 1918, ending Russian involvement in World War I.[4]

The United States participated in the Allied Expeditionary Forces that supported the White armies in the Russian Civil War and participated in the Allied blockade until 1920. The most famous American observer of the Russian Revolution was American radical journalist and poet John Reed whose *Ten Days that Shook the World* was an eyewitness account of these events.[5] Other observers from both the right and the left wrote eyewitness accounts on the Revolution, often influenced by their own ideological viewpoints.[6]

American Communism and American Trotskyism

American radicals were profoundly affected by the Russian Revolution with American socialism being the cradle of the Communist Party USA. In 1918 Lenin published his "Letter to American Workers" in *Pravda* which was then translated and distributed in the United States. The Letter was a call to action for American workers and praised the American Revolution and Civil War, praised socialist Eugene V. Debs, condemned President Wilson and the capitalist-imperialist "robbers," defended the Russian Revolution (and its "mistakes"), and predicted that the "world proletarian revolution is invincible."[7] The Socialist Labor Party supported the Bolsheviks and created the Party's Left Wing Branch in 1919. However, the Socialists expelled the left-wing members, and American Communist parties began. According to the Communist Party of America's 1919 constitution, the purpose of the Party was "The education and organization of the working class for the establishment of the Dictatorship of the Proletariat, the abolition of the capitalist system, and the establishment of the Communist Society."[8] According to a brief history of the American Communist Party published by the Library of Congress:

The Americans were so divided they created two parties instead. One group consisted primarily of relatively recent Russian and East European immigrants, who emphasized adherence to Marxist orthodoxy and proletarian revolution. The other group, dominated by native-born, somewhat more pragmatic American radicals, sought mass influence.[9]

The Comintern (the Communist [Third] International) forced the two American parties to merge in 1922 and to follow Moscow's party line. Although membership in the American party rose to about 75,000 by 1938, many members left the party after the signing of the Nazi-Soviet Non-aggression Pact of 1939.[10] Comintern sent directives to the American Party on internal party issues and on what stands to take on national and international affairs. American Communists had representatives on its Executive Committee. During the 1920s and 1930s, the American Party was concerned with the following issues: the Sacco-Vanzetti case, labor organizing, fighting unemployment, civil rights for African Americans (especially the Scottsboro case), the Spanish Civil War, and the creation of the Popular (People's) Front against fascism. As part of its antiracist and anticolonialist rhetoric, the Bolsheviks courted radical African American leaders.[11] The American Party held conventions, mass meetings, and public demonstrations throughout this time.[12]

American Communists (also known as the Workers' Party) were outspoken, fractious, and hard to keep unified in the 1920s. They engaged in disputes, splintered into separate groups, were ordered by the Comintern to reunite, reunited, and then split off again.[13] The major split came with the expulsion of the Trotskyists in 1928, an action justified in the anti-Trotsky tract, *The Trotsky Opposition*, published by Workers Library Publishers, the American Party's publishing house.[14] The Comintern Executive Committee ordered the American Party to "liquidate" all factionalism and to defeat Trotskyism.[15] In addition to Trotskyists, other dissidents were expelled as well, most notably Jay Lovestone, a supporter of Nikolai Bukharin. These dissidents then formed their own oppositionist Communist Party. Other splinter groups were the Revolutionary Workers Party and the Leninist League. During the 1930s, under General Secretary Earl Browder, the Communist Party USA supported the Moscow show trials and the purges and continually criticized the exiled Trotsky, his supporters and other Communist dissidents.

The Communist Party USA's Workers Library Publishers published accounts of the show trials in its periodicals, including *Daily Worker*, the Party's official newspaper. Communists also published the weekly *New Masses* and *The*

Communist, the Party's monthly journal of Marxist theory (later renamed *Political Affairs*). The Friends of Soviet Russia, established in 1921, published the monthly *Soviet Russia Pictorial* after taking it over from the Russian Soviet Government Bureau. Friends was renamed Friends of the Soviet Union, and the magazine was later renamed *Soviet Russia Today* and then *New World Review*. These publications' editorial policies adhered to the Stalinist line, supported the Moscow show trials, and criticized Trotsky and his supporters.

American Trotskyists formed the Communist League of America. The League later merged with the American Workers Party, forming the Workers Party of the United States in 1934. The Workers Party was dissolved in 1936, and its members briefly joined the Socialist Party as the Left Wing Branch. In 1937 they were expelled from the Socialist Party. After a convention in January 1938, they formed the Socialist Workers Party (SWP) and became the American section of the Trotskyist Fourth International.[16] Their stated purpose was to shape "the indispensable weapon of the working class in its struggle against a powerful and merciless class enemy, the exploiter of labor and oppressor of the people."[17]

The SWP condemned capitalism, advocated Trotsky's anti-bureaucratic sentiments and his theory of permanent world revolution, and opposed Joseph Stalin's theory of "socialism in one country." The SWP tirelessly defended Trotsky against the accusations made by the Soviet government and by the Communist Party USA and was unfailingly critical of American Communists who supported the Soviet government and the Moscow show trials. The SWP published pamphlets and translations of Trotsky's writings. Leading periodicals of the Trotskyists were *New International* and *Socialist Appeal*. *Labor Appeal* was another Trotskyist newspaper that was published in San Francisco as the self-proclaimed "Voice of Socialism in the West."

Both American Communists and Trotskyists were active in organizing workers during this time and in supporting labor strikes throughout the United States, perhaps unaware of the irony that workers in the Soviet Union were not allowed to strike. The Bolsheviks had established the Red International of Labor Unions (Profintern) and the short-lived International Council of Trade and Industrial Unions which had an American Bureau. They also established the Trade Union Education League in the United States, headed by leading Communist William Z. Foster. An American trade delegation met with Stalin in 1927. Walter Reuther, later head of the United Auto Workers and one of the most influential labor leaders of the mid-twentieth century, had been employed in a Ford factory in the Soviet Union in 1933. Communists were influential in the Organizations (CIO) during the 1930s. Harry Bridges, head of the International

Longshore and Warehouse Union on the West Coast, was accused of being a Communist and threatened with deportation back to his native Australia. Bridges escaped deportation, but later research in the Communist archives proved that he was a Communist.[18] This history led to dire warnings about the Communist infiltration and control of labor unions.[19]

The Red Scare

After the First World War the threat of Bolshevik revolution and the forming of the Communist Party USA led to the "Red Scare," a backlash against labor strikes and against the perceived threat of Bolshevism, socialism, and anarchism. The Department of Justice hunted down alleged conspirators, and there were government hearings on the threat of Bolshevism in the United States, including testimony on the fact that some of the Bolsheviks, most prominently Trotsky, had lived in the United States.[20] These hearings gave the media material for articles on the "mass terror," on the "horrors" of Bolshevism in Russia and on the menace at home.[21]

The Red Scare included a wave of arrests and deportations of suspected and convicted radicals as the US Congress passed an amendment to the immigration law that singled out anarchists and others who advocated the overthrow of the government. The House of Representatives held a series of hearings in 1920 on the deportations of aliens deemed threats to the US government. These hearings included testimony on the purposes of the Communist Party USA and its relationship with the Comintern, citing the American Party's constitution and manifesto as proof of the Party's advocacy of the violent overthrow of the US government.[22] Twenty members of the Communist Party were tried in 1922 for "teaching and advocating the overthrow of the United States government by force and violence."[23]

US Contacts with the Soviet Union

In spite of the lack of formal diplomatic contact, the Department of State had a Division of Russian Affairs, later part of the Eastern European Division. Its purpose was to monitor and analyze developments in the Soviet Union. In 1922 the United States had listening posts when the US government formally recognized the independence of the three Baltic states—Estonia, Latvia, and

Lithuania. The US legation in Riga, Latvia, closely monitored events in the Soviet Union. The US legation in Tallinn, Estonia, was also a listening post, and American diplomats who later served in Moscow during the show trials were stationed at these sites.

As an example of US monitoring of events, a lengthy communiqué was sent from the legation in Riga, Latvia, in November 1923. This communiqué was critical of the Bolshevik government and was intended to counter the sentiments of Americans who were in favor of establishing diplomatic relations. The communiqué included the opinion that the so-called government was controlled by the Russian Communist Party, that the aim of the government was to foment international revolution, and that the relationship between the Russian Communist Party, the government, and the Comintern was part of a "Communist Interlocking Directorate." The author also claimed that the government engaged in international propaganda to overthrow foreign governments, that the Red International of Trade Unions (also part of the "Communist Interlocking Directorate") was a vehicle to foster labor unrest around the world and cited the subversive activities of the Comintern. This communiqué listed several prominent Soviet leaders who would later be exiled, purged, put on trial, or driven to suicide. Ironically, Joseph Stalin barely rated a mention. The author made a point of listing the original surnames of those leaders of Jewish descent.[24] In spite of the US government's official hostility toward Bolshevism, the United States was part of an international effort to send food aid, seed, and medical supplies to the Soviet Union during the famine of the early 1920s that was centered in the Volga region.

One point of contention between the US and the Soviet government in the early 1920s was the persecution of organized religion in Russia. In 1922 Russian Orthodox clergy in the United States petitioned President Warren G. Harding to protest the imprisonment and impending trial of Tikhon, Patriarch of Moscow and All the Russias. President Harding took a "we-can't-do-anything" attitude.[25] In 1923 the Soviets also tried Catholic clergy for counter-revolutionary activities. Outrage over this trial led the US government to informally protest and also led to a series of Department of State memoranda on how to deal with the public outcry against this trial, the death sentences, and the execution of the Vicar General Msgr. Butchkavitch. This trial was covered in the American press, and Secretary of State Charles Evans Hughes directed the US ambassador to Germany to informally contact Soviet ambassador Nikolai Krestinsky in order to convey the Secretary's view that such executions would make an "unfortunate impression" in the United States.[26]

In spite of this official antipathy, there were advocates for trade with the Soviets, and, when the trade embargo was lifted, US companies were allowed to do business there. By 1924 US exports exceeded the amount of goods exported in 1912, while imports from the Soviet Union were far less, reflecting the weakened state of its economy.[27] The American-Russian Chamber of Commerce was reorganized in 1926 with offices in New York City and in Moscow, and the Soviets set up Amtorg, its official purchasing agency, in New York City. During this time, American engineers, agronomists, and industrial workers went to the Soviet Union to work in the rapidly reorganized and expanding economy. Unfortunately, many American workers became trapped during the purges and disappeared into the Gulag.[28]

One important source of contact for the United States during this time was a group of Moscow-based correspondents for American media. In 1921 journalists for US newspapers were accredited in the Soviet Union.[29] Their cabled articles had to go through Glavit, the Soviet censorship agency; foreign correspondents who ran afoul of Glavlit faced deportation. The most famous correspondent for the American press was the English-born Walter Duranty, who reported from Moscow for the *New York Times* throughout the 1920s and 1930s. He also wrote books on his time there.[30] Louis Fischer reported on the Soviet Union and was an editor of the liberal weekly *The Nation* and also wrote books on the Soviet Union.[31] While Duranty wrote articles critical of the Soviet government in the early 1920s, both Duranty and Fischer came to be seen as pro-Soviet by the US Embassy staff.[32] Journalist Anna Louise Strong, a founder of the *Moscow Daily News*, was a tireless supporter and defender of the Soviets, the purges, and the show trials.[33]

Two American journalists who became disillusioned with communism due to their years in Moscow were Eugene Lyons (United Press International) and William Henry Chamberlin (*Christian Science Monitor*).[34] The major news weekly magazines were anticommunist in their coverage. The liberal weeklies *The Nation* and *New Republic* covered the show trials with articles, editorials, and letters to the editor and received criticism from both the right and radical left for their commentaries.

Much has been written about American intellectuals and their fascination with socialism, communism, and the Soviet Union during the 1920s and 1930s.[35] Some joined the Communist-backed League of American Writers.[36] There have been many theories about the reasons for their interest, including liberals' curiosity about the Soviet experiment in bringing state socialism to a vast nation perceived to be backward and "Asiatic." The Soviet system was implementing a planned economy in conjunction with a total revamping and expansion of the education system and the implementation of a new cultural model. When the Great Depression hit and the fascists consolidated power in Germany and Italy, intellectuals looked to the Soviets to overcome the faults of capitalism, to create a centrally planned economy and full employment and to be a bulwark against fascism.

Famous writers published in the Communist weekly *New Masses*, including novelists Thomas Wolfe, John Dos Passos, James T. Farrell, Nelson Algren, Ralph Ellison, Richard Wright, Erskine Caldwell, and Ernest Hemingway, playwrights Clifford Odets, George F. Kaufman, Sherwood Anderson, and Lillian Hellman, and poets Edna St. Vincent Millay, William Rose Benet, Archibald MacLeish, and William Carlos Williams. Other arts represented in *New Masses* were screenwriters Dalton Trumbo and Ring Lardner, Jr., artist Rockwell Kent, composers Aaron Copeland and Marc Blitstein, and humorists S. J. Perelman and Dorothy Parker.

Partisan Review, a literary journal with communist origins, published short essays by American writers on the United States and communism. The February 1936 issue included a series of essays on the meaning of Americanism and any relationship of American revolutionary literature to Marxism.[37] Among the contributors were novelist Theodore Dreiser and poet William Carlos Williams. *Partisan Review* later published some writings of Leon Trotsky.

The intellectuals who supported the Soviet Union faced criticism from American Trotskyists. Leading Trotskyist George Novack published two essays in the Trotskyist journal *New International*, in which he wrote the following about intellectuals who turned to communism during the Depression: "Few of these intellectuals had any previous acquaintance with Marxian thought or the history of the revolutionary movement. However, this did not deter them from blossoming forth overnight as dyed-in-the-wool revolutionists and authorities on Marxism."[38]

The Soviet government was mindful of the advantages of courting foreign intellectuals and had established the All-Union Society for Cultural Ties Abroad (VOKS). The purpose of VOKS was to show the achievements and potential of the new Soviet society to Westerners active in the arts.[39] American writers, artists, and traveling journalists made their way to the Soviet Union, including novelist Theodore Dreiser, African American writer Langston Hughes and singer and actor Paul Robeson, novelist Sinclair Lewis, short story writer Fanny Hurst, modern dancer Isadora Duncan, architect Frank Lloyd Wright, civil libertarian Roger Baldwin, and journalist Dorothy Thompson. Comedian and mime Harpo Marx performed there in 1933 to much acclaim.[40]

The Debate over Diplomatic Recognition

In 1919 the Department of State held that a government should be established in Russia that was "expressive of the will of the people and capable of performing its international obligations" and that "Russian resources should be no longer at the disposal of adventurous revolutionaries" intent on subverting other governments.[41] In their efforts to gain diplomatic recognition, the Bolshevik government established a Government Bureau in New York City, headed by Russian-born radical Ludwig C. A. K. Martens. Martens tried unsuccessfully to obtain official recognition from the Department of State, and he protested the deportations of radicals. The Government Bureau's office was raided, Martens was the subject of a Senate investigation and hearing and was deported.[42] In addition to Martens's efforts, the Bolshevik government both officially and unofficially stated a desire for diplomatic recognition while still criticizing "capitalist-imperialist" countries at home.[43]

The debate over US recognition of the Soviet government ran into the early 1930s. The American Socialist Party supported recognition and declared that "the Russian people have given inspiration and incalculable aid to the working class movement in all lands."[44] From the early 1920s, American left-wing groups and the Communist publications *Soviet Russia Pictorial* and *Daily Worker* were active in promoting recognition.[45] The liberal weeklies *New Republic* and *The Nation* were also early advocates for recognition.[46] Secretary of State Charles Evans Hughes issued a press release in 1923 that stated that while concerned about the welfare of the Russian people and the need for trade and investment, the US government opposed recognition because of the Soviet government's stated goal of world revolution.[47]

There was also opposition from Samuel Gompers, the legendary labor leader and president of the American Federation of Labor. Gompers sent a letter to Secretary of State Hughes in which he stated: "The soviet power cannot be recognized because it is an autocracy forced upon the people of Russia against their will and maintained in the same manner."[48] Father Edmund Walsh, the influential founder of the School of Foreign Service at Georgetown University, also opposed recognition, writing: "There are no rights for citizens or foreigners in Soviet Russia" and that Lenin showed "contempt for existing international law."[49]

In 1924 Senator William Borah of Idaho, a pro-recognition advocate, held Congressional hearings on recognition.[50] In a 1928 letter to Senator Butler of the Committee on Foreign Relations, Secretary of State Frank B. Kellogg wrote that Soviet interference in the internal affairs of other countries was an effort to spread "world revolution."[51]

In 1923 concern about labor unrest in the United States led to a series of hearings by the House of Representatives Special Committee to Investigate Communist Activities in the United States, known informally as the Fish Committee. These hearings were held in several cities to investigate groups alleged to be advocating the overthrow of the US government and alleged to be inciting riots, sabotage, and unrest.[52] Soviet ambitions toward establishing communist governments in foreign countries were still troubling to the Department of State in 1931 when Acting Secretary of State William R. Castle, Jr. sent a directive to US diplomatic and consular officers which barred entry to the United States for any members of any Communist Party that was part of the Comintern, members of the Communist Unions of Youth that were sections of the Communist International of Youth and members of other Communist-backed organizations.[53]

In 1932 *Congressional Digest* devoted an entire issue to the pros and cons of recognition, including brief essays by senators and former government officials.[54] This debate continued almost up to the day that the Roosevelt administration established diplomatic relations.

Diplomatic Recognition

The policy of non-recognition changed with the election of Franklin D. Roosevelt in 1932, and diplomatic relations were reestablished in 1933. According to the Office of the Historian of the US Department of State:

> Roosevelt hoped that recognition of the Soviet Union would serve U.S. strategic interests by limiting Japanese expansionism in Asia, and he believed that full diplomatic recognition would serve American commercial interests in the Soviet Union, a matter of some concern to an Administration grappling with the effects of the Great Depression. Finally, the United States was the only major power that continued to withhold official diplomatic recognition from the Soviet Union.[55]

A series of high-level negotiations, known as the "Litvinov Conversations" (named for People's Commissar for Foreign Affairs Maxim Maximovich Litvinov), involved William C. Bullitt (a future ambassador) and *New York Times* Moscow correspondent Walter Duranty.[56] President Roosevelt sent a letter to Soviet President Mikhail Kalinin on October 10, 1933, in which he stated that he wanted to "end the present abnormal relations" between the two countries.[57] Roosevelt's official announcement of diplomatic relations, issued on November 16, 1933, included the following: "I trust that the relations now established between our peoples will forever remain normal and friendly and that our nations henceforth may cooperate for their mutual benefit and for the preservation of the peace of the world."[58]

The recognition of the Soviet Union included the Soviets' "Pledge on Propaganda" and the US pledge of reciprocity. The official communications also included protocols on the two governments' stands on religion, the protection of nationals, "economic espionage," the settling of previous claims, the Soviets' waiving of any claims from the US military expedition in Siberia and the pledge of further discussions.[59]

Recognition was headline news in the American press.[60] While diplomatic recognition had been a long-sought goal of the Communist Party USA, dissident communists and Trotskyists criticized the governments of both countries.[61] The establishment of diplomatic relations was celebrated in Moscow, including a laudatory article by leading Soviet journalist Karl Radek, a future purge victim.[62]

The Ambassadors

The US ambassadors to the Soviet Union during this time had to tread the line between President Roosevelt's desire for rapprochement with the Soviets and the realities of dealing with the Stalinist government. The first US ambassador to the Soviet Union was William Christian Bullitt, Jr. In 1919 he had visited the Soviet Union on a secret mission, met with Vladimir Lenin, reported back to the US Senate Committee on Foreign Relations and advocated a rapprochement with Lenin's government, an effort which failed.[63] Upon becoming ambassador, Bullitt was initially hopeful for a positive relationship with the Soviets. However, by the end of his tenure in 1936, he had become disillusioned and wrote the following:

> This is a hard climate, and an American finds many things to try his patience, but few that are capable of winning his affections. One of the most disagreeable features . . . is the secrecy with which everything is done. He can rarely obtain accurate information, until events have transpired, and he may rely upon it, that his own movements are closely observed, by eyes that he never sees. The Russian mind seems naturally distrustful, and this is especially so with the Government officers. . . . Nothing is more striking to an American here on his first arrival, that of the rigor of the police. It would seem that the capital was in a state of siege.[64]

Ambassador Bullitt's disillusionment with the Bolshevik government continued after he left Moscow. He published *The Great Globe Itself* in 1946 in which he expressed anti-Stalinist sympathies, comparing Stalin and the NKVD (the secret police) to Ivan the Terrible and the Oprichnina, Ivan's secret police which terrorized the Russian populace.[65]

Bullitt was succeeded by Joseph Edward Davies, a friend of President Roosevelt and a purely political appointment. Davies had no previous diplomatic experience, was more of a "brandy and cigars" ambassador, and was not always popular with the Embassy secretaries. Davies was married to Marjorie Merriweather Post, heiress to the Post cereal fortune and one of the richest women in the United States. She accompanied Davies to Moscow where they entertained lavishly. They left the Soviet Union in 1938. In 1941 he published *Mission to Moscow*, his bestselling memoir, which later was made into a film.[66] Davies later came under criticism for publicly accepting the Stalinist line and for his belief that the defendants in the Moscow show trials were involved in anti-Stalinist plots.

Stalin appointed Alexander Antonovich Troyanovsky, a former Red Army officer and ambassador to Japan, as the first Soviet ambassador to the United States.

Embassy Personnel

There were three Embassy secretaries who attended the Moscow show trials. They were all Russian speakers and Eastern European specialists who had served in the US legation in Riga, Latvia. These secretaries (known formally as *chargés d'affaires* and consuls and vice consuls) are listed with their years in Moscow during the show trials: Charles Edward ("Chip") Bohlen (1937–40), Loy Wesley Henderson (1934–8), and George Frost Kennan (1933–7). These men witnessed the effects of the purges on Soviet society and sent lengthy, thoughtful communiqués. They all continued in long careers in diplomacy and discussed the show trials in their memoirs.[67] Due to his influence on postwar foreign policy, Kennan is the best-known. He was the author of the famous "Long Telegram" and the "X" article in the July 1947 issue of *Foreign Affairs*.[68] His writings were important foundations of the US postwar policy of the containment of communism. Kennan and Bohlen were postwar ambassadors there, although Kennan's tenure there was short and unhappy.

During the purges, Lt. Col. Philip R. Faymonville was the military attaché in Moscow and reported to the Military Intelligence Division of the War Department General Staff. He spoke Russian and had served in the Allied Expeditionary Force Siberia during the Civil War. Faymonville was praised by Ambassador Davies, but Embassy secretaries Bohlen and Henderson considered him to be too anxious to be friendly with the Soviets.[69] Faymonville sent communiqués on the state of the Soviet military and on the trial of top army leaders.

Initial US–Soviet diplomatic relations were occupied by the negotiations for the debts and claims accrued by the previous Russian government, trade and commercial treaty negotiations, and the plans for building a new embassy. In 1935 there were also concerns about speeches by American Communists at the Seventh All World Congress of the Comintern and at the Sixth Congress of Communist International of Youth in Moscow. Reporting back to Washington, the Embassy staff considered these speeches to be proof of the violation of the protocol of diplomatic recognition regarding noninterference with the internal affairs of both countries. Ambassador Bullitt made a formal protest to the People's Commissariat for Foreign Affairs.[70]

Conclusion

These early years of renewed diplomatic relations took place against the international backdrop of the worldwide depression, the rise of fascism in Nazi Germany and Italy, German expansionism, the Italian invasion of Ethiopia, the Spanish Civil War (in which the Soviets were officially involved), and Japanese military expansion into China. The long debate over recognition was a symptom of official wariness toward the Bolshevik government as it spurred the development of a communist political party in the United States, advocated for world revolution, and advocated for the end of capitalism. The official recognition of the Soviet government made the presence of American diplomats at the Moscow show trials possible, providing the opportunity for eyewitness accounts of these historic proceedings and to the upheaval of the purges.

Plate 2.1 Vladimir Lenin, the first Bolshevik head of state. "Lenine," n.d., https://commons.wikimedia.org (accessed June 30, 2022).

Plate 2.2 Joseph Stalin. "Stalin before 1929," n.d., https://commons.wikimedia.org (accessed June 30, 2022).

Plate 2.3 Leon Trotsky in exile, n.d., https://commons.wikimedia.org (accessed June 30, 2022).

Plate 2.4 Sergei Kirov, assassinated leader of the Leningrad Communist Party. Kalashnikov, Mikhail Mikhaylovich, "Sergei Kirov," January 1934. http://commons.wikimedia.org (accessed June 30, 2022).

2

Prelude to the Moscow Show Trials (1917–35)

Introduction

This chapter is a brief summary of the events in the Soviet Union that led to the Moscow show trials, American reactions to these events, and a summary of the conduct of the trials.

The Rise of Joseph Stalin

The tsarist government was overthrown in 1917 and replaced by a provisional government that was in turn overthrown by the Bolsheviks in the October Revolution. Vladimir Ilyich Lenin became the head of the Bolshevik state. In 1924 Lenin died after a period of incapacitation. Before dying, he left a testament that recommended that Joseph Stalin be removed from power; Stalin had it suppressed. The American press was mindful of the impact of the death of Lenin on the future of the Soviet Union and speculated as to who would emerge as Lenin's successor.[1]

A power struggle ensued that eventually led to Party General Secretary Joseph Vassarionovich Stalin's rise to power when he succeeded in removing his chief rival People's Commissar of the Army and Navy (War) Leon Davidovich Trotsky. Stalin, general secretary of the Central Committee, acted in collusion with Grigori Zinoviev and Lev Kamenev to first push Trotsky out and to expel him from the Politburo in 1926, sending him into internal exile, recalling him and then expelling him from the Soviet Union in 1929.

Stalin and Trotsky had different philosophies on the future of the communist movement. Trotsky believed in permanent worldwide revolution with success only possible if all countries were communist. He was also opposed to an entrenched bureaucracy, believing that bureaucrats should be sent into the field before they became too powerful. Stalin settled on the philosophy of "socialism in one country," protecting the Soviet state at home while trying to spread communism overseas. Stalin also used his position as general secretary of the Party to appoint people beholden to him to the bureaucracy, thus having supporters to sustain his power. Stalin had characterized Trotsky's theory of permanent revolution as "another variety of Menshevism" at the Party Congress of 1924. Zinoviev and Kamenev had aided Stalin in removing Trotsky from power but were then themselves removed from the Politburo, sent into internal exile but were later returned.[2] The American press followed the fall of Trotsky and his allies in 1926 and 1927. Trotsky, Kamenev, and Zinoviev publicly retracted their "opposition" to the Party Central Committee in front of the Politburo in 1926.[3] When Trotsky later tried to defend himself at a Comintern meeting, he was "violently assailed" by Nikolai Bukharin.[4] Bukharin had aided Stalin in removing Zinoviev and Kamenev, but he also was expelled, sent into internal exile, and later returned. As reported in a skeptical editorial in the *New York Times*, in 1930 Bukharin himself publicly recanted his "heresies." The editorialist linked these recantations to laying the blame for the failures in the early years of the first Five Year Plan and speculated that the Soviet populace was living "under the sword of terror."[5] Kamenev, Zinoviev, and Bukharin would be defendants in the Moscow show trials.

The general populace was not spared during the early 1930s as Stalin instituted a central purge commission to conduct a *chistka* (cleansing), the purging of state institutions, and Party rolls.[6] High-ranking officials were forced to undergo *samokritika*, forced admissions of guilt and repentance in closed sessions, while rank-and-file members of the Communist Party and employees of state institutions underwent public rituals to decide whether they were deemed worthy of keeping their jobs. Anticommunist journalist Eugene Lyons termed this purging to be a "pitiless public inquiry" and a "sword of Damocles."[7] The American press followed Stalin's rise to power which *Literary Digest* characterized as the "expulsion of his foes" and the liberal weekly *New Republic* called him the "new Lenin."[8]

In 1928 Stalin introduced the first Five Year Plan for the collectivization of agriculture and for rapid industrialization. The excesses of the Five Year Plan have been well documented, including the elimination of the *kulak* class of prosperous peasants, deportation of populations into internal exile, and the devastating famine that was centered in Ukraine. One of the reactions to the Five Year Plan was the 1932 Riutin Platform, a document circulated by Siberian-born Party functionary Martemian Riutin, which criticized Stalin and his rule and cataloged the excesses of Stalin's policies. Supporters of the Riutin Platform would be marked as enemies of the people, and the Platform was cited in the Moscow show trials as example of Trotskyist opposition. Riutin was arrested and executed in 1937.

According to *The Soviet Union: Facts, Descriptions, Statistics*, in 1929 the Soviet Union had a population of 131,000,000 people and was governed by the constitution of 1924. The structure of the central government was as follows: the All-Union Congress of Soviets ("the supreme organ of authority"), the Central Executive Committee (the Council of the Union and the Council of Nationalities), the Presidium of the Central Executive Committee, and the Council of People's Commissars (the "executive and directive organ of the Central Executive Committee").[9] *The Soviet Union* also listed the members of the Council of People's Commissars, members of the Presidium of the Central Executive Committee, and Soviet diplomats as of December 1, 1928. Several of the listed officials and diplomats would either be purged, tried, and executed or would die under mysterious circumstances, the most prominent being Alexei Rykov, Lenin's successor as Chairman of the Council of People's Commissars.[10]

The Role of the Secret Police

Stalin's chief instrument of terror was his secret police. The arrests, imprisonment, and interrogations of the accused in the Moscow show trials were handled by the NKVD (People's Commissariat for Internal Affairs). The NKVD had evolved from the Cheka, the brutal secret police established by the Bolsheviks after the Russian Revolution, later becoming the Government Political Administration (GPU). The GPU became the NKVD in 1933 and administered the Gulag (Main Directorate for Corrective Labor Camps), the vast network of forced-labor camps. The horrors of the arrests, interrogations, and conditions in the prisons and in the Gulag have been well documented. Accused individuals were jailed under harsh conditions, including inadequate food, sleep deprivation, overcrowding, and either cold or overheated cells. The accused were subjected to marathon interrogation sessions (the "conveyor") conducted by teams of interrogators, sometimes under glaringly bright lights. They were also subjected to beatings and torture. To further induce confessions and the implication of alleged accomplices, the accused had "confrontations" with other defendants who urged them to confess, or the accused were falsely promised that they would not be executed or that their families would be spared. However, in many cases, the close relatives or even the extended families of the accused were also arrested, either exiled or sent to the Gulag or executed.

Three men headed the NKVD during the era of the show trials—Genrikh G. Yagoda, Nikolai Ivanovich Yezhov, and the Georgian Lavrenti Pavlovich Beria. These men were eventually purged and liquidated. Yagoda was demoted, arrested, tried, and shot in the third show trial in 1938. Nikolai Yezhov [also transliterated as Ezhov] was known as the "Bloodthirsty Dwarf" or the "Bloody Dwarf," due to his short stature, replaced Yagoda. While Harold Denny of the *New York Times* had speculated that the purge might be dying down, Yezhov's tenure as head of the NKVD came to be called the Yezhovshchina and saw an increase in the number of informants, arrests, and prisoners in the Gulag[11]. Yezhov was demoted from his post at the NKVD and later arrested and executed. Beria lasted until Stalin's death. He was purged and executed in 1953.

Previous Show Trials

Even in Lenin's time, show trials were used to humiliate and eliminate dissidents. One such trial was of the Socialist Revolutionaries who had been political rivals of the Bolsheviks. A Socialist Revolutionary had tried to assassinate Lenin in 1918. Thirty-four Socialist Revolutionaries were tried in 1922 with the charges of the "organization of and participation in armed insurrections to overthrow the government, supporting foreign intervention, the assassinations of government leaders, and the organization of money expropriations." This trial resulted in death sentences for twelve of the accused, but the executions were stayed and commuted into prison terms. Prominent Bolsheviks who would later be purged played key roles in this trial. They included Georgi Pyatakov (chief judge), Nikolai Krylenko (state prosecutor), and Nikolai Bukharin (counsel for the defendants who turned state's evidence). Future victims Grigori Zinoviev, Karl Radek, and Trotsky supported this trial. The Bolshevik government staged a public demonstration against the defendants; such demonstrations would be repeated during the Moscow show trials. Mainstream American press coverage of this trial was critical of the Bolsheviks ("an anti-treason show").[12] Leading American socialist Eugene V. Debs protested the death sentences; Debs was condemned by American Communists.[13] In the same vein that they would use in the Moscow show trials, American Communist leaders supported this trial. They termed it to be "another phase of the social revolution."[14] This trial's accusations, the attendant self-condemning confessions, and recantations of the defendants would be replicated in the Moscow show trials.

Three later trials laid the foundation for the accusations of "wrecking" (sabotage) and conspiracy against the Soviet state, major themes of the Moscow show trials. These were the Shakhty trial for economic crimes in 1928, the Industrial Party (Prompartiya) trial in 1930 and the Metropolitan-Vickers trial in 1933. These trials would blame the defendants for mining and industrial accidents, train derailments, and crop failures by means of "wrecking"—the sabotage of industrial and agricultural production and transportation at the behest of foreign governments and exiled former owners. Andrei Vyshinsky, the state prosecutor in the three Moscow show trials, was a judge or a prosecutor in two of these trials.

Walter Duranty reported on these trials for the *New York Times*, including the large and lengthy Shakhty trial that included charges of "economic counter-revolution" in the coalmining region of Donbas in eastern Ukraine. The trial was also called the "technicians' plot," and the defendants were denounced by Stalin.[15] Fifty-two defendants were charged with sabotage and contacts with foreigners, especially Germans. Vyshinsky was the chief judge, and the trial was held in the same venue that would be used in the Moscow show trials. While Duranty was somewhat skeptical of the charges and the lack of proof, he later praised the prosecution as being "admirably conducted."[16] The anticommunist news magazine *Time* was skeptical and quoted Alexander Kerensky, the exiled former head of the 1917 provisional government, who termed the trial to be a "rehearsed drama with hired 'conspirators.'"[17] In contrast, the liberal weekly *The Nation* praised Duranty's trial coverage in an editorial that expressed belief in the conspiracy charges.[18]

The 1930 Industrial Party trial of eight engineers and industrial planners was for wrecking and counter-revolutionary plotting to overthrow the government in collusion with foreign governments. Duranty reported that their plotting allegedly included a planned invasion by Britain and France. 500,000 people demonstrated against the defendants at the beginning of the trial. Again, the defendants' confessions were the major proof against them.[19] The trial was denounced by Russian exiles and in the mainstream American press as "fake."[20] It was also the first trial to be broadcast over the radio, and, according to *Literary Digest*, aroused "ridicule and scorn . . . in the outside world."[21] Anticommunist journalist Eugene Lyons, who attended the trial, slammed the trial as part of the "embattled desperation within the Soviet frontier" in his 1941 book *Assignment in Utopia*.[22]

American Communists supported the trial for "espionage and wrecking in full bloom" by publishing two pamphlets on this trial—*The Wreckers Exposed* and *Wreckers on Trial*.[23] The pro-Stalinist magazine *Soviet Russia Today* published an article that tied the Shakhty trial and the Industrial trial together in a tangled tale of conspiracy for a foreign invasion to be led by the French.[24] Continuing their support of this trial, in 1938 *Soviet Russia Today* published a confession by "Ivanov," one of the alleged conspirators in the Industrial Party trial, who claimed to have been rehabilitated.[25]

In a purely political trial in 1931, fourteen former Mensheviks were tried for trying to restore their party to power and for trying to overthrow the Soviet government.[26]

The Metropolitan-Vickers trial of 1933 concerned a group of engineers (including British citizens) who were accused of "wrecking activities at power stations in the Soviet Union," bribery, and other crimes against the state.[27] Andrei Vyshinsky was the prosecutor. This trial was also covered in the American press.[28] Eugene Lyons later described it as a "shadow play on a screen."[29] The trial was supported by American Communists as an example of "British imperialism in the conspiracy to break down Soviet industry in preparation for an attack on the Soviet Union."[30] It received a great deal of coverage in Great Britain because British engineers had been accused. Lengthy accounts in *The Times* (London) described the use of the "conveyor" (marathon interrogation sessions) against the accused and the "confrontation"—encounters with other defendants who claimed to have confessed in an effort to get other accused to confess. These articles were later compiled into a pamphlet and were among the first widely circulated descriptions of the use of these techniques in obtaining confessions and guilty pleas.[31] Two British engineers got prison sentences, one was acquitted and the rest were deported.

Foundations of the Moscow Show Trials

Stalin's rise to power, the role of the secret police, and the earlier show trials laid the groundwork for the Moscow show trials. The principals were all in place—Stalin in charge, Leon Trotsky in exile, Old Bolsheviks in disgrace, the secret police browbeating defendants to confess, and Vyshinsky ready to prosecute. The trial charges of espionage and collusion with foreign powers reinforced Stalin's theme that the Soviet Union was surrounded by capitalist enemies and was riddled with spies. Sabotage ("wrecking") was blamed for industrial accidents and agricultural failures.

One person and one event were continuing themes throughout the show trials. The one person was Trotsky, Stalin's chief rival for power after Lenin's death. The one event was the murder of Sergei Mironovich Kirov, the head of the Communist Party in Leningrad.

Trotsky (born Lev Davidovich Bronstein) had been imprisoned by the tsarist government and had spent time in internal exile and in exile in Europe and in New York City. He returned to Russia in 1917 and joined the Bolsheviks. Known for his skills as an orator and as an organizer, he had been People's Commissar for Foreign Affairs and was a founder of the Workers and Peasants Red Army (RKKA). He was the People's Commissar for the Army and the Navy (War) during the Civil War and during the war with Poland. He was well known in the West and was often photographed in American newspapers as one of the faces of the Bolshevik government. A prolific writer, his books were published and reviewed in the West.

The American press chronicled the ups and downs of Trotsky's career. After expulsion from the Party, Trotsky was sent into internal exile in Kazakhstan, then recalled.[32] The Communist Party USA (then called the Workers [Communist] Party) supported Stalin's actions, calling Trotskyism "the negation of the Leninist revolutionary theory and practice."[33] In 1929 Stalin deported Trotsky from the Soviet Union in order to "preserve national unity."[34] For good measure, 150 of Trotsky's alleged followers were arrested and put in isolation cells in 1929.[35]

Trotsky did not go quietly into exile as he spent time in Turkey, France, and Norway before finally settling in Mexico in 1937. He constantly spoke out and wrote against Stalin, the persecution of alleged Trotskyists, the trials, and his hardships in exile.[36] In his defense, Trotsky published the journal *Bulletin of the Opposition* and established the Fourth International in opposition to the Comintern. American Trotskyists were outraged by Trotsky's deportation, terming it to be a "shameful banishment."[37]

Throughout the Moscow show trials, the defendants were accused of being Trotskyists, which the Soviets equated with being fascists. They were accused of plotting with him and his exiled son Lev Sedov against Stalin and the Soviet state, often in collusion with foreign powers, usually Nazi Germany or Japan.

The assassination of Sergei Kirov was the one event that is considered to be the beginning of the purges. Kirov was the popular secretary of the Communist Party in Leningrad and a member of the Politburo. Disaffected Communist Leonid Vasilievich Nikolaev shot and killed him on December 1, 1934. Immediately upon Kirov's murder, the Soviet government revised Article 58 of the 1927 Penal Code of the Russian SFSR; this was the article under which the defendants in previous show trials had been tried. The revised Article 58 outlined counter-revolutionary crimes by both civilians and the military. These crimes included treason, armed uprising, dealings with foreign states to undermine the revolution, espionage, sabotage ("wrecking"), anti-Soviet propaganda, and failure to inform or denounce counter-revolutionary crimes. Punishment for these crimes included imprisonment from six months to ten years, the confiscation of property, and execution.[38] Adult family members of those convicted were subject to the loss of voting privileges and to exile in Siberia. Minor children were sent to state-run homes. The defendants in the trials for Kirov's murder and in the Moscow show trials of 1936–8 were tried under this article.

American reactions to Kirov's death came in three phases—his murder and funeral, trials and executions of condemned plotters, and the arrests of veteran Party leaders Zinoviev and Kamenev. Kirov's death was headline news and was touted by the Soviet government as part of an anti-government conspiracy.[39] American Communists devoted several articles in *Daily Worker* celebrating Kirov's life and career as "one of the greatest leaders of the proletariat" and as a "passionate revolutionary."[40] Harold Denny of the *New York Times* cited "informed foreigners" who doubted that Nikolaev was part of any conspiracy.[41]

The murder also led to a rapid wave of arrests, perfunctory trials, and guilty verdicts, resulting in over 100 executions and prison terms. The Soviet government initially blamed Kirov's murder on "white guard" elements, which led to accusations against thirteen accused plotters and to a speedy trial before the Military Collegium of the Supreme Court. The draconian aspects of the first trials for Kirov's murder were not lost on Harold Denny, who reported that "terrorists and plotters are to be tried swiftly and to be executed immediately without opportunity for appeal." Denny sent a steady stream of articles, reporting on the trials and executions, noting that those convicted had no right of counsel or right of appeal of their sentences. He also reported on arrests and spreading fear in other parts of the Soviet Union.[42] The defendants were accused of being part of the traitorous "Leningrad Centre," and the Communist Party and NKVD in Leningrad were heavily purged. *Time* characterized the trials and executions as "drastic Bolshevik terror" and "state butchery."[43] The US-based Russian Progressive Political Committee, a group of non-communist socialists and liberals, sent a telegram to President Roosevelt to ask him to intervene to stop the mass executions; the Committee also held a protest rally in New York City.[44]

Nikolaev and 13 others were found guilty and executed on December 29, 1934, part of a string of executions that numbered 117 by January 1935.[45]

Moscow correspondent William Henry Chamberlin wrote a critical article in which he stated that the "Soviet government places its own supposed interests above the rights of its individual citizens to fair and open trial." Chamberlin also speculated that these trials and executions may lead to a "new opposition" in the Party ranks.[46]

Smashing the alleged "Leningrad Centre" was not enough as the blame for Kirov's assassination later morphed into accusations against a second group of accused plotters—the "Moscow Reserve Centre"—which was part of an alleged plot of fascist elements and Trotskyists. Old Bolsheviks Zinoviev and Kamenev were arrested in December 1934 and accused of participation in plotting Kirov's murder and in plotting the murders of Stalin and other high officials, including Vyacheslav Molotov, head of the Council of Commissars and People's Commissar for Transportation Lazar Kaganovich. This was the first time that leading Bolsheviks were accused of a capital crime and were called part of the "Trotskyist Left opposition." Harold Denny speculated they would share Trotsky's fate and be sent into exile, but the Soviets announced that they would be put on trial. Denny termed their trial to be a "dramatic change," "caused great surprise," and cast the arrests of Zinoviev and Kamenev as being part of a strategy to stifle dissent and to "cleanse" the Communist Party.[47]

They were brought to trial in January 1935. *Time* published two cynical articles on this trial, calling Zinoviev "tousle-haired, barrel-chested," and summarized his up-and-down relationship with Stalin. This article also ridiculed the official Soviet pronouncements on the defendants' guilt.[48] A second article called Zinoviev the "Bomb Boy of Bolshevism," repeating a characterization of him from 1924.[49]

There was some division among the editorialists and reporters for the liberal weeklies concerning the arrests and trials. A short editorial in *The Nation* took a rather hard line against the arrests and executions (the "ruthless and bloody reprisal of the Soviet government").[50] Oswald Garrison Villard, grandson of nineteenth-century abolitionist William Lloyd Garrison and an editor of *The Nation*, wrote editorials that condemned the executions and compared Soviet leaders to Hitler.[51] Louis Fischer, *The Nation*'s Moscow correspondent, painted a rosier picture of conditions in the Soviet Union with a tamed G. P. U. (secret police), more consumer goods, and a "trend toward normality." He called the mass executions a "frank effort to intimidate terrorists."[52] *New Republic* published two editorials on the arrests and executions. In the first, brief editorial, the writer expressed some doubt about the existence of any conspiracy.[53] The second editorial answered public criticism about the trials and executions by theorizing that the Soviet government feared other assassinations which indicated a "dangerous amount of hostility to them."[54]

American Communists dutifully followed directives from the Comintern in blaming the assassination on the "remnants of the former Zinoviev-Trotskyist opposition." The Comintern also exhorted American Communists to extol the virtues of the "great leader" Stalin.[55] *Daily Worker* published several articles which condemned the accused for being "leaders of the Zinoviev-Trotskyite counter-revolutionary cliques" that inspired the assassination of Kirov.[56] *Daily Worker* also supported the contention that Trotskyism was an "agent of international fascism."[57] To reinforce the idea that the trials and executions were supported by the Soviet public, *Daily Worker* reported that Soviet workers were clamoring for the executions of the "dastardly dregs" and "enemies of the proletarian revolution."[58]

Other American Communist publications eulogized Kirov, initially blamed the "white guard" elements, defended the trials and executions, and later blamed Trotsky, Zinoviev, and Kamenev.[59] A pamphlet published by the Communist Party USA eulogized Kirov as "one of the most beloved leaders of the Soviet working class," reported that his assassin was a member of the "former Zinoviev-Trotsky opposition," and slammed critics of the trials and executions.[60] Another pamphlet entitled *Trotskyism: Counter-Revolution in Disguise* accused Zinoviev and Kamenev of being part of a counter-revolutionary group. The writer portrayed Kirov's death as follows: "A great hero was destroyed. New Russia was robbed of a talented, courageous and universally beloved working-class builder of the Socialist system." The author also condemned Trotsky for plotting against Lenin and condemned American Trotskyists as a "small band of petit-bourgeois individuals" with "one aim — to discredit revolutionary theory and revolutionary practice."[61] Even dissident American Communists who had been expelled from the main party defended these trials and condemned leading American Socialist Norman Thomas for criticizing the "Soviet Terror" and for comparing Stalin to Hitler.[62]

Kirov's assassination caused an escalation in the war of words between American Communists and Trotskyists. American Trotskyists denied that the assassination was part of any counter-revolutionary plot, picked apart the official accounts, and decried the lack of public trials for the accused.[63] The Trotskyist newspaper *Socialist Appeal* concluded: "Stalin took advantage of the act of an unbalanced individual and executed and exiled those who were dissatisfied with his policies."[64] American Trotskyists also published a pamphlet by Trotsky in which he denied any involvement and asserted that the assassination was being used as an excuse to destroy Trotskyism.[65]

The three US Embassy secretaries—Charles "Chip" Bohlen, Loy W. Henderson, and George F. Kennan—later wrote that Kirov's assassination was a shock to everyone, was the start of the purges, and created a climate of fear. They were unsure about the theories behind it, including the theory that Trotsky was the mastermind.[66] In his memoir *I Write as I Please*, *New York Times* correspondent Walter Duranty deviated slightly from the Kremlin line and wrote: "Many of those shot were not implicated in the plot to assassinate Kirov, but were 'hostile elements' whose elimination was meant to strike terror; it was not even an act of revenge, but a symbol and a warning."[67]

State Prosecutor Vyshinsky referred to Kirov's murder during his questioning of the defendants in the Moscow show trials, and Nikita Khrushchev referred to it in his famous "secret speech" denouncing Stalin in 1956. Kirov's death has been the object of study, speculation, and debate for decades as scholars have tried to unravel the course of events, to identify who was responsible and the reasons behind it.[68]

The Conduct of the Three Moscow Show Trials

The three Moscow show trials, held from 1936 through 1938, were conducted under similar procedures. The accused were usually demoted from their official positions, then arrested, dismissed from all positions, and purged from the Communist Party. The trials were held under the auspices of the Military Collegium of the Supreme Court. There were three judges, and the chief judge for all of the show trials was the Latvian-born General Vasily Vasilyevich Ulrich, chairman of the Military Collegium and a judge in the Kirov murder trials. During the trials he was referred to as the "President." Vyshinsky was the chief prosecutor, called the state prosecutor or procurator. He served as Chief Prosecutor of the Soviet Union from 1935 through 1939. Vyshinsky, a former Menshevik, had joined the Bolsheviks in 1920, and in 1928 Stalin appointed him as head of the office to investigate and prosecute cases of sabotage. He had also been the prosecutor in the Kirov murder trials. Unlike others who did Stalin's bidding but were still purged, both Ulrich and Vyshinsky survived the purges and lived until the 1950s. The trials were held in the ornate October Hall of the House of Trade Unions, formerly the Noblemen's Club in tsarist Russia. There were seats for spectators, including limited seating for foreign journalists and diplomats.

The defendants were listed in the indictments with the designation "employee" and were addressed as "accused" (e.g., "Accused Radek"). The defendants were asked if they wanted defense counsel; most declined. Almost all of them pleaded guilty. Vyshinsky's courtroom examinations of the defendants and his lengthy summations at the ends of the trials included strident harangues of accusation and derision. He railed at the defendants, forced them to repeat their confessions (often the only evidence against them), and forced them to denounce themselves and others. The defendants' self-incriminating confessions and recantations of heretical beliefs had their basis in the Bolshevik ritual of *samokritika* (public self-criticism).

The defendants were allowed to cross-examine witnesses, usually their co-defendants. The trials ended with Vyshinsky giving lengthy summations, filled with name-calling and recriminations against the defendants and calling for guilty verdicts and executions for their alleged villainous crimes against Stalin, the state, and the Soviet people. The defendants could make final pleas, which had no effect on the judges' verdicts. They could also make pleas for clemency to the Presidium of the Supreme Soviet; clemency was never granted. Verdicts were quickly rendered, and executions were quickly carried out. The few defendants who received prison sentences died while incarcerated.

Before, during, and after these trials, Soviet media excoriated the defendants and praised their convictions. As in earlier trials, the Soviet government arranged for public demonstrations and public meetings with speakers vilifying the defendants and the crowds calling for the death penalty. In his memoir *Mission to Moscow*, US ambassador Joseph E. Davies reported on such public meeting during the second trial.[69]

US Reporting on the Show Trials

Foreign Relations of the United States: Soviet Union, 1933-1939, a compilation of official diplomatic communications, included a "List of Persons" which named several of the Moscow show trial defendants and their fates. In some cases, US diplomats did not have definite information on the fates of some of the officials who were victims of the purges. The "List of Persons" listed only the years that they were arrested or purged or using speculative terms, such as "missing and presumed executed," "probably executed," "disappeared," or "removed."[70] The Embassy staff had met several of the accused (e.g., Karl Radek and Marshal Mikhail Tukhachevsky). The Soviets allowed either one or two US diplomats to attend the trials. Loy W. Henderson's and George F. Kennan's official accounts of the trials reflected their perplexed reactions to the proceedings and reflected their incredulity concerning the trial charges and the defendants' self-condemning confessions. Ambassador Davies accepted the charges, confessions, and guilty verdicts.

On a daily basis, Walter Duranty and Harold Denny of the *New York Times* sent lengthy articles that passed through Soviet censorship that described the demeanor of the defendants as well as trial testimony. By the time of the third trial, mainstream American news magazines had adopted a skeptical, "here-we-go-again" tone about the charges, the confessions, and the verdicts. Liberal publications varied in their analyses of the trials, ranging from believing in the alleged conspiracies to considering the trials to be a necessary evil in the evolution of the world's first socialist state. Reporters for these publications also criticized the shortcomings of the Soviet justice system in its lack of protection of individuals' rights. Some liberal journalists eventually condemned the trials. The Communist Party USA sent its members to report on the trials. Their accounts vilified the defendants, Trotsky and trial critics. Limited to secondhand accounts, American Trotskyists railed against the trials, published Trotsky's rebuttals to the charges, and railed against Stalin and the Communist Party USA for its unwavering support for Stalin and the trials. American intellectuals were divided on the trials.

Conclusion

Before 1936 the stage was set for the Moscow show trials. Stalin held absolute power, and Trotsky was in exile. These events were chronicled in the US press and informed the US public about these happenings and the workings of Soviet justice, and further solidified the beliefs of the radical left and divided them into pro-Stalinist and pro-Trotskyist camps. Such divisions would last throughout the three Moscow show trials, causing bitter actions and recriminations among the various radical factions. While powerless, Trotsky's exile gave him a platform for frequently denouncing the Stalinist regime and the charges against him, allowing him coverage in the mainstream American press that he may not have gotten otherwise.

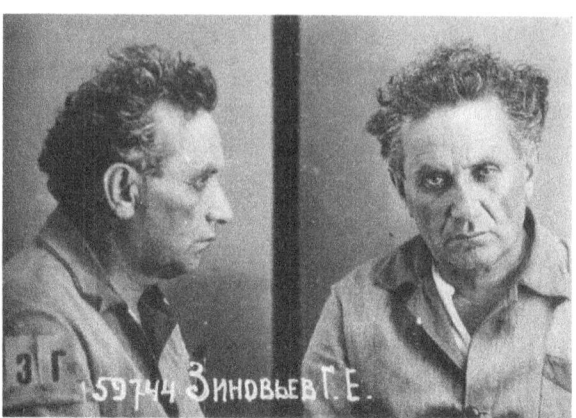

Plate 3.1 Lev Kamenev, defendant in the first Moscow show trial. "Lev Kamenev 1920s." Wikimedia Commons, n.d., http://commons.wikimedia.org (accessed July 1, 2022).

Plate 3.2 Arrest photograph of Grigori Zinoviev, defendant in the first Moscow show trial. "Ficha Politica de Zinoviev." Wikimedia Commons, December 1, 1934, http://commons.wikimedia.org (accessed July 1, 2022).

Plate 3.3 Andrey Vyshinsky, state prosecutor for all three Moscow show trials. "Vyshinskiy AYA." Wikimedia Commons, 1938, http://commons.wikimedia.org (accessed July 1, 2022).

Plate 3.4 Loy W. Henderson, the only American diplomat to attend the first Moscow show trial. "Loy Henderson," US National Archives and Records Administration photograph, public domain, https://archives.gov (accessed June 23, 2022).

3

The First Moscow Show Trial

The Case of the Trotskyite-Zinovievite Terrorist Centre (1936)*

The Conduct of the Trial

The first Moscow show trial was held from August 19 through August 24, 1936. There were sixteen defendants, charged under Articles 58 and 19 of the Criminal Code of Russian SFSR. According to the official trial transcript, the indictment was read, followed by the "definition of the charge" (the description of the "Trotskyite-Zinovievite United Terrorist Centre") and the connecting of the members of the alleged Centre to the assassination of Sergei Kirov. This was followed by accusations that the defendants were plotting to assassinate Joseph Stalin, Klementi T. Voroshilov (People's Commissar for Defense), Andrei A. Zhdanov (Communist Party leader in Leningrad), Lazar Moiseyevich Kaganovich (a member of Politburo), Grigori Konstantinovich Orjonikidze [also transliterated Orzhonikidze] (People's Commissar for Heavy Industry who later committed suicide), and Communist Party officials Stanislav Kossior and Pavel P. Postyshev.[1] Kossior and Postyshev would later be purged.

The indictment accused four men of being the ring leaders—Grigori (Yuri) Zinoviev, Lev Borisovich Kamenev, Ivan Petrovich Bakayev, and Grigori E. Ekdokimov [also transliterated as Yevkokimov]. The defendants were accused of being complicit in the "foul murder" of Sergei Kirov and of being under orders from Leon Trotsky and his son to form a counter-revolutionary group to take power and kill Stalin and other Soviet leaders. The most prominent of the accused were Zinoviev and Kamenev, well known in the West and had previously been convicted in the murder of Sergei Kirov. Zinoviev was a Communist Party

---

* Union of Soviet Socialist Republics, People's Commissariat of Justice, *The Case of the Trotskyite-Zinovievite Terrorit Centre: Report of the Court Proceedings Heard before the Military Collegium of the Supreme Court of the U.S.S.R.. Moscow, August 19–24. 1936* (Moscow: The Commissariat, 1936).

veteran and a companion of Lenin in exile. Among his former positions were head of the Petrograd (later Leningrad) Soviet, held memberships of the Central Committee, the Politburo, the Central Committee of the Russian Communist Party and was an organizer and president of the Comintern.[2]

Lev Kamenev had married Trotsky's younger sister Olga Davidovna. He was also a veteran Communist leader, a former member of the Politburo and had held a variety of other Party and government positions. In 1925 Zinoviev and Kamenev had joined Stalin in removing Trotsky from power. Stalin then turned on them. Kamenev underwent a public repenting (*samokritika*) and was removed from his position on the Council of Labor and Defense and as People's Commissar for Trade in 1926. Zinoviev was well known in the West. Both were found guilty and executed on August 24, 1936. *The New York Times* published articles which chronicled their careers and persecution by Stalin, terming the final years of these veteran revolutionaries as being spent in "degradation and imprisonment."[3]

Bakayev had been a member of the Central Committee and the Central Control Commission and head of the NKVD in Leningrad. Ekdokimov had been a leader of the Communist Party in Leningrad and a member of the Central Committee. Both had been defendants in the Kirov murder trial.

Other prominent defendants are listed in the following paragraph with their former positions:

> Isak I. Reingold—Head of the Cotton Division in the People's Commissariat for Agriculture;
> Sergei Vitalevich Mrachkovsky—Commander in the Civil War;
> Ivan Nikitich Smirnov—Member of the Central Committee; commander in the Civil War;
> Vagarshak Arutyanovich Ter-Vaganyan—Leader of the Armenian Communist Party and member of the Central Committee; editor of *Under the Banner of Marxism*, a Communist Party journal.

Reingold's fall from grace came in 1935 when he was expelled from the Party when the Cotton Division was purged over his alleged membership in the "Trotsky-Zinovieff opposition," held responsible for a lax Party organization in the Division and blamed for trouble with harvesting the cotton crop.[4] Reingold tried to defend himself against some of the charges.

Lesser defendants were: Latvian Communist Konon Borisovich Berman-Yurin, Fritz David, Civil War hero Ephim Alexandrovich Dreitzer, Edouard Solomonovich Holtzman, Moissei Ilyich Lurye, Nathan Lazarevich Lurye, Valentin Pavlovich Olberg, and Richard Vitoldovich Pickel (Zinoviev's former secretary).

Mikhail Pavlovich Tomsky, a former member of the Politburo, the Red International of Trade Unions, the Presidium of the Central Executive Committee, president of the All-Russian Central Soviet (Council) of Trade Unions, and head of OGIZ (State Publishing House), was implicated in this trial and committed suicide on August 22, 1936.[5]

This assassination plot was alleged to be carried out with the assistance of the German-born defendants—Berman-Yurin, David, Nathan Lurye, and Olberg—who purportedly had been sent by Trotsky to be assassins. Witnesses, including Smirnov's former wife, backed up the accusations of the organization of the traitors' group and the plot to kill Stalin. There was little physical evidence presented. During the trial the defendants made extensive, self-incriminating confessions and implicated other leaders who would be defendants in subsequent trials.

State Prosecutor Andrey Vyshinsky gave a long summation, demanding death for each defendant, calling them "a gang of contemptible terrorists," "sworn enemies of the Soviet Union," and guilty of "double-dealing deception and provocation." Vyshinsky condemned the accused with these words, the most famous quotation from the show trials:

> These wreckers are a contemptible base, vile, despicable, rotten band of murderous scoundrels ... mad Fascist dogs—the dregs of humanity—the scum of the underworld—traitors and bandits. They planned to walk to power over the corpses of leaders of this country. *They are mad dogs and must be shot—every one of them.*[6] [Italics added.]

The defendants were allowed to make final pleas, but they were all found guilty and sentenced to death. Trotsky and his exiled son Lev Sedov were "convicted by the evidence" *in absentia* and declared to be subject to arrest and trial if they ever returned to the Soviet Union. In October 1936, the *New York Times* published a rare account of the executions of seven of the defendants; this account had reached London by a "roundabout route." This article detailed the executions of Kamenev, Smirnov, and Zinoviev. This article claimed that Kamenev died bravely while Zinoviev blubbered and "screamed for mercy."[7]

Joseph Stalin did not let Kamenev and Zinoviev rest in peace. In a 1938 letter in *Pravda*, Stalin condemned them, took a swipe at Trotsky's belief in worldwide revolution, and condemned the "gentlemen" (defendants) by claiming that they "later became spies and agents of fascism, denied the possibility of constructing socialism in our country without the previous victory of the socialist revolution in other countries, in the capitalist countries."[8] US Embassy Secretary Loy

Henderson was of the opinion that this letter was for "internal consumption," with an eye as well to "radical groups abroad" to demonstrate that the Soviet government had not "departed from the original principles of Leninism."[9]

In the aftermath of this trial Gengrikh Yagoda, head of the NKVD, was removed from office and downgraded to head the People's Commissariat of Ways of Communication. He would be a defendant in the third show trial. Nikolai Yezhov became head of the NKVD.

Official US Reactions

Embassy secretary Loy W. Henderson was the only American diplomat to attend this trial. He wrote:

> The few foreign journalists and diplomats permitted to attend the trial . . . were *puzzled and astonished at the manner in which the defendants denounced themselves and Trotski* and dragged in the names of other prominent Soviet leaders who in the past had been opposed to Stalin. It is difficult to state with any degree of certainty the extent to which the accused were guilty of the crimes to which they confessed or to explain the motives prompting their behavior at the trial.[10] [Italics added.]

Henderson went on to express the skepticism of the other Embassy secretaries concerning the charges and listed the Embassy staff's conclusions as to the true reasons for the trial. Their theories included that the trial was to prevent expression of any dissatisfaction within the Party, to show that there would be no room for criticism under the new constitution, to eliminate the influence of former leaders, to blame Trotskyists for any economic failures, to kill Trotsky's influence in international circles, and to increase hatred for Germany. Henderson also surmised that the defendants testified to escape torture, to get lesser sentences, and to spare their families.

Henderson also reported the rumor of the arrests of "hundreds of active or former Party members" and speculated on the fates of Nikolai Bukharin, Yuri Pyatakov, Karl Radek, and Alexei Rykov. Henderson cited a "usually well-informed Soviet official" who incorrectly predicted that they would "probably be exonerated to varying degrees from complicity in terroristic plots."[11] These men would be tried in the second and third show trials.

In another communiqué on September 1, 1936, Henderson expressed skepticism about any assassination plots, especially in league with Nazi Germany, as eleven of the defendants were Jewish. He commented on the climate of fear that resulted from the announcement of the executions of the defendants, including the reluctance of Russians to speak to foreigners. He concluded his analysis by writing:

> It is reported . . . that hundreds of persons have been arrested on charges of disloyalty to Stalin and the Party and that some of them are being tried in secret at the present time. The announcement of the execution of all sixteen of the condemned men within 24 hours of the passing of the sentence has made a profound impression, and a *wave of fear, almost equal to that noticeable following the assassination of Kirov in December 1934, is said to be sweeping over the country.* It is understood that members and former members of the Communist Party who . . . may have been on friendly terms with persons now branded as adherents of Trotski or with any of the persons accused or mentioned in the trial are now terror-stricken. . . . Many Soviet officials who a few weeks ago spoke to them with an air of self-confidence are now most diffident and are apparently afraid to come to any decisions without protracted consultations with their superiors.[12] [Italics added.]

In his memoir Henderson devoted several pages to this trial and wrote that, during one trial session, he sat directly behind Karl Radek, the Soviets' most prominent journalist. Henderson stated that Radek "flushed" when his name was mentioned during the trial. Radek would be a leading defendant in the second show trial. Henderson also wrote that the trial and executions were a shock to Communists and other leftists.[13]

Reactions of American Journalists

Shortly before the trial began, Harold Denny of the *New York Times* wrote a steady stream of articles about the "enmity" between Trotskyists and Stalinists with Trotskyists joining with "external foes" to overthrow the government. This resulted in a "hunt for subversive elements within the Communist party."[14] This theory was the foundation for the trial charges of collusion with Nazi Germany. The trial was front-page news in the *New York Times*.[15] Denny's articles were subject to Soviet censorship and lacked the same level of skepticism as Henderson's reports, but they gave interesting details on court procedures and the demeanor of the defendants. Denny reported on the indictment which directly linked Zinoviev and Kamenev to Sergei Kirov's assassination. Denny correctly predicted that the defendants would receive the death penalty.[16] Writing from the safety of Paris, *New York*

Times correspondent Walter Duranty believed in the existence of the Trotskyist plot while the Soviet government was "doing its utmost to maintain peace."[17]

As the trial progressed, Denny reported on the defendants' seeming eagerness to confess and to implicate each other and other leaders who would be defendants in future trials He reported that the testimonies "rocked and shocked the breathless audience." As the defendants made their self-condemning confessions, Denny reported that Kamenev looked "animated and distinguished" while Zinoviev looked "utterly beaten, chagrined and apathetic."[18] He also reported that Trotsky was the "real conspirator."[19] Denny concluded that the trial demonstrated that the old-line intellectuals were being replaced with "practical, realistic iron-willed executives."[20] Denny's article on the defendants' final pleas, guilty verdicts, and death sentences characterized most of them as "apparently reconciled to death" and included his opinion that this trial was the "most notable in the history of the Soviet Union."[21]

Immediately after the verdicts, Denny reported that industrial workers were summoned to meetings to pass resolutions of approval of the verdicts, and *Pravda* and *Izvestia* published editorials endorsing the verdicts and that the verdicts were approved by Soviet workers.[22] At the same time there was "great skepticism" among foreign observers, and he was also incredulous about the self-condemning confessions and termed the leading defendants to be "remnants of various opposition movements" of men who hated Stalin.[23]

The *New York Times* editorialists did not share their reporters' opinions and published two brief editorials on this trial. The first quoted from Kamenev's testimony and Trotsky's denials; the second criticized the Soviets' rule "by secret police and firing squad."[24]

The major news magazines published several articles on this trial. *Time* published a sardonic article on the announcement of one of "Dictator Stalin's" "great propaganda trials" as a ploy to distract the populace from Soviet activities in the Spanish Civil War. The article also included Trotsky's accusations of "fraud, fakery and framing innocents" and his call for an international investigation.[25] A second article was a ridicule-filled eyewitness account that concentrated on Zinoviev, Kamenev, and the defendants' seemingly eager, sometimes lengthy, self-condemning confessions ("confessing by the yard"). The reporter mocked Zinoviev and Kamenev and pointed out the irony of the defendants confessing to plotting to kill Stalin but then praising him in court. The reporter also made a point of listing their original Jewish surnames.[26]

Newsweek published three articles on this trial and a follow-up article on the exiled Trotsky. The first was a brief account of the announcement of the trial and the fact that this was the first time that leading Bolsheviks could face the death penalty.[27] The second article was a longer account of the trial which characterized the defendants as confessing like "Gilbert and Sullivan puppets," highlighted Reingold's ratting out his fellow conspirators and how the defendants "heaped accusations on Trotsky," their alleged leader in the conspiracy. The reporter termed Andrey Vyshinsky's summation as "frenzied" and reported that the defendants "cracked" and "buried their heads in their arms and wept."[28] The follow-up article concentrated on Trotsky's exile in Norway, his railings against Stalin and speculation on the fates of other Old Bolsheviks, including journalist Karl Radek, a future trial defendant. This article included an account of Moscow's attempt to have the Norwegian government expel Trotsky.[29]

Literary Digest published a skeptical article that termed the proceedings to be an "orgy of confessions." The reporter also quoted Trotsky's vehement denials.[30] The anticommunist monthly *American Mercury* published a scathing article by Eugene Lyons, a former Moscow correspondent, in which he ripped the Soviet justice system to shreds and called it the "fantastic trial" with its "weird" and "bizarre" proceedings. He portrayed the trial as a "sort of morality play" with the defendants playing their assigned roles after being in the hands of the "refined cruelty of the GPU."[31]

Both liberal weeklies published articles on this trial. *New Republic* accepted the trial charges "at face value," consigned the defendants to their fate because of their failure to see the futility of their doomed plots and dismissed criticism of the trial as "labored hypotheses."[32] An article in *The Nation* at the beginning of the trial had an optimistic tone with the new Soviet constitution being an indication that a "new democracy is slowly being born." The reporter considered this trial to be a symptom of the Soviets' sense of being surrounded by enemies and that the demise of the Old Bolsheviks was the inevitable result of the consolidation of revolutionary gains.[33] After the executions, a brief editorial in *The Nation* considered the trial to be "peculiarly to Russia and to a revolutionary psychology" and attributed the trial to the "discipline and purposes of the party," a trait of "revolutionary Russia." The editorialist also put the trial within the context of Russia's reactions to the rise of fascism, the Spanish Civil War, and the need to be unified and have "every opposition stamped out."[34] When the trial transcript was released in English, *The Nation* was more skeptical of the proceedings, including the lack of evidence. The reporter termed Soviet propaganda to be "shocking" in calling for the deaths of the defendants before the trial had started. The reporter also supported Trotsky's call for an international commission to investigate the charges against him.[35]

Reactions of American Radicals

The leaders of the Communist Party USA dutifully followed the directives of the Comintern, and *Daily Worker* reported extensively on the trial. Using reports from the official Soviet news agency TASS and from *Pravda*, *Daily Worker* published several articles and editorials with headlines that excoriated the defendants, Trotsky, and critics of the trial. With headlines about the "terrorist plot," *Daily Worker* reported that Soviet workers were asking for "no mercy" for the defendants and reported that Trotsky had issued orders to kill Stalin.[36] A cartoon depicted Trotsky and Kamenev holding a bomb labeled "Terrorism" with a dark, menacing, swastika-bearing shadow looming over them.[37]

One article included a letter by the Bulgarian-born Soviet diplomat Khristian Rakovsky in which he stood with Stalin and expressed shame for his own past associations with these "counter-revolutionaries, criminals and murderers."[38] This public denunciation and confession did not save Rakovsky; he would be a defendant in the third Moscow show trial. *Daily Worker* also published editorial-style articles on Trotskyism using the term "Nazi aid" in condemning the alleged plot, and, in response to criticism of the trial by the American Socialist Party, urged all socialists to repudiate Trotskyists.[39] A third editorial condemned the "double dealings" of Kamenev and Zinoviev for their alleged contact with Trotsky and for their alleged roles in Kirov's assassination.[40] The Communist Party USA dutifully reported back to the Comintern, listing all of the articles that it had published and justifying their use of "capitalist" American newspapers and "bourgeois press services" to beef up their coverage.[41] Pro-trial articles were also published in the American Party's Yiddish-language newspaper *Morgen Freiheit* and *Western Worker*, the Party's newspaper for the western states.[42]

Joshua Kunitz attended the trial and published four articles in the Communist weekly *New Masses*.[43] At the end of his final article, he wrote this contempt-filled statement about the defendants: "They were once Bolsheviks. One feels that they realize all the more sensitively, here, in the presence of death, that history is with communism. . . . They killed Kirov, one of their best beloved leaders. Trust the murderers? Not even when they sob recantations in the face of death."[44] Kunitz's articles had been reviewed by Communist Party USA leaders who considered his original drafts as too full of sympathetic descriptions of the defendants, criticized the prosecution, and "wrote a series of articles that were very much against us."[45] The Comintern emphasized the need for "thorough control with writing articles against Trotskyism" in a directive sent to foreign communist parties in December 1936.[46]

New Masses also published a series of editorials that disparaged Trotsky, trial critics, and Trotsky's defenders in three editorials. The first editorial concentrated on Trotsky as an "unscrupulous adventurer" and the "degenerate, counter-revolutionary madness" of the plots and called the trial a triumph of Soviet democracy.[47] Two more editorials targeted the newly formed Provisional American Committee for the Defense of Leon Trotsky as being biased in favor of Trotsky and targeted the liberal weekly *The Nation* for its opinion on the trial, calling the editorial writer a "Trotskyite mouthpiece."[48]

The Communist, the American Party's journal of Marxist theory, published an editorial by Alexander Bittelman that condemned the defendants and Trotsky for their "dastardly plans" and used the Stalinist line that Trotskyism was fascism.[49] *Soviet Russia Today*, the monthly magazine of the Friends of the Soviet Union, published several articles supporting the trial, writing that the trial was necessary so that the Soviet Union could "preserve its unity and strength."[50] *Soviet Russia Today* also published an article by Anna Louise Strong, one of America's most famous expatriates in the Soviet Union. Strong was prone to florid, overly dramatic prose, and she described the defendants' confessions as evidence of their descent into the "pit of self-acknowledged degradation in which they declared themselves worthy of death."[51]

Following a directive from the Comintern, the American Communist press also published pamphlets on the trial, a practice that continued during later show trials. These included pamphlets by Comintern head Georgi Dimitrov, summaries of the indictment, State Prosecutor Vyshinsky's summation and the verdicts, and an eyewitness account by D. N. Pritt, a British barrister and MP.[52] Pritt's account was praised in *Soviet Russia Today* by radical lawyer Alexander Unger as an answer to all complaints and criticism of the trial.[53]

Dissident American Communists, who had been expelled from the Communist Party USA and had formed the Communist Party (Opposition), reported the trial in *Workers Age*, their official newspaper. The first article on the trial was a brief account that included the belief that there was a connection between the defendants and the "Nazi Gestapo."[54] While no admirer of Trotsky, the author of the second article believed the charges but deviated from the Party line by disagreeing with the death sentences for "such personages as Zinoviev, Kamenev, Smirnov, etc." Perhaps because *Workers Age* had been founded by Communists who had been expelled from the Party, the author stated the need for a "healthy, constructive critical opposition" within the Soviet Communist Party.[55]

New Militant, the official newspaper of the Workers Party of the United States, laid the groundwork for its criticism of the Moscow show trials in late 1935 when it began a campaign to expose the harsh conditions of the imprisonment and internal exile of Soviet dissidents and veteran revolutionaries. It published first-person accounts, terming these conditions to be the "torture of real Bolsheviks in Stalin's prisons" and "Stalin's anti-Bolshevik terror." Trotsky applauded the publishing of these accounts, and the Trotskyist *New International* reported that these prison accounts showed the "savage and treacherous persecution" of the "proletarian revolutionists."[56] *New Militant* also condemned *Daily Worker* for "waging a hysterical and poisonous campaign" against these revelations.[57] In February 1936 the Workers Party organized a meeting in New York City with a speech given by the *New Militant*'s editor James P. Cannon and A. J. Muste on "Stalin's Terror Against Bolsheviks."[58]

When this trial began. Trotsky vehemently denied the trial charges and attacked the Stalinist regime. From his exile in Norway, Trotsky called the trial "humbug," "for political vengeance," and based on forced confessions.[59] The Trotskyist newspaper *Socialist Appeal* published Trotsky's emphatic denials of the charges and his call for an investigation by an "impartial international commission."[60] Trotskyists published articles and pamphlets condemning this trial, using Trotsky's term "frame-up" in their articles. *Socialist Appeal* also published an editorial in September 1936, which supported Trotsky's denial of the charges. The editorialist dismissed the defendants' confessions and wrote: "It is a shameful spectacle to see the first workers' government resorting to a political frame-up" and compared it to the Nazis setting fire to the Reichstag.[61]

The October 1936 issue of *Socialist Appeal* devoted several pages to this trial. In an interview, Trotsky blamed Stalin and again called the trial a "frame-up" that began with Kirov's assassination.[62] Leading Trotskyist Max Shachtman blamed the bureaucracy (a favorite target of Trotsky) for a "clumsy and cynical frame-up" and gave a rationale for the defendants' confessions as attempts to spare their lives. He asserted that the purposes for the trial were to distract the public from Soviet failures in the Spanish Civil War, to further Stalin's "socialism in one country" philosophy, to "behead . . . possible experienced leadership" against the bureaucracy, to stifle opposition, and to discredit Trotsky and Trotskyism.[63] Shachtman expanded this article into *Behind the Moscow Trial*, a pamphlet that placed the trial within a historical context and included a detailed analysis of the trial transcript. Shachtman concluded that the reasons for the trial were for Stalin to "Further his reconciliation with the world bourgeoisie, particularly with the so-called 'democratic' imperialism. The other was to strengthen the shaky foundation of his own power in the Soviet Union."[64] This pamphlet earned a scornful review in *New Masses* as the reviewer rejected Shachtman's characterization of the trial as a frame-up because the defendants made such full confessions; the reviewer also dismissed criticism of the lack of evidence.[65]

Socialist Appeal did not end its criticism after the trial was over. It also reprinted a letter from Menshevik Theodore Dan to the *Manchester Guardian* in which he condemned Stalin for his "personal dictatorship."[66] Shachtman's pamphlet and Trotsky's discourses proved to be too much for the news magazine *Time* which ran an anti-Trotsky article with the reporter writing that Trotsky ("Russia's Great Exile") "expectorates in print upon Dictator Stalin on all occasions." Perhaps reflecting the mainstream press's tiring of Trotsky and his endless denials, the reporter wrote that the purpose of Shachtman's pamphlet was to "keep up the notion that Stalin regards him [Trotsky] as a serious enemy."[67]

Socialist Appeal published an article in 1938 by Soviet defector Walter Krivitsky, in which he described the marathon interrogation (the "conveyor'") of defendant Mrachkovsky and Mrachkovksy's "confrontation" with his fellow defendant Smirnov, urging Smirnov to confess.[68] Trotsky's exiled son Lev Sedov also wrote a book dissecting this trial.[69]

The Trotskyists continued to criticize this trial even after Trotsky's assassination in 1940. The Revolutionary Workers League, a splinter group, published an excerpt from Trotsky's journal in *Fourth International* in which he described Zinoviev and Kamenev as his "bitter enemies" who had succumbed to "unprecedented pressure."[70] *New Militant* editor James P. Cannon wrote in 1956 in the *International Socialist Review* that he thought that Zinoviev confessed "primarily because he thought he could serve the cause" so that the opposition leaders could live in order to overthrow Stalin and restore a "revolutionary leadership of the Russian party and the Comintern."[71]

The Revolutionary Workers League also published *Stalinism Betrays the Spanish Revolution: Behind the Murder of Zinoviev, Kamenev, Smirnov and the Frame-Up of Trotsky*, a pamphlet that used Trotsky's favorite terms "frame-up" and "amalgam," calling the trial "monstrous" and the confessions the results of "terrorizing" the defendants.[72] Amalgam was Trotsky's term for the NKVD's method of constructing a conspiracy among the accused through their confessions.

American socialists had their doubts about this trial. The Party's weekly newspaper *Socialist Call* published two articles in opposition to this trial. The first article stated: "Credulity is strained by the thought that men who had won the confidence of the international working class through years of revolutionary activity could thus betray their own past and their hopes for labor's future." The reporter urged the establishment of an "international labor commission" to investigate the charges against Trotsky.[73] The second article consisted of excerpts from the Austrian Friedrich Adler's anti-trial pamphlet *The Witchcraft Trial in Moscow*.[74] *American Socialist Monthly*, the short-lived Party journal of socialist theory, published an article by David P. Berenberg in which he stated that the trial proved nothing. He dissected the defendants' confessions and concluded that the "irresponsible dictatorship of Stalin in Russia" would never lead to socialism.[75]

In 1937 the American Socialist Society's Rand School of Social Science published *Letter of an Old Bolshevik* by Boris Nicolaevsky, an exiled Menshevik. Purportedly based on conversations with Nikolai Bukharin in Paris, *Letter* included a thoughtful and thorough introduction, accounts of the inner workings of the Politburo concerning Kirov's murder, the ensuing trials, and the downfall of Zinoviev and Kamenev.[76] The authenticity of *Letter* has been a topic of debate among scholars and was denied by Anna Larina, Bukharin's widow.[77]

Conclusion

The first show trial set the pattern for future trials—the outrageous charges, the vilifications of the defendants in the Soviet press and in public demonstrations, the defendants' self-condemning confessions, their implicating of others, and the lack of physical evidence. It also established the pattern of Vyshinsky's ranting closing statements, calling for guilty verdicts, the death penalty, and swift executions. It also saw the beginning of the pattern of the Embassy secretaries' and mainstream news magazines' skepticism about the trials.

Reactions to this trial had a major impact on the American radical left, widening the fault lines among the various factions concerning the Soviet Union. The Communist Party USA's leadership maintained its utter loyalty to the Stalinist line, blaming Trotsky and criticizing his American supporters. Taking the opposite view, American Trotskyists condemned the trial, Stalin, and his American supporters while defending their ideological leader and publishing Trotsky's ceaseless and forceful denials. Various radical splinter groups were also critical of this trial.

This trial also set the pattern of American responses that would be repeated throughout the subsequent trials and started the process of crystalizing American attitudes toward the Soviet Union. History would eventually prove the Trotskyists to be right with the exposure of the falseness of the charges and the forced confessions, but during this time, Trotsky, his supporters, and other American critics of the trials could do nothing to change the course of events.

Plate 4.1 Karl Radek, defendant in the second Moscow show trial. "Karl Radek in Moscow in 1930s." n.d., Wikimedia Commons, http://commons.wikimedia.org (accessed July 20, 2022).

Plate 4.2 US ambassador Joseph E. Davies, an American diplomat who attended the second and third Moscow show trials. Harris and Ewing. "White House Caller." July 18, 1939. Wikimedia Commons, http://commons.wikimedia.org (accessed July 20, 2022).

Plate 4.3 George F. Kennan, an American diplomat who attended the second Moscow show trial. "George F. Kennan, 1947." 1947. Wikimedia Commons, http://commons.wikimedia.org (accessed July 20, 2022).

4

The Second Moscow Show Trial
The Case of the Anti-Soviet Trotskyite Centre (1937)[*]

The Conduct of the Trial

With a great deal of fanfare, the Soviets unveiled a new, seemingly more liberal constitution at the end of 1936. Harold Denny of the *New York Times* wrote articles in which he was cautiously optimistic about its more liberal aspects and as it being a sign that Stalin was slightly relaxing his "iron hand."[1] However, this new constitution did not stop the Moscow show trials, and the year 1937 is considered by scholars to be the height of the purges with this bigger show trial and the "Yezhovshchena"—the arrests of thousands of citizens—directed by NKVD head Nikolai Yezhov (the "Bloody Dwarf").

Preparations for the trial began in August 1936 when the Soviet government announced investigations into the activities of six prominent Bolsheviks who had been named in the first trial, most notably Karl Radek and Nikolai Bukharin, as well as others who would be defendants in this and in the third show trial. The second trial was announced on January 19 ("another great public treason trial") at the same time as the announcement of Nikolai Bukharin's removal as editor of *Izvestia*.[2]

The second show trial, also known as the "Parallel Centre" trial, was held from January 23 through January 30, 1937. There were seventeen defendants who were charged with "treason against the country, espionage, acts of diversion, wrecking activities and the preparation of terrorist acts."[3] The defendants were alleged to have been a reserve group that was to proceed with their counter-revolutionary plotting if the first group failed. The trial was conducted in a similar fashion to the first trial, with the exception of the ineffectual presence of three defense attorneys from the Moscow Collegium of Defence. The alleged conspiracy was characterized by

---

[*] Union of Soviet Socialist Republic, People's Commissariat of Justice, *Report of the Proceedings in the Case of the Anti-Soviet Trotsky8te Centre: Heard before the Military Collegium of the Supreme Court of the U.S.S.R.. Moscow, January 23–30, 1937* (Moscow: The Commissariat, 1937).

State Prosecutor Andrey Vyshinsky as the "vile, treasonable, anti-Soviet activities of the Trotskyites, and the contemptible fascist hirelings, traitors to their country and enemies of the people."[4] The indictment charged the following:

> The main task which the parallel centre set itself was the forcible overthrow of the Soviet government with the object of changing the social and state system existing in the U.S.S.R. L. D. *Trotsky*, and on his instructions the parallel Trotskyite centre, aimed as seizing power with the aid of foreign states with the object of restoring capitalist social relations in the U.S.S.R.[5]

The most prominent defendants were Karl Berngardovich Radek and Georgy (Yuri) Leonidovich Pyatakov. Balding and bespectacled, the Polish-born Radek had been a prominent journalist and editor, a former secretary of the Comintern and his writings had been published in the West. He used sarcasm and ridicule toward critics of the Soviet state.[6] In 1927 Radek was expelled from the Communist Party and suffered internal exile to Siberia for being a Trotskyist. While in exile he pleaded that he and his fellow exiles, including Trotsky, be allowed to return.[7] To get back into Stalin's good graces, he wrote *Portraits and Pamphlets*, which included a laudatory profile of Stalin.[8] He also wrote one last article in *Izvestia* in which he confessed his heresies and denounced Trotsky; in his defense he claimed that he had personally sabotaged one of Trotsky's plots in 1928. An Associated Press reporter claimed that Radek wrote this to spare himself from execution.[9] This article did him little good as he, Pyatakov, and Grigori Sokolnikov were denounced in *Pravda* before the trial began.[10]

One of the highlights of the trial was Radek's verbal sparring with State Prosecutor Vyshinsky, which was in contrast to the other defendants' abject confessions. These lively exchanges were remarked upon in the Western press. Radek was found guilty and sentenced to ten years in prison where he died. Such was his reputation in the West that in 1955 American ex-Communist Louis Budenz wrote "What Has Become of Karl Radek?" Budenz claimed that Radek had become another non-person "among the long lines of men who have been lost in the Soviet unknown, in the vastness of the prison camps and in possible secret liquidation."[11]

Georgy Pyatakov [also transliterated as Piatakov] had been the Assistant People's Commissar for Heavy Industry and a member of the Party's Central Committee. Pyatakov had also been Chairman of the Supreme Tribunal of the Central Executive Committee. He had presided over the controversial treason trial of the Socialist Revolutionaries in 1922. Accused of being a Trotskyist, Pyatakov recanted his heresy in 1928; and both he and Radek recanted their heresies at the Seventeenth Party Congress in 1934.[12] In 1936 they published articles in *Pravda* that vilified Trotsky and the defendants in the first show trial. As directed by the Comintern, *Daily Worker* published a translation as one article.[13] According to historians William J. Chase and Vadim A. Staklo, the Comintern directive to publish this article was part of its international campaign against Trotsky and was an effort to validate the first show trial.[14] Sentenced to the fate that he had once ruled for others, Pyatakov was found guilty and shot.

There were two other prominent defendants who had also been implicated in the first public show trial—Leonid Petrovich Serebryakov and Grigori Yakovlevich Sokolnikov. Serebryakov had been Director of the Central Administration for Highway and Road Construction and Auto Transport, secretary of the Communist Party, and Assistant People's Commissar for Ways of Communication. He was shot. Sokolnikov had been ambassador to the United Kingdom and to France, Assistant People's Commissar for Foreign Affairs, and Assistant People's Commissar for the Timber Industry. He was sentenced to ten years and died in prison. His case was indicative of the government's anti-foreigner campaign which persecuted Soviet citizens who had been abroad or who had contact with foreigners in the Soviet Union. Walter Duranty of the *New York Times* incorrectly speculated that Radek and Sokolnikov would be witnesses in future trials.[15]

Other defendants were Valentin Volfridovich Arnold, Mikhail Solomonovich Boguslavsky, Yakov Naumovich Drobnis, Ivan Yosifovich Hrasche [also transliterated as Grasche], Ivan Alexandrovich Knyazev, Yakov Abramovich Livshits, Nikolai Ivanovich Muralov, Boris Osipovich Norkin, Gavril Yefremovich Pushin, Stanislav Antonovich Rataichak, Alexei Alexandrovich Shestov, Mikhail Stepanovich Stroilov, and Yosif Dmitrievich Turok. American diplomat George F. Kennan attended this trial and characterized these lesser defendants as a "somewhat motley company" with Muralov, Drobnis, Boguslavski, and Livshits, as "four other fairly well-known Trotskyites" and "nine lesser lights."[16] Thirteen defendants were sentenced to death. In addition to Radek and Sokolnikov, Arnold and Stroilov were given prison terms and were never heard from again. The judges were Vasily V. Ulrich, I. O. Matulevich, and N. M. Rychkov.

Witnesses verified alleged acts of espionage and sabotage. Two accusations momentarily tripped up the prosecution. The first was that in 1935, while in Germany on official business, Pyatakov had flown to Norway to meet with the exiled Trotsky. The Norwegian and German governments officially disputed this charge, stating that no flights took place between the airports in Germany and Norway during that time. Trotsky and his supporters also denied this charge. The prosecution also alleged that Trotsky's son Lev Sedov had met with conspirators in Copenhagen at a hotel that Trotskyists claimed did not exist at the time. Vyshinsky gave a lengthy closing statement in which he demanded the death penalty.

A side note to this trial was the death of Grigori Konstantinovich ("Sergo") Orzhonikidze [also transliterated as Orjonikidze], one of the senior government officials, who was allegedly a potential victim of the conspiracy. Orzhonikidze had been a member of the Politburo, the People's Commissar for Heavy Industry and head of the Supreme Economic Council. He committed suicide on February 18, 1937, echoing the fate of Mikhail Tomsky at the time of the first show trial. In reporting his death, *Time* described Orzhonikidze as "cold, brusque" and "Russia's greatest uprooter of bureaucracy and slasher of red tape."[17] The Soviet public was told that his death was from natural causes and overwork, and the government decreed a big state funeral in freezing weather.[18] According to Robert Conquest, Orzhonikidze committed suicide because he was shocked by the arrest of Pyatakov, his subordinate in the People's Commissariat of Heavy Industry. He had protested vehemently to Stalin about Pyatakov's arrest, was harassed, and shot himself.[19]

Official US Reactions

Without knowing who the defendants in the second show trial would be, Embassy secretary Loy W. Henderson predicted the fall of Radek in "The Meaning of Party Democracy," part of a communiqué that he sent on October 12, 1936. During this time, Kremlin officials were still talking to foreign diplomats, a situation that would change during the government's anti-foreigner campaign. Henderson reported on a conversation with a "Soviet official who is known to enjoy the confidence of the Kremlin" in which Henderson characterized this official's attitudes toward Radek as follows: "Men like Radek . . . whose loyalty to Stalin was believed to be more that of the mouth than of the heart were likely to fare badly."[20]

Embassy secretary George F. Kennan attended this trial to act as an interpreter for the newly arrived Ambassador Joseph E. Davies. Kennan assumed the existence of Trotskyists in a lengthy communiqué sent on February 13, 1937. However, his critique of the trial proceedings reeked of skepticism as to the veracity of the testimony against the defendants and as to the lack of evidence, other than their self-condemning confessions. He also remarked upon Radek's verbal sparring with Vyshinsky, and he speculated as to how much of the trial was "bona fide" and whether the participants were "talking in symbols." He was skeptical of the charges of sabotage while considering the charges of espionage to be "almost inevitable."[21]

Kennan then turned to four leading defendants—Serebryakov, Pyatakov, Sokolnikov, and Radek. Kennan considered Radek to be the main defendant and did not believe that he had been part of any active conspiracy. Kennan concluded that the theory of an international conspiracy was weak and speculated as to why the defendants confessed to the charges. Kennan disbelieved the charge that the main defendants were in a conspiracy with the lesser defendants. Mincing no words, he wrote:

> *The fact that some of these lesser defendants—evidently spies and stool pigeons— were people whom Radek and the other leading defendants had obviously never seen before in their lives or even heard of, caused little surprise among the public.* It had long since been a practice of the Soviet Government . . . to emulate the practice of the old Romans to crucify its most dangerous oppositionists in company with common thieves.[22] [Italics added.]

Kennan also read an account of the trial in the Soviet press and found a discrepancy between the "stenographic record" of the proceedings and this published account.[23] In a 1996 interview with CNN, Kennan sympathetically described the defendants as follows: "These were the faces of men who had been, if not tortured, then terrified in many ways, and often by threats to take it out on their families if they didn't confess. But they had been through hell, and they knew that these were likely to be their last hours."[24] In one of his memoirs, Kennan described State Prosecutor Vyshinsky's "thundering brutalities" and the "cringing confessions of the accused."[25] Kennan's views were in contrast to Ambassador Davies's opinion of Vyshinsky's performance and *New York Times* reporter Walter Duranty's rather positive appraisal of Vyshinsky's conduct in this trial.

Ambassador Davies devoted a section of his bestselling memoir *Mission to Moscow* to this trial.[26] He believed in the presence of a conspiracy and in the defendants' guilt. On February 4, 1937, Davies sent a letter to President Franklin D. Roosevelt in which he remarked upon the pervasive propaganda about this trial, including members of Party cells "working overtime" in discussing the trial with local residents and on the radio.[27] On February 17 he sent a long communiqué to the Secretary of State in which he termed the trial to be "terrific in its human drama." He described the demeanor of the leading defendants and described Vyshinsky's summation as a "scholarly, able presentation." However, he was critical of Soviet jurisprudence, considered the guilty verdicts to be inevitable, and "reluctantly" believed in the existence of a conspiracy.[28] In his diary Davies also described a public demonstration in Red Square in support of the verdicts.[29] In a letter to Senator James Francis Byrnes of South Carolina, Davies concluded that, while the rights of the accused were subordinated to those of the state, the court had established the fact of a conspiracy against the government.[30] No fan of Davies, Kennan characterized Davies's reports as placing "considerable credence in the fantastic charges leveled at these unfortunate men."[31]

Official concern about this trial continued throughout 1937. In June Embassy secretary Henderson sent another communiqué that summarized the purges thus far with their "waves of dismissals and arrests" and offered several theories for the purges. Regarding the first two trials, he surmised that Stalin had hoped to "discredit Trotsky at home and abroad and at the same time to eliminate a number of personalities who in case of a *coup d'état* might become influential overnight." Henderson also claimed that Stalin "was infuriated when he found that the trials resulted in increasing Trotsky's prestige abroad and were even greeted with considerable incredulity in the Soviet Union, particularly on the part of the new intelligentsia."[32]

Concern about the two public show trials reached the highest level of the Department of State when Secretary of State Cordell Hull had a meeting with Soviet ambassador Alexander Troyanovsky on October 26, 1937. Hull issued a memorandum which included his skepticism concerning the charges of spying. Hull was also incredulous about the defendants' confessions to crimes that were certain to result in the death penalty. Troyanovsky replied that he had consulted with FBI Director J. Edgar Hoover, who stated that most criminals confessed. Hull remained unconvinced.[33]

Another official source of information on this trial was *U. S. Military Intelligence Reports: Bi-Weekly Intelligence Summaries, 1928-1938*, a compilation of reports by the Military Intelligence Division of the War Department. These reports included analyses of internal politics. An extensive 1937 report included a comprehensive survey of the rise of the Bolsheviks, the rise of Stalin, and the trials. This conjecture-filled and bluntly worded report tied the trial to the Metropolitan-Vickers trial of 1933 and to the first show trial, summarized the charges, and characterized the defendants' confessions as an "orgy of self-accusation in extensive detail. Arrogance and humility vied with pedantic exposition and cynical flippancy." This may have been a reference to Radek's verbal sparring with Vyshinsky.

The author had little respect for the charges of conspiracy and plotting. The report listed a full page of reasons as to why the defendants confessed and listed the trial's "incongruities" in the light of the Soviet justice system. It included a series of questions on the status of the "Stalin regime," Stalin's motives, why the defendants played their "roles," the possibility of anti-Semitism as a cause and whether Stalin used the trials to lead the Soviet public "away from the first direction of the Revolution." The author also included sections of "what ifs" that questioned the defendants' motives and discussed whether the charges were true and the possible significance of the trials, including Stalin's belief that "Trotsky had engineered a formidable movement" and whether Stalin suffered from a "tyrannical phobia" and thus had eliminated all opposition. The author bluntly concluded that the alleged acts of sabotage "could very well have resulted from typical Russian ineptitude and inefficiency" and dismissed the alleged plots as "amateurish and ridiculous." The report ended with rendering a verdict of "Not Proven." This conclusion again illustrated the difference of opinion concerning the veracity of the trial charges and confessions within the US diplomatic establishment in Moscow. It echoed Kennan's skepticism and disagreed with Davies's belief in the existence of a conspiracy.[34]

Reactions of American Journalists

The *New York Times* provided extensive coverage by Walter Duranty, including coverage of Pyatakov's detailed, self-condemning confession which Duranty characterized as a "tale of black treason" given in a "clear, colorless voice." Duranty characterized such testimony as showing the defendants pleading guilty to crimes that guaranteed the death penalty.[35] He gave a sympathetic account of Radek's testimony, calling him "the greatest of European journalists" and a "delightful conversationalist" who delivered his confession with "rapier wit" in his "tilt of wits" with Vyshinsky.[36] Further testimony by Radek included confessions of the extensive sabotage of the railroads and a planned German-Japanese war against the Soviets with Trotsky involved in plotting to cede territory and resources to them. One of the witnesses was former Washington correspondent for *Izvestia* Vladimir Romm who also confessed to involvement in the plot.[37,38] Both Germany and Japan denied any war plotting with Trotsky.[39,40]

Vyshinsky's lengthy summation and the guilty verdicts were front-page news with Duranty praising Vyshinsky's handling of the prosecution.[41] A companion article described how some of the defendants "slumped forward in their chairs when the death penalty was demanded."[42] While an excellent writer who provided concise descriptions of the defendants' demeanor and the courtroom atmosphere, Duranty believed in the defendants' guilt and in their involvement in these unbelievable plots to overthrow the Soviet government in collusion with Trotsky and Nazi Germany.

The verdicts, death sentences, and prison terms were also front-page news, along with the last statements of the defendants, ranging from an abject confession from Shestov to Pyatakov's claims that, being "crushed and covered with filth," he had broken with Trotskyism.[43] Short *New York Times* articles reported that some of the defendants wept as the verdicts were read.[44] Another article reported that Radek's mother in Poland collapsed while listening to the trial on the radio.[45] Another short article reported Trotsky's denial of meeting Pyatakov in Norway.[46] Duranty considered Pyatakov's death to be a "great loss to Soviet Russia."[47] Duranty reported on the rejection of the defendants' pleas for clemency and the announcement of the 3:30 a.m. executions.[48] A companion article by Duranty reported that workers' meetings were held to demand another trial and also correctly speculated that Nikolai Bukharin and Alexei Rykov were to be the most likely defendants, adding that the trial was a warning to Soviet citizens and to Trotskyists abroad that Trotskyism was "tantamount to counter-revolution or fascism."[49] Duranty briefly reported on the announcement of the executions and reported that 200,000 Soviets filled the streets in freezing weather to demonstrate for the sentences to be "carried out pitilessly and speedily." Duranty also wrote that he was sure that Pyatakov "died with courage" and that his death would be a "great loss to Soviet Russia."[50] A companion article summarized the executions as part of the regime's "lengthening list of enemies wiped out . . . in its ten-year fight to eradication of what it calls 'Trotskyism.'" The reporter also speculated that the executions took place in Lubianka Prison's basement with no notification to the defendants' relatives and that the bodies were immediately cremated.[51]

In follow-up articles, Duranty reported on the Soviet government's pervasive anti-Trotsky propaganda and the "savage, sincere" public resolutions condemning the defendants. He claimed that these resolutions were based on the public's belief in the trial charges of sabotage which hurt Russian workers and soldiers and weakened the Soviets against Germany and Japan.[52] Duranty's beliefs in the veracity of the charges and confessions culminated in an article in the *New York Times Magazine* in which he chronicled the history of Stalin's "merciless war" on Trotsky, rationalized that the trial charges were based on the belief that "Trotskyism was great in the U.S.S.R.," that Trotsky had "staked everything" on a "palace revolution," and that there existed "underground" communications and the threat of a "terroristic campaign."[53]

After the trial the Associated Press reported that throughout the Soviet Union hundreds of "former Communist leaders" were purged from the Communist Party rolls and lost their jobs for taking part in the "Trotskyist wrecking conspiracy."[54] This assertion of a mass purge of Trotskyists was downplayed by Duranty as a "minute investigation ... of former oppositionists, especially Trotskyists, the majority of whom would probably get a clean bill of health."[55]

In contrast to Duranty's opinions, the *New York Times* published two skeptical editorials on this trial. In the first, the editorialist dismissed the theory that the "Russian character" was the reason for the self-condemning confessions of "these wretched Trotskyist bunglers."[56] After the trial transcript was published, another editorial focused on a letter allegedly sent by Trotsky to Radek that outlined ceding Soviet territories and resources to Germany and Japan. The editorialist was incredulous that the erudite Trotsky would write such a letter; the editorialist wrote that it read like a "well-informed editorial by a California high school boy."[57] For good measure, the *New York Times* published a letter to the editor from its European correspondent Joseph Shaplen who claimed that the false confessions in the 1936 and 1937 trials were echoes of similar confessions in a 1931 trial. He quoted Léon Blum, the socialist prime minister of France, who compared the Soviet secret police to the Spanish Inquisition.[58]

In addition to the suicide of Orzhonikidze, there was another tragic side effect to this trial. One of the witnesses was journalist Vladimir Romm who was called to testify to verify Radek's confession of contact with Trotsky. Romm had been the first permanent *Izvestia* correspondent in Washington, DC, and had been given a send-off to his new assignment at a luncheon in Moscow; Karl Radek had attended.[59] During his time in the United States, Romm had been an effective advocate for the Soviet government.[60] Duranty gave a sympathetic account of Romm's testimony, writing that he spoke with "charm" and "courage," as he admitted to carrying correspondence between Trotsky and Radek.[61] American journalists who knew Romm were shocked by his confession, and they tried to come to his defense as to his being a loyal Communist, in spite of Ambassador Troyanovsky's claim that Romm had been a Trotskyist.[62] Ambassador Davies also tried to come to Romm's aid and was informed by People's Commissar for Foreign Affairs Litvinov that Romm "had been sent to do work in the interior."[63] Trotsky also denied knowing Romm.[64] A *New York Times* editorial considered Romm's testimony to be among the more "impossible" of all of the allegations in the first and second show trials and pondered why the defendants in this trial ("this month's batch of breast-beaters") were being put through "this comedy."[65]

By this time some American news magazines have grown increasingly skeptical of the trial charges and confessions. *Time* published two articles on this trial. The first was a long account of the trial in a world-weary tone as the reporter recited the charges, the self-incriminating confessions, Romm's testimony, Trotsky's incessant denials, and the opposite reactions of journalists Walter Duranty and Eugene Lyons. The reporter described Judge Ulrikh as "ponderous" and Vyshinsky as "pouncing." The reporter also mentioned the Communist Party USA's mass meeting at which Party leader Earl Browder condemned the Trotskyists and "that Monkey Radek."[66] The second article concentrated on Radek being spared execution in spite of being excoriated in the Soviet press and during a mass demonstration in Moscow. This article also included a map of the places where the defendants allegedly had committed their crimes of assassination, sabotage, and conspiracy.[67]

Prior to the trial, *Newsweek* published an article on the purges (the "Stalin Steam Roller") reaching into the intelligentsia and threatening Ivy Low Litvinov, the English-born wife of People's Commissar for Foreign Affairs Litvinov.[68] *NewsWeek* published an eyewitness account which compared this trial to "eighteenth-century witchcraft trials whose tortured victims often admitted conniving with the devil himself," reported that Radek looked "shabby and broken," and that the defendants admitted to "selling their souls" to Trotsky. The reporter characterized the trial as Stalin settling old scores and eliminating Trotskyists and potential rivals.[69]

Literary Digest termed the trial to be "grim, incredible court-room follies" and called Pyatakov's confession of conspiring with Trotsky and Nazi Germany "bland" but given "in hair-raising detail."[70] *Saturday Evening Post* took both sides in regard to this trial. It published an editorial that concluded that the defendants had confessed in order to protect their families, citing the medieval precedent of an entire family suffering for the misdeeds of one of its members.[71] In contrast to this editorial, the *Post* published a series of articles by John. D. Littlepage, an American mining engineer who had worked in the Soviet Union. Littlepage asserted that there was "deliberate sabotage" in the mining industry, thus implicating defendant Leonid Serebryakov who had been head of the Gold Trust. He also asserted that Pyatakov had engaged in corrupt practices when he led a trade commission to Germany. He expanded his recollections into a book, *In Search of Soviet Gold*.[72] Predictably, his writings were praised by American Communists and derided by American Trotskyists.[73,74]

New Republic published several articles on this trial. The first discussed the various interpretations of the meaning of the trials, called the crimes "even more amazing" than the alleged crimes in the first trial, and noted Trotsky's "daily denials." The reporter dismissed Trotsky's call for an international investigation and supported Walter Duranty's belief in the defendants' confessions. The reporter wrote that whether the charges and confessions were true or not, the presence of so many "implacably hostile enemies within its ranks" gave "aid and encouragement to the fascist forces" and highlighted the Soviets' need for "free political expression."[75] *New Republic* also took notice of the "hot controversy" among American liberals and progressives concerning the show trials. The editorialist contended that Americans did not know enough facts to take either side on the guilt of the defendants and should stick to "matters nearer home."[76] This editorial elicited a rebuke in the American Communist press.

The third article by a *New Republic* editor Malcolm Cowley was a lengthy review of the trial transcript as "the most exciting book I have read this year" and as a "true detective story and high Elizabethan tragedy." Cowley drew several conclusions from the "undoubtedly sincere" confessions and characterized the defendants ("professional wreckers") as guilty and "ashamed." He ended with criticism of Trotsky but wrote that, while we do not owe "blind loyalty" to the Soviet Union, it was the "most progressive force in the world."[77] A fourth article included a brief review of the trial transcript by Yale University law professor Fred Rodell. Rodell found both the State's case and Trotsky's denials as lacking solid proof and called himself "completely neutral, or agnostic" on the facts portrayed in the trial.[78]

One of the most famous contemporary analyses of this trial was Walter Duranty's "The Riddle of Russia," published in *New Republic* on July 14, 1937. He asserted that the alleged conspiracy came from Trotsky, Germany, Japan, and "disaffected elements" within the Communist Party, all going back to Kirov's assassination. He believed that the confessions proved the existence of this conspiracy and also proved collusion with Germany and Japan. He asserted that "foreign bewilderment" over the trials had been used by the "Kremlin's enemies" to weaken the Soviets' international prestige.[79] In October 1937 *New Republic* published an article by an unnamed American working in a Soviet tractor plant. His claim that this factory had been the target of "subversive activity" gave credence to the trial's charges of sabotage. He analyzed the political beliefs of the factory workers and concluded that a "vast majority" of the Soviet populace approved of the show trials and that the trials strengthened the Soviet Union.[80]

The Nation published an article on this trial that considered the key issues to be the authenticity of the confessions and the fairness of the trial procedures. The reporter highlighted the differences between the Soviet and Anglo-Saxon legal systems and placed this trial within the context of the first show trial and previous trials, going back to the Socialist Revolutionaries trial in 1922. The reporter gave credence to the alleged conspiracies and surmised that all of these trials were part of a bitter struggle for power. The reporter examined the possible reasons for the defendants to conspire with hostile powers and called the trials "publicity exhibits" to discredit Trotskyism. The article ended with the assertion that the regime "sows the seeds of conspiracy," due to the stifling of opposition.[81]

There were two other legal analyses of the trial transcript with both noting the differences between Soviet and Anglo-Saxon jurisprudence. *Foreign Affairs*, the official publication of the US Council for Foreign Relations, published an analysis of the trial transcript by legal scholar Max Radin. He wrote that the main charges were announced in court in an "elaborate and somewhat denunciatory recital." Radin cited Trotsky's denials as an "emphatic" not-guilty plea by an absent defendant. Radin questioned several aspects of the proceedings, including the role of confessions and the lack of corroborating evidence. He also questioned the rationale for the lenient sentences for some defendants and slammed Vyshinsky for his abusive name-calling and distortions of Trotsky's relationship with Lenin. Radin posed vague theories about the defendants' confessions. He concluded by siding with the prosecution in spite of any "repugnance to capital punishment inflicted" on thirteen defendants.[82]

Another legal analysis by Canadian jurist William Renwick Riddell was published in the *Journal of Criminal Law and Criminology*. Riddell summarized the trial proceedings, citing differences with Anglo-Saxon judicial procedures. He concentrated on the testimony of one of the most minor defendants, Valentin Arnold, to show what he considered to be the thoroughness of the prosecution's investigations. Demonstrating that even distinguished jurists can be wrong, Riddell echoed those who believed the defendants' confessions, and he concluded that they deserved the death penalty.[83]

Reactions of American Radicals

The Comintern sent out a stream of directives that ordered foreign Communist parties to explain this trial according to the Stalinist line, to deflect any criticism and to work to destroy Trotskyism. Articles on the conduct of the trial were to be published under the byline of a "special correspondent."[84] The obedient leadership of the Communist Party USA went into overdrive and supported this trial with articles, pamphlets, and a major speech at a mass meeting in New York City. Under banner headlines, *Daily Worker* devoted a great deal of space to the trial proceedings, portraying Trotsky and the defendants as agents of fascism and as plotting war against the Soviet Union in league with Germany and Japan so that they could take over the government and cede Soviet territory and resources.[85] *Daily Worker* also devoted several pages to lengthy excerpts from the indictment, the defendants' and witnesses' testimonies and Vyshinsky's summation.[86] It also published several pro-trial editorials; these editorials echoed the condemnations in the Soviet press by citing the "hideous Trotskyite crimes" and the "terrible degradation, the counter-revolutionary rottenness and brutality of these men."[87] For good measure, *Daily Worker* also published articles with comments by Soviet ambassador Troyanovsky, including a radio broadcast in which he condemned Trotskyists. In a second article Troyanovsky denied that the defendants had been under any undue pressure to confess and stated that any criticism of the trial was to "create prejudice and hatred against the country of Socialism."[88]

American Party leader Earl Browder's speech at a mass meeting at Madison Square Garden on February 5, 1937, culminated their efforts. In an effort to build up interest and attendance prior to the speech, *Daily Worker* published four articles, beginning with Browder's condemnation of "Trotzky and the fascist conspiracy" and condemnation of Trotsky's American supporters.[89] Browder entitled this speech "Trotzkyism and World Peace." It was delivered to answer the "poisonous propaganda" of Trotsky's supporters, to condemn Trotsky for plotting war so that he could take over the Soviet government ("that bulwark of peace and democracy") and cited the "horrible nature of the Trotskyist-fascist alliance." For good measure he excoriated President Lázaro Cárdenas of Mexico for granting Trotsky asylum.

Daily Worker reported that the attendees unanimously supported this trial as Browder denounced Trotskyists and their plots. *Daily Worker* printed Browder's entire speech, and it also was published as a pamphlet.[90] According to the *New York Times*, more than 15,000 people attended this meeting which was marked by fistfights between Communists and Trotskyists that had to be broken up by the police.[91] In tandem with coverage of this speech, *Daily Worker* claimed that Trotsky publicly "confessed" to wanting to use force against the Soviet regime in an article in the *New York Herald-American*, a Hearst-owned newspaper that was loathed by communists.[92]

The publication of the trial transcript was another opportunity for *Daily Worker* to condemn Trotsky and the trial defendants. Using the common vehicle of a book review to defend the trial and to vilify Trotsky, the review was by Sherwood Eddy. Eddy was a well-known American evangelist who became a pacifist and socialist during the First World War, traveled to the Soviet Union, and claimed to have met Radek. He believed in Radek's guilt and in the plot to kill Soviet leaders. Eddy considered Stalin to be the "best living leader" for the Soviets and considered Trotsky to be "the most dangerous would-be dictator that the Soviet Union could possibly have."[93]

In February 1937 the Communist weekly *New Masses* published three articles and three long editorials in support of this trial. The first article was a brief mention of the verdicts and sentences and quoted a Danish source who called Trotsky "enemy Number One of the whole of humanity and democracy."[94] The second article by *Daily Worker* correspondent A. B. Magil compared this trial to the earlier Shakhty and Industrial Party trials. Magil cited Radek's commentary on the Industrial Party trial which condemned the defendants on the same charges for which he was now confessing; Magil also explained away the defendants' confessions in these earlier trials as being reluctantly made after months in prison.[95] For good measure, *New Masses* reprinted an article by English barrister Dudley Collard who had been convinced of the defendants' guilt. Collard called Pyatakov "the master-mind behind the gang," called Radek a "poseur," and praised Vyshinsky's "remarkable restraint and courtesy."[96] The editorials dissected the careers of the defendants ("the terrorists") as oppositionists to Lenin which was the ultimate sin, called American socialists who defended Trotsky "mouthpieces," dissected Trotsky's career as an oppositionist, and dismissed the call for an international inquiry.[97]

New Masses did not let up on this trial. Charles Recht, a lawyer who had represented the Soviet Union in the United States in the years before recognition, wrote a review of the trial transcript that defended the trial proceedings and concluded that the defendants confessed because there was so much evidence against them. He slammed Trotsky's theory of permanent revolution and contended that, in addition to the confessions, there was "incriminating correspondence and other collaborative data."[98] American Comintern representative Sam Darcy demonstrated the American Party leadership's obedience in a comprehensive article in which he justified the charges of sabotage and espionage by echoing the claims that thousands of "German fascist spies" and a "Japanese-German-Polish espionage apparatus" had entered the Soviet Union during the massive industrialization projects of the first Five Year Plan. These alleged spies conspired with "certain degenerate elements," "right-wingers," and "Trotskyist elements" to conduct their campaign of industrial sabotage and espionage while posing as engineers or as tourists. Darcy claimed that, in addition to Trotsky, Pyatakov, and Radek, Nikolai Bukharin headed these espionage groups. He also claimed that the defendants' confessions took his "breath away to see the utter cynicism which these criminals represented." He asserted that because the "success" of the first Five Year Plan belied the Trotskyists' belief that the Plan would fail, they turned on their "fellow conspirators" and confessed. Darcy concluded by predicting the triumph of the third Five Year Plan and making dire warnings about the Trotskyists being the "chief weapons of the fascists."[99]

In 1938 *New Masses* published an eyewitness account by Joshua Kunitz, who had also reported on the first Moscow show trial. Kunitz justified the charges of sabotage as he portrayed the defendants as betrayers of Soviet workers, quoting from the writings of John D. Littlepage who considered the defendants to be guilty of sabotage. Kunitz called criticism of the trial an attempt to undermine "the prestige and influence of the Soviet Union" and, like Sam Darcy, predicted the Soviets Union's triumph.[100] In August 1939 *New Masses* published another article by A. B. Magil that referred back to this trial in which he cited Radek's testimony that "master fink" Trotsky was plotting to cede Ukraine to Germany.[101] In publishing these articles, *New Masses* did an about-face concerning Radek. In 1935 *New Masses* published a rave review of his writing, calling him "courageous and honorable" as a revolutionary and "adventurous" and talented as a writer who produced "outstanding expressions of Soviet journalism."[102] *New Masses* had published an article by him in May 1936.[103] These facts were omitted in their coverage of this trial.

In March 1937, *The Communist*, the American Party's journal of Marxist theory and practice, published two articles which defended the trial, called the defendants the "Trotskyite agents of fascism," attacked Trotsky's theory of permanent revolution, and slammed Trotsky's American supporters, including the American Committee for the Defense of Leon Trotsky. The first article was by Israel Amter, a founding member of the Party and a former representative to the Comintern, who defended the trial as "open and above-board," accepted the charges as proven, and described the "degeneracy" of the Trotskyists. Amter also slammed American critics of the trial and rehashed Trotsky's early differences with Lenin.[104] The second article by veteran Communist Clarence A. Hathaway began as a response to "Russian Politics in America," the *New Republic* editorial that suggested that Americans stay out of the debate over the defendants' guilt. Hathaway called the *New Republic*'s editorial an example of "criminal indifference" to the "renegades from Communism" who have allied themselves with the fascists. Following the Comintern directive to denounce Trotsky's defenders, he excoriated them as "Trotskyist rats" who sowed dissention within the progressive and labor movements.[105]

Prior to the trial proceedings, *Soviet Russia Today* published an editorial that cited Walter Duranty's reporting on the "widespread" Trotskyist conspiracy.[106] The March issue devoted a great deal of space to the trial with small articles reprinted from other sources, including a reprint of Collard's account of the trial with a sidebar of an endorsement of the trial by German novelist Leon Feuchtwanger who had attended the trial.[107] It printed an abridged version of Vyshinsky's summation and excerpts from the final statements (final pleas) of Pyatakov, Radek, and Serebryakov, in which they again proclaimed their guilt and repented. An "Editor's Note" supported the trial and listed the defendants' sentences.[108] A final article was in the form of a question-and-answer column. It refuted the charge that there was no solid evidence except the confessions, disputed claims that the trial was a frame-up and refuted the claim that the alleged conspiratorial meetings never took place.[109]

When the trial transcript was published, *Soviet Russia Today* published an article, which quoted a surprising source—Newton D. Baker, a longtime colleague of Woodrow Wilson, a controversial US Secretary of War during the First World War for his supposed pacifist views and a proponent of the League of Nations. In a radio address in which he reviewed the trial transcript, Baker believed in the conspiracy theory that Trotsky and his supporters were plotting war with Germany and Japan so that they could take over the government. The reporter praised Baker's analysis and called Trotsky a "deliberate war-monger" and "an ally of Hitler and the Japanese generals."[110]

The Communist Party USA also followed the Comintern directive by publishing pamphlets on this trial. These pamphlets included an eyewitness account by Sam Darcy in which he called the trial a "triumph of socialism" and included a summary of alleged acts of sabotage and a summary of Kirov's assassination.[111] Alexander Bittelman, editor of *The Communist*, wrote *Trotsky the Traitor* which employed a standard Party tactic of comparing the trial defendants to American traitors Benedict Arnold, Aaron Burr, and John Wilkes Booth.[112] Prominent Communist William Z. Foster also wrote a long, anti-Trotsky pamphlet in which he also disparaged the international inquiry into the charges and wrote that Trotsky should never be allowed into the United States.[113] As was the practice in other trials, Workers Library Publishers reprinted the trial indictment as a pamphlet entitled *Traitors Accused*.[114]

As with the first trial, Trotsky incessantly denied the charges, both in person and in print. The *New York Times* gave Trotsky a platform to defend himself against the accusations that he had conspired with the defendants, Germany, and Japan to take over the Soviet Union and to kill its leaders. He particularly denied that he had ever met with Vladimir Romm. He again called for an international investigation of the charges against him.[115] *Newsweek* published an article which quoted Trotsky on the methods that the secret police used to get prisoners to confess; the reporter expressed total disbelief in the trial charges and also speculated on the fates of Nikolai Bukharin, Alexei Rykov, and Khristian Rakovsky, who would all be defendants in the third show trial.[116] The anticommunist *American Mercury* published an article by Trotsky in which he condemned Stalin's persecution of the oppositionists.[117] In continuing its "pamphlet wars" with the Communists, the Trotskyists published Trotsky's anti-trial pamphlet *Truth about the Moscow Trials*.[118]

In February 1937, the Trotskyist weekly *Socialist Appeal* published an article by labor lawyer Albert Goldman, who would be Trotsky's attorney during the Dewey Commission's Inquiry in Mexico. Goldman succinctly stated the Trotskyists' arguments against the trial in blunt terms ("the greatest frame-up in history"), writing that the trials were "serious blows to the revolutionary movement" and were meant to "discredit revolutionary Marxism" by discrediting Trotsky. He characterized the defendants as "degraded wretches" and Stalin as a "monstrous usurper." He also called the proposed Inquiry a "means to defend the integrity of the revolutionary idea," not just a defense for Trotsky and his son.[119]

In March 1937 the Trotskyist Socialist Appeal Institute passed a resolution criticizing the trials as attempts "to stamp out the traditions of Bolshevism . . . and to destroy the independent revolutionary working-class movement." The resolution condemned the Soviet bureaucracy, another favorite target of Trotsky. The resolution also called for an international inquiry into the charges.[120] In December 1937 *Socialist Appeal* published an article on the revelations of the American media's two favorite Soviet defectors—Walter Krivitsky and Alexandre Barmine. They claimed that the defendants were innocent and supported the Trotskyist claim that the trials were "frame-ups," one of Trotsky's favorite terms.[121]

The Trotskyists published *Why Did They "Confess"?* a translation of a French dissident Communist publication that contended that the confessions were false. This pamphlet included an introduction by American Trotskyist and political theorist James Burnham, who wrote that the trials were part of Stalin's strategy to enlist support in a coming war with Germany and Japan. He also took a swipe at the intellectuals who signed the "Open Letter to American Liberals."[122] Max

Eastman, one of Trotsky's most loyal American defenders, published *The End of Socialism in Russia*, a condemnation of the Soviet government. He termed the defendants' confessions as their attempts to have Stalin spare them and their families, but "when they got through publicly dishonouring themselves, and each explicitly implicating Trotsky, [Stalin] led them out and shot them."[123]

This trial also earned condemnations from dissident Communists, from other radical splinter groups and from the American Socialist Party. Jay Lovestone, the most famous of the dissidents, wrote a scathing article on this trial in *Workers Age*, the official newspaper of the Communist Party (Opposition). Lovestone echoed Trotsky in that he compared the trials to the aftermath of the French Revolution when the revolutionaries turned on each other. He asserted that the trials must be seen in a political, not criminal, context. With the charges being "manifestly impossible or self-contradictory," he termed the trial an "act of political suppression."[124] *Workers Age* then published an editorial that acknowledged the possibility of the existence of a Trotskyist conspiracy but condemned Stalin's one-man rule, his stifling of dissent and asserted that these trials impaired Soviet prestige. The editorialist called the trials an "unmitigated disaster" to the cause of world revolution but disparaged the idea of an international inquiry for Trotsky.[125] *Workers Age* also used the trial as an opportunity to attack the Soviet-dominated Comintern with a call to reform it from the "present ruinous policies of the Stalin leadership" and termed the trials to be a "bloody circle" of "misrepresentation . . . to character assassination, from character assassination to physical extermination." The writer asserted that the trials have "exposed the crisis and rottenness in the Communist International" and were part of its "long course of mistakes and defeats." The writer proposed the "organization of a new international center," free of the influence of the Soviet Communist Party.[126]

Fighting Worker, the official newspaper of the Revolutionary Workers League US, correctly predicted the downfalls of Radek and Bukharin, claiming that "desperately frightened bureaucrats" were "finishing off" the last veterans of the Revolution.[127] However, the League was no fan of Trotsky, and in the same issue dismissed the Trotskyist Fourth International as a "paper set-up to hide the bankruptcy of Trotsky's attempt to build a movement."[128] In 1937 the Revolutionary Workers League published an article in the form of an open letter to the Socialist Party that roundly condemned the trial and asserted that the defendants' confessions had been obtained by force and pressure.[129] The League also published a pamphlet *The Truth about the Moscow Frame-Up Trials*, a reprint from the March 1, 1937, issue of *Fighting Worker*, which proclaimed that "Stalinism must be destroyed." The writer also supported the establishment of an "impartial commission" but criticized the efforts of the American Committee for the Defense of Leon Trotsky. The writer asserted that, while Trotsky was not guilty of the charges, the League was opposed to his "opportunistic policies."[130]

An extended and virulent anti-Stalinist rant came from George Spiro, an American Communist who became embittered and disillusioned by the treatment that he had received from American Party leaders in dismissing his proletarian novel *The Road*. Writing under the pseudonym George Marlen, he wrote *Earl Browder, Communist or Tool of Wall Street: Stalin, Trotsky or Lenin*. This book was replete with accusations and name-calling and included a chapter that dealt with the Kirov murder, previous trials, and the two show trials. In the section on the second trial, Spiro concentrated on Radek. In melodramatic terms he blamed Stalin for torturing the defendants into confessing and "becoming helpless tools of the Usurper in his revolting crimes."[131]

To the chagrin of the Communist Party USA, American Socialists also condemned this trial and published *The First Two Moscow Trials—Why?* by labor lawyer Francis Heisler. Heisler criticized the indictment as politically motivated and correctly predicted future trials.[132] *Labor Action* was the official newspaper of the Western Federation of the Socialist Party and the self-proclaimed "Voice of Socialism in the West." It was edited by Trotsky's supporter James P. Cannon. It published an anti-trial cartoon showing Stalin digging Radek's grave and published articles and editorials that continued the grave-digging theme, portraying the trials as "digging the grave of the Russian Revolution."[133]

Conclusion

The second Moscow show trial solidified the positions of American friends and enemies of Stalin and Trotsky. The US Embassy secretaries did not believe that the trials were legitimate while Ambassador Davies accepted the Stalinist line. The mainstream press became increasingly skeptical of the charges and of the confessions. This trial further exacerbated the gulf between pro- and anti-Stalinists on the radical left. American Communists continued their lapdog-like loyalty to Stalin and their antagonism toward Trotsky and his supporters. Trotskyists continued their unending support of their hero and attacked the trials. Opposing sides continued to voice their opinions through press and radio attacks, mass meetings, name-calling, literary feuds, and the vehicles of letters to the editor and dismissive book reviews to swipe at their opponents. Meanwhile, in the Soviet Union the purge and the show trials continued.

Plate 5.1 John Dewey, American philosopher and educator, the chair of the Dewey Commission. Courtesy of Wikimedia Commons, http://commons.wikimedia.org (accessed March 16, 2023)

5

Other American Reactions to the Second Trial (1937)

American liberals and intellectuals were fascinated with the Soviet Union as the world's first socialist state. Three of the most famous reactions of American liberals and intellectuals to the trials occurred in 1936 and 1937—the formation of the American Committee for the Defense of Leon Trotsky, the formation of the Committee's Commission of Inquiry (the Dewey Commission), and the "Open Letter to American Liberals."

This chain of events started in 1936 when Trotsky was going to be expelled from Norway and needed a new country of asylum.[1]

The American Committee for the Defense of Leon Trotsky

A group of liberals, headed by leading socialist Norman Thomas, founded a Provisional Committee for the Defense of Leon Trotsky to assist him in finding another country of asylum and to form an international commission of inquiry to investigate the trial charges made against him and his exiled son Lev Sedov.[2] Renamed the American Committee for the Defense of Leon Trotsky, prominent liberals joined. The American Committee held mass meetings, gave radio addresses, and published a *News Bulletin*. Through the Trotskyist Pioneer Press, the American Committee published a compilation of articles on the trials from liberal publications.[3] Similar committees were formed in other countries, and subcommittees were formed in other US cities.

At the urging of the renowned Mexican painter Diego Rivera, Mexico's left-wing president Lázaro Cárdenas granted Trotsky asylum, a decision opposed by Mexican Stalinists and also opposed by American Communists, who were ordered by the Comintern to oppose the asylum.[4] The decision to grant Trotsky asylum was praised by Norman Thomas who considered Trotsky's asylum in

Mexico as a step toward an international inquiry.⁵ The Committee held a public meeting in New York City on December 18, 1936, which the Trotskyist newspaper *Socialist Appeal* described as a standing-room-only triumph and praised the American Committee, especially Thomas who called the American Communists' opposition a "Stalinist lynch campaign." The reporter singled out American Party leader Earl Browder for criticism.⁶ Trotsky did not arrive in Mexico quietly, publicly demanding an inquiry and criticizing Stalin.⁷

In its January 27, 1937, issue of its *News Bulletin*, the American Committee announced a call for an "impartial commission of inquiry" ("Let the truth be known!"), called for the support of American liberals and asked for donations.⁸ This issue also included an article by Trotsky in which he declared that he was "ready to denounce Stalin before any impartial and authoritative international commission."⁹ The Committee was controversial from the start with accusations from American Communists that it was far from impartial and consisted of supporters of fascism and defenders of the "murderers of Kirov" and called it an "organized assault on the Soviet Union" and "serving the cause of fascism."¹⁰ Liberals split over conducting an inquiry into the trial charges, and, starting with prominent journalist and editor Mauritz A. Hallgren, ten members of the American Committee very publicly resigned. Hallgren cited his belief in the guilt of the defendants, challenged Trotsky to produce proof of his innocence and called the Committee an "instrument of the Trotskyists." These resignations were gleefully reported in the Communist press, and the Communists reprinted Hallgren's resignation letter.¹¹ Prominent Communist William Z. Foster included a section on the concept of an international hearing in his pamphlet on the second show trial. Foster called the proposal a "sham" and asserted that Trotsky would not go back to Russia to stand trial because he had "no case" and that he was guilty of the charges. Foster also called any inquiry an "attack upon the integrity of the Soviet government" and claimed that the American Committee was full of Trotskyists, thus negating any impartiality. He criticized Trotsky for not producing any proof to discredit the trials; Foster also cited Hallgren's resignation.¹²

The American Committee's responses to Hallgren's resignation were swift. Committee secretary George Novack sent a letter to Hallgren that reiterated the Committee's goals of finding Trotsky a new place of asylum and getting him a hearing; he urged Hallgren to reconsider his resignation.¹³ Committee treasurer Suzanne La Follette, a relative of Senator Robert La Follette of Wisconsin, sent a letter to the editor of the *New York Times*, reiterating the Committee's goals of finding Trotsky a new place of asylum and conducting a "fair and impartial hearing."[14] The American Committee's *News Bulletin* defended itself against Hallgren's resignation and responded to the "Open Letter to American Liberals."[15]

The Committee's efforts were spurred by the executions of the defendants in the second show trial. In order to protest the trial, the Committee announced mass meetings in New York City, Chicago, and Boston. The mass meeting in New York City was scheduled for February 9, 1937. It was attended by 6,500 people, and, perhaps mindful of the fistfights at Earl Browder's speech, the meeting had police protection.[16] The highlight of this meeting was to have been a telephone address by Trotsky from his home in Mexico. This telephone address, which had been initially opposed by the Roosevelt administration but finally allowed, never took place as Mexican trade unionists sabotaged the telephone lines.[17] His address was read by Max Shachtman and was later published as a pamphlet *I Stake My Life!* Trotsky refuted the charges and criticized the trials ("frame-ups") and the "spirit of the Inquisition" in the Soviet Union.[18] The American Committee proclaimed this meeting to be "one of the most impressive labor defense meetings this city has ever seen."[19]

The Committee published letters of both support and disagreement and more resignations in its *News Bulletin* and stated that its goal was to secure for Trotsky: "Those plain human rights before the court of public opinion and under the law of the land to which, according to international liberal tradition, all people in similar circumstances are entitled."[20] The *News Bulletin* also included a short letter from novelist Sinclair Lewis, the first American to win the Nobel Prize for literature, who endorsed a "public hearing before a distinguished international jury."[21]

The Committee launched the Commission of Inquiry into the Charges against Leon Trotsky in the Moscow Trials at its February meeting. The Commission of Inquiry planned to send a delegation to Mexico in order to question Trotsky about the trial charges in a courtroom-style setting. Due to the controversy caused by the Commission. John Dewey and other liberals on the Committee claimed that its members were targets of blackmail attempts and were hounded in order to make them resign. They also claimed that they wanted Communist Party participation, a proposal that was ridiculed by Soviet ambassador Troyanovsky.[22] *Daily Worker* called it a "whitewash."[23] *New Masses* wasted no time in labeling the Commission an attack on the Soviet Union, contended that such an inquiry could not be impartial, and stated that the Soviet courts should hold any inquiry.[24] Again showing the splits within American radicalism, the Revolutionary Workers League's *Fighting Worker*, while not believing that

Trotsky was guilty, did not endorse the Commission, contending that only a Marxist "proletarian court" could provide justice.[25]

The Dewey Commission

The Commission of Inquiry became known as the Dewey Commission after John Dewey, its chairman and one of America's best-known philosophers and educators. The Commission formed a "Sub-Commission" of five members, headed by Dewey, to go to Mexico in order to question Trotsky. Other members of the Sub-Commission were Benjamin Stolberg, Suzanne La Follette, German socialist Otto Ruehle, radical journalist Carleton Beals, and Italian-born antifascist Carlo Tresca. Their lawyer was John F. Finerty. Albert Einstein had been invited to join the Commission but declined, claiming that such a public venue would only "serve Trotsky's purposes."[26] Prominent American historians Charles Beard and Carl Becker also declined to serve on the Commission. In declining, Beard conceded that he did not believe that the confessions were "positive proof," due to the lack of corroborating evidence and that the conspiracy charges had not been proven beyond a reasonable doubt.[27]

Prior to the hearings, *New York Times* correspondent Frank L. Kluckhohn wrote an extensive and less than flattering article on Trotsky's life in Mexico, calling Trotsky's visitors "pilgrims," reporting that people around him "must pay him constant homage" and remarking upon his "continued diatribes." Kluckhohn portrayed Trotsky as a "master propagandist," "hopeful revolutionary," and the "world's most prominent exile."[28] Before the Inquiry began, Kluckhohn expressed some skepticism about the Commission's impartiality ("a trial without prosecutors").[29] His skepticism led to defensive responses from Albert Goldman, Trotsky's attorney, and from John F. Finerty, the Commission's attorney. Finerty stated that Trotsky would be treated as a "hostile witness."[30] However, Kluckhohn's reporting during the hearings was a matter-of-fact, quoting liberally from Trotsky's testimony.[31]

In April 1937 the inquiry held thirteen hearings. At the opening session, Chairman Dewey claimed that the Sub-Commission was not going to pass judgment but was only an "investigative body." Dewey stated: "Our sole function is to ascertain the truth as far as is humanly possible."[32] The inquiry was largely Trotsky's stage to recite his revolutionary past, to refute the accusations made against him and his son Lev Sedov, and to call for an end to the Stalinist regime. Two of the sessions concentrated on the show trials. Trotsky made a special point of denying having ever known Vladimir Romm, the *Izvestia* correspondent who had confessed to carrying correspondence between Trotsky and Karl Radek. Trotsky stated that the "whole tissue of the trial is rotten," claiming that he had never met Romm and that the "GPU compelled him [Romm] to lie."[33] Trotsky's closing statement lasted for hours. On the tenth anniversary of Trotsky's assassination in 1950, American Trotskyists published his closing statement as a pamphlet entitled *Stalin's Frame-Up System and the Moscow Trials*.[34]

American reaction to the Dewey Commission came in several phases—eyewitness accounts of the proceedings, reactions to the American Committee's mass meeting after the hearings ended, publication of the hearing transcripts, a mass meeting to announce its conclusions and the publication of its conclusions.

As with the resignations from the American Committee, the Dewey Commission had a very noisy and very public resignation by radical journalist Carleton Beals, who had verbally sparred with Trotsky during the hearings. Beals left Mexico and became a vocal critic of the Inquiry for not being a "truly serious investigation" and that the other members of the Commission had "hushed adoration" for Trotsky.[35] Trotsky did not let Beals's comments go unchallenged; he issued a statement in which he implied that Beals was "working for the Soviet."[36] Throughout the rest of the year, the American Committee defended itself against Beals's criticisms.[37]

Trotsky was also the subject of a critical account of his past in a *New York Times* editorial that included the fact that while Trotsky portrayed Stalin as ruthless, Trotsky himself had been criticized by Lenin as a "severe and unpopular disciplinarian."[38] American Committee member Lorine Pruette published a sympathetic account of the hearings as having an "academic air" with Dewey allowing Trotsky to dominate.[39] *The Nation* reported that, although Trotsky may be innocent, the proceedings were a "waste of time, effort, and money," lacked impartiality and were ultimately unconvincing in establishing Trotsky's innocence.[40] The American Committee devoted the entire May 3, 1937, issue of its *News Bulletin* to the hearings ("an unprecedented historical event"), criticizing negative press coverage, defending itself against Carlton Beals's criticism, and promoting the American Committee's upcoming public meeting to discuss the hearings.[41]

American Communist leaders were unrelenting in their criticism of the Inquiry. *Daily Worker* characterized Dewey as a "deluded old man," who had been "duped by the enemies of socialism" and was now the "enemy of peace and progress."[42] An editorial in *New Masses* claimed that Trotsky was essentially investigating himself; this editorial ridiculed the members of the Dewey

Commission as a group ("a little band of Americans") and disparaged their lack of impartiality.[43] *New Masses* published a long article by two spectators at the Inquiry who wrote that the hearings consisted of Trotsky's previously stated denials, produced nothing new and that the members of the Commission were biased toward Trotsky. They also highlighted Beals's questioning of Trotsky and his resignation from the Commission. This article was accompanied by a cartoon of Trotsky in lockstep with Hitler and Mussolini, a reinforcement of the assertion that Trotskyism was equated with fascism.[44] Predictably, Ambassador Troyanovsky called the Inquiry a "flop."[45] *Soviet Russia Today* called the Inquiry the "farce in Mexico."[46]

On a side note, in 1937 American socialists were wrestling with ways to end Trotskyist influence within the Socialist Party.[47] However, Trotsky supporter James Cannon P. was still the editor of *Labor Action*, the official newspaper of the Western Federation of the Party. *Labor Action* headlined the Inquiry, highlighting the fact that the Soviet government and the American Communist Party had not responded to offers to participate.[48] The Socialist Party finally expelled the Trotskyists.

In May, Dewey gave his first interview since leaving Mexico in which he defended the Inquiry, stating that he was not a Trotskyist but wanted an Inquiry as to whether the defendants "had actually betrayed the revolution."[49]

The American Committee held a public meeting at which the Commission submitted a brief report on the Inquiry and on Beals's resignation; the report concluded with a recommendation for additional investigations. Dewey gave additional remarks to answer the Commission's critics. The report and Dewey's remarks were later published in a pamphlet grandly titled *Truth Is on the March!* The report itself was very short, just a summary of the proceedings and a call for "further investigation." In his remarks Dewey criticized Malcolm Cowley's review of the trial transcript in *The Nation*, and criticized Ambassador Troyanovsky's characterization of the trial as a "flop."[50] Dewey later told the press that "powerful sources" were still trying to disrupt the Commission's work.[51] He pledged to continue the inquiry, and the Commission continued to hold hearings in New York City, receiving much less publicity than the hearings in Mexico.[52]

The public meeting and Dewey's remarks elicited reactions in the mainstream and radical presses. An article in *Time* was an example of a less than admiring take on the American Committee and on the public meeting, portraying Dewey as "kindly, grizzled" and stating that the "committee had proved nothing at all," characterizing Trotsky as a "disowned and virtually impotent revolutionist."[53]

Soviet Russia Today published an editorial that ridiculed the Dewey Commission in general and Dewey in particular ("he acts like a stooge"). This editorial also criticized Oswald Garrison Villard, an editor of *The Nation*. Villard earned the editorialist's wrath when he termed the show trials "political murders."[54] In the same issue, the editorialist criticized the National Executive Committee of the Socialist Party for endorsing the American Committee; the editorialist called the Dewey Commission the "laughing-stock of the continents."[55]

On a side note, in May 1937 Communist journalist Waldo Frank visited Trotsky in Mexico where Trotsky told him that he would not return to the Soviet Union because the trials were a "trap." While Frank wrote that the Soviet Union was a "kind of fatherland for all good revolutionists," there were doubts created by Trotsky's accusations that the trials were frame-ups. Frank proposed a second Inquiry to be conducted by "jurists and lawyers," a proposal dismissed by both the American Committee and the Communist Party USA, including a sneering rebuttal from American Party leader Earl Browder.[56]

The Inquiry gained more public attention in September 1937 when the hearing transcript was published as *The Case of Leon Trotsky*.[57] The transcript received glowing reviews from American Committee members novelist James T. Farrell and literary critic Edmund Wilson; Farrell had attended the Inquiry.[58] Wilson termed it to be "one of the greatest political interviews ever printed."[59] Dissident Communist Bertram D. Wolfe gave the transcript a less favorable review but considered the trial charges to be absurd.[60] Wolfe's review elicited a defensive response from Trotsky.[61] The Trotskyist newspaper *Socialist Appeal* proclaimed *The Case of Leon Trotsky* to be the triumph of truth over falsehood and urged its readers to buy copies in order to spread the word.[62]

The Dewey Commission was in the spotlight again in December when the Committee held a mass meeting in New York City to discuss its final report.[63] In anticipation of this meeting, the Trotskyist *New International* published an article that praised members of the Dewey Commission for their "courage and integrity" in not bowing to outside pressure. The reporter denounced the Moscow show trials ("the most gigantic frame-up in history") and denounced Stalinism as a "counter-revolution."[64]

Dewey was the meeting's lead speaker and declared that Trotsky and his son were not guilty, using the Trotskyist term "frame-up" to describe the Moscow show trials and citing the evidence that they had collected which refuted the trials' charges and the defendants' testimonies. The final report was divided into five parts—a summary of findings, the history and procedures of the Commission, the two Moscow show trials, conclusions, and final conclusions. Regarding the trials and the defendants' confessions, the Commission concluded the trials made no effort to "ascertain the truth" and that the confessions "do not represent the truth, irrespective of any means used to obtain them." The attendees voted in favor of a resolution to endorse the findings, condemn the trials as frame-ups, and circulate the report.[65] The Commission's findings received a "wait and see" response in an editorial in *New Republic* and a cautiously positive review in *The Nation*.[66]

American Communists dismissed the findings and disparaged Dewey personally. *New Masses* published three articles on the Committee's findings that criticized Dewey and the conduct of the American Committee's mass meeting. The first article summarized the Committee's public meeting and concluded that the Committee had not proven anything.[67] A column by Robert Forsythe sarcastically picked apart both the report and a radio address given by Dewey, terming him both a "most disarming old cuss" but "capable of great viciousness." Forsythe wrote that Dewey was "playing into the hands of the fascists."[68] The third article was another Forsythe column that again attacked Dewey and mocked Commission member Benjamin Stolberg (the "well-known parlor fink").[69] *The Communist* published an editorial that derided the Inquiry as being dominated by Trotsky while the Commission members sat "in awe and admiration and swallowing everything presented by Trotsky." The editorialist asserted that Dewey was "in the camp of the Trotskyite fascist gangsters" and that he spewed "poisonous hatred of the Soviet peoples."[70] Soviet ambassador Troyanovsky used the standard Communist term "whitewash" to describe the Committee's conclusions.[71]

American Trotskyists were jubilant and headlined the not-guilty findings, devoting much of the December 18, 1937, issue of *Socialist Appeal* to reactions to the report and its "firm and unassailable conclusions" which proved that the trial was "flimsy and vicious." This issue included extensive sections from the Dewey Commission's final report and a telegram from Trotsky in which he triumphantly stated that the Commission had "served the liberating struggle of all mankind."[72] In this vein, *Socialist Appeal* published an interview with Trotsky in which he stated that, while there may be no immediate consequences: "The judgement of the Commission demonstrates once more that the correct idea is stronger than the most powerful police force. In this conviction lies the unshakable basis of revolutionary optimism."[73]

Soon after the mass meeting, Dewey engaged in a national radio broadcast with his former student Corliss Lamont, the head of the Friends of the Soviet Union. Dewey warned liberals not to fall for Communist propaganda that equated Trotskyism with fascism.[74] Lamont slammed the Inquiry, calling it a "political weapon to advance their fanatical cause and to stir up hatred against the Soviet Union" and termed Dewey's involvement to be a "tragic mistake."[75] Lamont's criticism of the Dewey Commission led to a mild rebuke in a *New York Times* editorial.[76] Lamont also earned the enmity of the anticommunist journalist Eugene Lyons. In his 1941 book *The Red Decade*, Lyons singled out Lamont as the "generalissimo" of the "frantic campaign to smear" and to discredit the Dewey Commission.[77]

Dewey also gave an interview to the *Washington Post* in which he stated that the purges and the show trials demonstrated the "complete breakdown of revolutionary Marxism."[78] Journalist Heywood Broun, a signer of the "Open Letter," wrote a column in the *New Republic* in which he criticized Dewey for "hanging Soviet Russia" and claimed that Dewey advocated for the Congress of Industrial Organizations to bar Communists from membership.[79] Leading Trotsky supporter and former Dewey student Sidney Hook then wrote a letter to the editor of the *New Republic* that was a rebuke of Broun's article.[80]

In 1938 the Commission published its findings in *Not Guilty*, a comprehensive work that also included the hearings held outside Mexico and supporting documentation to disprove the charges.[81] Suzanne La Follette has been credited with principal authorship. American Committee member and prominent Protestant theologian Reinhold Niebuhr wrote a thoughtful review in *The Nation* in which he praised the Commission's work while criticizing Trotsky for his "fantastic" political theories, his pathetic "messianic ego" and regarded his "present political influence as confusing."[82] American Trotskyists hailed *Not Guilty* as a vindication of their leader and as a condemnation of the show trials ("frame-ups"), Stalin, and the Soviet regime.[83]

The American Committee for the Defense of Leon Trotsky continued to be active in 1938 during the third Moscow show trial. It sent a request to Ambassador Troyanovsky, asking for a six-week delay to the start of the trial and for permission to send observers. The Committee called this trial a "frame-up," the favorite Trotskyist term.[84] The Committee also sent a letter to Soviet ambassador Troyanovsky which included a deposition disproving the testimony of one of the defendants as to meeting with Trotsky in Paris in 1934.[85] The Committee held another public meeting on March 9, 1938, to pass resolutions to condemn the third trial as a "frame-up."[86] Lead speaker Bertram D. Wolfe barely mentioned Trotsky while denouncing the trials and "Stalin's bloody deeds." He concluded that Stalinism must be destroyed in order to "redeem the Russian Revolution."[87]

These Committee activities were condemned in *Daily Worker* which published an article stating that some of the signers of the Committee's request to Troyanovsky were people who later claimed that their names had been used without their permission.[88] Corliss Lamont also piled on to the criticism of the Committee, terming it to be a "mouthpiece" for Trotskyists.[89] In response, the Trotskyist *New International* published an open letter from Trotsky supporter and former Dewey student Max Eastman to Lamont in which Eastman termed the trials to be the "whole cult, art, ideology and technique of political and party lying" and called Corliss Lamont a "public defender of a deliberate policy of falsification."[90]

There was also a sad footnote concerning one of the members of the Dewey Commission. On January 1, 1943, Carlo Tresca, an Italian-born anti-Fascist and radical labor leader, was shot dead in broad daylight on a New York City street. The radical press suspected both Fascists and Stalinists, but his murder was never solved.[91]

The American Committee and the Dewey Commission were two contemporaneous reactions to the Moscow show trials that have been cited, if only briefly, in comprehensive studies of the show trials. They gave Trotsky and his American supporters a forum to refute the show trials' confessions and verdicts and to air their condemnations of Stalinism. While history did prove the Commission's findings to be correct, the American Committee and the Commission of Inquiry received mixed reviews at the time. Partly due to the prominence of John Dewey, the American Committee and the Commission of Inquiry have been objects of study to this day.[92]

In 1968 *The Case of Leon Trotsky* was republished by Merit Publishers, the successor to the Trotskyist Pioneer Press. This reprint included an introduction by Committee secretary George Novack who had attended the Inquiry.[93] Novack recounted the history of the Inquiry, defended the not-guilty findings, and concluded with the following: "Enlightened opinion . . . has come to recognize the monstrous falsifications perpetrated by Stalin against his political opponents. Thus, history has already vindicated the work and conclusions of the Dewey Commission."[94] In 1984 Trotsky supporter Sidney Hook defended the Inquiry in an article which he slammed the Moscow show trials' defenders and singled out Corliss Lamont for leading the opposition to the Inquiry and for composing the "Open Letter."[95]

Later revelations vindicated the Commission's findings, but at the time the Inquiry did nothing but give Trotsky another forum to refute the trial charges and to rail against the Stalinist regime. Stalin retained power and the purges and show trials continued.

The "Open Letter to American Liberals"

The founding of the American Committee for the Defense of Leon Trotsky elicited one of the most famous US responses to the Moscow show trials—the "Open Letter to American Liberals." Prior to the publication of the Open Letter, *New Republic* published two pro-Trotsky letters from Socialist Norman Thomas and American Committee members John Chamberlain and James T. Farrell.[96] In the same issue, it published an abridged copy of the Open Letter which criticized the American Committee for its "violent attacks" on the show trials and its "bitter denunciations" of the Soviet government.[97] The full Open Letter was published in March 1937 in *Soviet Russia Today* with a preface by Corliss Lamont, who characterized the Soviet Union as the target of "Fascist" and "semi-Fascist governments" who wanted the "smashing of the Soviet Union."[98]

The letter was addressed to "liberals who may be approached by the American Committee." It again criticized the "violent attacks" on the Moscow show trials and the "bitter denunciations" against the Soviet government. The Open Letter defended the trials and posed four questions to the "liberal members" of the American Committee—why they joined the Committee ("out of interest in Trotskyism or wholly in defense of the right of asylum and free speech"), whether they were willing to "ally themselves" with opposition to the Soviets' Five Year Plan and its foreign policy of "peace and international understanding," were they mindful of "lending support to the fascist forces which are attacking democracy," and whether the Soviets should be able to defend themselves "against treasonous plots." The Open Letter also quoted Mauritz Hallgren who had resigned from the American Committee. The letter ended with a call for liberals to support the Soviet Union against Hitler.[99]

The Open Letter was signed by a wide range of liberal intellectuals. One of the most famous signers was playwright Lillian Hellman. Other signers were journalist Heywood Broun, then president of the American Newspaper Guild, Malcolm Cowley, literary editor of *New Republic*, journalists Louis Fischer, Maxwell Stewart, and Max Lerner of *The Nation* and journalist Anna Louise Strong, one of the Soviet Union's leading American advocates. Academics included sociologist Robert S. Lynd, author of the landmark "Middletown" studies, and economist Mary Van Kleeck. Writers included Theodore Dreiser, Carey McWilliams, Dorothy Parker, and Nathaniel West. Artist Rockwell Kent was also a signer. Hollywood was represented by director Lewis Milestone and by screenwriters Ring Lardner, Jr. and David Ogden Stewart. However, the invitation to sign the Open Letter also elicited some high-profile refusals.

Playwright Sidney Howard, later credited as the screenwriter for *Gone with the Wind*, declined to sign the letter and allowed that Trotsky deserved to defend himself and that the show trials could be questioned.[100]

The Communist Party USA saw the propaganda value of the Open Letter. Party leader Earl Browder reported on it at a meeting of the Comintern Executive Committee. Browder referred to the signers as "88 outstanding public figures" and the "cream of the American intellectual and artistic world" and as "the most outstanding list of names ever signed on one document in the United States for the defense of the Soviet Union." Browder also cited the danger of American Trotskyists as "reactionary forces."[101]

In 1941 anticommunist journalist Eugene Lyons defended the Dewey Commission and criticized the Open Letter. He referred to the show trials as telling a "lunatic tale," chastised liberals who did not support the Dewey Commission and characterized the Open Letter as "mass support of a far-off and bloodthirsty dictatorship by otherwise sane and largely well-meaning people." Lyons singled out Corliss Lamont for criticism for his "command of the anti-Dewey campaign."[102]

Open Letter signer Theodore Dreiser, who had spent three months in the Soviet Union in the 1920s, was also part of a 1937 literary symposium which discussed three questions about the significance of the purges and the show trials, Trotsky's guilt, and the international impact of "Stalin's repressions." Dreiser expressed some doubts about the confessions but believed that Trotsky was capable of "planning the very vastest schemes," had wanted to run Russia, and believed that Trotsky hated Stalin. Dreiser concluded that while the trials lessened any favorable opinions of the Soviet Union at the present time, they would be beneficial in the long run.[103] Dreiser also participated in a brief exchange with novelist John Dos Passos, a member of the American Committee, in which Dos Passos referred to the purges as a "terrible terror," and Dreiser expressed doubts based on events of the past year but still cited the Soviets' achievements.[104]

Throughout 1937 pro- and anti-Trotskyists, including individuals involved in the American Committee and in the Dewey Commission, engaged in a war of words in the literary and opinion journal *Southern Review*. It began with an anti-Trotsky essay by political scientist Frederick L. Schuman. Schuman was a well-known college professor, a prolific author on international relations, and an expert on German and Soviet affairs. He characterized Trotsky as always "too early or too late," as a "political blunderer," and he characterized the Soviet Union as an ally of democracies and as a bulwark against fascism.[105] [Schuman later ran afoul of the House Un-American Activities Committee for his "Communist affiliations."] Schuman's essay elicited five letters in response—anti-Trotsky letters by Malcolm Cowley and Carleton Beals, pro-Trotsky letters by Max Eastman and James T. Farrell (American Committee members), and a short, non-committal response by Dewey.[106] Schuman's essay also elicited an essay in rebuttal by American Committee member Sidney Hook who defended the Dewey Commission.[107] Hook's essay caused another round of letters, including back-and-forth arguments by Hook, Beals, Schuman, and Farrell.[108]

Some of the intellectuals who signed the Open Letter would become embroiled in the US government's anticommunist investigations after the Second World War.

Plate 6.1 Five Soviet marshals, 1935. Front row: Mikhail Tukachevsky (trial defendants, later executed), People's Commissar for Defense Klementi Voroshilov (ousted in 1957), Aleksandr Yegorov (trial judge, later executed); back row: Semyon Budyenny (trial judge, survived) and Vasily Blyukher (trial judge, later executed). "5 marshals." Wikimedia Commons, November 11, 1935, https://commons.wikimedia.org (accessed July 6, 2022).

Plate 6.2 People's Commissar for Foreign Affairs Maxim Litvinov (ousted in 1939, survived). "Maxim Litvinov, 1932." Wikimedia Commons, February 11, 1932, https://commons.wikimedia.org (accessed July 6, 2022).

6

The Army Trial

The Case of the Trotskyist Anti-Soviet Military Organization (1937), the Navy Purges (1937–8), and the Anti-Foreigner Campaign (1937–8)

Joseph Stalin's next move was to purge the Soviet armed forces and to decimate the officer corps. In addition, the Soviet government conducted an intense anti-foreigner campaign that painted the country as riddled with foreign spies, saboteurs ("wreckers"), and counter-revolutionary plotters planning to overthrow the government. Foreigners and Soviet citizens who dealt with foreigners were accused and arrested. This chapter discusses American reactions to the military purges and the anti-foreigner campaign.

The Army Trial

Known formally as the Workers and Peasants Red Army (RKKA or Krasnya Armiya), the Soviet Army was established in 1918 as part of the People's Commissariat for War. Leon Trotsky had been a leading organizer of the Red Army and had been People's Commissar for War during the Civil War. The Army grew in size and prestige as part of the renamed People's Commissariat for Defense. By 1937 the Soviets had a standing army of over 1,000,000 men and was reported in the West to be the largest standing army in the world.[1] Stalin promoted five generals and People's Commissar for Defense Klementi Voroshilov to the equivalent rank of field marshal, and *Izvestia* published brief, propaganda-laden, laudatory profiles of them (e.g., "Tukhachevsky rose like an eagle in the battles") in 1935. In one of the ongoing ironies of the purges and the trials, future trial defendant Karl Radek wrote these profiles.[2] A signal that the Army was next to be purged came when Army Corps Commander

Vitovka Kazimirovich Putna, a military attaché who had served in London and Berlin, was recalled to Moscow and arrested in 1936; he had been implicated in the first show trial and was suspected of plotting with Grigori Zinoviev.[3] A more serious sign that the military was targeted came when Joseph Stalin began a campaign of increased Communist indoctrination in the military by the reintroduction of political commissars into the military councils of the armed forces. These commissars were equal to officers in making command decisions as two members of any military council must approve any actions. Such councils had been introduced during the Russian Revolution and, after the poor showing of Soviet troops in the Winter War with Finland, were abolished in 1940.[4]

The purge of the armed forces was under the direction of People's Commissar for Defense Klementi E. Voroshilov who headed the Military Council and reported directly to Stalin. The signal that the armed forces were about to be purged came at a meeting of the War Council and the government, held by Voroshilov and new NKVD head Nikolai Yezhov from June 1 to June 4, 1937. The *New York Times* reported on Marshal Voroshilov's statement to the Red Army on the alleged crimes of the defendants, stating that all treason, sabotage, and plots against the government would be eliminated. He asserted: "The ultimate aim of this band was to liquidate by any means the Soviet order, to destroy the Soviet regime, to crush the workers and to restore the U.S.S.R. to landlords and capitalists."[5]

The purge of the military began in earnest with the Army trial in June 1937. It should be noted that while this trial became known as the "secret" Army trial, it was not secret. The Soviet press announced the arrests and the trial, but the proceedings were closed to spectators. The defendants were top generals (called Army Commanders or Corps Commanders) and Marshal Mikhail Tukhachevsky. Tukhachevsky was the most prominent victim of the Army trial. He was a veteran of the First World War, the war with Poland, and a hero of the Civil War. As late as 1936 he was writing for *Pravda* and giving official reports on military preparedness to the Soviet government's Central Executive Committee.[6] He was the Soviets' most highly regarded and best-known military strategist ("the most talked of army leader in Europe").[7] He had first been demoted to a lesser command, a sign that he was on the way out.

In addition to Putna and Tukhachevsky, the other defendants were:

> Corps Commander Robert Petrovich Eideman—Head of the Osoaviakhim (Society for Air and Chemical Defense, civil defense, and reserves);

Army Commander B. M. Feldman—Chief of the Bureau of General Affairs, People's Commissariat for Defense;
Army Commander August Ivanovich Kork—Head of the Frunze Military Academy (war college);
Corps Commander V. M. Primakov—Assistant Commander of the Leningrad Military District;
Army Commander Jeronim Petrovich Uborevich—Commander of the White Russian (Byelorussian) Military District;
Army Commander Iona Emanuilovich Yakir—Commander of the Leningrad and Kiev Military Districts, member of the Central Committee.

The defendants were demoted, recalled to Moscow, expelled from the Party, arrested in May, and tortured until they confessed. They were charged with the usual crimes of espionage for foreign powers, plotting a *coup d'état*, and plotting to restore capitalism and large landownership. They all pleaded guilty, were condemned to death, and were summarily shot on June 12, 1937.

This trial was unique in that top Army officers were judges alongside chief judge Vasily Vasilyevich Ulrikh. These military judges were:

People's Vice Commissar for Defense Yakov Ivanovich Alknis (Chief of the Air Forces of the Red Army);
Army Commander I. P. Belov;
Marshal Vasily Konstantinovich Blyukher [also transliterated as Bluecher];
Marshal Semyon Mikhailovich Budyonny [also transliterated at Budyenny];
Army Commander Pavel Efimovich Dybenko;
Corps Commander E. I. Goryachev;
Army Commander I. D. Kasharin;
Army Commander Boris Mikhailovich Shaposhnikov.

Several of these military judges would later face the same fate as the defendants, including People's Vice Commissar Alknis and Marshal Blyukher. General Alknis was rumored to have been arrested soon after the trial.[8] Marshal Blyukher (the "Red Bonaparte") was purged in 1938 and executed in 1939.[9] In May 1938, after months of rumors, the *New York Times* published a report of rumors that other judges—Army Commander Dybenko ("one of the most romantic figures of the Bolshevik revolution"), Army Commander Belov, and Marshal Alexander Ilyich Yegorov, Tukhachevsky's successor—had been removed from their posts.[10] Belov had been profiled in the Soviet press and praised for his achievements during the Civil War and for his "willingness to sacrifice himself for the cause of Revolution."[11] Both Marshal Blyukher and Marshal Budyonny had been profiled in the West.[12]

There was one marshal who did not serve as a judge. The *New York Times* reported the suicide of Marshal I. B. Gamarnik, the People's Vice Commissar for Defense, Chief of the Political Administration of the Workers and Peasants Red Army and a member of the Party Central Committee. The Central Committee claimed that he had been "involved with anti-Soviet elements in a plot against the government" and that he had committed suicide on May 31, 1937.[13] According to Gamarnik's daughter, he shot himself rather than serve as a trial judge.[14]

The haste and lack of spectators at this trial led to speculation that no trial was held and that the judges were simply ordered to sign the guilty verdicts. However, historian Stephen Kotkin included a detailed account of this trial in the second volume of his biography of Stalin.[15] At the Eighteenth Party Congress in 1939, Stalin vilified the defendants when he referred to Tukhachevsky, Yakir, and Uborevich as "fiends."[16]

The effect of the Army purge on the highest level of Soviet military officers was summarized in a 1964 US Central Intelligence Agency report. The report stated that within eighteen months of the June 1937 meeting held by Voroshilov: "75 of the 80 members of the [War] Council were purged, according to Soviet sources."[17]

During the destalinization period of the 1950s, the reputations of Marshals Tukhachevsky, Gamarnik, and Yegorov and Generals Dybenko and Bluykher were restored when their biographies were included in the *Great Soviet Encyclopedia*.[18] Nikita Khrushchev also mentioned the innocence of the executed marshals and generals ("splendid commanders and political officers") in his speech to the Twenty-Second Party Congress in 1961.[19]

Official US Reactions

The Army trial and purge of the officer corps were of great interest to the United States as the government considered the Soviet armed forces to be a counterbalance to the growing military might of Nazi Germany. Thus, there were several US Embassy communiqués in reaction to the official announcements of the removals, arrests, verdicts, and executions. Embassy secretary Loy W. Henderson sent a communiqué that predicted the purge of senior officers when it included a report on the demotion of Marshal Tukhachevsky, the reported suicide of Marshal Gamarnik, and the reintroduction of political commissars. The communiqué also speculated on the arrests of several other high-ranking military officers who would be defendants, Stalin's "lack of confidence" in the loyalty of the Red Army and the adverse effect of the political commissars on the Army's efficiency. The communiqué ended by stating that these events were a "severe shock" to the "morale and self-confidence of the armed forces."[20]

When it was announced in *Pravda* that these officers had been arrested and would be tried, Henderson sent a communiqué that speculated that Germany was the "foreign nation" involved in the charges of espionage. Perhaps indirectly expressing incredulity at the charges of espionage against defendants Yakir and Feldman, Henderson noted that "both Yakir and Feldman are Jews and the former has a reputation of being an extreme Jewish nationalist."[21] This statement cast doubts on the charges that these men would spy for the German government with its avowed anti-Semitism.

After the death sentences were announced, Henderson sent a longer, speculative communiqué in which he stated that the Embassy had not heard of any disturbances in Moscow after this announcement. He offered the opinion that "higher officers" in the Red Army had been friendly toward Germany as many of the defendants had been trained at the German General Staff College in the 1920s, and they had "acquired a respect for the efficiency and fighting power of the Reichswehr and considerable admiration for German military traditions." These officers had publicly expressed such friendly feelings. Taking this into consideration, Henderson wrote the following in condemnation of the trial and his sorrow for the defendants:

> It is the practice of the Kremlin to stretch into heinous crimes certain known views of persons whom it has decided to destroy. It distorted the known friendly feelings for Germany shared by the condemned officers into treason.... The character and reputations for professional integrity of the condemned are such that it does not seem possible that all of them could have been guilty of the crimes for which they have been condemned.... Their loss is a severe blow to the efficiency and morale of the Red Army.[22]

Henderson speculated that Stalin's motive for condemning these men "was that Stalin had become suspicious of them" as they were "becoming too independent in their attitude and that he could not be sure of their unconditional loyalty to himself." Henderson further speculated that the generals had resisted any political influence or penetration by the NKVD and that the military judges were shown the confessions and were commanded to sign the verdicts. He repeated the rumor of a German conspiracy to overthrow the government. Henderson ended by stating: "The Embassy nevertheless is not convinced that the condemned men were guilty of the crimes attributed to them."[23]

Henderson's short communiqué on June 23, 1937, stated that "not one diplomatic mission here, nor a single foreign observer in Moscow whose opinion bears weight, believed that the executed Red Army officers were guilty of the crimes attributed to them." Henderson went on to speculate that these men objected to Stalin holding his own career over the "welfare of the State," that they had "become alarmed at the havoc" Stalin had caused and that they held conversations for the "purpose of either getting rid of Stalin or curbing his power." The communiqué ended by quoting from discussions with other foreign diplomats as to the veracity of the charges against the defendants and with Henderson's disbelief in any formal conspiracy.[24] By using the phrase "not a single observer in Moscow whose opinion bears weight," Henderson may have been indirectly stating a difference of opinion with Ambassador Joseph E. Davies, whose own writings on the Army trial reflected the view that the defendants were guilty.

The Embassy's interest in the Army trial continued into 1938. Henderson summarized the effect of the purges on the Red Army, referring to Stalin's decision to reintroduce political commissars and stated the belief among military attachés that the reintroduction of these commissars rendered the Red Army less effective as a military organization and that it should be reorganized on a non-political basis.[25] In his memoir, *A Question of Trust,* Henderson surmised that there were differences between Stalin and the high-ranking officers over military strategy with Stalin being a proponent of an offensive strategy and the officers in favor of a more defensive policy. Henderson had met Marshal Tukhachevsky at a Kremlin reception and wrote that Tukhachevsky (a "gregarious sort of person") believed in a defensive war strategy.[26]

Ambassador Davies published his own opinions on the Army trial. Because of his marriage to the wealthy Marjorie Merriweather Post, Davies entertained lavishly at the Embassy. He had met Army leaders at an Embassy dinner in the spring of 1937; among the invitees were both future trial judges and defendants. In his diary he described them as follows: "Strong, healthy, and with fine faces. Their uniforms were perfectly tailored and were quite resplendent with the various insignia of rank and various decorations."[27] In a section of *Mission to Moscow* Davies included a communiqué to Undersecretary of State Sumner Welles. In contrast to the doubts expressed by Embassy secretary Henderson, Davies wrote that there was probably a "definite conspiracy in the making looking to a *coup d'état* by the army—not necessarily anti-Stalin, but anti-political and anti-party, and that Stalin struck with characteristic speed, boldness, and strength. A violent 'purge' all over the country seems to be going on."[28] In a private letter to his daughter, Davies wrote that Moscow was calm but that there was "much agitation and excitement and gossip in the Diplomatic Corps," and he ended this letter with the question of the morale of the army being "destroyed" or "whether its loyalty has been alienated from Stalin." Davies speculated that "if Stalin retains the loyalty of the army he will be more strongly entrenched politically than ever before because he has smashed all potential rivalry and leadership."[29]

An entry in his diary included his description of a Fourth of July reception held at the Embassy at which People's Commissar for Foreign Affairs Maxim Litvinov was a guest. The ambassador informed him that the reaction of the United States and Western Europe to the purges and the Army trial "definitely was bad, and harmful to the outside reputation of the U.S.S.R."[30] In a letter to White House press secretary Stephen Early, Davies wrote that the loyalty of the army did not seem to be weakened and that, if so, the "government will be stronger than ever internally, because he has with characteristic speed killed off all potential leadership."[31]

In a later section of his memoir, entitled "Why They Shot Tukhachevsky," Davies wrote a long analysis of the trial to Secretary of State Sumner Welles. He recounted the rumors about the army plotting with Germany and its alleged anti-Stalin sentiments. Davies defended Stalin as devoted "to communism and the elevation of the proletariat." Davies characterized the Army trial as part of a "cleansing and purging" and as a "bitter internecine struggle . . . between the army and the secret police." He concluded that, because the defendants had been found guilty by their fellow marshals and generals, they "had been guilty of some offence" while other members of the diplomatic corps doubted any German conspiracy. He surmised that the defendants resented the political control being imposed on them, including more secret police, and that party leaders considered them to be a "serious threat." Davies again acknowledged that a major purge was happening in all sectors of the Soviet economy and the provinces.[32]

There was another official US source on the Army trial. The United States had military attachés in its embassies and legations. The Army attaché in Moscow was Lt. Col. Philip R. Faymonville. Faymonville wrote that the Army had strong support from the Soviet government. However, he reported that the two previous show trials revealed "counter-revolutionary elements" and plotting to overthrow the government, which were a shock to the nation and lowered the army's prestige. He characterized the Army high command as recovering from the shock of the first two show trials and trying to rid the Army of subversive elements and to "reinvigorate the patriotic feelings."[33] He wrote a long report on the trial, recounted the events that led to it, and briefly recounted the careers of the defendants. This report expressed doubts about such a trial taking place in just one day and expressed doubts about the charges. He not only termed the guilt of the defendants as "improbable" but also surmised that defendants Putna and Primakov may have involved with Trotskyist plotters.

Faymonville was convinced that the defendants had opposed greater Party control of the military. He had opinions on the effects of the trial as weakening the morale of the Red Army and weakening Soviet foreign relations, especially with Germany and Japan. He reported that the trial vindicated Communist Party discipline and that it had little effect on the Soviet populace. He concluded: "The recent weakening of the Red Army . . . leaves the forces working for peace definitely weaker and renders the prospect of Japanese and fascist aggression definitely more probable."[34] Faymonville's reporting made its way up the chain of command in the Department of War's Military Intelligence Division. In his summary report to the Chief of Staff, Col. E. W. R. McCabe called the executions of the defendants "the most serious army crisis since the Revolution" and echoed Faymonville's conclusions.[35]

Reactions of American Journalists

For a trial held in closed session, the Army trial was well covered in the American press. The *New York Times* kept up a running commentary as the noose tightened around the Army, including rumors about Marshal Tukhachevsky and about General Putna, Tukhachevsky's demotion, and the reintroduction of political commissars.[36],[37] *New York Times* Moscow correspondent Harold Denny wrote on the ramped-up search for spies and saboteurs in the military reserves, the alleged "political laxness" in the Far Eastern Army, and the scathing condemnations in the press that singled out Marshal Gamarnik for his "counter-revolutionary activity of a spy and Fascist bandit."[38] As with other articles that passed through Soviet censors, Denny's reporting was non-committal, but one article contained a sidebar posted from Berlin about the "unusually strict censorship had been put on dispatches from Moscow dealing with the alleged plots in the Soviet Red army."[39]

Denny wrote three front-page articles on the removal of Marshal Tukhachevsky and the accused generals ("this extraordinary list"), the trial and the guilty verdicts. He reported on the skepticism of foreign military observers as to any such anti-government plotting within the Army, the vehement condemnations of the defendants in the Soviet press which he termed as strident as those for the defendants in the previous show trials and that ordinary citizens seemed to be unaffected by this turn of events, echoing the observations of US Embassy officials.[40] The Associated Press reported the executions of the defendants, terming Tukhachevsky as "one of the Soviet Union's most brilliant military leaders." The reporter further stated that the trial had led to vicious editorials in the Soviet press ("dogs die like dogs").[41] A companion article by Frederick T. Birchall, the *New York Times*'s Pulitzer Prize-winning European correspondent, reported on a spate of rumors in Europe about additional executions of Army officers, mutinies, and the rumored assassination of the German ambassador in Moscow.[42]

The fact that two such high-profile trials were held within six months led the *New York Times*' Russian-born reporter Elias Tobenkin to consider the alleged crimes and conspiracies to be evidence that Stalin's rule may be in "crisis" and to denote the stress between Stalin and the military as the secret police tried to infiltrate the armed forces. He considered the prestige of the army to have suffered.[43]

The *New York Times* published an editorial that praised Marshal Tukhachevsky, lamented his fate ("degradation and execution") and considered his execution and the increased political influence within the military to be detrimental to the Soviet Army, thus destroying Tukhachevsky's life's work.[44] Predictably, Soviet ambassador Alexander Troyanovsky stated that the government's swift action "bolstered the morale" of the Soviet people; he also echoed the charges of the defendants' being conspirators and Trotskyists.[45] Frederick T. Birchall of the *New York Times* analyzed a theory that the Army wanted to stage a *coup d'état*, and he concluded that the prestige of Army had suffered in the eyes of other European powers. This article was accompanied by a map showing economic resources and where alleged "dissatisfaction has brought death sentences."[46]

Denny wrote several follow-up articles. The first reported on the widening of the purge of the Osoaviakhim, the reserves and civil defense unit, for alleged wrecking (sabotage) and for being full of spies; it had been headed by the executed General Eideman. He also reported on the Soviet press reports of "alarming disorganization in many key industries," listing a litany of troubles, including a collapse of "labor discipline."[47] Denny's true opinion about the Army trial and the purges was revealed in an uncensored, front-page article on June 24. Denny bluntly reported on the "cloud of anxiety and bewilderment" hanging over the Soviet Union, and he condemned the purges and. reported on the disarray within Soviet industries, including worker unrest. He also reported on the growing skepticism within the diplomatic community about this trial; Denny began to reverse his previous writing that the Soviet people were indifferent to this trial. He also praised the records of the defendants and attributed their downfall to their protests over the reintroduction of political commissars, their belief in a defensive strategy, and Stalin's fear of a Napoleon rising from the Army. He stated that the "tension in Moscow is great" as the purge expanded with Soviet citizens denouncing each other. He bluntly stated that the constitution of 1936 was proving to be no protection and that the hunt for "political offenders is merciless."[48] In an article on June 26 that did not have the "Uncensored" designation, Denny speculated that the Army seemed to have "withstood the shock" of the purges, and he expressed belief in the charges in the earlier purge trials but defended the condemned generals' records in the Civil War. He again reported that foreign observers believed that the purge of the military was based on opposition to the reintroduction of political commissars, disagreement with Stalin on military strategy, and Stalin's fear of the concentration of power in the military.[49]

Editorial comments in the *New York Times* backed up Denny's opinions stated in his uncensored article of June 24.[50] However, in contrast, the *New York Times* published an article by Pertinax, the pseudonym of André Géraud, the foreign editor for *Echo de Paris*, a conservative French newspaper. He accepted the theory of pro-German sentiments among the defendants and further theorized that the generals had rebelled against Stalin's new anti-German stance. He further stated that Tukhachevsky had secretly visited Berlin and that General Putna had "closely cooperated with his German colleagues" while posted to the Soviet Embassy in London.[51]

Denny reported that political commissars were to hold power equal to regimental commanders and that this was part of "Stalinizing" the Red Army, an opinion that Denny reported was held by "foreign observers." Denny also reported that the Kremlin was continuing its denunciations of the trial defendants for allegedly opposing the political commissars.[52] The *New York Times* reported on further Army purges throughout 1938 and 1939 with little editorial comment, only summaries of mentions in the Soviet press.[53] The *New York Times* also quoted Ambassador Troyanovsky's characterization of the purge as shooting the conspirators before they "shot government leaders."[54]

Denny sent a series of uncensored reports that began with an article on September 13, 1937, that bluntly summarized the "cleansing"—the purges of the Old Bolsheviks, the Army and the reserves, the secret police, other government agencies, and Party organizations and the arts, reaching down to all levels of society. He termed 1937 to be the "bloody year." He cited a list of state and Party agencies that had been purged and cited the arrests or departure of foreigners, including Americans, a symptom of the government's anti-foreigner campaign. He also wrote that the Soviet public had become accustomed to the purges.[55]

Both *Time* and *Newsweek* reported rather skeptically on the Army trial. In a short article, *Time* reported on widespread purges and referred to the propaganda about Marshal Gamarnik's suicide with the Kremlin's official line about his connection to "'anti-Soviet elements.'"[56] In a much longer article, the *Time* reporter referred to the defendants as "eight dead dogs," echoing a name-calling reference to them in a *Pravda* editorial. The reporter summarized the downfall of Marshal Tukhachevsky and highlighted the theory of foreign correspondent Hubert R. Knickerbocker that the general staffs of both Germany and the Soviet Union felt that a war between the two would be "suicidal" and wanted a secret agreement which Adolf Hitler had dismissed. However, Stalin showed "his horror of any compromise with Fascism" that led the Army trial. The reporter also cited a theory that People's Commissar of Defense Klementi Voroshilov had made a deal with Stalin to succeed him in exchange for the reintroduction of the political commissars and for the death of the eight defendants.[57] *Time* followed up with an article on the Soviet Union "sweltering in a lather of treason trials, executions and suicides" and quoted from Harold Denny's uncensored reports on the "chaos" in Soviet industry as company executives had disappeared.[58]

Newsweek reported on the suicide of Marshal Gamarnik, noting that he had been treated as a national hero until May Day of that year. The reporter wrote that Stalin had feared the growing power of the Soviet Army and had "humiliated" Marshal Voroshilov by reintroducing political commissars into the armed forces.[59] An article after the trial described the downfall of Marshal Tukhachevsky.[60] A subsequent article described "Stalin's steam roller" and the Germans' muddled assertion that the trial defendants had collaborated with Germany to rebuild the Reichswehr, that Tukhachevsky himself reported this collaboration to Stalin who panicked, thus weakening the Soviet Union in the eyes of the West, especially France.[61] *Newsweek* also quoted from an uncensored report from Harold Denny. The *Newsweek* reporter termed the purges to be "Stalin's Reign of Terror" and used such terms as "undiminished bloodlust" in detailing the arrests of top government officials and Army leaders and the mass arrests conducted under Yezhov. The reporter characterized the military purge as a struggle over difference in strategy between the military leaders and "Czar Stalin."[62]

Literary Digest reported on the demotion of Marshal Tukhachevsky and correctly predicted his execution. The reporter was incredulous about Tukhachevsky's dismissal as Vice Commissar and was unimpressed with his successor Marshal Alexander Yegorov. The reporter grimly described the reintroduction of political commissars as keeping the army "safe for Stalin" and predicted future purges.[63] A second article led off with the death of Stalin's mother and reported on the executions of the defendants, citing a theory that Russian and German military officers had been "chummy" before 1934 and wanted to remain so.[64] A third article pondered the meaning of the purges, their impact on international relations, and Stalin's motives. These possible motives included Stalin being "mentally quirky," wanting to eliminate opponents, fearing a "mammoth Trotsky plot" or an Army *coup d'état* and that the Germans and Japanese were bribing "everyone in Russia." The reporter compared Stalin to Hitler in their both being "personal, nationalist" dictators.[65]

Living Age reprinted an article by British historian Sir Bernard Pares who misread the situation and was "convinced that there is a deep-rooted and many-sided conspiracy against the supremacy of Stalin," but he was skeptical of the charges of plotting to "restore landlordism." He praised Stalin and Yezhov "who is now being congratulated on the discovery of the danger."[66] *Current History* published an article by the anticommunist journalist Eugene Lyons who condemned the show trials and the purges and characterized the Army as being the "latest victim of Russia's panicky house-cleaning" and the purge as part of an "orgy of authoritarian violence." Lyons attributed all of this to the government's "fear of the Russian masses" with the reintroduction of political commissars in the military as one manifestation.[67] In the same anti-Stalinist vein, *American Mercury* published an article on "Ten Years of Soviet Terror" by an unnamed "Moscow Correspondent" who reported ten "episodes of terror" that included the Army trial. The reporter also praised the uncensored articles by Harold Denny and wondered if he would share the fate of reporters Paul Scheffer and Nicholas Basseches ("dean of the press corps") who had been deported by the Soviets.[68]

The liberal weeklies also weighed in on this trial. *The Nation* published an anti-Stalin column by editor Oswald Garrison Villard in which he called the trials a "genuine disaster" and "legal murders." Villard dismissed Stalin apologists' rationale that the defendants had "sold out to Germany" because they were former tsarist officers. Villard considered the trial to be giving the "greatest aid and comfort to the dictators--notably Hitler." He concluded that the trials and the purges were detrimental to European diplomacy in dealing with Hitler and were demoralizing to the Soviet populace who were trying to build a "great new world order" while under the "threat of death."[69]

In contrast to Villard's anti-Stalin stance, *New Republic* had more mixed reactions. It published "Soviet Chills and Fever," an article which did not question Soviet justice and dismissed Trotskyist criticism. The reporter pondered what the widespread cases of treason said about "weak morale," citizens' loyalty, and confidence in the Soviet Union twenty years after the Revolution. The reporter concluded that the purges have dealt a blow to Soviet prestige.[70] *New Republic* published an article by London correspondent and contributing editor H. N. Brailsford, who had met Marshal Tukhachevsky during the Soviets' war with Poland. He praised Tukhachevsky and derided the charges against the defendants. Brailsford cited an alleged memorandum that put the charges within the context of the friendship of the Soviet high command with their counterparts in the German Army and with the defendants' opposition to alliances with "bourgeois governments." Brailsford concluded that after the "bloodbath" of the purges, the Soviet Union would never be stable or healthy without the presence of a loyal opposition.[71]

Foreign Affairs published a strange article by an author with the pseudonym "Balticus" who denigrated critics of this trial, gave credence to the accusations against the defendants, and concluded that the trials were held to end "pro-German tendencies," to "impress the masses," and to "keep conspirators" from stirring up "public opinion against the Government." He concentrated on Tukhachevsky and praised Stalin as "faithful to Lenin" but admitted that Stalin used the "most violent and cruel means." Balticus blithered about the "new generation" of Russians and quoted extensively from a conversation with an "orthodox Stalinist" who repeated the charge that some Old Bolsheviks may have been German spies as far back as 1917.[72]

Reporting on the Army purges continued into 1938 and 1939 with continued speculation about the effects of the purges on the strength and morale of the Red Army. Writers argued on both sides of the issue. Military analyst George Fielding Eliot wrote that the purge was caused by opposition to the reintroduction of political commissars and that it was impossible to assess the impact of the purge on the "morale and efficiency" of the Army. He also incorrectly predicted that Marshal Bluykher would not be affected.[73] Blyukher was later purged.

In 1939 the *Saturday Evening Post* published an article entitled "Why Stalin Shot His Generals" by Walter Krivitsky, the Soviet defector who claimed to have been the former head of Soviet military intelligence (GRU) in Western Europe. In his first-person account, Krivitsky blamed Stalin for instigating a conspiracy with the Germans to bring down the generals, a charge that he repeated in his memoir *In Stalin's Secret Service*. Krivitsky claimed that Stalin was settling accounts over policy differences with the Army leadership.[74]

Reactions of American Radicals

Predictably, American Communist leaders supported the Army trial. *Daily Worker* published a long article that excoriated critics of this trial and outlined the "treachery" of the defendants ("gang of spies, wreckers, murderers") as part of the struggle between socialism and capitalism.[75] *New Masses* published a brief editorial that echoed *Daily Worker*, dismissed the criticism of the "capitalist press," and considered the defendants to be traitors who revealed war plans to Germany ("their employers").[76] *New Masses* condemned the defendants, citing a British source who accused the defendants of pro-German and anti-French sympathies, singling out Marshal Tukhachevsky as wanting a change in the Soviet government to forestall a war with Germany which he and his colleagues allegedly believed would lead to defeat.[77] *Soviet Russia Today* published a brief editorial that quoted a correspondent for the *Chicago Daily News* who maintained that the purge had not "impaired the efficiency or mobility of the army." The editorialist concluded that this report refuted the claims of innocence by Trotsky (the "traitor in Mexico") and his supporters.[78]

Opposition Communists, including the Independent Communist Labor League, were critics of the Army trial. Jay Lovestone considered the Army trial to be different from the Moscow show trials in that it was not within the context of internal Party politics. He rejected the official accounts of the charges as being "obviously absurd." Lovestone considered the purges to be symptomatic of "great discontent in the USSR" and called Stalin an "expert of trumping up charges." He also claimed that Stalin was attempting to stifle discontent in order to preserve "his leadership and regime." Lovestone believed that Stalin had contributed to the "growth and progress of the USSR" but also listed the faults of his regime, including "corruption . . . incompetency, favoritism and callous bureaucracy." Being a true believer in class solidarity, he concluded that, in spite of everything, the "workers movement" in capitalist nations would defend the Soviet Union if it were threatened.[79]

As with the show trials, Trotsky reacted strongly to the trial of the leaders of the Army that he had helped to create and had led during the Civil War. He called the execution of the generals an "assassination" of the "heroes of the civil war, the pride of the country." He attributed their executions to opposition to the reintroduction of political commissars, and he debunked the charges against them and tied the charges to the previous Moscow show trial defendants.[80]

The Trotskyist newspaper *Socialist Appeal* published short columns by Joseph Vansler, writing under the pseudonym of John G. Wright, that referred to the purge of the military. He incorrectly speculated that there would be another Army trial but correctly speculated that other Army leaders would be purged.[81] In subsequent columns, he reported that the Army "has been decimated by the purge" and placed the Army purge within the context of other government purges and purges of members of the Young Communists League (Komsomol) who were in the military. He cited a Menshevik publication in Paris for what he called the "crisis in the Soviet armed forces." He pondered the fate of the trial judges and other high-ranking generals. He also mentioned the purge of the Soviet Navy.[82] *Socialist Appeal* published a front-page article by Soviet defector Krivitsky in which he discussed the Soviets' diplomatic negotiations with Germany and asserted that Stalin had framed the defendants with the assistance of the Gestapo.[83]

Soviet Navy Purges

These purges also affected the Workers' and Peasants' Red Navy, known informally as the Red Fleet (Krasny Flot). The Navy had been politically active during the last years of tsarist rule, and sailors fought in the Revolution and in the Civil War. However, in 1921 the sailors at Kronstadt, the home of the Baltic Fleet, staged a revolt against the Bolsheviks that was brutally crushed. As a result, the Navy was purged and downgraded to an auxiliary service of the Red Army. The Soviet government was keenly aware of the political history of the Navy, and the Navy went through another purge in 1930. The Navy regained independent status within the People's Commissariat for Defense at the end of 1937. During the 1920s and 1930s there had been a debate on Soviet naval strategy between having a defensive navy consisting mainly of submarines and smaller craft or a more offensive strategy with submarines, battleships, and other larger ships in order to challenge other nations, specifically Germany. Stalin eventually favored the plan for the offensive strategy and used their advocacy of the defensive naval strategy as one reason to purge "defeatist" naval officers.

There was no announced trial of any naval officers, and information about purges and executions came out in bits and pieces in brief announcements and mentions in speeches throughout 1937 and 1938. Admirals, including commanders-in-chief, fleet commanders, and officers of the Frunze Red Naval Academy, were purged, and the purges reached deeply into the officer corps. Admiral Vladimir Orlov, the best-known Navy commander-in-chief and a Vice Commissar for Defense, was purged.[84] Soon Orlov's successor Admiral M. V. Viktorov was purged.[85] Finally, People's Commissar for Defense Voroshilov gave a speech in which he stated that the purged admirals Orlov and A. K. Sivkov were "fascist bandits, traitors, and spies" and that they had "been wiped off the face of the earth." A sidebar to this article reported that no trial had been announced for Orlov.[86] After this speech, the People's Commissariat of the Navy announced a list of admirals who were "traitors" and "enemies of the people." A sidebar in the *New York Times* reported the executions of Admirals Orlov and Sivkov and that Admiral Viktorov was reported to be in "disfavor."[87] Another brief announcement accused advocates of the defensive naval strategy of having "defeatist theories" and that other high-ranking officers had been stripped of their decorations.[88] Another indication of admirals in disgrace was made when the Soviet government's *Official Gazette* listed seventy-nine government and military officials who had been stripped of their decorations, including a rear admiral and the former political commissar of the Frunze Red Naval Academy.[89] The Trotskyist newspaper *Socialist Appeal* published a brief announcement of the purge of the top admirals.[90]

While much has been written about the Army trial, there was less contemporaneous information published in the United States about the Navy purges. A report from the US military attaché in Riga, Latvia, cited a Russian émigré newspaper in Paris which listed the names of the purged admirals. The official Soviet press labeled them "traitors and people's enemies." This brief report concluded with the following: "The purge in the Red Navy seems to have been as radical as that in the Red Army."[91] During the Second World War, the US government studied conditions in the Soviet Navy. The Eastern European Division of Naval Intelligence issued a report which included the following section on the purges: "It was the most far-reaching purge ever instituted, and when it was over, every high-ranking officer with the exception of Admiral Galler had been 'liquidated.'"[92] Admiral L. M. Galler, an acting commander-in-chief during part of this time, survived the 1930s but was purged after the Second World War.

In 2008 the *Journal of Slavic Military Studies* published a thorough study of the purge of the Pacific Fleet. The author wrote: "The beating of those who were arrested and the falsification of materials from the investigations were the norm for the activities of the NKVD workers." The author concluded that the lack of professionalism among the personnel who replaced the purged officers had a negative effect on the fleet's combat capability.[93]

People's Commissar for Defense Voroshilov responded to foreign opinion that the purges had weakened the military. He maintained that the army had not been weakened, defended the introduction of the political commissars, and asserted that the Army was "fully equipped and prepared to defend the Soviet Union against any attack."[94]

The executions of the Army marshals and generals and Navy admirals may be considered among the most tragic episodes of the purges, especially the case of Marshal Tukhachevsky, and the Army purges have been studied extensively.[95] Tukhachevsky's tactics were eventually implemented during the Second World War. According to a paper from the Institute of Land Warfare of the Association of the United States Army: "Few come close to Tukhachevsky in depth and breadth of applicable concepts from the tactical to strategic levels. . . . He merits a place in the hall of fame of practice and theory of military operations in history."[96]

On the other hand, as with the defendants in the show trials, these men had participated in the establishment of the Bolshevik regime, fought in the war with Poland and in the Civil War, and carried out the Soviet government's repressive programs, including the suppression of peasant rebellions and the forced relocation of local populations. In *Stalin's Hangmen*, a critical study of Soviet leaders during Stalin's rule, British author Donald Rayfield wrote: "Tukhachevsky and his fellow Civil War commanders were up to their necks in blood."[97]

The causes of the purge and its effects on the Soviet Union's military preparedness during the Second World War have been studied and debated by military historians to this day. Stalin biographer Stephen Kotkin concluded: "The combination of Communist ways of thinking and political practice with Stalin's demonic mind and political skills allowed for astonishing bloodletting."[98] Some scholars attributed the heavy Soviet losses in the beginning of the Winter War with Finland and in the disastrous opening days of the German invasion in June 1941 at least in part to the loss of an experienced officer corps and to the subsequent promotions of less-prepared underlings.[99]

The Soviet Anti-Foreigner Campaign (1937–8)

Two of Stalin's main themes were that the Soviet Union was surrounded by capitalist enemies and that the country was facing a growing fascist threat. As a backdrop to the Moscow show trials and to reinforce the charges of espionage, sabotage, and counter-revolutionary plotting, the Soviet government conducted a relentless anti-foreigner campaign. The campaign had four main aspects: anti-foreigner propaganda, the arrests of Soviet citizens who dealt with foreigners, the arrests of foreigners in the Soviet Union, and harassment in day-to-day operations for foreign diplomats.

The Department of State was concerned about Soviet attitudes toward American diplomats as early as 1936 when Acting Secretary of State R. Walton Moore sent a memorandum to Soviet ambassador Troyanovsky to protest efforts to blame US ambassador William C. Bullitt "by throwing on him all responsibility for the failure of establishing closer relations between our Government and the Soviet Government."[100] The Soviet press had published two surprisingly friendly articles about the visit of US Navy ships to Vladivostok in 1936. These articles exasperated the Embassy staff, and Embassy secretary Henderson sent a "don't you believe it" communiqué that stated the following:

> The expressions of friendliness . . . have not been accompanied thus far by a noticeable change in attitude of the Soviet authorities towards this Mission or towards American citizens in general. The anti-foreigner campaign which continues to be waged unceasingly makes no exceptions. . . . At no time since the establishment of this Mission have foreigners, including Americans, been so isolated from Soviet life as they are at the present time.[101]

Henderson concluded: "One is inclined to wonder whether . . . that Government seriously desires genuinely friendly relations between the Soviet Union and any other country."[102]

A steady stream of US Embassy communiqués ensued, complaining about the anti-foreigner campaign. Henderson sent a long communiqué, reporting that the campaign "continues with little relaxation" and may be "one phase of the broader campaign of terror which has been sweeping the country for months." He cataloged the continuous barrage of pamphlets, posters, public speeches, and radio broadcasts. He also reported that Soviet employees of the US Embassy had been arrested or interrogated by the secret police, officials of Soviet agencies that dealt with foreigners had disappeared, and hundreds of foreigners have been arrested, including foreigners who worked for the Comintern.[103]

The American press was also mindful of the attitude of the Soviet government toward foreigners. As far back as 1935, Harold Denny of the *New York Times* reported on foreigners being watched by the secret police, their telephone calls monitored, and their mail opened.[104] The *New York Times* reported on Soviet press warnings about spies and saboteurs luring Soviet citizens into their service and warned them that foreign companies in the Soviet Union were "anti-Soviet bases."[105] In an uncensored article, Denny expressed puzzlement over the hunt for "wreckers, spies and enemies of the people" when the Stalinist regime seemed firmly in power. He theorized that either the government was staging a "frame-up on a gigantic scale" or that the country was seething with discontent and that opposition has "alarmed the Kremlin." He also described the Russian people as "bewildered" by the arrests of so many prominent people and foreigners and he was mainly unbelieving in any plots against the government.[106]

Dealings with foreigners had led to tragic consequences for Soviet citizens, including those who worked in the US Embassy, resulting in a memorandum from Acting Secretary of State R. Walton Moore to Ambassador Troyanovsky in which Moore stated that such arrests show the Soviet Union as not acting as a "civilized" country.[107] Those arrested included not only Soviet employees of the US Embassy but also employees of Soviet government agencies that dealt with foreigners, including the People's Commissariat for Foreign Affairs (the "Foreign Office") and VOKS (the agency for arranging tours for foreign writers and artists) and Intourist.

Henderson sent a communiqué in which he stated their concerns about these arrests: "Practically all Soviet citizens who have had . . . relations with members of foreign diplomatic missions or with foreigners who keep in touch with their diplomatic missions appear to be in constant fear of being arrested on charges of espionage or terrorism." He cited the arrests, exile, or "terrorizing" of Soviet citizens who dealt with foreigners, the arrest or expulsion of foreign citizens who might bring information to the foreign missions and a "closer surveillance" of diplomats and foreigners. He brought up the Embassy staff's concerns to the People's Commissariat for Foreign Affairs and received the rationale that the show trials had "aroused popular indignation" among Soviet citizens and that it was advisable to "reduce the number of foreigners." Not mincing words, Henderson attributed this campaign to "Stalin's tirade against the capitalist encirclement and espionage."[108]

In a tragic side effect to the anti-foreign campaign, American workers who had come to the Soviet Union for either jobs or ideological reasons were also caught up in the purges. This sad chapter is chronicled in *The Forsaken: An American Tragedy in Stalin's Russia* by Tim Tzouliadis.[109]

Henderson again reported in 1938 on the reluctance of Soviet citizens to have contact with foreigners, police interrogations, and arrests of Soviet citizens who were Embassy employees or married to Embassy employees and the disappearances or arrests of Soviet professionals (e.g., doctors, dentists, and lawyers) who served the diplomatic community. He also referred to reports of other embassies as to the number of their foreign nationals who had been arrested. He discussed his attempts to get any information from the People's Commissariat for Foreign Affairs regarding the arrests of Soviet employees of the Embassy. He informed Commissariat officials that such arrests were hindering the operations of the Embassy.[110]

Ambassador Davies met with People's Commissar for Foreign Affairs Maxim Litvinov and "unofficially" discussed the following situations: the government's refusal to allow the Soviet wives of American citizens to go to the United States, the arrests of the Soviet employees of American foreign correspondents, and the eviction of the American-Russian Chamber of Commerce from its offices.[111] The Embassy staff were also informed that Soviet employees of the Embassy were pressured to be NKVD informants, and mysterious wires and a microphone were discovered in the attic above the ambassador's office which they suspected were for surveillance.[112,113]

George F. Kennan, then stationed in Washington, DC, wrote a memorandum that outlined the restrictions placed on foreign embassies and described the deteriorating situation in the Commissariat for Foreign Affairs. He listed complaints about the treatment of diplomats as a result of the anti-foreigner campaign, including the portrayal of diplomats as "accredited spies," the disappearance of Soviets who had contact with foreigners and the arrests of Soviets who worked at the US Embassy. He stated that a "deliberate anti-foreign campaign of unparalleled intensity has been in progress for some time and shows no signs of abating." He described the "high mortality rate" in the Commissariat as affecting the Embassy's dealings with People's Commissar Litvinov, including Litvinov's "reluctance to discuss topics." He reported that Soviet employees of the Embassy had been arrested. Kennan also wrote the following about Soviet efforts to paint all diplomats as spies: "It is a rare Soviet propaganda trial which does not contain some reference to contacts of the accused with the representatives in Russia of foreign powers." He also listed the Soviet government officials who dealt with foreigners who had been "disgraced and removed."[114]

The purge of Soviet citizens who had contact with foreigners reached the highest level of the Soviet government with the December 1937 trial of eight prominent officials of the People's Commissariat for Foreign Affairs (Narkomindel) which American diplomats called the "Foreign Office." The condemned men in this trial included People's Assistant Commissar Leo Karakhan, the Soviet Union's most famous expert on the Far East. Embassy secretary Henderson wrote that they had been accused of "betraying their country, terrorist activities and systematic espionage on behalf of a certain foreign power," as well as selling intelligence to fascists and a "certain foreign power."[115] Henderson sent two communiqués on this trial. In the first, he surmised that the morale of the Commissariat would take a long time to be restored.[116] In the second communiqué, he discussed the purge within the context of deteriorating Soviet foreign relations and reported that the purge "has resulted in the replacement of many of the most skilled Soviet diplomatists by persons who, as far as can be ascertained, have had little or no experience in international affairs."[117]

The American press reported on the purges and executions "for high treason" in the Commissariat, especially the execution of the high-profile Karakhan.[118] The Soviet government also recalled its ambassadors from their posts, and they were never heard from again.[119] A *New York Times* editorial termed these recalls the "grim summons."[120]

Both *Time* and *Newsweek* reported on the recalls and disappearances within the Soviet diplomatic corps. *Time* detailed the recall of the Soviets' Finnish ambassador and his family and the very public resignation of Alexandre Barmine, the Soviet *chargé d'affaires* in Athens, who melodramatically stated that he had "signed my death warrant and exposed myself to the bullets of professional killers."[121] Barmine defected to the United States, and in a series of articles in the *New York Times*, he lambasted Stalin, condemned the trials as "frauds," and called the Stalinist regime a "reactionary dictatorship," much to the chagrin of Ambassador Troyanovsky.[122] He joined Walter Krivitsky in being the most vocal Soviet defectors in the United States during this time, and, contrary to his prediction of a violent death, he lived in the United States until his death in 1987. *Newsweek* concluded that the diplomatic corps was now "entirely under Stalin's thumb."[123] In a thoughtfully-written article *New Republic* posed two theories about this purge—the Russian leadership had "succumbed to fear" or there was "bitter opposition" to the government and plots against it.[124]

The Trotskyist *Socialist Appeal* had a few articles on the purge of the Commissariat and the disappearance of the recalled diplomats. John G. Wright's "International Notes" column listed several recalled diplomats in the "grip of purge" and reported that Nikolai Krestinsky, a future trial defendant, had "confessed."[125] *Socialist Appeal* called Karakhan's execution an "assassination."[126] Soviet exile Victor Serge speculated on the recall of Soviet Consul-General to Spain Vladimir Antonov-Ovseyenko, a veteran Bolshevik who led the assault on the Winter Palace in 1917, correctly predicting that he would be executed.[127]

The purge of the Foreign Office culminated with the sudden resignation of People's Commissar Maxim Litvinov in May 1939. His resignation was discussed in conjecture-filled communiqués from Embassy secretary Alexander C. Kirk and former Ambassador Davies, then the ambassador to Belgium, who wrote that the sudden resignation "created a sensation in the diplomatic corps." Both men speculated on Litvinov's resignation in terms of future changes in Soviet foreign policy.[128,129] According to Stephen Kotkin, Litvinov had tried to "blunt the murderous rampage but he, too feared for his life."[130] His "removal" had been predicted in *Socialist Appeal* in February 1938 as part of a "change of Soviet foreign policy."[131] He was replaced by Stalin's crony Vyacheslav Molotov. Embassy secretary Stuart Grummon estimated that under Molotov, 90 percent of the Commissariat's minor officials had been replaced. Grummon echoed Henderson's opinion of the lack of qualifications of their replacements by writing that they "have no experience with matters pertaining to foreign affairs, no knowledge of foreign languages nor any contacts in general with foreigners or foreign countries."[132]

Litvinov's resignation did not go unnoticed in the American press. Harold Denny of the *New York Times* reported the official explanation of "ill health."[133] Litvinov's resignation elicited a scathing article in *Social Justice*, the publication of Father Charles E. Coughlin, the right-wing, rabblerousing Catholic priest who promoted anti-Semitism in print and on the radio. This article portrayed Litvinov as a Jewish radical, criminal, and spy.[134] *Socialist Appeal* framed his resignation as a "foregone conclusion" and as an attempt by Stalin to "come to an understanding" with Hitler by removing the Jewish Litvinov.[135] A 1996 study of Litvinov included an account by Litvinov's daughter in which she stated that upon being removed from office, he was subjected to a humiliating harangue from Molotov.[136] However, Litvinov survived the purges.

One study of the purge of the Commissariat by old Russia hand Louis Fischer called it "negligible" compared to the decimating purges in other government agencies and within the Communist Party.[137] In contrast, scholar Terry J. Uldricks concluded that the purge caused the "near total destruction of that talented and urbane corps of diplomats."[138] Stephen Kotkin wrote that many of the purged officials and diplomats were Jewish, and their removal altered the "image of the regime" and made way for the "promotion of the young, the humble, and the Slavic."[139] British historian Alastair Kocho-Williams wrote that the Commissariat was rendered effectively "impotent" by the purges.[140]

Continuing their campaign against Soviets who dealt with foreigners, the People's Commissariat for Foreign Trade was also purged, and former People's Commissar Arkady P. Rosengoltz would be a defendant in the third Moscow show trial.

Dealing with the Soviets was especially distressing when the Embassy staff attempted to assist American citizens who had difficulties with the Soviet government. In his memoir, Embassy secretary Henderson wrote that from the very beginning of diplomatic relations, the Embassy staff was "besieged by U. S. citizens in distress who were requesting assistance."[141] The establishment of diplomatic relations included a protocol that stipulated that an American citizen under arrest in the Soviet Union could be interviewed by "consular representatives" within three days of the notification of arrest in a major city and within seven days if arrested elsewhere.[142] The Soviets did not live up to the protocol, and the Embassy staff was continually frustrated by delays in meeting with detainees.[143] This concern over arrested American citizens reached Secretary of State Cordell Hull who instructed Embassy secretary Henderson to try to get the release of an American who had been granted Soviet citizenship.[144]

In 1937 a husband and wife entered the Soviet Union with a false US passport for the husband, and they were arrested. This became a minor *cause célébre* known as the *Robinson-Rubens* case, made the front page of the *New York Times* and reached the highest levels of the Department of State.[145] The husband was found not to be an American citizen and disappeared. His American-born wife was tried and pleaded guilty to entering the Soviet Union under false pretenses. She was sentenced to time served and allowed to remain in the Soviet Union for six months when the usual punishment for illegal entry included a fine and deportation.[146]

This case reinforced the Soviet government's contention that the country was beset by foreign spies. In an unintended irony, it had a similar effect in the United States by causing a minor spy scare. Finding out how the couple got their passports from the New York County Clerk's office led to a federal investigation and to the arrests, trial, and convictions of three men for conspiring to forge US passports.[147] The anticommunist monthly *American Mercury* published allegations of a "passport mill" in the United States run by Soviet spies.[148] Soviet defector Walter Krivitsky claimed that the husband was a Soviet spy sent to the United States to establish a passport forgery ring.[149]

American Trotskyists took a special interest in this case with weekly articles in *Socialist Appeal* that asserted that the *Robinson-Rubens* case was another "frame-up" as the Soviets claimed that Trotsky and American Trotskyists were somehow involved. *Socialist Appeal* considered this claim to be an attempt to discredit Trotsky, his American supporters, and the Dewey Commission.[150]

In addition to the arrests of Soviet employees of the embassy, the Soviet government inflicted a host of petty annoyances upon US diplomats, including the seeming arbitrariness of the Soviets' handling of visa requests for American tourists, either dishonoring them for no reason or not issuing them at all.[151] Embassy secretary Henderson complained about the difficulties that American citizens had in dealing with Soviet customs which he contended was "closely tied up with an anti-foreigner movement which undoubtedly accounts for the present attitude of the Soviet customs authorities."[152]

Foreign Relations of the United States devoted a lengthy section to these issues.[153] This section included memoranda of conversations between Secretary of State Hull and Soviet ambassador Troyanovsky about the "irritating experiences" in dealing with the Soviet government. Among other complaints listed were the customs inspections and fees for the personal effects of Embassy personnel. As these inspections and fees affected the Embassy staff directly, they sent lengthy communiqués complaining about Soviet actions. Troyanovsky either claimed ignorance, was dismissive of complaints, or denied specific difficulties.[154]

George F. Kennan and Edward Page, Jr., wrote a memorandum in response to Troyanovsky's denials. The memorandum included this condemnation of the anti-foreigner campaign which summed up the frustrations in dealing with the Soviet government:

> The population has been taught that all foreigners are to be regarded as being engaged in espionage under the immediate direction of their own diplomatic mission. Every effort had been made by the Soviet regime to isolate foreign diplomatic officials. . . . People who have had personal dealing with foreigners have been persecuted. . . . Employees of the Embassy Chancery as well as a number of servants, chauffeurs, and gardeners employed by members of the Embassy staff have been arrested. Many others have suffered inconvenience through their connections with the Embassy. Practically every Soviet official who has ever had any personal connection with any member of the Embassy has disappeared from the scene in circumstances which indicated exile, imprisonment, or disgrace, if not execution.[155]

Conclusion

The Army and Navy purges and the anti-foreigner campaign were further proof that 1937 was the "bloody year" as the purges reached almost insane proportions. The United States wondered about the effect of the military purges on the effectiveness of the Soviet military during the rising military threat of Nazi Germany. In addition to the anti-foreigner campaign reinforcing Stalin's propaganda that the Soviets were beset by enemies, US Embassy personnel felt its impact as Embassy operations were hampered by the arrests of Soviet employees, the growing ineffectiveness of the People's Commissariat for Foreign Affairs, the arrests of Soviet-born Embassy personnel, and the petty annoyances inflicted on the Embassy staff.

Plate 7.1 Nikolai Bukharin. "N. Bucharin." Wikimedia Commons. 1900, http://commons.wikimedia.org (accessed July 6, 2022).

Plate 7.2 Charles Bohlen, American diplomat who attended the third Moscow show trial. "Charles Bohlen at Desk." Harry S. Truman Library & Museum accession no. 87-21-3. 1953? http://trumanlibrary.gov (accessed July 6, 2022).

The Third Moscow Show Trial

The Bloc of Rightists and Trotskyites (1938) and The Moscow Trials: A Statement by American Progressives (1938)*

Introduction

The year 1937 was also the twentieth anniversary of the Russian Revolution, and American journalists took the occasion to analyze conditions in the Soviet Union. Soon after the Army trial, Walter Duranty of the *New York Times* wrote an article that examined Western assumptions about the show trials, based on the theories that dictatorships refuse to "admit the opposition" and that Trotskyism was a magnet for malcontents. He also cited the Russians as being prone to "excitement and exaggeration" and to blaming enemies for the failures of the Five Year Plans. In an uncensored report Harold Denny of the *New York Times* again contrasted the new constitution with the wave of secret trials and the overwhelming power of the "political police."[1] A *New York Times* editorial questioned conditions in the Soviet Union since the Revolution.[2]

The mainstream American press published articles on the escalating purges. One of the longest articles was by former Moscow correspondent William Henry Chamberlin. Writing in the anticommunist *American Mercury*, Chamberlin was critical of Stalin, called him a "degenerate," compared him to Al Capone, and used the Trotskyist tactic of comparing the purges to the aftermath of the French Revolution when the revolutionaries turned on each other. He called farm collectivization the "new serfdom." Chamberlin incorrectly predicted that Stalin's "cruel and capricious despotism" would lead to his downfall.[3] In a 1938 article, Chamberlin called Stalin "Russia's worst czar" and considered the Soviet regime to be the bloodiest since the time of Ivan the Terrible.[4]

---

* Union of Soviet Socialist Republic, People's Commissariat of Justice, *Report of the Proceedings in the Case of the Anti-Soviet Trotskyite Bloc of Rights and Trotskyites: Heard before the Military Collegium of the Supreme Court of the U.S.S.R.*(Moscow: The Commissariat, 1938).

Other mainstream American press outlets chronicled the widespread purges throughout the fall of 1937, often laying them at Stalin's doorstep, citing Chamberlin's article.[5] *Literary Digest* published a brief overview of the purges, listing the heads of the various Soviet republics who had been purged, while portraying Stalinism as "increasingly . . . moderate," in contrast to the radical Bolshevism of Trotsky.[6] In November 1938 the liberal weekly *The Nation* published an article by editor Maxwell S. Stewart which summarized industrial and agricultural conditions, discussed the still low standards of living and inequalities in income, and condemned the "ruthlessness" of the purges. He blamed the purges on festering "popular discontent" and that the alleged crimes grew from "anti-bureaucratic feeling." At the same time, Stewart acknowledged the "ruthless treatment of thousands" but praised the government's campaign to "raise the cultural level." He urged the Soviet government to address the needs of ordinary citizens and to listen to workers' ideas. He concluded that the Soviet Union "will greatly influence the entire world."[7] The same issue included an editorial that lamented the Soviet government's censorship and the "lack of open political discussion."[8]

In January 1938, perhaps mindful of negative international reporting, the Communist Party's Central Committee passed a resolution on the excessive purges of the Party's rank and file. As reported by Embassy secretary Loy W. Henderson, this resolution criticized Party functionaries for their "mass exclusions" and distortions of Party directives, blaming either "masked enemies" or "Communist careerists" within the Party. Henderson went on to report that this was similar to Stalin's placing the blame for the excesses of agricultural collectivization in the first Five Year Plan on local overzealousness, that this was a signal to ease up on Party members and absolving the NKVD and Stalin of any blame. Henderson speculated that some of the local Party functionaries would themselves be purged, but he hedged his bets as to whether the purges were ending. He wrote: "It is as yet too early to state whether this resolution which concerns itself only with activities within the Party signifies the beginning of the end of the campaign of dismissals, arrests and executions which during the past year has affected every phase of Soviet life."[9] Harold Denny also reported on this resolution, citing incidents of the unfair treatment of purge victims.[10]

The Conduct of the Trial

The Party resolution on the excesses of the purges did not save the Old Bolsheviks in the last and largest Moscow show trial which was held from March

2 through March 13, 1938. This trial was also known as the "Trial of the Twenty-One" and the "Treason Trial." The defendants were charged with the following crimes under Article 58 of the Criminal Code of the Russian SFSR: "Treason to the country, espionage, committing acts of diversion, terrorism, wrecking, undermining the military power of the U.S.S.R. and provoking a military attack of foreign states upon the U.S.S.R."[11]

The leading defendant and the "big fish" among the Old Bolsheviks was Nikolai Ivanovich Bukharin, the Party's leading theorist and the former editor of both *Izvestia* and *Pravda*. He had spent time in exile in New York City before the Revolution. He was well known and had been published in the West as late as 1936. During his year-long incarceration, he sent several pleading letters to Stalin.[12] He also sent a plea for mercy to the Presidium of the Supreme Soviet.[13] According to Stalin biographer Stephen Kotkin, Stalin went so far as to edit Bukharin's final statement in the trial transcript.[14] As a result of his prominence, his downfall was chronicled in the American press.[15,16] He has been a continuing object of scholarly study.[17]

Other prominent defendants were Alexei Ivanovich Rykov [also transliterated as Alexis Ryoff or Rykof], Khristian Grigorievich Rakovsky, Nikolai Krestinsky, and Genrikh Grigorievich Yagoda. Rykov had replaced Vladimir Lenin as Chairman of the Council of Commissars and was also known in the West. The American press also reported his downfall.[18] Upon being sentenced to death, he sent a plea for mercy to the Presidium.[19]

The Bulgarian-born Rakovsky had been a well-known diplomat and had been published in the West, and his exile to Siberia in 1930 had been reported in the American press.[20] In 1936, he had written a spirited condemnation of Trotsky and the defendants in the first trial in *Pravda*. This was translated and published in the *Daily Worker*. He called Stalin the "beloved leader and teacher of the toiling masses" and condemned the defendants as "counter-revolutionaries, criminals, and murderers."[21] Krestinsky had been the Soviet ambassador to Germany and a Vice Commissar of the People's Commissariat for Foreign Affairs. Yagoda had been head of the NKVD before being demoted to People's Commissar for Ways of Communication. Due to his fearsome reputation, his downfall in 1936 and his obviously disintegrating physical appearance during the trial were chronicled in the American press.[22] Unlike other Old Bolsheviks, Yagoda's reputation was never restored during destalinization. Other defendants known in the West were these former People's Commissars: Arkady Pavlovich Rosengoltz (Foreign Trade), Mikhail Alexandrovich Chernov (Agriculture), and Grigori Fedorovich Grinko (Finance). Grinko had been denounced by the Ukrainian-born Vlas

Chubar, his successor as Commissar.[23] Chubar was purged and executed in 1939. Other defendants included these former officials in the Soviet Union and in Uzbekistan: Sergei Alexeyevich Bessanov, Pavel Petrovich Bulanov, Akmal Ikramov, Vladimir Ivanovich Ivanov, Faizulla Khodjayev, Venyamin Adamovich Maximov-Dikovsky, Vasily Fomich Sharangovich, Isaac Abramovich Zelensky, and Prokopy Timofeyevich Zubarev.

This trial had an additional component not found in the previous show trials—the charge of medical murder. Charges were made against three prominent doctors—Ignaty Nikolayevich Kazakov, Lev Grigorievich Levin, and Dmitri Dmitrievich Pletnev. Allegedly under threats from Yagoda, they were charged with the poisoning of Maxim Gorky, the Soviet Union's most prominent writer and president of the Union of Soviet Writers, and two prominent Soviet officials. Gorky had died in 1936; Dr. Levin had been his physician. Levin had also been a consultant to the Kremlin Medical Sanitary Administration. Dr. Pletnev was the country's leading cardiologist. This especially sad aspect of the trial forced these distinguished physicians to confess to poisoning plots at the behest of their co-defendant Yagoda. An "expert commission" of five doctors was formed by the prosecution in order to provide evidence against them. While the physicians had defense lawyers, all were found guilty. Two were shot, and one was sentenced to prison where he died. Gorky's personal secretary Pyotr P. Kryuchkov was also charged in the medical murder plots.

The judges were V. V. Ulrich, I. O. Matulevich, and B. I. Yevlev. Perhaps in anticipation of this trial, *Izvestia* published a laudatory profile of State Prosecutor Andrey Vyshinsky which exalted his revolutionary past, his career in jurisprudence, and his performance in the two previous show trials (directing "the implacable searchlight of justice"). This propaganda piece was reprinted in the monthly *Living Age* for American consumption.[24]

The trial followed the same procedures as the preceding trials which included the naming of the defense counsel for the physicians, asking the other defendants if they had refused counsel and the reading of the lengthy indictment. There was one variation from the usual scenario of guilty pleas from the defendants when Krestinsky did not plead guilty to the charges. State Prosecutor Vyshinsky hastily called other defendants as witnesses to verify Krestinsky's guilt.[25] An eyewitness account in *Time* entered the realm of the slightly macabre when the reporter surmised that Krestinsky was speaking to "The Box," a darkened space above the judges' bench where the reporter assumed that Stalin was watching and that Krestinsky was hoping that Stalin would intervene. The reporter also called Chief Judge Ulrich the "hanging judge."[26] The next day Krestinsky ("this one-time brilliant Soviet diplomat") recanted his not-guilty plea and pleaded guilty to all charges. According to later research, Krestinsky was tortured into changing his plea and confessing, an assertion that had been made in the German press during the trial.[27,28]

After the state prosecutor had examined the defendants, they heard the report of the expert commission of physicians to confirm the charges of poisoning Gorky and the other alleged victims. Vyshinsky gave a lengthy summation that was full of contempt for the defendants, referring to them as "dogs" and referring to the alleged conspiracy as an "accursed reptile," stating: "The graves of the odious traitors will be overgrown with weeds and thistle, covered with the eternal contempt of honest Soviet citizens, of the entire Soviet people."[29] As in the previous trials, the defendants were allowed to make final pleas for clemency. All were found guilty and were either shot or given prison sentences from which none survived.

Official US Reactions

As with the previous show trials, American diplomats attended this trial. With the exception of the first day, Ambassador Davies was accompanied by Embassy secretary Charles "Chip" Bohlen who served as Davies's translator. On the opening day of the trial, Ambassador Davies sent a communiqué that was a matter-of-fact description of the charges and proceedings and had a "wait and see" attitude as to how the trial would progress. Davies stated that he had met four of the defendants and that in 1937 he had lunch at the dacha of People's Commissar for Foreign Trade Rosengoltz. In a case of irony, State Prosecutor Vyshinsky had also attended this lunch.[30] Davies reported that three of the defendants (Krestinsky, Rosengoltz, and Dr. Pletnev) "seemed haggard, drawn, and under great nervous tension."[31] While elements of the trial gave the "impression of propaganda," Davies concluded that, if the charges were true, a "terrible sordid picture of human nature at its worst is being unfolded."[32] This communiqué was in sharp contrast to the skeptical communiqués that the Embassy secretaries had sent about the previous trials.

Ambassador Davies sent another communiqué after the verdicts had been rendered. Despite stated reservations about the trial procedures and about the guilt of the physicians, he accepted the guilty verdicts concerning the alleged terrorist plots. He ended the communiqué with this condemnation of the Soviet judicial system: "Aside from the natural horror instilled by this exhibition of intense drama and human tragedy, the trial affords a shocking realization that there does exist still a modern system of jurisprudence which affords so little protection to the accused and to the rights of the individual."[33]

Ambassador Davies was ending his appointment as ambassador, and in April 1938 he submitted what he termed a "brief résumé," a lengthy report to the Secretary of State on Soviet foreign relations and internal conditions. This report included sections entitled "Security," "The Purge," and "The Treason Trial." Concerning the purges, it was his opinion that the purges were subsiding but that "arrests are still going forward all over the country, but perhaps not with the violence of a few months ago." He gave a mixed review to the trial, stating that there was opposition caused by the "constantly growing oppression of the Stalin regime" but that the defendants "actually did conspire to act and overthrow the Stalin Government."[34] This report included a section on "The Terror" that is discussed in Chapter 9.

In his 1941 memoir *Mission to Moscow*, Davies included several entries on this trial. Before the trial, he was incredulous about several prominent purge victims being guilty of treason.[35] He noted in his diary that the defendants that he knew "sat not more than ten feet from me in the prisoner's box. I hope they saw in my eyes the sorrow which I felt in seeing them again under these conditions." One defendant, the heart specialist Dr. Pletnev, had treated Davies during the previous year.[36] In a March 8, 1938, diary entry Davies related the testimony of Dr. Levin as to being pressured by Yagoda into poisoning Maxim Gorky, Gorky's son, and others. Davies described this confession as "gruesome and bizarre." He also speculated that the poisoning was due to a love triangle between Yagoda, the wife of Gorky's son, and Gorky's son.[37] In a letter to his daughter, Davies wrote that he believed the testimony concerning a planned *coup d'état* involving Marshal Tukhachevsky, Germany, and Japan, thus justifying the executions of the generals, the purges, and the hostility toward foreigners.[38] In a brief entry on March 12, 1938, he characterized the "last words" (i.e., final pleas) of the defendants as "harrowing in their interest and tragedy."[39]

Davies sent a communiqué to the Secretary of State on March 17, 1938, stating that the defendants had all been found guilty and that the executions had been carried out at 5 a.m. While he again stated reservations about the Soviet judicial system, he believed that they were guilty of treason.[40] Davies adhered to this position when he added a section to his diary in 1941 after the German invasion of the Soviet Union. He concluded that the invasion was the result of a "fifth column" of traitors who had conspired with Germany and Japan. He cited the confessions of the defendants as proof of their participation in plots to overthrow the government and as proof of the other charges against them. In his words: "The purge had cleansed the country and rid it of treason."[41]

Embassy secretary Chip Bohlen was no fan of Davies, and, perhaps mindful of the thoughtful communiqués sent by his colleagues during the previous trials, he wrote the following in his memoir: "Ambassador Davies was not noted for any acute understanding of the Soviet system, and he had an unfortunate tendency to take what was presented at the trial as the honest and gospel truth. *I still blush when I think of some of the telegrams he sent to the State Department.*"[42] Bohlen devoted an entire chapter of his memoir to the trial, and he had little good to say about the proceedings. He characterized State Prosecutor Vyshinsky as "one of the most unsavory products of Bolshevism . . . mercilessly pursuing, mocking, and prodding the defendants." He also wrote that Vyshinsky had a "ferretlike quality" and that Chief Judge Ulrich looked like a "sadistic pig." Bohlen concentrated on Bukharin and Yagoda. While he praised the defendants' composure, Bohlen was dismissive of the testimonies of the defendants and of the witnesses. After the death sentences had been announced, Bohlen wrote that he "felt that the top of my head was coming off. I could not go to sleep easily for almost a month after that." He also wrote that the trial was a "subject of endless discussion in the Embassy" and claimed that, with the exception of military attaché Lt. Col. Philip Faymonville, they "were dubious about the trials." Bohlen claimed that he knew that the trial was a "phony" but that he could not prove it. In later years Bohlen came to the conclusion that Stalin had several purposes for the trial, including that he "purged the true believers . . . in order to avoid the possibility of a revolt." Bohlen echoed Trotsky's claim that the trials were frame-ups.[43]

Reactions of American Journalists

Perhaps because of the trial coming so soon after the twentieth anniversary of the Revolution, the number of defendants, the prominence of Bukharin and the added charges of medical murder, this trial was extensively covered in the American press. Walter Duranty of the *New York Times* called it the "greatest and most startling of the Soviet treason trials" and that it marked the disappearance of the last of the Old Bolsheviks.[44] Duranty reported on the vilification of the defendants in the state-run media. He surmised that this trial was for domestic consumption to show the defeat of "internal enemies" because the Soviets were certain that a war was coming.[45] Seemingly fed up with the fantastic charges in all of the trials, a March editorial in the *New York Times* reeked of disbelief. The editorialist considered this trial to be as ridiculous as executing our founding fathers for conspiring "to hand over the United States to George III."[46] The *New York Times* also published the text of the indictment.[47] Another *New York Times* editorial compared the trials to the aftermath of the French Revolution and compared Stalin's actions to Trotsky as Trotsky had taken their families hostage in order to pressure tsarist officers to join the Red Army during the Civil War.[48]

Harold Denny did most of the *New York Times*'s reporting on the trial. His first article described the alleged military plot to take over the Kremlin and the NKVD headquarters as "weird" as a plot as in the "days of Ivan the Terrible and Boris Godunoff." Denny also reported that Krestinsky implicated foreign correspondents, including an unnamed American correspondent. Upon hearing this, American correspondents went to a "high Soviet official" to protest. The official brushed them off.[49]

The second article was an overview of the court setting and proceedings, highlighting the demeanor of the defendants and their self-condemning confessions. He described Vyshinsky's manner toward the defendants as alternating between "gentle" and "savage" and remarked upon Yagoda's disintegrating appearance.[50] His third article was an extensive recounting of the witnesses' testimonies in which he called Bukharin a "spirited witness," called Yagoda "stoop-shouldered, a wreck of a man" and reported that Rakovsky implicated two British nationals as being his contacts for espionage, as did Zelensky.[51] In a sidebar, the two British nationals denied any such espionage activities.[52] Reporting on the fifth day of the trial, Denny called Krestinsky's testimony about the alleged military plot to stage a *coup d'état* as "startling" and reported on the vicious Russian press attacks on the defendants, especially Bukharin.[53] Bukharin's testimony was the highlight of the trial and was extensively quoted. On the last day of his testimony, Denny reported that while Bukharin knew that he was doomed, he fought for his reputation and his place in history.[54]

Denny reported on the testimony of the doctors accused of poisoning Gorky and two Soviet officials ("this particular complicated drama") in which they claimed that they were forced to do so by the coercion of Yagoda who had an alleged "secret poison laboratory."[55,56] Denny also reported on the attorneys' summations and the defendants' final pleas for clemency. He characterized Vyshinsky's lengthy summation as his "most vigorous and frequent in vituperation" of any of the trials and that this summation was met by thunderous applause while the defendants were "sitting dejectedly and even disinterestedly."[57] Denny also reported on the guilty verdicts, the death sentences, and the prison sentences.[58]

Rykov reportedly wept upon hearing his death sentence while Bukharin stared at the floor.[59] In a wrap-up article, Denny believed in the charges of conspiracy and gave three reasons for the trial—the Old Bolsheviks held strong convictions that were stifled because of the lack of any legal opposition, they wanted to regain their power and they disapproved of "conditions that had risen under Stalin's rule." He was also skeptical of the confessions and the testimonies of the witnesses.[60] Predictably, Soviet ambassador Alexander Troyanovsky defended the trial as a blow against fascism and called American liberals' pleas for clemency for the defendants as either an "honest misunderstanding" or as "bitter hostility."[61]

The anti-foreigner campaign also affected this trial when a Soviet woman who had worked for Denny for several years as a translator was suddenly arrested in the middle of the proceedings.[62] In a meeting with People's Commissar for Foreign Affairs Maxim Litvinov, Ambassador Davies brought up the arrests of Soviets working for Americans. Davies stated that these arrests caused inconvenience and cast aspersions on their American employers. Litvinov brushed their concerns aside.[63] This trial also elicited a long letter to the editor of the *New York Times* from the exiled Alexander Kerensky, the head of the short-lived provisional government that was overthrown by the Bolsheviks in 1917. Kerensky believed in the innocence of Bukharin and Rykov and believed that they had been doomed for speaking against Stalin.[64]

Time and *Newsweek* continued their skeptical reporting with this trial. *Time* compared this trial's charges to the US government accusing members of President Roosevelt's cabinet and other prominent Americans of such heinous crimes. The reporter quoted from Moscow correspondent Joseph Barnes who stated that the indictment "read like a Biblical denunciation of Lucifer."[65] *Time* reported the guilty verdicts and derided the defendants who were accused of trying to kill Stalin who then constituted a "cheering section for Stalin" in their praise of him during their final statements. The reporter also detailed the poison accusations.[66]

Newsweek called the Old Bolsheviks the "special objects of Stalin's wrath."[67] A second *Newsweek* article summarized the defendants' confessions and called the trial part of a pattern set by the previous trials but with "frightful embellishments."[68] *Newsweek* called Yagoda a "miserable figure crouching in the last row of prisoners." The reporter termed Yagoda's testimony on the poisoning plots to be a "mixture of Oriental poison orgy and detective-fiction."[69] *Saturday Evening Post* published an article entitled "Why Did They Confess?" by Soviet defector Walter Krivitsky. He summarized events going back to the Kirov assassination and termed the trials to be a "political device" that had nothing to do with justice. He called the defendants' confessions their "last desperate attempt" to be of service to the Party. Krivitsky based the confessions on four factors—physical and mental torture, blackmail, confessions from prison informants, and the defendants' "bargaining" to spare their families and associates.[70]

The liberal media published several articles on this trial. *New Republic*'s first article called the list of defendants "breath-taking," had a world-weary tone with predictions of confessions and guilty pleas and acknowledged that American commentary on the trials fell along ideological lines. The reporter concluded that the Soviet Union was not weakened militarily.[71] A second article took a more critical tone. The reporter conceded that the defendants had opposed Stalin's policies but maintained that they were not guilty of the charges. The reporter asserted that the purges and the trials had weakened any alliances with Western democracies, weakened other leftist movements, and lessened the Soviet Union's prestige. The reporter editorialized that the trial also highlighted the lack of protection for the accused with the flaws in the Soviet judicial system. This article elicited several letters to the editor.[72] An editorial by *New Republic* editor Bruce Bliven, in the form of a long, open letter to Stalin, was an example of some liberal thinking. Bliven claimed that these trials had "unhappy repercussions in many parts of the world," strengthened the aggressive stance of the fascist powers, and caused the belief that the "Soviet Russia had turned to a bloody-handed dictatorship." Bliven gave Stalin four suggestions concerning any future purge trials—follow Western procedures in treason trials, publish all documentary evidence, abolish the death penalty, and offer amnesty that included allowing an open opposition.[73] In 1984 *New Republic* reviewed Bliven's letter and opined that he "scrounged for any scrap of logic that might excuse his hero" [Stalin], and he admitted that the editors "were unforgivably slow to realize what was happening."[74] Another article in *New Republic* by a "Moscow Observer" believed in the conspiracy theory and divided the defendants into two groups—defendants pressured into participating and genuinely confessing and the unrepentant leading defendants who confessed to save their families and in the hope of "carrying on the fight."[75]

Malcolm Cowley wrote a review of the trial transcript that, except for the lack of Communist rhetoric and name-calling, read as if it had been dictated by the Comintern. He accepted the allegations of a conspiracy, wrote that Yagoda "snapped and whined like a cornered jackal" and called the crimes "mean and repulsive." He claimed that this trial reinforced the charges in the Army trial.[76] Cowley wrote a subsequent article with his conclusions on the meaning of this trial. He believed that the alleged conspiracy came from the threat of

Japan occupying Manchuria, from a bad wheat harvest and from the pride of the defendants. He also wrote that communism had the status of a religion in the Soviet Union.[77] Decades later, Cowley regretted his pro-Soviet stance which he claimed was due to his efforts to protect the Popular Front against Nazi Germany.[78]

The Nation published two columns by Oswald Garrison Villard, who once had been considered friendly to the Soviets. He claimed that this brand of Soviet justice undermined the Russian Revolution and called the trials "appalling." He claimed that they were proof of "madness" and likened them to the Salem witchcraft trials. He also signed the telegram sent by the American Committee to Ambassador Alexander Troyanovsky, asking for a delay of the trial so that an international commission could attend and report.[79] His second column was a satirical set of "telegrams" from the future to show the absurdity of the trial charges. He dated these "telegrams" in 1940 and 1941, reporting on "trials" in which Vyacheslav Molotov, Soviet ambassador Troyanovsky, Stalin's mother, and Stalin himself pleaded guilty.[80]

The German journalist Paul Scheffer, a former Moscow correspondent who had been expelled from the Soviet Union, wrote a thoughtful article in *Foreign Affairs*. He noted that the history of the Revolution could be rewritten with the demise of almost all of the Old Bolsheviks who had been close to Lenin. Scheffer summarized the various opposition movements within the Party and gave revenge, jealousy, and ambition as the reasons for Stalin's actions which Scheffer claimed were part of a "premeditated scheme." He also surmised that Stalin wanted "complete unity" within the Party.[81] The *American Bar Association Journal* published a thoughtful, dispassionate article by Harvey T. Mann that was based on the trial transcript. As with other foreign observers at the trial, he criticized Soviet justice as "obviously open to the gravest abuses." Mann noted that no documentary evidence was produced, concluded that the court was not independent, questioned the verdicts, and disbelieved the charges of medical murder.[82]

Pacific Affairs, the left-leaning journal of the Institute of Pacific Relations, published several letters on this trial, starting with a letter in support of the trials by economist Mary Van Kleeck, one of the signers of 1937 "Open Letter."[83] Her letter started a minor literary feud when it elicited a negative response from William Henry Chamberlin, a former Moscow correspondent, and then a rebuttal to Chamberlin by *Pacific Affairs*' controversial, communist editor Owen Lattimore.[84,85] In the same issue, *Pacific Affairs* published a review of the trial transcript by John N. Hazard, a leading scholar on Soviet law. Hazard came to several conclusions, including that the defendants were speaking to the country as a whole; he discounted the theory that the defendants had been tortured and considered their confessions and final pleas as making the final sacrifice for the revolutionary cause.[86]

Walter Duranty and Moscow correspondent Louis Fischer discussed the trial in separate books in 1941. In a chapter entitled "The Bukharin-Yagoda Trial," Duranty wrote that foreign public opinion "received the Trials with skepticism and disgust" and hurt the Soviet Union's "prestige and reputation." He believed that the trials heightened the Soviet public's suspicion and showed signs that a "virus of frenzy was working in the nation's blood." He found that parts of the testimony were "strange and horrible" but still believed in a conspiracy with Trotsky at the center.[87] Fischer published his autobiography *Men and Politics* in the same year. While he once had been considered to be a Kremlin mouthpiece by the Embassy secretaries, he studied the trials and claimed that the defendants had been coerced into confessing, calling them the victims of "slow-motion destruction." He wrote that the purge and the trials led the Soviet people to live lives of lies, "produced a crisis of faith" and that the Communist Party was becoming a "rubber stamp."[88]

Reactions of American Radicals

Following a detailed directive from the Comintern, American Communists relentlessly covered this trial, again relying heavily on *Pravda* for content.[89] *Daily Worker* warmed up its coverage of the proceedings with the announcement of the trial in a lead-off article, an editorial on the "monstrous plot" and a translation of a *Pravda* column that recited the defendants' alleged crimes going back to 1921.[90,91] The defendants' guilty pleas were front-page news.[92] *Daily Worker* also published the text of the indictment.[93] Krestinsky's recantation and subsequent admission of guilt were also front-page news.[94] The trial continued to occupy the front page as the defendants' testimonies linked them and Trotsky to the Nazis and to a plot to kill the leaders of the Revolution in 1918.[95,96]

Daily Worker instituted a running column called "Word-for-Word Testimony at Trial of Bukharin-Trotskyist Traitors" with extensive quotations from the defendants' testimonies.[97] Final coverage included State Prosecutor Vyshinsky's summation, quotes from a *Pravda* editorial, the defendants' final pleas, and the guilty verdicts.[98] The testimony of Yagoda and the physicians accused in the poisoning plots received special treatment with *Daily Worker* using the word "fiendish" to describe their alleged conspiracy.[99] *Daily Worker* also published articles that trumpeted NKVD chief Yezhov's "valiant work" in exposing the alleged planning for an "imperialist attack" on the Soviet Union.[100] Another article also vilified Yagoda (an "abnormal and evil figure").[101] Other articles described the defendants as a "rogue's gallery" and refuted the criticism of the trial by Trotsky and by the "capitalist" press.[102,103]

The Communist Party USA's public support for this trial culminated in a speech by Party Secretary Earl Browder in New York City on March 18, 1938. Browder used the Communist Party tactic of comparing the defendants to traitors in American history, recited the charges, and dismissed Trotskyist criticism. He called Joseph Stalin "the greatest leader of democracy that mankind has ever produced" and concluded that the trials were a "blow for peace" that would make the Soviet Union stronger. This speech was reprinted in *Daily Worker* and in *The Communist*, the Party's journal of Marxist theory. It was also reprinted as a pamphlet, entitled *Traitors in American History: Lessons of the Moscow Trials*.[104]

In March 1938 anticommunist journalist Eugene Lyons and socialist Upton Sinclair engaged in a debate that was chronicled in the press. On March 4, 1938, *Daily Worker* published Sinclair's "A Letter to Eugene Lyons" in which Sinclair defended the show trials and stated his belief in the charges.[105] Lyons responded with "The Terror in Stalin's Russia: An Open Letter to Upton Sinclair," an indictment of Sinclair's seeming willingness to excuse the excesses of the purges and to continue "defending the indefensible." These open letters were later published together as a pamphlet which received a rather dismissive review in the literary weekly *Saturday Review*.[106]

In its March 7, 1938, issue *Daily Worker* had a front-page article that cited Rakovksy's testimony in which he alluded to Max Eastman, one of Trotsky's leading American supporters, as being a British spy.[107] In May 1938 Eastman filed a lawsuit against *Daily Worker* and Earl Browder, the leader of the American Party.[108]

Other Communist publications also enthusiastically supported this trial. The weekly *New Masses* published editorials that criticized the trial's detractors for their "obscene campaign of slander and vile insinuations," praised the Soviet government for exposing the "conspiracies" and called Soviet defector Alexandre Barmine a traitor.[109] *New Masses* also published two eyewitness accounts of the trial by Joshua Kunitz. The first article focused on Krestinsky, Bukharin, and Rykov and was accompanied by a full-page cartoon of Trotsky, Hitler, Mussolini, Neville Chamberlain, and Japanese Emperor Hirohito looking worriedly at a newspaper with a headline on the trial.[110] Kunitz's second article condemned

Trotsky, the oppositionists and the capitalist press. This article was accompanied by a full-page cartoon of a naked reporter with a swastika tattooed on his buttock as he churned out headlines about the trials being a "fake."[111] To give additional validity to the charges, *New Masses* published a unique account by John Sutton, an African American agriculturalist in Tashkent in Central Asia. Sutton traced his frustrations in dealing with the People's Commissariat for Agriculture to the "enemies of the people" who had been removed in the purges.[112] As with second trial defendant Karl Radek, *New Masses* did an about-face with Bukharin, having previously published Bukharin's writing in 1934.[113]

The Communist's editor Alexander Bittelman wrote a long commentary on the trial in which he stated his belief in the defendants' confessions, singled out Bukharin, and called the defendants "spies and provocateurs" who were working for Hitler and Japan. He also slammed Trotsky, Trotsky's American defenders, and the capitalist press, calling them the "apologists for reaction and fascism."[114] *The Communist* published two more articles that concentrated on Bukharin, characterizing him as being against Leninism as far back as the Revolution.[115] The second article condemned him and Rykov for their opposition to the "socialist construction" of the first Five Year Plan and for participation in the Riutin platform ("a *kulak* organization with the design of restoring capitalism").[116] *Young Communist Review*, a short-lived journal of the Young Communist League of the United States, published an article by Joseph Starobin in which he defended the trial, compared the defendants to famous traitors in American history (a common Party theme), and warned against Trotskyism. This article was accompanied by two anti-Trotsky cartoons. The first portrayed Trotsky as a forked-tongue and swastika-covered snake about to be struck down by a hammer-wielding worker; the second showed him in lockstep with Hitler and Mussolini.[117]

Soviet Russia Today devoted much of its April 1938 issue to this trial. This included two editorials that defended the confessions as genuine and criticized journalist Eugene Lyons and Oswald Garrison Villard, editor of *The Nation*.[118,119] John Garnett published an article in which he trumpeted the "trial of traitors" as a "blow in defense of peace and democracy everywhere," concentrated on Bukharin's testimony and quoted from several defendants' self-condemning confessions. Garnett concluded by comparing them to strike-breaking spies who had infiltrated American trade unions.[120] *Soviet Russia Toady* also published a translation of State Prosecutor Vyshinsky's summation which condemned the "foul dogs" and "accursed vipers."[121] Columnist Theodore Bayer answered several questions about the trial, including how the defendants' confessions were obtained through the "weight of gathered evidence" and that the cause of the defendants' "degeneration" into "fascist agents" was because they had lost all of their followers.[122] *Soviet Russia Today* continued to defend the trial in June 1938 with John Garnett's favorable review of the trial transcript, using the standard Communist Party tactic of comparing the trial defendants to Tories (Loyalists) during the American Revolution and to notorious traitors in American history.[123] In its July 1938 issue the editors published an open letter to the editors of the "*New Republic*—and Others." This letter chastised the *New Republic* correspondent for his coverage of the trial.[124] A second, short editorial called Trotskyism a "worldwide conspiracy against peace and progress."[125]

Dutifully following the Comintern directive, the American Party also published pamphlets by Boris Nikolayevich Ponomorev of the Soviet Party's Central Committee. For good measure it also published a pamphlet by Central Committee member Emilian Yaroslavsky included the text of the indictment.[126,127] Yaroslavsky's pamphlet had an introduction written by the radical labor leader and prominent American Communist William Z. Foster who compared the defendants to the American traitor Aaron Burr. Foster also slammed American critics of the trial for their "lies and slanders." This pamphlet included an article by Yaroslavsky that had previously been published in *Daily Worker* in which he smeared the defendants; the pamphlet also included the text of the indictment.

As with other trials, Trotsky and his supporters did not let this trial's charges go unanswered. The Trotskyist weekly newspaper *Socialist Appeal* reported on Yagoda's arrest (a "scape-goat"). It also reported on the spread of the purges into the provinces in 1937.[128,129] In a series of daily articles in the *New York Times*, Trotsky analyzed the motives for this trial and attacked everything about it.[130] His US supporters published Trotsky's attacks on Stalin and the trial and held public protest rallies. At the beginning of the trial, *Socialist Appeal* published articles that used the Trotskyist term "frame-up" to describe the trial and used the terms "facing death" and "face doom" to describe the defendants.[131] Articles near the end of the trial pointed out flaws in the testimony and condemned the trial with these words which sum up their view of the trial: "The Prosecuting Attorney continues to drag the moral wrecks seated in the prisoners' dock through an orgy of lies and self-abasement."[132] The newspaper's editor Max Shachtman held a workers' meeting in New York City at which he made a "withering analysis" of the evidence.[133] The Party also organized picket lines outside the Soviet consulates in New York City and San Francisco.[134,135]

A special supplement to *Socialist Appeal* devoted to the trial included a column by Trotsky and an editorial attacking liberal criticism for not seeing the trials as contradictions to the "great and deathless ideal of the socialist revolution."[136]

Socialist Appeal reported the guilty verdicts and the executions of the defendants and used the device of an open letter to urge Communists to reject the "illusions, shams, treacheries" in the trial and to urge them to join the newly formed Socialist Workers Party.[137,138] Not letting go of the issue, *Socialist Appeal* reported that the trials were causing dissension within the Communist Party ranks in the United States and overseas.[139] Trotskyist James Burnham condemned the trial and castigated American liberals who were finally questioning the trials.[140] Burnham later became disillusioned with communism and became one of the founders of the conservative *National Review*. Before and throughout the trial, the "Soviet Union Notes" column by Joseph Vansler, writing as John G. Wright, referred to the Soviet "blood purge" and called the trial a "frame-up."[141]

Socialist Appeal published articles in opposition after the trial, including a letter from Trotsky to Freda Kirchwey, an editor of *The Nation* considered to be pro-Soviet, in which he defended the accused and slammed Stalin and Vyshinsky.[142] *Socialist Appeal* also published an anti-Stalinist article by French communist Alfred Rosmer in which he asserted that the trials were "coarsely fabricated" and refuted Krestinsky's testimony concerning Rosmer's involvement, claiming that he had only met Krestinsky once in 1924.[143]

Socialist Appeal also published a letter from Trotsky to the Juridical Section of the League of Nations. Mindful of his supposed importance on the world stage, Trotsky requested that the League hold a special tribunal to hear his case because Stalin was the "head of an international terrorist band."[144] As with the supposition that Karl Radek was spared the death penalty in the second trial in order to have him testify in the future, *Socialist Appeal* incorrectly speculated that Rakovsky was spared in order to testify again at some future trial.[145] Both men were never heard from again. This article was accompanied by a cartoon that showed the black stain of the "Moscow Murders" on the "Stalinist Constitution." *Socialist Appeal* also chimed in on the literary feud between Upton Sinclair and Eugene Lyons. In a review of *Terror in Russia*, the reviewer severely criticized Sinclair and praised Lyons.[146]

The Trotskyist monthly *New International* published several articles on this trial. Trotsky defender Max Eastman wrote an open letter to Corliss Lamont, president of the Friends of the Soviet Union and a supporter of the trials, in which Eastman made a string of personal accusations against Lamont and called him a "public defender of a deliberate policy of falsification."[147] In the same issue, the editors cited Trotsky's longstanding blaming of the Soviet bureaucracy and the need to cover up the regime's mistakes. The editors also blamed the "war in the Far East," shifting European alliances and "international dissatisfaction with Stalinism." They called the trials "political instruments," a "political fabrication," and the favorite

Trotskyist term—"frame-up." The editors also followed Trotsky's line that Hitler felt emboldened to annex Austria because the trials had supposedly weakened the Soviet Union.[148] *New International* also published an article by George Novack, a member of the American Committee for the Defense of Leon Trotsky, that employed a common tactic of criticizing a political opponent through the means of a book review. In this case Novack reviewed Earl Browder's pro-trial pamphlet *Traitors in American History*. He called the trials "judicial assassinations" and called Browder "one of the masters in the Stalin School of Falsification."[149] A June 1938 article by Trotsky skewered everyone who had written a kind word about the trials, including *The Nation, New Republic*, and journalists Walter Duranty and Louis Fischer ("prostitutes of the pen"). He also had no kind words for Eugene Lyons and Walter Krivitsky, two critics of Stalin's regime.[150]

Fighting Worker, the official newspaper of the Chicago-based, anti-Stalinist Revolutionary Workers League, called the trial a "frame-up" and turned on both defenders of the earlier trials and turned on Trotskyists. The article ended with a call for the destruction of Stalinism.[151] The Leninist League US, an anti-Stalinist and anti-Trotskyist splinter group, published *In Defense of Bolshevism*, a monthly newsletter. Its April 5, 1938, issue included articles in which the writers accused everyone associated with both support of and criticism of the purges as being anti-Leninist, including Stalin, Trotsky, and American Communist dissident Jay Lovestone. The issue ended with an article on an open letter that the League had sent to other leftist groups, asking them to participate in public demonstrations in New York City. This letter included a denunciation of "the monstrous gang headed by Stalin" and a call for the "formation of a united front." When the "Trotskyites" and "Lovestoneites" did not reply to this call, the writer denounced their leaders.[152]

Reactions of American Liberals

The American Committee for the Defense of Leon Trotsky opposed this trial, and, when the trial was announced, a group of liberals sent a telegram to Ambassador Troyanovsky in which they requested that the trial be postponed for six weeks. Perhaps in a symbolic gesture or in an act of naïveté, the Committee wanted the trial to be delayed so that an "international committee" could go to Moscow to witness the proceedings and report back.[153] In a swipe at the American Committee, *Daily Worker* published a condemnation of this request by Corliss Lamont, who called the Dewey Commission a "mere mouthpiece" for American Trotskyists.[154]

While the American Committee claimed not to be pro-Trotsky, it held a mass meeting and invited members of the Socialist Workers Party to speak. This meeting included a message from Trotsky who praised them for leading to the ultimate victory of this "great liberating struggle" against Stalinism. This meeting included addresses by Max Shachtman, the editor of *Socialist Appeal*, and Bertram D. Wolfe of the Independent Labor League of America, a group of dissident Communists.[155] Wolfe roundly condemned the purge and the trials as a danger to the labor movement and as being against Lenin. He also condemned Stalin's "bloody deeds" and "fearful crimes" against the Soviet state, the Party, and the Soviet people. He considered it to be the labor movement's task to "redeem the Russian Revolution from its destroyer."[156] Wolfe continued his condemnation of this trial in a lecture in November 1938.[157]

Another denunciation of this trial came from socialist Norman Thomas, one of the founders of the American Committee. He called the trials "the most dreadful single chapter in the story of the degradation of a self-proclaimed socialist movement." He echoed Wolfe's assertion that the trials had hurt the labor movement, due to Stalin's "perversion" of socialism. He called the one-party rule the "dictatorship of the lie" and called the Soviet Union a "totalitarian state under a monolithic party."[158] Thomas continued his criticism in a pamphlet co-authored with Joel Seidman, in which they considered the "carefully staged" trials to be propaganda and the defendants to be scapegoats.[159]

The Communist press took the liberals to task for this criticism of the Soviet Union. Singling out Norman Thomas and the "righteous arrogance" of liberal critics, Robert Forsythe asserted that: "A liberal is one who wastes no word of sympathy over the assassination of Kirov but who later keeps the cables hot with demands that his murderers go unpunished."[160]

New Masses and *Soviet Russia Today* published a second statement by American intellectuals in support of the trials in May 1938. "The Moscow Trials: A Statement by American Progressives" was signed by 150 intellectuals and affirmed the guilt of the defendants and accused Trotskyists of weakening anti-fascism and discrediting the Peoples (Popular) Front, the Congress of Industrial Organizations (CIO), and the Soviet Union. They called on liberals to support the Soviet Union and to support the fight against fascism. The statement condemned the trial defendants as "opponents" of Soviet policies who "resorted to duplicity and conspiracy" with "long-standing enemies of the Soviet Union." Among the signers were leading writers Nelson Algren, Vera Caspary, Dashiell Hammett, Lillian Hellman, Langston Hughes, Dorothy Parker, and Irwin Shaw. Actor Morris Carnovksy, composer Marc Blitzstein, and artist Arnold Blanch represented other arts. Communist journalists Louis Budenz of *Daily Worker*, Joshua Kunitz of *New Masses*, Malcolm Cowley of *New Republic*, and the pro-Soviet journalist Anna Louise Strong were also signatories.[161]

Soviet Russia Today published an attack on Malcolm Cowley, cited as "among those who initiated this statement" and one of its signers. In spite of his participation in the framing of the Statement, Cowley, who had written a positive review of the trial transcript, had later written another article with rather mild criticism of the lack of legal opposition in the Soviet Union. The reporter for *Soviet Russia Today* criticized Cowley for his second article, upheld the Statement, and condemned the trial defendants.[162]

Trotskyists did not let the Statement go unchallenged. *Socialist Appeal* published "Street-Walkers of the G. P. U.," a brief article on the efforts of intellectuals to get signers for the Statement. The reporter called this effort a "nauseating piece of mendacity" and called the signers "street-walkers" and "running dogs of the G.P.U." The article named specific signers, including Malcolm Cowley of *The Nation*.[163] Decades later, co-signer Corliss Lamont, a critic of the American Committee, admitted that during this time he had made the "biggest mistake" in underestimating the "extent of Stalin's terrible tyranny" and in defending the trials.[164] In the left-wing *Partisan Review*, the Ukrainian-born literary critic Philip Rahv condemned the signers as being "taken in by the professional illusionists of the Comintern." He called the trials "performance plays, fiction," and he did not believe the defendants' confessions.[165]

The Statement did not go unnoticed in anticommunist circles. In his 1941 book *The Red Decade*, journalist Eugene Lyons skewered the Statement's signers, calling them "American apologists for the G.P.U." and "bogus radicals." Lyons called the Statement an "amazing whitewash of Stalin." He also defended the Dewey Commission and criticized signers of the earlier Open Letter.[166]

Several of the signers were caught up in the postwar McCarthy era and were either blacklisted, called before the House Un-American Activities Committee, or put on trial for their pro-Soviet sympathies.

Conclusion

Chip Bohlen, the only Embassy secretary to attend this final show trial with Ambassador Joseph E. Davies, later used the words "fantastic" and "unbelievable" to describe the alleged plots and the defendants' testimony; he considered Stalin's "overall purpose" was to "blacken the opposition . . . and render it incapable of organizing any movement against him."[167] Loy W. Henderson, who had observed the first show trial, later wrote that Stalin did not want the Old Bolsheviks to rewrite history, and he set out "to eliminate them one by one."[168] After service in Moscow during the Second World War, George F. Kennan looked back at this trial and wrote: "Vyshinsky is sounding the cry of suspicious, secretive Russia against the fancied hostility of the outside world."[169]

Plate 8.1 A photograph of Leon Trotsky and American followers in Mexico in 1940. US Court of the Fourth (Minneapolis) Division of the District of Minnesota, "Leon Trotsky and American Admirers." US National Archives and Records Administration, no. 283462, April 4, 1940, http://nara.gov (accessed July 12, 2022).

Plate 8.2 Stalin funeral. Stalin's disease first reported by Pravda. Wikimedia Commons. March 4, 1953, http://commons.wikimeda.org (accessed March 21, 2023).

8

The Aftermath of the Moscow Show Trials
Part I—1939–55

Introduction

This chapter discusses American reactions to events in the Soviet Union in the years after the last Moscow show trial and prior to Nikita Khrushchev's "secret speech" of 1956. Events included the Eighteenth Communist Party Congress resolution that was the "official" end of the purges, the purge of NKVD chief Nikolai Yezhov, and the assassination of Leon Trotsky. In the United States, the publication of Arthur Koestler's *Darkness at Noon* and Ambassador Joseph E. Davies's memoir *Mission to Moscow* (and subsequent film) caused another set of reactions to the show trials. Radical political parties suffered a decline and their leaders were prosecuted during this time. Another aspect of the aftermath in the United States were the postwar anticommunist crusade, including investigations by the House Un-American Activities Committee (HUAC) and the trial and executions of Julius and Ethel Rosenberg for espionage. Events in the Soviet Union tied to the show trials included the Doctors' Plot, Joseph Stalin's death, and the purge of Lavrenti Beria.

The Eighteenth Party Congress and the Purge of Nikolai Yezhov

At the Eighteenth Communist Party Congress in March 1939, Stalin heaped scorn on the trial defendants as "spies, assassins and wreckers" and "fiends" engaged in espionage for foreign governments. Stalin also condemned the "bourgeoisie and its agents" who had "succeeded to a certain extent in contaminating the spirit of the working class." He also ridiculed the foreign "drivellers" who claimed that the purges had weakened the Soviet Union.¹ Stalin's speech was front-page news in the *New York Times*.² This Party Congress passed a resolution that called for an end to the purges, stating that the purges were ineffective and unjust, using the Stalinist tactic of blaming local functionaries and underlings. *Newsweek* used this Party resolution as an opportunity to report on the devastation that the purges had caused to Party membership and claimed that the Party was run by Stalin and the Politburo. The reporter also asserted that Britain and France feared that the purges had weakened the Soviet Union (a "second civil war") and that the Party was trying to "remedy its internal ailments in preparation for war."³ The business weekly *Barron's* reported on the end of the purges by condemning the Politburo for engendering a climate of fear and "inexhaustible suspicion." The reporter cited the devastation of the officer class in the military and concluded by wondering if the Soviets could ever restore efficiency. Oddly, the reporter blamed the Politburo but never mentioned Stalin by name.⁴

As a sign of the lessening of the purges, in January 1939, Harold Denny of the *New York Times* wrote on the Kyiv trial and execution of five Moldovan "political police officers" for extorting confessions. While Denny wrote that the purges caught foreign agents, saboteurs, and oppositionists, he acknowledged that the purging of "thousands of innocent victims" had caused resentment among the Soviet population. Denny questioned whether the secret police had used torture and intimidation because they had only to hold prisoners indefinitely until they confessed. He also acknowledged that they used overcrowded cells and marathon interrogation sessions (the conveyor) to break down the accused.⁵ The Trotskyist weekly newspaper *Socialist Appeal* quoted from Denny's article, labeled the show trials the "Moscow frameups" and editorialized that the Kyiv trial was confirmation of the excesses of the "blood purge" and the "murderous onslaught of the degenerate bureaucracy." This trial was also a demonstration that even those who had done Stalin's bidding were not safe. In a prime example of Trotskyist animus toward the Stalinist regime, the article ended with the following: "Nothing but the removal of the Stalinist bureaucracy, the revival of the Soviet and the establishment of a new revolutionary party can save the Soviet Union from destruction."⁶

In January 1939, Joseph Barnes, a former Moscow correspondent, wrote an insightful, comprehensive essay on the purges for *Foreign Affairs*. Barnes described the history and scope of the purges within the Communist Party, gave statistics, and stated that "Bolsheviks have been executing each other on a large scale." He cited the Party resolution winding down the purges and also mentioned the publication of *History of the Communist Party of the Soviet Union*

(Bolshevik), (Short Course), an official history of the rise of the Party, in which he noted that Trotsky was portrayed as disloyal to Lenin, that the executed military leaders were not mentioned at all and that Bukharin was accused of trying to "arrest and murder Lenin, Stalin and Sverdlov in 1918."[7] Barnes was referring to a section of Chapter 12 of *A Short History* entitled "Liquidation of the Remnants of the Bukharin-Trotsky Gang of Spies, Wreckers and Traitors to the Country." In this section the trial defendants were either vilified as spies, the "dregs of humanity," "Trotsky-Bukharin fiends," "Whiteguard pigmies," "Whiteguard insects," and "contemptible lackeys of the fascists" or they were not mentioned at all, in spite of their roles in the rise of the Party and in winning the Civil War.[8]

NKVD head Nikolai Yezhov was demoted during this time and was on his way out. In 1937 Embassy secretary Henderson had written the following about him:

> Ezhov by playing upon Stalin's fears and prejudices is responsible for what seems to be the decision of the Dictator to eliminate not only all opponents, former, present, potential, or fancied together with their friends and adherents, but also all persons whose unconditional loyalty to Stalin is at all in doubt.[9]

In 1939 Embassy secretary Alexander Kirk described Yezhov's downfall from being the "chief instrument of the reign of terror," the possible shift of policy under Beria's tenure (a "possible modification of repressive measures") and ended with the following cautionary note:

> Any definite statement . . . to the end of the purge in the Soviet Union must be made with the greatest reserve. . . . Nor is there any reason to believe that individual officials who may in one way or another incur the displeasure or arouse the distrust of Stalin will be treated with any greater leniency than in the past or that any greater degree of freedom in word or deed will be permitted in the Soviet Union. . . . The functions of [the] secret police are being returned to those of control and surveillance rather than to the conduct of the active "witch hunt" for "Trotskiist-Bukharinist spies, wreckers and diversionists" which characterized Soviet internal political and economic life during the past two years.[10] [Yezhov was transliterated as Ezhov in these communiqués.]

Yezhov's downfall was also reported in the American press. In an uncensored report from London, Harold Denny bluntly described Stalin's dictatorial power ("oriental despotism") and stated that, during his "disastrous career," Yezhov had purged the country to the "edge of disaster," with the secret police everywhere and with Stalin in charge of everything through his control of the police. Denny also wrote that Soviet citizens have amazing endurance and that the Soviet Union suffered under an inefficient and "strangling" bureaucracy.[11]

In an article condemning Stalin and the purges, the Trotskyist *Socialist Appeal* asserted that Stalin knew of the scope of "Yezhov's activity" and had been prepared to "renounce" him when his work was done. The reporter incorrectly predicted the downfall of the regime.[12] Yezhov's downfall was also predicted by Embassy secretary Chip Bohlen who had witnessed the third show trial in which Yezhov was portrayed as a potential victim of Yagoda's poisoning plots. In his memoir Bohlen wrote that when it was asserted that Yezhov's "ill health" had been caused by the poisoning attempt, it was a sign that he was on his way out.[13]

In 1939 Stalin signed a non-aggression pact with Nazi Germany, an event that stunned the West. At the end of the same year, the Soviets went to war with Finland. These two events proved to be too much for President Roosevelt who had previously wanted a rapprochement with the Soviets. In a radio address to the American Youth Congress in 1940 he bluntly stated: "The Soviet Union . . . is a dictatorship as absolute as any other dictatorship in the world. It has aligned itself with another dictatorship, and it has invaded a neighbor so infinitesimally small that it could do no conceivable, possible harm to the Soviet Union."[14]

The Assassination of Leon Trotsky

In the first and second show trials, the court ruled that if Leon Trotsky or his exiled son Lev Sedov ever returned to the Soviet Union, they would be subject to arrest and trial. Sedov died in Paris under mysterious circumstances in 1938. While under police protection in Mexico, there had been an unsuccessful attempt on Trotsky's life in May 1940. In August 1940, in spite of having bodyguards as well as police protection, Ramón Mercader, a Spanish Communist and NKVD agent from Catalonia, assassinated Trotsky by striking him in the head with an ice axe. Trotsky died on August 21. Mercader was apprehended, confessed, tried, convicted, and sentenced to prison for 19 ½ years. Upon the completion of his sentence, he was released, went to Cuba, and then to the Soviet Union.

Trotsky's assassination was front-page news around the world.[15] Liberal weeklies characterized Trotsky as an idealist with a small following, as Stalin's great rival and as being killed by Stalin's secret police.[16] Literary critic Dwight Macdonald and exiled writer Victor Serge eulogized him in *Partisan Review* which also published a long memorial poem to Trotsky by Paul Goodman.[17,18,19]

Daily Worker portrayed Trotsky's death as the result of an argument between Trotsky and his disillusioned "follower."[20] In a "serves him right" tone, an editorial in the Communist weekly *New Masses* accused Trotsky of a barrage of crimes, ridiculed those who "mourn the loss," and stated that he had been killed by a member of his "irresponsible gang" in an "atmosphere of recrimination and bitter hostility."[21]

American Trotskyists eulogized him at a meeting in New York City, exalted his revolutionary past, and blamed Stalin and the Soviet secret police for his murder.[22] For years after his death, Trotskyists revisited the assassination and denounced the purges and the Moscow show trials.[23] Leading Trotskyist Max Eastman published an article in *Foreign Affairs* that was full of reminiscences of his encounters with Trotsky and defended his reputation (a "great place in history"), his achievements, and his "consecration to the cause of socialism." He also cited Trotsky's strengths and flaws ("coldness and unreasonable impatience and irascibility"). Eastman ended with a lamentation that Trotsky was "inadequate" to continue the "heritage of Lenin."[24] The radical splinter group the Revolutionary Workers League also blamed Stalin for this assassination.[25]

The Federal Bureau of Investigation (FBI) had kept a file on Trotsky for years and had investigated the assassin Mercader's movements through the United States on his way to Mexico. The FBI also investigated his associates while in the United States and investigated an alleged American plot to help him escape from prison.[26] The House Un-American Activities Committee (HUAC) held hearings in 1950 to investigate whether the Soviet government and the Communist Party USA had "played any part in the murder of Trotsky" and whether there was an "unsuccessful attempt to secure the release of the killer from a Mexican prison." The Committee concluded that Trotsky's assassin was "possibly an NKVD agent" and that American Communists had ties to NKVD agents in the United States.[27] A Senate Subcommittee held hearings in 1955 on Soviet espionage that included Trotsky's assassination.[28] In 1994 the Central Intelligence Agency (CIA) compiled an analysis of Trotsky's life and assassination entitled *Leon Trotsky: Dupe of the NKVD*. The author took a "blame the victim" stance by concluding that their analysis "reveals . . . Trotsky's own gullibility, arrogance, and waywardness."[29] In 1961 Trotsky's widow Natalia asked for the Soviet government to review the Moscow show trials, investigate Trotsky's murder, and publish his writings.[30] His assassination has been the object of scholarly study to this day.[31]

On a side note, in 1941 Soviet defector Walter Krivitsky was found dead of a gunshot wound to the head in a hotel room in Washington, DC. He had been denounced by American Communists, testified before a Congressional committee, and had been tracked by the FBI. His death was ruled a suicide, a controversial finding.[32]

Darkness at Noon and *Mission to Moscow*

In 1941 two books concerned with the purges and the Moscow show trials were published in the United States. The first was Arthur Koestler's *Darkness at Noon*, the fictional account of the imprisonment and interrogations of Rubashov, a high government official purportedly based on Nikolai Bukharin. Koestler described the prison conditions and marathon interrogation sessions through Rubashov's first-person narrative as he awaited his inevitable execution.[33] *Darkness at Noon* was well-received in the mainstream American press and is considered to be one of the great novels of the twentieth century.[34] However, the Trotskyist *Fourth International* published a critical review by Albert Goldman, Trotsky's lawyer during the Dewey Commission. Goldman called the novel a "complete failure" for not adhering to Trotsky's theories.[35]

At the end of 1941 former Ambassador Joseph E. Davies published the bestselling *Mission to Moscow*, a memoir of his time in the Soviet Union.[36] Davies's overall support of the show trials elicited reviews along ideological lines as many reviewers referred to Davies's belief in the trials' charges.[37] The Communist press endorsed the book.[38] However, a review in the radical *Partisan Review* derisively lumped Davies together with Stalin apologists Walter Duranty of the *New York Times* and with journalist Anna Louise Strong. The reviewer concluded by blaming Stalin for wiping out the "most intelligent section of the population."[39] The Trotskyist journal *New International* published a denunciation of *Mission to Moscow* by leading Trotskyist Max Shachtman who derided Davies's lack of knowledge of Russia, his acceptance of the trials' charges, and his praise for Soviet leaders.[40] The publication of *Mission to Moscow* led to John Dewey engaging in a war of words with art critic Arthur Upham Pope in letters to the editor of the *New York Times*. Dewey criticized Davies's acceptance of the Stalinist line. Pope characterized Dewey's letter as a "savage assault on Stalin."[41]

Davies also published an article entitled "How Russia Blasted Hitler's Spy Machine" in the December 1941 issue of *American Magazine*. This article included Davies's belief that a Nazi fifth column had been destroyed by Stalin.[42] The Trotskyist *Fourth International* published a scathing critique of this article, terming it an attempt to "place a stamp of approval" on the show trials.[43] By the time *Mission to Moscow* was published, the United States had entered the Second World War and was supporting the Soviet Union as an important ally. At Davies's urging, Warner Brothers released a film adaptation of *Mission to Moscow* in April 1943.[44] Davies himself appeared at the beginning to introduce the film, and it included sinister scenes that hinted at sabotage and espionage.

The scene portraying a show trial showed several of the defendants on trial at the same time when in reality they were defendants in different trials. As with the book, the filmed version of *Mission to Moscow* was a cause of ideological controversy, including its portrayal of a show trial. The film received mixed reviews in the mainstream press.[45] The Communist weekly *New Masses* gave it a glowing review and praised the trial scene.[46] The Trotskyist press panned the film and termed its show trial scene to be the "greatest forgery of the picture."[47]

The film version of *Mission to Moscow* also caused another war of words between John Dewey, Suzanne La Follette, and Arthur Upham Pope in letters to editor of the *New York Times*.[48] The Communist weekly *New Masses* came to the film's defense and accused Dewey and La Follette of being allied with groups bent on disuniting the United Nations and exterminating the Soviet Union.[49] The continuing controversy elicited an explanatory "letter to the screen editor" of the *New York Times* by Howard Koch, a Hollywood veteran and the film's screenwriter. Koch defended his dramatic license in combining the show trials into one scene in order to save screen time.[50] In his memoir, former Embassy secretary Chip Bohlen, who had attended the third show trial and was no fan of Davies, lambasted *Mission to Moscow* as full of factual errors and "one of the most blatantly propagandistic pictures ever screened."[51]

In the postwar United States, *Mission to Moscow* and other pro-Soviet wartime films became part of a US congressional investigation into suspected Communist infiltration and influence in Hollywood. In his testimony to HUAC, Warner Brothers studio head Jack L. Warner wrapped himself in the flag and stated that such pro-Soviet films were patriotic parts of the war effort.[52] Screenwriter Howard Koch was later blacklisted. For such a forgettable film, *Mission to Moscow* has been an object of much scholarly study as both an example of wartime pro-Soviet filmmaking and as part of the postwar HUAC investigations.[53]

The State of Radical Political Parties in the United States

Radical political parties in the United States took a beating from the late 1930s to the early 1950s. Some American Party leaders and leading left-wing intellectuals had been expelled from the Party or had become disillusioned with communism and publicly turned against it, especially after Stalin signed the non-aggression pact with Adolph Hitler in 1939. The Communist Party USA and American Trotskyists had been targeted by anticommunist legislation, such as the Smith

Act in 1943, which outlawed advocating the overthrow of the government. Party leaders had been tried, convicted, and imprisoned. The Communist Party had been infiltrated and placed under surveillance by the FBI, as was the Socialist Workers Party.[54] Membership had declined, and there was internal dissension within both groups. Longtime Communist Party leader Earl Browder was expelled from the Party in 1946.

In 1949 American writers stated their falling out with communism in *The God that Failed*, a compilation of essays by Western intellectuals.[55] In 1954 Trotsky supporter Sidney Hook, then head of the Department of Philosophy at New York University published an article in the *New York Times Magazine* in which he took a kindly look at ex-communists and fellow travelers as motivated by "early idealism" and that they could be useful in combating communism as "intelligent advisors" on "Marxist-Leninist-Stalinist theory."[56]

Congressional hearings in the 1940s and 1950s, including the infamous McCarthy hearings, were the most well-known examples of the postwar anticommunist atmosphere in the United States. Cold War fears were also stoked by the trial and executions of Julius and Ethel Rosenberg. They had been arrested and tried in 1951 for being part of an espionage plot to pass secrets about the atomic bomb to the Soviets. They were executed in 1953. Their trial and executions were media sensations.

The Doctors' Plot

George F. Kennan, an Embassy secretary during the purges, returned to the Soviet Union during the Second World War and was named the US ambassador in 1952. However, his time in Moscow was short and unhappy, and he was declared *persona non grata* and left.[57] Jacob D. Beam served as interim ambassador. Charles "Chip" Bohlen was named ambassador and arrived in 1953.

Echoing the charges of medical murder in the third show trial, in January 1953, *Pravda* announced the arrests of nine physicians in the "Doctors' Plot." Returning to the playbook of the Moscow show trials, this announcement was full of name-calling ("saboteur doctors," "monsters," and "gang of poisoners-doctors") and full of sensational accusations that resurrected the old charges of poisoning. They were charged with causing the deaths of prominent Soviets Andrei Zhdanov and Alexander Shcherbakov and plotting to kill military leaders as part of a foreign conspiracy.[58] The doctors were to be put on trial for "wrecking, espionage and terroristic activities." Two of the accused doctors had been on the

Kremlin's Commission of Experts during the third show trial, another example of even those who did Stalin's bidding not being safe from persecution.

The US Embassy, the Department of State, and the Central Intelligence Agency (CIA) did analyses of the charges in the Doctors' Plot. Embassy secretary Jacob Beam sent a communiqué that was matter-of-fact in its analysis, stating his disbelief in the charges and citing the "reversion to techniques of 1930s." He also cited the "patent lack of reality of the charges" as the "ruling group lives in an atmosphere of constant psychotic mistrust and suspicion." As several of the defendants were Jewish, he also speculated that Stalin's anti-Semitism was a cause, and Bean wondered about the status of Lavrenti Beria, head of the MGB (the renamed NKVD), as the MGB had been criticized for failing to uncover the plot earlier.[59] Based on a draft co-authored by Chip Bohlen, Secretary of State John Foster Dulles sent a communiqué to the Embassy in which he theorized that the charges represented a "dramatic effort to increase vigilance and tighten discipline among Soviet people" and possibly reflected a "political or power problem in top Soviet hierarchy." Dulles also commented on the resemblance to the "techniques employed in the great purge of 1936 through 1939" and commented on the possible anti-Semitism.[60] The doctors' arrests were also covered in the US press with speculation about insecurity within the Soviet leadership, anti-Semitism, and the possibility of a new round of show trials.[61] The Trotskyist weekly newspaper *Labor Action*, now calling itself an "independent Socialist weekly," branded the Doctors' Plot as part of an anti-Semitic campaign.[62] Eventually the number of the accused doctors increased from nine to fifteen.

The Doctors' Plot abruptly ended with Stalin's death. A communiqué from the Embassy on April 4, 1953, reported that the accused had been vindicated and released. Calling the dismissal of all charges a "startling event," Jacob Beam speculated about a possible internal power struggle and a possible break with Stalinism.[63] A *Pravda* editorial on the dismissal of the charges blamed the Ministry of State Security for fabricating the case and blamed the "medical-expert commission" for giving "incorrect conclusions" regarding the charges of poisoning.[64] The dismissal of the charges also caused another round of press coverage with speculation about the dismissal being part of a Kremlin power struggle.[65] In 1954 the CIA produced a working paper on the Doctors' Plot and considered it to be anti-Semitic and to be part of a "hate America" and intensified propaganda campaigns, harkening back to the 1930s. The author also speculated about a power struggle within the Kremlin.[66] Years later interest in the Doctors' Plot was renewed when one of the surviving doctors published a memoir.[67] The Doctors' Plot has been a continuing subject of scholarly study.[68]

The Death of Stalin

Stalin's illness was announced on March 4, 1953, as the Soviet government prepared the populace for his death by issuing pessimistic bulletins about his declining health. Embassy secretary Beam sent a communiqué on the announcement, noting possible caution among the ruling group, a lack of reaction among Soviet citizens, and speculation that Stalin's illness may have affected "Stalin's already abnormally suspicious mind" and may have caused the Doctors' Plot.[69] The *New York Times* published an article that compared Stalin's ailments to those of Vladimir Lenin.[70] The National Committee of the Communist Party USA called his illness a "tragedy for all democratic humanity" and sent a message of "deepest grief."[71] *Daily Worker* also published an editorial expressing shock and proclaiming that collective leadership would "carry forward the great tasks of socialist construction."[72] Stalin's death was announced on March 5 by the Soviet Party's Central Committee as a "tremendous loss to the party, to the workers of the Soviet Union and to the whole world."[73]

The Department of State had been trying to prepare for Stalin's death for years and had organized a Working Group (Stalin) in 1951. The Department's most frequently cited paper was the "Program of Psychological Preparation for Stalin's Passing from Power," issued by the Department's Psychological Strategy Board in November 1952. It set the tone of speculation and cautious conjecture as to how the Soviet populace would react, future Soviet government policies, new Party leadership, and how the West should react.[74] The Department held meetings and produced other papers, an "Intelligence Estimate" and memoranda on the possible impact of his death, all while waiting for word that "Stalin was dead as hell." The National Security Council met with President Eisenhower on the day before Stalin's death was officially announced and discussed the possible ramifications.[75] All of the US government's official meetings, working papers, and memoranda may be considered to be exercises in futility and can be summarized by President Eisenhower's statement at a Cabinet meeting on March 6: "The President told the Cabinet that *no specific plan for Government action or policy has been developed in advance,* despite continuous talk since 1946 about the possibility of Stalin's death."[76] [Italics added.]

In spite of the ineffectiveness of their previous efforts, US government agencies began another round of meetings, memoranda, and papers, sometimes contradicting each other as to proposed courses of action.[77] Newly appointed Ambassador Bohlen was still in Washington, DC, and bluntly asserted that "naked Soviet imperialism" was still powerful in Eastern Europe.[78] Meanwhile,

Embassy secretary Beam sent reports on the subdued response to Stalin's death, on tightened security during funeral arrangements and on the funeral itself.[79] A meeting of the National Security Council on March 11 included another discussion of Stalin's death. According to an official account, President Eisenhower, who had met Stalin after the war, made this rather surprising statement:

> "*Stalin had never actually been undisputed ruler of the Soviet Union.* Contrary to the views of many of our intelligence agencies, the President persisted in believing that the Government of the Soviet Union had always been something of a committee government."[80] [Italics added.]

Joint government agencies issued a "Special Estimate" that concluded that the new Soviet leadership would make no radical changes.[81] Voice of America, the government's international radio broadcasting arm then under the Department of State, issued a cautious statement that asserted that Stalin's death did not end Russian "extermination and suppression."[82] Congress held a briefing on the impact of Stalin's death on Soviet domestic and foreign policy in April 1953, which included a discussion of anti-American propaganda by the Soviets.[83] In July the CIA compiled *Death of Stalin*, a working paper that analyzed Stalin's last days, the mystery surrounding his death, his funeral, the Soviet government and Communist Party reorganization, and possible successors, noting Nikita Khrushchev's rise to prominence.[84]

Stalin's death was headline news around the world and led to reviews of his life and career and speculation about his successors.[85] Echoing the revelations of Soviet defector Walter Krivitsky in the 1930s, *Life* published a series of articles by Soviet defector Alexander Orlov about Stalin and the purges. Orlov gave an unflattering insider's look at the personalities of the Soviet elite, including Andrei Vyshinski, the state prosecutor in the show trials ("one of the chief architects of those judicial frame-ups").[86]

The liberal weekly *New Republic* portrayed Stalin as a completely political creature and "always given to doubt and suspicion."[87] Isaac Deutscher, one of Stalin's best-known biographers at the time, wrote an article on the succession of Georgi Malenkov to power and on Stalin's legacy of an expanded Communist world. Perhaps harkening back to the purges, Deutscher surmised that there must be anxiety among "leading Stalinists" as to "whether the cult is not going to have its final revenge on them."[88] Dissident Communist Bertram D. Wolfe published a negative article in *Foreign Affairs* on the problems for the successors of Stalin. Wolfe bluntly condemned everything about the Soviet system, the "blood purges," and the Doctors' Plot. He had nothing good to say about Stalin ("jealous, resentful, envious, capricious and suspicious"). Wolfe concluded that the world was a safer place while this "total dictatorship" went through "convulsive struggles" to provide a succession of power.[89]

New World Review (formerly *Soviet Russia Today*) published eulogies for Stalin which were examples of American Communists' reactions. Editor Jessica Smith cited Stalin's "great and living heritage" and praised his knowledge and wisdom in guiding the Soviets "along the path charted by Lenin."[90]

American Trotskyists wasted no time in vilifying Stalin. In an article in *Fourth International* that was filled with historical references to the French Revolution and to Marxist theory, George Clarke claimed that Stalin must go down in history as a "usurper, a hangman, hated and despised," and proclaimed the "coming vindication" of Trotskyism as the "science of working class victory."[91] Writing under a pseudonym, Albert Glotzer, the stenographer during the Dewey Commission's Inquiry, claimed that Stalin used his "dictatorial rule" to "wipe out every trace of the old party." Glotzer also cataloged Stalin's personal failings, including his "personal cruelty, his sadism and his envy."[92]

After Stalin's death Georgi Malenkov became prime minister and party secretary in a triumvirate with Lavrenti Beria and Vyacheslav Molotov. Ambassador Bohlen sent a bluntly worded communiqué in July 1953 on internal conditions in the Soviet Union. He included a list of "fundamental premises," including the following:

> The Soviet Union remains a totalitarian police dictatorship, reinforced by a highly integrated ideology and consequently basically continues to regard all countries and organizations which it does not control as basically hostile and no change in this respect can be anticipated as long as [the] basic structure of Soviet society remains unaltered.[93]

In 2017 the dark comedic film *The Death of Stalin* was a fictional account of the scrambling by Kremlin insiders to conduct Stalin's funeral and to purge Lavrenti Beria.[94]

The Fall of Lavrenti Beria

Stalin's fellow Georgian Lavrenti Beria was head of the NKVD near the end of the purges and served as People's Commissar of the Interior throughout the rest of Stalin's rule. He also held other posts, including heading the Soviet atomic bomb project. He gave one of Stalin's funeral orations and had been profiled in the American press, both in terms of his being head of the secret police and as one of Stalin's possible successors.[95] Echoing the fates of his predecessors—Gengrikh Yagoda and Nikolai Yezhov—and using the tactics and charges leveled against the Old Bolsheviks in the 1930s, Beria and six of his associates were arrested, tried, and executed in 1953. His downfall was chronicled in the United States in two phases—his arrest in July 1953 and his trial and execution in December.

In July the Party Central Committee, under the leadership of Malenkov, removed Beria from his positions and ordered his trial before the Supreme Court for "criminal and anti-state action." The Party claimed that Beria had served the "interest of foreign capital" and had put the secret police above the government and the Party. *Pravda* went further by accusing him of impeding agriculture and causing dissension in the Soviet republics.[96]

The implications of Beria's arrest were discussed at a presidential cabinet meeting on July 10, 1953. CIA Director Allen Dulles speculated on the impact of Beria's arrest on internal conditions as being a "tremendous shock to the Russian people." Other speculation included the possibility of the United States being able to develop "passive resistance in the satellite states" [i.e., Eastern Europe] and sending a "series of notes concerning food, atrocities, trade unions, and slave labor" to the Soviet government.[97] On the same date, Ambassador Bohlen sent a communiqué concerning Beria's arrest, speculating as to whether it was the prelude to a possible "large scale purge." However, he hedged any predictions by writing: "It is not possible to assess the full political significance of his arrest."[98] Secretary of State Dulles considered Beria to be the "leader and symbol of the police state" and termed his arrest to be part of a "new convulsion."[99] Years later in his memoir, Bohlen stated that he did not believe that Beria's arrest would set off such a "convulsion."[100]

Beria's arrest was widely covered in the American press, including an insightful article by C. I. Sulzberger in the *New York Times* that compared Beria's downfall to that of Yagoda in the 1930s. He considered the arrest to be as yet another mystery about the direction of post-Stalinist Soviet policies.[101] In a cover story entitled "Purge of the Purger," *Time* chronicled the events that led to his arrest and his career, termed him to be Stalin's "sycophant," recalled the similar fates of his predecessors, and speculated that his arrest was part of a power struggle.[102] *Life* published an article by Soviet defector Alexander Orlov that chronicled Beria's career in unflattering terms, also labeling him to be a sycophant and showing Orlov's bias against Stalin's "Georgian cruelty and intrigue."[103]

The announcement of Beria's arrest coincided with a meeting of Western foreign ministers in Washington, DC. According to the *New Yorker*, the arrest was a leading topic of discussion at this meeting with no clear understanding as to whether it would be helpful or detrimental ("either gain or disaster") in the Cold War.[104] Isaac Deutscher published an article in *The Reporter* in which he considered Beria's removal an "incident of personal rivalry." Deutscher asserted that Beria's name was "associated with the darkest aspects of Stalinism in the last fifteen years" and labeled the charges to be an "amalgam of the Stalinist purges of the 1930s." Deutscher also reported that Malenkov had the support of the Soviet Army in removing Beria.[105]

Both liberal weeklies *The Nation* and *New Republic* reported on Beria's arrest. An article by Alexander Werth in *The Nation* chronicled recent liberalizing policies, unrest in East Germany and Hungary, and opined that Kremlin hardliners wanted to turn away from these reforms. Werth also wondered if Beria's arrest would lead to a "vast purge."[106] In an editorial written in a scolding tone, *The Nation* criticized the Department of State's seeming rush to judgment and mixed pronouncements on Beria's arrest during the meeting of Western foreign ministers.[107] *New Republic* published an editorial that was critical of the Soviet leadership, claiming that the "Soviet state must be weakened" and "overextended."[108] In the same issue, an article disparaged the accusations made against Beria but called him the "executioner of thousands" while crediting him with repudiating the "final excesses of Stalin's regime." Such reported repudiations made him a target of hardliners like Malenkov.[109] In an article in *Foreign Affairs*, dissident Communist Bertram D. Wolfe asserted that "Beria seemed to be on his way out at the moment of Stalin's death," doomed because of the resentment of the secret police and because the Soviets did not want another Georgian in power over Russians.[110]

The American Communist press dutifully repeated the Kremlin's charges against Beria. *Daily Worker* published an editorial, which applauded "exposing Beria" as the show trials of the 1930s had exposed Trotsky and Bukharin.[111] *New World Review* published an article in August 1953 that claimed that collective leadership would save the day, quoted extensively from the *Pravda* editorial on Beria's alleged crimes, and drew parallels to the show trials of the 1930s.[112] The Trotskyist *New International* chronicled Beria's last years in power, the "clash of personalities" within the regime, and predicted that Beria's arrest was the first "bitter fruit" of the new Kremlin leadership. The author also speculated that the Army's backing of Beria's removal gave them influence in preventing another military purge similar to the purge of officers in the 1930s.[113]

The second phase of American reactions came in December 1953 when the Soviet government announced that Beria and his associates had been tried in a closed trial before a Special Judicial Commission. They were tried under Article

58 of the Russian Criminal Code ("high treason"), the same law that had been used to try the Old Bolsheviks, were found guilty, and were executed. Ambassador Bohlen sent a communiqué in which he stated that the announcement of the verdict and executions "brought no surprises" and that Beria's downfall was due to the decision "to subordinate police to party." He also reported that Beria's "final liquidation . . . has been greeted by complete indifference and possibly secret pleasure by [the] Soviet population" without the "*signs of anxiety or apprehension which accompanied similar phenomena during Stalinist purges in Thirty's*" [Italics added.] Bohlen considered the case against Beria to be a "definitely half-hearted attempt" and speculated that the current leaders may not have wanted the populace to believe the charges against Beria due to their close association with him. Again recalling the purges in the 1930s and showing his own hardline attitude toward Stalin, Bohlen ended this communiqué with the following: "It would have been more fitting if retribution had been meted out by his victims rather than his accomplices. . . . Entire proceedings go to confirm [the] obvious fact that Stalin's successors have no greater semblance of morality or regard for truth than had Stalin himself."[114]

The Central Intelligence Agency produced a working paper on the purge of Beria in 1954. The report stated that the indictment charged that he had been in league with British intelligence since 1920. This was the same tactic used in the show trials to paint the Old Bolsheviks as foreign agents of Germany as far back as 1918. The author wrote that the charges against him included the charge that he had "waged a criminal campaign" against "Sergo" Ordzhonikidze, the People's Commissar for Heavy Industry who died in 1937 under mysterious circumstances, later termed to be suicide. The author concluded that this purge was "limited in scope and mild in its consequences." The author noted that there had been little propaganda surrounding the trial, unlike the "intensive, sustained propaganda campaign" at the beginning of the Doctors' Plot because "important officials" who had cooperated with Beria in the past may have wanted the "Beria case forgotten."[115]

The *New York Times* seemed prescient in predicting Beria's fate. A 1949 article in the *New York Times Magazine* anticipated the elements of any future purge by outlining the Communist script of trying a group of defendants together, waiting several months between arrest and trial, using propaganda to turn the public against the accused, and using vaguely drafted laws to convict them.[116] Another *New York Times Magazine* article by Godfrey Blunden reconstructed the trial of former NKVD head Gengrik Yagoda and predicted the same fate for Beria through an imagined interrogation session in which Beria ended up weeping and begging for mercy. Blunden concluded that the purpose of the purge of Beria was for the Communist Party to "show a strong ruling hand."[117]

Beria's trial and execution were front-page news. The *New York Times* published the text of the indictment and the verdict.[118] Two *New York Times* articles analyzed the trial with one reporter considering this trial to be the most important since the 1930s and to be a sign of the elimination of Georgians from high positions in state security, a theory that echoed other writers' opinions.[119] Also at this time, Nikita Khrushchev's name began to be mentioned in the campaign to discredit Beria.[120] The *New York Times* published additional articles on the repercussions of the fall of Beria and his associates, including later executions in Soviet Georgia in 1954 and 1955.[121] In an extensive article by Harrison Salisbury on the events surrounding Beria's arrest, he concluded that Beria was removed because he "had too much military power" in the "unstable coalition of party, police and Army."[122]

I. F. Stone's Weekly published a cynical article on the charges against Beria and considered his execution to be a "setback for the hopes of a more moderate regime."[123] Isaac Deutscher wrote a thoughtful article in *The Reporter* in which he concluded that Beria's downfall was part of a "personal rivalry" and gave examples of Beria's actions dating back to the Civil War that led to his purge. Deutscher also termed the trial to be a "political tribunal par excellence" that consisted of military men and Party "second-raters" as judges. He contrasted this trial to the show trials of the 1930s in that Beria did not have to confess to assassination or wrecking. While the announcement of his arrest led to nationwide meetings in the Soviet Union to denounce him as had been done to the Old Bolsheviks, there was a lack of public confessions and public demonstrations during the trial. Deutscher considered this trial to be part of a power struggle between the Party and the secret police.[124] An editorial in *New Republic* saw the trial as no surprise with the same tired charges, and the editorialist surmised that the trial indicated a rise in the power of the Army and a decline of the secret police.[125]

Daily Worker dutifully followed the Soviet line as it had in the 1930s and published excerpts from the indictment and verdict and reported the executions of the "traitor" Beria and his aides.[126] Perhaps the last word on Beria's downfall came from one of the people who danced on his grave. In 1957 Bertram D. Wolfe published an account in which Khrushchev claimed that the Presidium decided to shoot Beria even before they had "received sufficient and irrefutable evidence of his guilt."[127] Beria's downfall was among the last public uses of the tactics of the 1930s. Beria continues to be the object of scholarly study.[128]

Conclusion

Even though the Moscow show trials had ended in 1938, events during this period revived interest in these trials. Radical political parties in the United States suffered and declined under the anticommunist atmosphere in the 1940s and early 1950s. The Doctors' Plot, the death of Stalin, and the purge of Beria were causes of extensive analyses by the US government during the early stages of the Cold War. However, these events did not prepare the government or the radical political parties for the bombshells that were to come—Nikita Khrushchev's "secret speech" denouncing Stalin and signaling the start of destalinization.

Plate 9.1 Nikita Khrushchev and Joseph Stalin in 1936 when Khrushchev was a rising star in the Communist Party. "Joseph Stalin and Nikita Khrushchev, 1936." Wikimedia Commons, January 1936, http://commons.wikimedia.org (accessed July 7, 2022).

Plate 9.2 The Twentieth Party Congress of the Communist Party of the Soviet Union, 1956, where Nikita Khrushchev denounced Joseph Stalin. "20th Party Congress." Wikimedia Commons, February 1956, http://commons.wikimedia.org (accessed July 7, 2022).

9

The Aftermath of the Moscow Show Trials
Part II—1956 to the Present

Introduction

This chapter discusses Nikita Khrushchev's famous "secret speech" of 1956 and the ensuing destalinization, the effects of destalinization on American radicals, liberals, and intellectuals, and the discrediting of the reporting of *New York Times* Moscow correspondent Walter Duranty.

Nikita Khrushchev's Secret Speech and Destalinization

Georgi Malenkov's time in power would be short-lived with the rise of Nikita Khrushchev. Khrushchev had come to the attention of the United States in the 1930s when he was mentioned as a member of Politburo in the "List of Persons" in *Foreign Relations of the United States: The Soviet Union, 1933-1939*.[1] In 1953 the CIA considered him to be one of the possible successors to Stalin, writing: "Various biographical appraisals of Khrushchev stressed his ability to hew a center line, his opportunism and his blind obedience to Stalin; yet such appraisals are common to most Soviet leaders."[2]

In February 1956 the Soviets held their Twentieth Communist Party Congress, the first Congress since Stalin's death. As reported by *New York Times* correspondent Harrison E. Salisbury, open sessions of the Party Congress mentioned Stalin far fewer times than during the 1952 Congress. During the open sessions Party leaders, including Deputy Party Secretary Anastas I. Mikoyan, expressed different opinions from 1952 and made numerous "slurring references" to the cult of personality by praising collective leadership and criticizing Stalinist-era economic and foreign policies. Mikoyan also discussed Lenin's "Last Testament" in which Lenin expressed his doubts about Stalin.[3]

Mikoyan's speech was the warm-up act to the shocker that was to come. On the evening of February 24–25, 1956, Nikita Khrushchev delivered one of the biggest bombshells of the twentieth century in a lengthy speech to a closed session of the Congress. The speech was entitled "On the Cult of Personality and Its Consequences," which also came to be known as the "secret speech" in which Khrushchev condemned Stalin's one-man rule over the Communist Party and over the Soviet Union. This speech began by praising Lenin and quoted Lenin's various criticisms of Stalin, including Lenin's "Last Testament" in which he had warned against Stalin. Khrushchev condemned the elevation of one person to power as antithetical to the Marxist-Leninist principle of collective party leadership, condemned the purges of the members of the Central Committee elected at the Seventeenth Party Congress in 1934 as one of "mass acts of abuse," and enumerated the injustices of the purges and the deaths of innocent purge victims. He also blamed Stalin for the purges of the armed forces and for the military setbacks that occurred at the beginning of the Second World War (the "Great Patriotic War"). He also criticized Stalin's postwar rule, discredited the Doctors' Plot, and condemned Lavrenti Beria as an enemy of the people. Khrushchev cited Stalin's official biography that was published in 1948 as an example of his "self-glorification."[4] Party leadership still dictated official policy on June 30, 1956, when the Central Committee followed up on the secret speech by passing a resolution "On Overcoming the Cult of the Individual and Its Consequences" which approved the Twentieth Party Congress, listed Stalin's achievements and "errors," and pledged to work with foreign communist parties for the "flourishing of socialist democracy."[5]

Destalinization began after Khrushchev's speech, and amnesty was slowly extended to the survivors of the purges still in prison, in the Gulag or in internal exile. This began the official exposure of the horrors of the arrests, interrogations, imprisonments, and executions. The reputations of most of the defendants in the show trials were slowly rehabilitated, thus repudiating the trial verdicts.

Official US Reactions

While Harrison Salisbury may have suspected something was up in the open sessions of the Party Congress, the secret speech was a complete surprise to the American diplomatic establishment. The lack of official preparedness for this drastic change in the Soviet government's attitude toward Stalin was reflected in a memorandum from the US Information Agency, dated February 8, 1956 (prior to the speech), which stated the following: "The 20th Party Congress *will probably not bring any surprises on policy issues.* . . . *It is not in our interest to give the 20th Party Congress undue public attention.*"[6] [Italics added.]

When news of the secret speech leaked out, the Department of State went into overdrive, started a round of meetings, and issued a spate of communiqués and memoranda based on rumors and fragments of the speech that they were able to obtain. Official American reactions can be divided into two categories: getting an authenticated copy of the speech and analyzing the speech in terms of its meaning for the Soviet leadership and for future Soviet internal and external policies. This analysis also included the possible effects of the speech on Soviet satellites and foreign communist parties and how to exploit the speech to the West's advantage during the Cold War, such as fomenting dissent in Eastern European satellites and stopping the spread of communism elsewhere.

While still attempting to obtain an authenticated copy of the speech, a Department of State Intelligence report on March 6, 1956, stated that "The first public criticism of Stalin by his successors stands out as the highlight and main innovation of the Twentieth Congress," that "Stalin's stature has been progressively reduced," and that the "Soviet rulers are rewriting history and rehabilitating some of Stalin's victims." The authors portrayed what they knew about the speech as a criticism of one-man rule and as an effort to "underscore the virtue claimed for collective leadership."[7]

Ambassador Charles E. "Chip" Bohlen first heard about a copy of the speech being available while he was at a reception at the French Embassy on March 10, 1956, when a Western reporter told him that Marshal Josip Tito of Yugoslavia had received a "detailed summary" of the speech.[8] The US government began a drive to get an authenticated copy. The circumstances under which the US government got a copy have been a matter of dispute. According to the Department of State's Office of the Historian, Israeli intelligence agents delivered a copy of the speech to the US Central Intelligence Agency (CIA).[9] However, in 1976 James Angleton, head of CIA Special Operations and Counterintelligence, stated that the CIA received a copy from a "European Communist" and did not mention Israel as a go-between.[10] Vetting the authenticity of the speech, deciding whether and how to make it public and any official reactions were continuing topics of discussion between Bohlen, the CIA, and the Department of State.[11]

On March 22, 1956, the speech's importance was highlighted in a meeting of the National Security Council where CIA Director Allen Dulles described the speech as a "plain attempt to blast Stalin to pieces" while admitting that "no one knew precisely what had transpired at this meeting." Director Dulles also gave his impressions as to why Khrushchev "had deliberately undertaken in his speech to destroy Stalin, because he had cited chapter and verse on all of Stalin's crimes." Director Dulles's reasons for Khrushchev's speech included the "Communist penchant for self-criticism" and the "hope of the Soviet leaders to gain respectability aboard [sic]." Dulles also surmised that other reasons may be "Khrushchev's exuberant personality" or the "possibility . . . that Khrushchev had been drunk." He concluded that "Khrushchev and the other leaders had been guilty of a most serious mistake." In terms of the effects of the speech on US policy, both Director Dulles and President Eisenhower agreed that "these events would be definitely advantageous for the United States."[12]

The official meetings, memoranda, and briefings continued unabated. "The Desecration of Stalin," a long Department of State brief by the Office of Intelligence Research, analyzed the risks that the Soviet leadership took in publicly attacking Stalin and the Soviet leadership's cautious approach. It listed Khrushchev's charges against him and listed possible motives for this attack. The authors considered the impact of Khrushchev's speech on the "psychological effect on Party members at home and abroad" after the "sudden effort to eradicate a quarter century of indoctrination." They considered the speech to be a risk that Soviet leaders were willing to take but were moving "with some degree of caution." The authors gleaned from other Communist sources a list of the charges against Stalin. Among the brief's "errors" and "excesses" relating to the show trials were the following:

- Illegal use of the police and resultant excesses, including unjustified repression even of fellow Communists;
- Self-adulation, fabrication, and distortion of Soviet history and unjust maligning of veteran Communists;
- Unjustly liquidating a large number of Soviet military officers.

The authors gave these possible motives for this attack on Stalin: to besmirch one-man rule, to portray the current leadership as more reasonable, to undercut the position of Stalinists and to smear Stalin's reputation. The authors concluded that the Party leaders "have attempted to operate a totalitarian state without a single dictator and to refute the paralyzing sanctions of Stalin's rule."[13]

The Department of State established an Ad Hoc Committee on (the) Anti-Stalin Campaign under the Department's Operations Coordinating Board. This Committee met frequently to discuss the latest developments, examine editorials in Soviet publications, and make recommendations for future actions. The Committee urged caution to avoid seeming to be "gloating over their present embarrassment," but to try to "promote the destruction of communist credibility" and to create confusion in foreign communist parties.[14]

Embassy secretary Walter Newbold Walmsley, Jr., sent a long, thoughtful telegram on April 9, 1956, that, among its general impressions and cautious predictions, included assertions that the new leadership was laying the blame on Stalin, not on the Party, for "specific errors," thus both destroying the "myth of Stalinist infallibility and invulnerability" and giving the party "legality, morality and omniscience." He surmised that "professional military pride" was "deeply injured by the purges and by Stalin's assumption of credit for winning [the] war," and that the Party members, the bureaucracy, and "professional classes" who had rapidly advanced during the purges had developed vested interests in "privileges and positions."[15] Walmsley sent another communiqué on April 11 which outlined his conclusions, based on official Soviet sources. He wrote that among the goals of the new leadership were: reinvigorating the Party, disassociating themselves from "acts of Stalin," "repudiating certain acts of Stalinism," and removing the "onus which brutalities [of] Stalinism placed on [the] party." He added that the Party leadership also wanted to assure the populace that "police terror as it existed under Stalin is [a] thing of past." Walmsley also listed the risks that the Party leadership was taking, including "encouraging freedom [of] thought, expression beyond intended limits" and the fact that members of the Presidium were "Stalin's creatures and tools," thus making themselves vulnerable.[16]

In April 1956 Ambassador Bohlen gave a briefing on the reasons for the denigration of Stalin, the timing of Khrushchev's speech, and the effects of the speech on Soviet foreign policy. As a rationale for the secret speech, he cited the new leaders' need to establish collective leadership.[17]

Meanwhile, top US government officials began making official statements and giving public addresses on the secret speech. Deputy Undersecretary of State Robert Daniel Murphy gave an address at George Washington University in which he listed a catalog of Stalin's evil policies and stated that Stalin was "a few short years ago the demigod, the physical and spiritual ruler of all the Russians." Murphy stated that Stalin apparently has now become an "outcast, a pariah" because of his "arbitrariness in law enforcement" and that the purge of Beria "brought the police under firmer party control."[18] Secretary of State John Foster Dulles held a news conference on the significance of the secret speech without mentioning Khrushchev's name. He stated that the secret speech unmasked "the brutal and arbitrary rule of the Stalin era."[19]

CIA Director Dulles made a hard-hitting speech entitled "The Purge of Stalinism" at a meeting of the Los Angeles World Affairs Council. Dulles had little good to say about the Soviets' current leadership who "sat acquiescent in the seats of the mighty during all the period of Stalin's dictatorship" when the "price of non-conformity was a bullet in the head." Dulles stated the following about Stalin's purge of the military leadership: "He deliberately liquidated Marshal Tukhachevsky and thousands of his best officers in the Soviet Army, presumably to insure [sic] his political control of the military apparatus."[20] Deputy Undersecretary Murphy gave another speech to the American Society of Newspaper Editors in which he referred to the end of the "traditional worshipful reverence" of Stalin and to the start of a "campaign of defamation" against him. Murphy assumed that they had denounced Stalin after "careful and calculated preparation" and stated that the death of Beria and the rehabilitation of the reputations of purge victims "indicate deep subsurface disturbances" and a "radical transition to group dictatorship."[21]

The US government reports and memoranda kept coming. In contrast to the general impressions and cautious predictions in Department of State documents, CIA Deputy Director of Plans Frank C. Wisner sent a bluntly worded memorandum to CIA Director Dulles. This memorandum was identified as the "Views of a Leading Expert on Soviet Affairs;" later identified as George F. Kennan. Kennan did not make vague predictions or accept the premise that the new leaders were acting in harmony with a well-conceived plan. Kennan posed a hypothesis that "members of the present leading group" (with the exceptions of Molotov and Malenkov) were responsible for Stalin's death and had kept that fact quiet. Their plan was to "reduce his stature in the public eye" and to reveal "gradually and discreetly—the true frightfulness of Stalin's personality" in order to be able to justify the killing of a "semi-mad villain," if such a truth about Stalin's death ever became known. Kennan also believed that Lavrenti Beria had been purged because he knew of their complicity in Stalin's death. Wisner added that the belief that Stalin was murdered was held by other commentators on the Stalinist era.[22] The possibility that Stalin had been murdered was raised by Moscow correspondent Harrison E. Salisbury in the *New York Times* in 1954. Salisbury claimed that Stalin was on the brink of a new reign of terror worse than that of the 1930s and was killed by his inner circle who feared that they would be among the victims.[23]

The Department of State's Ad Hoc Committee became the Operations Coordinating Board's Special Working Group on Stalinism and held a meeting on May 17, 1956, to discuss the "exploitation of the anti-Stalin campaign." The

Working Group recommended making propaganda on the following aspects of the purges:

- Only a few of Stalin's victims have been rehabilitated to date;
- The Soviet Government has confirmed Western accusations of many years standing;
- Communist leaders have admitted that Soviet policies under Stalin involved "excessive costs."

The authors also stated that the motivations for the "anti-Stalin campaign" included a desire by Soviet leaders "to confirm their own positions by a dramatic break with the past" and a desire to "gain greater freedom of action" by emphasizing coexistence.[24]

Ambassador Bohlen met a rather subdued Khrushchev at a Kremlin reception in June 1956 and mentioned the "special speech." Khrushchev started to deny the speech but then stated that circulated versions were inaccurate.[25] Bohlen's belief in the importance of the speech was illustrated by the fact that in his memoir he devoted an entire chapter to "Khrushchev's Secret Speech." He summed up the speech as unmasking Stalin as the "instigator of the terror of the 1930s," among other accusations. Bohlen also noted that Khrushchev did not explain his own involvement with Stalin.[26]

The Department of State finally released what was considered to be an authenticated copy of the speech by leaking it to the *New York Times* in June 1956.[27] Then Secretary Dulles left diplomacy behind and went into full cold-warrior mode in a speech to the Kiwanis International convention in San Francisco. He bluntly condemned the Soviet system and summarized Khrushchev's accusations against Stalin as follows:

> Stalin, to satisfy his sadistic lusts, constantly invoked torture to procure false confessions which were then made the basis of judicial murder. He directed long tortures and habitually himself called the investigative judge, gave him instructions, advised him on which investigative methods should be used; these methods were simple—beat, beat, and once again, beat. . . . Mr. Khrushchev's speech portrays a loathsome scene. The speech cannot be read without horror and revulsion.[28]

Still guessing as to what it all meant, the National Security Council had a conjecture-filled meeting on June 28, 1956, to discuss the impact of the secret speech on Eastern Europe and on Western Communist parties. Secretary Dulles contended that the Kremlin leadership never intended the speech to have such far-reaching consequences and characterized Khrushchev as emotional and "obviously intoxicated much of the time and could be expected to commit irrational acts."[29]

The Department of State and the CIA then turned their attentions to the Central Committee's resolution on the cult of personality. The Department of State's Office of the Special Assistant for Intelligence issued a memorandum which analyzed the resolution's motives and possible impact on foreign communist parties. It termed the resolution to be "superficial, transparent, and hackneyed," having a "defensive tone, lack of frankness, and incompleteness" and blaming everything on "Stalin's vanity."[30] The CIA was still in contact with George F. Kennan who observed that this resolution harkened back to the Stalinist explanation of "capitalist encirclement" to justify his dictatorship.[31]

In a news conference Secretary Dulles referred to the Central Committee's resolution as follows: "It attempts to explain how, under the Soviet Communist system, the abuses of Stalinism were tolerated for so many years and what they say will prevent the recurrence of such abuses." Dulles expressed skepticism as he pointed out that the Soviet constitution of 1936 did not "prevent the policies of violence and the massive terrorisms, tortures, enforced confessions, and judicial murders."[32]

In July 1956 the CIA paper issued a paper that summarized the effects of the secret speech on foreign communist parties and had this skeptical tone about the resolution: "There is no evidence that a plenary meeting of the Committee actually took place. The document appears to have been hastily drafted; it is repetitive and apologetic." The authors also were skeptical about any "deterioration" of communism and surmised that "Communist encroachment is likely to increase."[33] The CIA also wrote an analysis of the Twentieth Party Congress that did not specifically address the show trials and the purges but maintained: "Totalitarian dictatorship had to be justified by alleging the necessity for an unending struggle against the 'class enemy' within and 'capitalist imperialism' without." This statement echoed the Stalinist rationale of the 1930s that enemies of the state were operating within the Soviet Union and that it was the target of hostile capitalists. The authors contended that the Soviets still had the long-range goal of the triumph of communism.[34]

The House Un-American Activities Committee (HUAC) responded to the secret speech by holding a symposium at the Twentieth Party Congress on May 19, 1956. Entitled *The Great Pretense*, its overall themes were anti-Soviet and skepticism about any radical change in Soviet policies. The symposium was almost a class reunion of Americans who were involved with the Soviet Union in the 1930s. They included former ambassador William C. Bullitt, Jr., former Moscow correspondents William Henry Chamberlin and Eugene Lyons, former American Committee for the Defense of Leon Trotsky member Max Eastman, and former Communist journalist Louis Budenz, Boris I. Nicolaevsky, a Soviet exile and the author of the *Letter of an Old Bolshevik*, and Whittaker Chambers, the controversial ex-Soviet spy who had accused Alger Hiss of espionage, also gave statements. Outspoken, anticommunist FBI director J. Edgar Hoover gave the closing statement. The purges received only a few mentions, but a recurring theme of several of the speakers was the complicity of Khrushchev and other current Soviet leaders in the crimes that they were now denouncing.[35] Nicolaevsky specifically cited the purge of the military and cited Stalin taking credit for Soviet victories in the Second World War, stating: "If the charges against Tukhachevsky were false, then the charges against other victims of the purges must also have been false—above all, those who were condemned in the three main trials of 1936-38."[36]

Problems of Communism, a journal of the US Information Agency for foreign consumption, but also distributed in the United States, published a series of articles on the Twentieth Party Congress and on the secret speech, occasionally relying on foreign observers for articles critical of the Moscow show trials and critical of the new Soviet leadership. This series began in March 1956 with a skeptical commentary on Stalin's "virtual dethronement" and "bleak legacy," as hinted at in the open sessions of the Congress. Abraham Brumberg, the journal's founding editor, echoed the theme that Stalin's denouncers had once been his accomplices: "Those who are now burying Stalin are those who brought him to power, who—though exposed to Stalin's paranoiac wrath—were also the beneficiaries of his exalted status . . . those who had, in the course of the past quarter of a century, taken the place of the men who made the revolution and then fell victim to it."[37]

A longer article in July 1956 was a summary of Stalin's crimes, and the author claimed that Khrushchev's accusations echoed the "more lurid efforts of the extreme anti-Communist school." The author referred to the purges as: "Stalin's dictatorship by terror, of mass injustice, of the execution of thousands of innocents, of cringing judges and confessions extorted by torture to crimes that were never committed, of the distortion of history, of the paralyzing rule of fear—all of it smothered under choking clouds of servile adulation." The author rejected any pleas of ignorance by the new leadership as he claimed that they "saw their colleagues, their superiors, and their subordinates fall by the thousand" and that with the new collective leadership came "collective guilt."

The author also blamed the communist system for allowing such excesses to occur and surmised that a regime of "controlled relaxation" of previous Soviet policies was being implemented.[38]

British Trotskyist Hugo Dewar had written a damning indictment of the Moscow show trials in his 1953 work *The Modern Inquisition*.[39] He published a scholarly article in *Problems of Communism* in 1957 in which he criticized the current Soviet leadership for not being able to "make a decisive, radical break with their Stalinist past." Dewar traced the history of the show trials back to the 1922 trial of leaders of the Socialist Revolutionists and to other earlier trials. Dewar cited Stalin's speech to the Sixteenth Party Congress in 1930 as providing the rationale for the trials by blaming foreign countries who allegedly worked with the Old Bolsheviks to turn on the Soviet government. Dewar wrote: "The Great Purge . . . served the double purpose of removing those who opposed Stalin and of providing for the population an 'explanation' of the continuing low standard of living." Dewar surmised that Khrushchev and the surviving Kremlin leaders were trying to revitalize the Party and that the postwar show trials in Eastern Europe echoed the damage done by the Moscow show trials by depriving those countries of their "ablest leaders." The trials also "failed dismally to destroy" nationalism, and they enhanced "anti-Soviet feeling." He termed Khrushchev's speech to be a "masterpiece of hypocrisy" as he and other Soviet leaders had known that the confessions were false and that the "trials were frame-ups." In his opinion Khrushchev's speech was an attempt to revitalize the Party and to assure the new generation that the "days of arbitrary terror were over."[40]

Problems of Communism did not let up on its coverage of the secret speech. It published "Terror in the Soviet System: Trends and Portents" by former communist Wolfgang Leonhard who had been a German refugee from Hitler and who had lived in the Soviet Union. He surmised that the new Kremlin leadership wanted to move away from an anticipated new "Stalinist reign of terror" that had put themselves in jeopardy during the last months of Stalin's life. Leonhard analyzed Khrushchev's denunciations of the terror under Stalin as efforts to bring the secret police under Party control. Leonhard also analyzed the show trials, the purge of Beria and the reforms in the Gulag.[41] In keeping with its anticommunist objectives, *Problems of Communism* continued publishing articles on the results of the secret speech into the 1960s. Leopold Labedz, a Senior Fellow of the Russian Institute at Columbia University, wrote on the tangled political aspects of destalinization and the "furtive" and "selective" rehabilitation of purge victims, including show trial defendants and purged military leaders. He echoed the charge that the current leaders had benefited from Stalin's crimes.[42]

Reactions of American Journalists

Mainstream American public reaction to the secret speech also came in two phases—discussions of the rumored contents of the speech in and after March 1956 and the release of the "official" version by the US government in June. *New York Times* correspondent Harrison Salisbury gave a front-page account of the rumors circulating in Moscow around the speech, emphasizing the injustices of the Army trial.[43] The *New York Times* began reporting on destalinization, including the rehabilitation of purge victims with the inclusion of their biographical entries in the *Great Soviet Encyclopedia*; this included the rehabilitation of the reputations of the purged Army leaders.[44] The *New York Times* followed up with an editorial that bashed the Soviet legal system and bashed the late State Prosecutor Andrei Vyshinsky for the use of false confessions, citing Arthur Koestler's novel *Darkness at Noon* to illustrate the defendants' hopes of sparing themselves and their families or their hopes of doing one last service for the Party.[45]

Mainstream news magazines and opinion journals began to chronicle the impact of the Twentieth Party Congress and its possible implications for Soviet leadership and policies, often joining the chorus in pointing out that the current leaders had been complicit in Stalin's crimes while now destroying the myths surrounding him. When rumors about the speech surfaced in March, *Time* published an eyewitness account of the closed session of the Party Congress in which the reporter, obviously no fan of Khrushchev, portrayed him as sometimes breaking into tears as he recounted Stalin's crimes and leaving a "profound hush" over the hall when he finished. The reporter reasoned that Khrushchev's motive was to absolve the present leaders of guilt. The reporter criticized Khrushchev for only condemning the purges of Party members and called Khrushchev as "merciless" as Stalin in his "downgrading" of Malenkov and his firing of Molotov. The reporter cited the difficulties in starting destalinization, both in the Soviet Union and among foreign Communist parties.[46] The second and third articles discussed the reactions of foreign communists as "angry and confused" about Khrushchev's "weeping and wailing" Time reported that Eastern European Party leaders who had been purged by Stalin had their reputations restored.[47,48]

At the same time, *Newsweek* published two articles on the denunciations in the secret speech, citing Stalin's "decimating party leadership to satisfy his own lust for power" and on the killing of the Stalinist myth.[49,50] *U.S. News & World Report* considered the secret speech to be a major news story and published two feature articles in its March 30, 1956, issue. The first was a summary of foreign reactions to the speech by the "impetuous Khrushchev," highlighted Khrushchev's accusations and listed other current Soviet leaders who were "deeply implicated in crimes committed by the late dictator."[51] The second article was a long interview with an unnamed "expert on Soviet affairs" who stated that the Soviet leadership was taking a risk in denouncing Stalin (a "megalomaniac, a paranoiac, a murderer"), that the Army was strengthened and considered the speech to be surprising in its "thoroughness, its violence." The interviewee was cautious in drawing any conclusions and in making predictions but stated that the Soviets still had the goal of world conquest through "political and economic warfare."[52] *I. F. Stone's Weekly* had a satirical tone toward American reactions to the secret speech, bashing political columnists Joseph and Stewart Alsop, President Eisenhower, the Department of State, the FBI and the American Communist Party. The reporter claimed: "The Communists stand exposed as prize idiots abroad and prize cowards within Russia; the hierarchy knew what was going on but dared not be speak up. When Stalin growled, Khrushchev danced the *gopak*."[53] [The *gopak* is a Ukrainian folk dance.]

Reflecting the anticommunism of the 1950s, *Life* published another exposé by Soviet defector Alexander Orlov. He related a tangled tale of the NKVD's discovery that Stalin had been an *agent provocateur* in the Okhrana (the czarist secret police) and that the Army had been involved in a plot to stage a *coup d'état* to oust him. Orlov asserted that the Army trial was held to eliminate anyone who knew about Stalin's past and asserted that Khrushchev chose to blacken Stalin's reputation before "Stalin's guiltiest secret" was exposed.[54] A companion article vouched for the authenticity of Stalin being an Okhrana agent.[55] The *Saturday Evening Post* published a brief editorial which harkened back to the Red Scare of the 1920s by listing the following alleged Soviet misdeeds on American soil: the killings of Walter Krivitsky and Carlo Tresca, the setting up of "Red cells in the Federal bureaucracy" and Communists influencing "many idealistic young people."[56]

The liberal weeklies *The Nation* and *New Republic* editorialized on the secret speech. A *New Republic* editorial reported that thirty delegates fainted during the speech, surmised that Khrushchev wanted to give the delegates a "shock treatment" to break with the past, and concluded that it was gratifying to see the myth of Stalin being destroyed.[57] *The Nation* published a major article by journalist Mark Gayn who called Stalin "spy-happy." In Gayn's opinion, while the Soviet Union had been transformed by industrialization and by more education, Stalin's rule had led to stagnation and decay within the Party. He concluded that the Soviets were only changing their methods, not their doctrine and that the anti-Stalin campaign was proceeding cautiously.[58] [In 1944 the Federal Bureau of Investigation (FBI) suspected that Gayn had been a Soviet spy.[59]] *The Nation* also took the opportunity to publicly scold other journalists in an editorial that called American press reporting on the speech "uniformly banal and unimaginative" and concluded that the speech was to end the myth of "infallibility in Soviet-satellite relationships."[60]

The liberal journal *Dissent* reprinted an article by Richard Lowenthal which had been originally published in the Anglo-American journal *Encounter* in May 1956. [*Encounter* was covertly supported by the CIA.] Lowenthal was a former German Communist and called the purges "covered by a slimy flood of lies and forgeries" and called Khrushchev "Stalin's representative during the Ukrainian purges." He characterized the reforms before the secret speech as efforts to "make peace with the Russian people" and claimed that the purpose of the speech and recent reforms was to "save the Party dictatorship." He asserted that the speech made the present Kremlin leadership "helpless tools" of Stalin's crimes. Lowenthal wrote that economic progress would be the proof of the success of destalinization, progress that Lowenthal deemed feasible only through the establishment of a market economy and through the end of central planning.[61] *Encounter* also published "After Stalin . . . A Symposium" which included a theory-filled article by literary critic Dwight Macdonald, a former member of the American Committee for the Defense of Leon Trotsky. He claimed to be surprised by the sudden turn of events in the Soviet Union and cited theories, including those of philosopher Hannah Arendt and the Trotskyists, that these events harkened back to the aftermath of the French Revolution when factions turned on each other. He wondered if the denunciation of Stalin and the ensuing reforms were only a temporary retreat as the Party and secret police still held power and wondered whether another Great Leader like Stalin would emerge.[62] [Macdonald later claimed that he had no knowledge of the CIA's covert support of *Encounter*.]

When the US government leaked a transcript of the speech to the *New York Times* in June, another spate of articles appeared in the American press. Many had the theme that the current Soviet leadership had been complicit in Stalin's crimes and questioned whether these revelations would lead to the lessening of the one-party dictatorship. Harrison E. Salisbury wrote a detailed analysis of the speech that was front-page news. He reported that Khrushchev had painted a horrific picture of Stalin as a "savage, half-mad, power-crazed despot" with "phobias" and "plots, counter-plots and intrigue" from which no one was safe. Khrushchev charged that Stalin's rule was "based on terror, torture and brute force" and that Stalin was about to embark on another purge of older Party leaders. Salisbury also reported that Khrushchev highlighted the false charges against the Army and in the "Leningrad case," a purge held in 1949. He also cited Stalin's use of the false charge of Trotskyism to purge Lev Kamenev and Grigori Zinoviev, the forced confessions, the mass deportations, and the Doctors' Plot. Salisbury also believed that the released text was an edited version of the speech.[63]

Washington-based columnist James Reston reported that "Washington is having a field day" with a "major propaganda offensive" against the Soviet regime, that "Soviet experts" pondered whether the new Soviet government was indeed allowing more dissent and pondered whether the US government was placing "so much emphasis on the theme that the new leaders were still carrying on the same old Stalinist system."[64] Soviet expert and *New York Times* editorial writer Harry Schwartz carried on the theme that Khrushchev, Marshal Klimenti Voroshilov, and Georgi Malenkov were complicit in Stalin's crimes.[65] A *New York Times* editorial reeked of suspicion and condemnation of the "present Soviet rulers as continuing their dictatorship."[66]

The news magazines maintained their anticommunist perspectives when reporting on the transcript. *Time* published two articles that included excerpts from the speech, the impact of the speech on European communist parties and critical comments about Khrushchev, calling him as "merciless as his old instructor."[67,68] *Newsweek* also published an article after the speech was leaked.[69] *U.S. News & World Report* published a May 1956 speech that former ambassador George F. Kennan gave to the World Affairs Forum of Pittsburgh and also published a response to Kennan's speech by former ambassador William C. Bullitt. They disagreed on the future of US foreign policy in light of changes in the Soviet Union. Kennan had a cautiously optimistic view of the changes and their potential effects on foreign affairs. He did not mention the purges or the show trials, but he condemned the harsh regimes in satellite countries. Bullitt was in cold-warrior mode and made dismissive remarks about Kennan and his theories in a pessimistic essay that called the new Soviet leadership "Kremlin gangsters" who wanted to shift the blame for all of the country's problems to Stalin and also aimed to "weaken the Western world." Bullitt was also dismissive of Kennan's previous foreign policy proposals and concluded that the United States should not "cringe or appease or submit" to Moscow.[70]

U. S. News & World Report also published *Soviet Crimes and Khrushchev's Confessions* by Chester S. Williams of the anticommunist Freedom House in New York City. This report was an indictment of Soviet crimes going back to 1918 (the "38-year criminal record of Bolshevism") and an indictment of current Soviet leaders who now blamed Stalin, Yezhov, and Beria when they themselves were Stalin's accomplices. Williams dissected the secret speech's references to the Moscow show trials, the Doctors' Plot, and the purge of Beria. It listed the types of crimes committed during the purges, condemned the show trials, and claimed that Khrushchev and his cronies supported Stalin throughout his rule. As an example of Khrushchev's complicity, Williams cited a speech that Khrushchev gave at a workers' rally in 1937 in which he denounced the defendants in the second show trial as traitors, spies, and fascist agents.[71]

Life editorialized that the speech was a "devastating indictment of communism" and condemned communism for allowing such a tyrant to rule. The editorialist also labeled the current Kremlin leaders as "arrant cowards, faceless men without spunk or spirit" and as "lackeys and lickspittles" as they tried to give themselves an "air of respectability." The editorial ended with a call for everyone to hold Kremlin leaders to account and for them to acknowledge that communism is the "root of their evil."[72] *Saturday Evening Post*'s short editorial cited Stalin's past affable demeanor with American diplomats and had a "don't be fooled" attitude toward any such demeanor from Khrushchev and Nikolai Bulganin whom the editorialist cited for their own past crimes and called them the "heirs of tyranny."[73] The business weekly *Barron's* published an article by Paul Wohl, a German-born associate of the deceased Soviet defector Walter Krivitsky. Wohl recounted Khrushchev's rise to power and the "systematic downgrading" of Stalin. He opined that Khrushchev and his cronies "surely weighed the implications" of their move against Stalin in terms of both foreign relations and in domestic affairs. Wohl concluded by wondering whether the Soviet Union would come out stronger or would the "whole empire" crumble with "Stalin's smouldering funeral pyre," dissolving the Soviets "weakened Communist shell."[74]

The liberal weekly *New Republic* published a thoughtful article by Soviet expert Alexander Dallin who chronicled the changes in Soviet education, law, and historiography. Dallin concentrated on the rewriting of history to downgrade Stalin and his henchmen, on the rehabilitation of the reputations of purge victims and on softened references to the West. He wondered how far the new regime would allow this revisionism to continue.[75] Isaac Deutscher wrote a thoughtful article in *The Reporter* in which he contended that the secret speech was rather impromptu in nature and he speculated about Khrushchev's reasons. Deutscher concentrated on Lenin's criticism of Stalin in his "Last Testament," Khrushchev's laying the blame for the purges without specific mentions of the victims in the three Moscow show trials and listed Stalin's wartime mistakes. Deutscher called Stalin a "huge, grim, whimsical, morbid monster," pondered why an entire nation bent to Stalin's will and contended that the "whole elite of the nation share in one degree or another Stalin's guilt."[76]

Soon after the release of the speech, Soviet scholar Philip E. Mosely published an article in *Foreign Affairs* on the goals of Soviet foreign policy, especially regarding its Eastern European satellites, Communist China, and Western Communist parties. He characterized the Western parties as "weak and insecure" as they jump "obediently through the hoop" of rejecting "Stalinist methods." He analyzed Khrushchev's stated policy of a more peaceful path to socialism and establishing "peace blocs" instead of military alliances, providing economic assistance and participating in international conferences, while keeping the goal of spreading its influence and ideology.[77] The political quarterly *Dissent* published two articles on the secret speech. The first was by sociologist Lewis Coser who opined that the Party Congress speeches showed a desire for normalization and stabilization among the new Soviet generation.[78] The second article by literary critic Irving Howe maintained that, in spite of the secret speech, Russia "remains a totalitarian or authoritarian society."[79]

Current History published an article by former Department of State official Julian Towster titled "Changing Russian Politics." He analyzed the reorganization of the Communist Party with Khrushchev's new cadre of officials, the Party's new ascendency and a new "diplomatic offensive." Towster asserted that after the speech there was turmoil among Soviet students and among the literati, prompting a strong reaction from the government, and, with the removal of Marshal Georgi Zhukov, the Party exerted its control over the military. He cataloged the steps in Khrushchev's consolidation of power and his goal of strengthening Soviet power, thus creating a challenge to the West.[80]

Former Moscow correspondent William Henry Chamberlin wrote a critique of the secret speech ("high drama and some political risk") in *Russian Review* in 1962. As in other commentaries, Chamberlin criticized Khrushchev for dwelling on Stalin's crimes against Party members, omitting crimes against the Soviet populace. Chamberlin cited the rift between the Soviets and Communist China where Stalin was still revered and claimed that there was "inner-Party in-fighting" as Khrushchev tried to "stigmatize" Stalin and his loyalists such as Malenkov, Molotov, and Voroshilov. Another possible motive was to rally support from those who had suffered during the purges. Chamberlin did not let Khrushchev go blameless and cited Khrushchev, Yezhov, and Molotov for conducting purges in Ukraine in 1937. Chamberlin vilified Stalin as a "figure of blood and horror" and as an "amoral monstrous tyrant, on the same level as Ivan the Terrible." Chamberlin singled out Ambassador Joseph E. Davies as being fooled by Stalin, and he pondered why the Communist Party allowed a "bloody tyrant" to rule.[81] Chamberlin also quoted from George F. Kennan's *Russia and the West under Lenin and Stalin* in which Kennan condemned Stalin and his crimes.[82]

Mainstream coverage of the purges and the show trials continued with new revelations about the purges in the writings of Alexander Solzhenitsyn who had spent eleven years in the Gulag. The *New York Times* published excerpts from *The Gulag Archipelago, 1918-1959*, his history and indictment of the system of forced-labor camps.[83] The Moscow show trials were also revisited due to the tireless efforts of Nikolai Bukharin's widow Anna Larina, a Gulag survivor. She worked to restore her husband's reputation, and he was finally rehabilitated in 1988 when a Party Commission stated that his "admissions of guilt" were "wrung from the accused through unlawful methods." During the same year his Party membership was reinstated in an acknowledgment of the "groundless" accusations and "gross violations of socialist legality."[84] The Communist Party acknowledged in 1991 that in the first Moscow show trial the "charges were false, the confessions extracted under torture and duress."[85]

Reactions of American Radicals

As would be expected, the secret speech had an immediate, stunning impact on Western Communist parties, including the Communist Party USA.[86] The revelations of the secret speech caused great turmoil within the American Party and led to a spate of Communist publications on the speech, both for and against accepting Khrushchev's denunciation of Stalin. There were differing opinions on how to react to Stalin's crimes, thus further exacerbating internal divisions with some factions favoring Khrushchev and others defending Stalin. Before the publication of the official version of the speech, Party leaders Eugene Dennis (born Francis Xavier Waldron and pro-Khrushchev) and William Z. Foster (pro-Stalin) published their initial reactions in *Daily Worker*. Foster especially warned against "tearing Stalin to political shreds."[87] Before the officially accepted text of the secret speech was published, the Communist Party USA held a meeting of its National Committee in New York City from April 28 through May 1, 1956. Party Education Director Max Weiss gave a report on the Twentieth Party Congress that cataloged recent reforms and included a section on "The Self-Criticism and Self-Correction of the XXth Congress." While not specifically mentioning the excesses of the purges, Weiss reported on the "deep shock" and wrote:

> This was, in itself, a reflection of how profoundly we had been affected by the cult of Stalin's infallibility. It had led us to a position where we had well-nigh ruled out the possibility of Stalin making any mistakes, or at any rate any serious ones. Hence, we had also ruled out the possibility of the CPSU making such mistakes since we identified the CPSU with Stalin.[88]

Weiss went on to criticize the Soviet Party for "developing the cult of the individual" and for abandoning collective leadership. He asserted the need for the American Party to develop inner-party democracy ("democratic centralism"). Weiss acknowledged Stalin's "important contributions" but enumerated Stalin's "violations of the principles of socialist democracy and legality." These included the persecution of innocent people and accepting confessions as the sole proof of guilt. Weiss also stated that Stalin had committed the cardinal sin of departing "from certain important Leninist concepts in his later years." Weiss also called for the American Party to acknowledge its own mistakes.[89]

Dorothy Healey, a lifelong Communist and labor activist from Los Angeles, was in the audience at this meeting. In her memoir she recounted that she was totally unprepared to hear that "wretched, bloody crimes had been committed" and that the American party had denied the crimes. She left the meeting distraught and in tears.[90] According to one discontented Party member who was not ready to denounce Stalin, the National Committee meeting split into left, central, and right factions.[91] Pro-Stalinist opposition to the secret speech and to the stance of the National Committee was swift and vocal. *Turning Point*, the magazine of the dissident Communist League, published several articles denouncing the "renegade Khrushchev," defending Stalin and lamenting the turmoil within the American Party (the "Khrushock").[92]

During June, *Daily Worker* published frequently on the secret speech, including a condensed version of the speech.[93] *Daily Worker*'s editors belatedly opened their eyes to Stalin's crimes and published editorials and lengthy columns. A long front-page editorial cited Khrushchev's "shattering revelations" of the "monstrous perversion of socialist principles under Stalin's brutal rule." The editorial also criticized the Department of State's opinion that the excesses of Stalin's regime were the fault of socialism. The editorialist criticized the lack of any mention of crimes committed against Soviet Jews and admitted that the *Daily Worker*'s "blind and uncritical attitude" damaged the goal of promoting socialism in the United States. The editorialist acknowledged the US Party's past mistakes, echoed the themes of critical self-examination, and asserted the need for independent thought within the American Party but ended on a note that was echoed in other Communist publications—the pledge to continue the struggle to establish "democratic socialism" in America.[94] As if the incessant denials of Trotsky and his followers and the Dewey Commission had never happened, a subsequent editorial was a *mea culpa* that claimed that members of the *Daily Worker* staff were "wholly ignorant," did not want to believe that such crimes could happen, and regretted their "harsh" and "vindictive" treatment of Stalin's critics.[95]

Party Secretary Eugene Dennis wrote a lengthy column on "The U.S.A. and Khrushchev's Special Report." Dennis wrote that Stalin's "crimes and brutalities" were "unforgiveable" and specifically noted that nothing "justified the tortures and rigged trials." He also blamed NKVD heads Nikolai Yezhov and Lavrenti Beria for the defendants' false confessions and for the false evidence against them, calling their actions alien to socialism.[96]

When the text of the secret speech was published, the American Party's National Committee issued a statement which slammed the Department of State for using the speech to slander socialism. While the Party's statement characterized Stalin's crimes as "alien to socialism," it repeated the Stalinist rationale that the Soviet Union had been surrounded by the "hostile capitalist world" and stated that the American Party was undergoing its own version of *samokritika* as it had previously justified "many foreign and domestic policies" that have now been proven wrong.[97] *Daily Worker* published another editorial which supported the American Party's statement. The editorialist stated that socialism in the United States would now differ from Soviet socialism.[98] The *New York Times* also published a lengthy analysis of the statement and mentioned William Z. Foster's *Daily Worker* article defending Stalin.[99]

Other Communist publications also chimed in on the secret speech. Seemingly oblivious to the fact that it was still following Moscow's line by now denouncing Stalin, *New World Review* published several articles on the secret speech, calling destalinization a series of "corrections." Before the text was made public, it published an article citing Moscow correspondents' reporting and a May 28 editorial in *Pravda*. It also reported recent reforms and the criticism of Stalin's wartime leadership. In terms of the purges, it put the blame on Gengrikh

Yagoda and cited the rehabilitation of Stalin's victims. The reporter termed the treatment of the Jews "among the most dastardly of the many excesses" of Stalin's rule, cited the liberalizing of thought in the sciences, economics, and the arts and cited revelations about Stalinist crimes committed in Soviet-satellite countries. It followed the line of other Communist publications in stating that Stalin's crimes went against the principles of Marxism-Leninism and credited Lavrenti Beria's downfall as putting an end to the "violations of socialist law."[100] "More on Corrections of Stalin Era" was a second article that again quoted other news sources on reforms to the Soviet legal system that included the abolition of quick trials and executions, lessened the powers of the secret police, and claimed that the purge's "trials by confession" had framed innocent victims. This article also reported on other reforms in satellite countries.[101]

When the text was published, *New World Review*'s editor Jessica Smith wrote a long column in which she gave formulaic praise for the achievements of the Soviet Union but then lamented the "needless suffering and sacrifices" and the "system of terror." In one of the strongest criticisms to appear in a contemporaneous Communist publication, Smith harshly condemned Stalin's "injustices," "terror and torture," and bad wartime leadership. Going back to the Moscow show trials, she blamed Stalin, citing his "pathological" suspicions and "mania." She minced no words in criticizing Stalin's American defenders for their "blind support" and their denunciations of all who disagreed with Soviet policies. Smith included a universal *mea culpa* for not recognizing and condemning Stalin's crimes and for heaping "exaggerated and all-embracing" praise for Stalin and wrote that *New World Review* now deeply regretted publishing "misleading or untrue" information. However, Smith ended on a positive note by endorsing the Soviets' "policy for peace" and disarmament.[102]

New World Review published a summary of the Soviet Party's Central Committee's resolution "On Overcoming the Personality Cult and Its Consequences" in its August 1956 issue.[103] A short companion editorial supported the released text of the secret speech and endorsed the Central Committee's resolution. The reporter expressed the hope for further explanations of the "tragic events," recognized that the process of examination and correction "cannot be completed within a brief period of time," and hoped that more facts would be forthcoming, especially about the recent persecution of the Jews in Poland.[104] *New World Review* published an article by former *New York Times* correspondent Ralph Parker on his recent visit to the Soviet Union. Parker described the reactions of Muscovites to the secret speech, noticed less "top down" management, and reported on the reforms to the penal code that were meant to curb the excesses of the 1930s. He wrote that these reforms were to prevent "Beria's methods of faking 'plots' to maintain the reputation of the secret police in the dictator's eyes," thus putting blame on Beria again.[105]

In September 1956 the American Party's National Committee submitted a *Draft Resolution* for the upcoming national Party convention. This was a compromise document that began with an apologetic introduction by Eugene Dennis who followed the Soviet Party's practice of self-criticism by acknowledging several failings of the National Committee; Dennis also referred to dissenting votes from this proposed resolution. In a section entitled "The Communist Party—Independent Party of American Workers," the Party leadership tacitly acknowledged the error of decades of obedience to Moscow by proclaiming itself to now be an "independent party of American workers." This section included a statement of recognition that "over the years it held certain wrong and oversimplified concepts" in its relationship "to other Marxist parties" [i.e., Moscow]. Without mentioning Stalin's name, the *Draft Resolution* stated that the Party "was entirely unprepared and deeply shocked by the admission of crimes, violations of socialist justice." This section ended with a call for allowing criticism, discussion, and independent thought throughout international communism. Perhaps unaware of the irony, the American Party was still taking its lead from Moscow in now advocating a more independent line of thought and adhering to Moscow's new policy of destalinization in order to stay in line with the international communist movement.[106]

According to an inciteful report by the American Jewish Committee, the secret speech had a "crushing impact" on the American Party and led to internal turmoil, including calls to allow more dissent, to examine its relationship with Moscow, or even to dissolve the Party. The report quoted from letters to *Daily Worker* that gave opinions on both sides of the issue. The author considered the *Draft Resolution* to be vague, showing "failure to reach real agreement."[107] The fractured American Party held its sixteenth national convention in 1957. In spite of internal opposition, the convention adopted this *Draft Resolution*.

The internal dissension caused by the secret speech was not lost on the Federal Bureau of Investigation (FBI) which compiled summaries of the Party's activities that included discussions of the speech's effects on the Party and the resulting "internal factionalism."[108] The US Senate held hearings on the Party convention that were skeptical and derogatory in tone, steeped in postwar anticommunism, and included testimony from FBI director J. Edgar Hoover.[109] Hoover repeated his skepticism and warnings from the hearing in an article in *Elks Magazine* in which he warned every "decent American citizen" to remain wary of the "current propaganda" line of the Party meeting because its aims were still the same—to take over the United States and to "wipe out Judeo-Christian principles."[110]

In November 1956 *New World Review* published Ralph Parker's article that discussed the reexamination of the court cases from the 1930s, the rehabilitation of victims and liberal reforms in the arts, education, and in local administration.[111] This issue included an article by British Fabian Socialist G. D. H. Cole who lauded the Soviet Union's survival and Trotsky's exile. However, Cole condemned the Stalinist regime as a "ruthlessly repressive parody of workers' democracy." He criticized Stalin's Western supporters for believing the "simple fantastic charges" made against Stalin's enemies. He concluded that while the West should recognize Soviet achievements under Stalin: "Nothing can remove the stain of the gross inhumanities that have been practiced in the Soviet Union . . . or of the sheer murder on trumped-up charges of a host of persons whose offense was simply that they were displeasing to the half-demented new autocrat of all the Russias."[112] ["Autocrat of All the Russias" was an honorific reserved for the tsars.] In the same issue, Corliss Lamont, a founder and president of the Friends of the Soviet Union, a tireless defender of Stalin and the purges in the 1930s and a strong critic of the Dewey Commission, still supported the Soviet Union but acknowledged Stalin's "blunders and misdeeds." He did not apologize for his personal attacks on his former professor John Dewey. He wrote: "It is the duty of friends to criticize defects as well as praise virtues." He concluded by endorsing the policy of peaceful coexistence.[113]

Soul-searching among Communists and former Communists continued for years, exacerbated by the Soviets' suppression of the Hungarian Revolution and by the suppression of the Posnan Riots in Poland. Dissident Communist Bertram D. Wolfe published *Khrushchev and Stalin's Ghost* which included a long section on "The Crimes of the Stalin Era." Wolfe included the text of the secret speech with commentary on each section. Wolfe was relentlessly critical of Khrushchev and emphasized the fact that Khrushchev concentrated on the purge of the Old Bolsheviks and did not dwell on the victimization of ordinary Soviet citizens. Wolfe wrote: "Not one word is wasted on the crimes against the peasants nor against the rest of Stalin's subjects."[114] In 1958 *Political Affairs* (formerly *The Communist*, the American Party's journal of Marxist theory) published an article by American Party leader Dorothy Healey on "Khrushchev's revelations on Stalin."[115]

In 1960 the Soviets published an English translation of the massive new Party history entitled *History of the Communist Party of the Soviet Union*.[116] Bertram D. Wolfe, never relenting in his hostility toward Stalinism, wrote a stinging review of the new *History* in *Foreign Affairs*. Wolfe began by philosophizing about the writing of history and compared this new *History* to the 1939 *History of the Communist Party of the Soviet Union (Bolshevik) (Short Course)* in which the Old Bolsheviks were either denounced or completely omitted. Wolfe slammed the original *Short History* as "virtually unreadable" as well as full of "malevolence, the pathological boasting, envy, and vengeance." He considered the newer *History*'s treatment of the purges to be too brief and too vague with its slight acknowledgment of the suffering of the purge victims ("mistakes were made"), in the lessening of the role of Trotsky and the omission of Marshal Mikhail Tukhachevsky, the most famous victim of the Army purges. He also wrote that Khrushchev inflated his own role, much as Stalin did in the past.[117]

In 1966 former *Daily Worker* editor Joseph Starobin, a past defender of the Moscow show trials, wrote a memoir in *Problems of Communism* in which he chronicled the demise of the American Party and called the revelations of the secret speech a "searing shock." He cited Khrushchev's admissions that the "Moscow Trials had no substance whatsoever," especially citing the transcript of the second show trial that supposed a "great conspiracy against Soviet Russia" but which now turned out to be a "monstrous concoction." He also called the American Party "hapless and helpless." Starobin not only lamented that loyal Communists suffered but also that the Soviets had denied the purges. He discussed the effects of the speech on other communist parties and concluded: "One need not be devoted to Kremlinology to realize that the claim of uniqueness for communism stands out . . . as but a hollow boast, one of mankind's most cruel mockeries of man's eternal hope."[118] Harry Haywood, a prominent African American Party member, looked back on the National Committee meeting of April 1956 and on the ensuing factionalism and debate throughout the year and during the 1957 Party Convention as the "secret revelations stunned the American Party."[119]

The effects of the secret speech on the American Party were profound and are remembered to this day. Author Vivian Gornick had been a "red diaper baby," the daughter of committed Communists who were among those devastated by the revelations of Stalin's crimes. In 2017 she wrote: "The 20th Congress report brought with it political devastation. Within weeks of its publication, 30,000 people in this country quit the party, and within the year it was as it had been in its 1919 beginnings: a small sect on the American political map."[120] Italian academic Sergio A. Rossi succinctly reported that Western Communist parties were completely in the dark about the fact that a "sweeping change was in the making" because these parties never brought "their critical faculties to bear on anything pertaining to the U.S.S.R." and "within their ranks things can never be the same.... The leaders may try to cover up the scandal, but it is there and cannot be erased from the pages of history."[121] According to a scholarly article in the Marxist journal *Science & Society*, the years from 1956 through 1958 left the Communist Party USA, once the "most important left-wing organization in U. S. history ... to the periphery of U. S. political life."[122]

American Trotskyists had also suffered trial and imprisonment in the 1940s, and many of their publications had ceased.[123] The Trotskyist Socialist Workers Party (SWP) suffered from factionalism with some members splitting off to form the Socialist Union of America. In spite of these difficulties, Trotskyists continued to defend their assassinated leader, expose the fraud of the Moscow show trials, and defend the Dewey Commission. Two major US Trotskyist publications were still in business—*The Militant* (the successor to *Socialist Appeal*) and the journal *International Socialist Review*.

American Trotskyists were jubilant about the revelations of the secret speech as vindication of their twenty years of denouncing the trials. Trotskyist writings on the secret speech fell into these categories—trumpeting the revelations as the justification of their condemnations of the trials, thus restoring Trotsky's reputation, skewering the Communist Party USA for its blind support of Stalin and vilification of Trotsky and his supporters and criticizing the Soviets for the excesses of the Stalinist era and for the lack of meaningful internal reforms.

The Militant had non-stop coverage of the secret speech for months. The April 30, 1956, issue was devoted in large part to Khrushchev's revelations. Trotskyist theoretician Joseph Hansen, who had been one of Trotsky's secretaries in Mexico and was with him at his death, wrote the lead article in which he cited an article in *Soviet State and Law*, which condemned the practice of convicting the accused on the basis of confessions alone. Hansen also cited a *Pravda* article which mentioned Old Bolshevik Alexei Rykov without the usual invectives of calling him a "traitor" and "enemy of the state." Hansen lauded these concessions by the "Stalinist bureaucracy," a favorite target of Trotsky, in that they proved that the trials had been frame-ups. Hansen also cited a 1922 letter from Lenin to Rykov that was published for the first time. It included Lenin's complaint about "stinking red tape," echoing Trotsky's railings against Soviet bureaucracy. Hansen also reported on Kremlin attacks on State Prosecutor Andrei Vishinsky (a "sinister figure") as part of the destruction of the Stalin cult.[124] An accompanying article by Myra Tanner Weiss skewered the leaders of the Communist Party USA, condemned the anti-Leninism of the Soviet bureaucracy, and extolled Trotsky.[125]

The Trotskyists also held a May Day meeting on "The Stalin Frame-Up System and the Moscow Trials."[126]

Mrs. Weiss was the wife of *The Militant*'s editor Murray Weiss, and she was the SWP's candidate for vice president in the 1956 presidential election. She made several speeches about Khrushchev's revelations during her campaign tour. She stated that the Kremlin leaders needed to explain their role in "beheading the world revolution that would rid the world of capitalism."[127] In a "we told you so" move, *The Militant* began reprinting Trotsky's final statement to the Dewey Commission and reprinted his writing from 1937 to demonstrate that Trotsky's calling the trials frame-ups had been validated.[128]

The May 7 issue of *The Militant* included the SWP's National Committee resolution on "The New Stage of the Russian Revolution and the Crisis of Stalinism." The resolution started with the theme that the Soviet masses had "forced far-reaching concessions" from the bureaucracy and that Trotsky's contention that the trials were frame-ups had been proven at long last. The resolution ended with a call to bring all communist parties to Trotsky's brand of revolutionary socialism as the true path to Leninism.[129] In the same issue, Daniel Roberts reported that the Soviets warning that "rotten elements" in their Party who criticized the regime was proof that there was still no room for criticism in the Soviet Union. He also reported that Red Army leaders and Party leaders were stifling dissent and that there was dissent in Hungary over past trials.[130] Roberts also reported that the Soviet Supreme Court repealed the laws under which the Moscow show trials were held, again proving that the show trials were "frame-ups and unspeakable bloodlettings."[131]

Impatient to get the text of speech, an editorial asked why the speech had not been published and accused the Department of State of sitting on it. The editorialist also slammed the Soviet and American Communist parties for not having open discussions of these revelations and their implications.[132] Several articles condemned American Communist Party leaders and *Daily Worker*, not only for their blind support of Stalin but also for their preventing open discussion and debate and for belatedly recognizing Lenin's Last Testament with its anti-Stalin sentiments.[133]

When the text of the secret speech was published, the spate of articles and editorials continued on the triumphant note that Khrushchev had validated Trotsky's accusations. The June 11 issue of *The Militant* was almost completely devoted to the revelations from the speech which it reprinted.[134] A front-page editorial entitled "Trotskyism Vindicated!" proclaimed that Trotsky had exposed all of Stalin's crimes, rehashed Lenin's Last Testament, cited the ongoing struggles in foreign communist parties, and slammed the "Stalinist bureaucracy," one of Trotsky's favorite targets.[135] The lead headline proclaimed that the trials were frame-ups and that the Communist Party USA was being "rocked by Khrushchev's confessions."[136]

The Militant republished an open letter from its editor Murry Weiss to his parents that had originally been published in *Daily Worker*. Weiss, who had been expelled from the Young Communist League in 1932, wrote on Stalin's persecution of Trotskyists and the lack of open discussion within the Communist Party USA. He condemned Stalinism's "unbelievable crimes," but as an anti-capitalist, he labeled Stalinism the "product precisely of the capitalist encirclement of the Soviet Union."[137] *The Militant* also went after one of Stalin's most ardent American supporters in the same issue and lambasted journalist Anna Louise Strong for her speech to the National Council of Soviet American Friendship. Still a true believer in spite of being expelled from the Soviet Union by Stalin, she was dismissive of the published draft of the speech. She blamed the secret police and its "unbridled power" as the most important factor in the crimes of the Stalinist era. The reporter concluded that her speech was an "attempt to justify absolute and slavish acceptance" of the Stalinist bureaucracy's actions.[138]

The Militant published an editorial on the crises in the French and Italian Communist parties which included *The Militant*'s position that the "powerful pressure" of the Soviet working class forced the bureaucracy to make concessions, reinforcing the Trotskyists' belief that they spoke for the proletariat and would lead to the "world socialist victory."[139] SWP leader James P. Cannon gave a speech to Trotskyists in Los Angeles in which he asked three questions: how was "such a monstrous regime possible," who spoke out against it and what happened to them, and "why weren't we told this before?" Cannon surmised that it had been "dangerous to speak" and that Khrushchev and company were Stalin's "handpicked accomplices," enjoying the privileges of the regime's leaders. He excoriated the leaders of the Communist Party USA for belatedly admitting their "mistakes," and he urged open discussions toward the goal of a "common struggle for a socialist America."[140] *The Militant* then issued a challenge to Party General Secretary Eugene Dennis for a public debate.[141]

The Trotskyist *International Socialist Review* continued the condemnation of Stalinism. It devoted part of its Summer 1956 issue to the Moscow show trials and to the secret speech. It published "The End of the Stalin Cult," the text of a speech given in New York City in March 1956 by Morris Lewit, using the pseudonym Morris Stein. He echoed one of Trotsky's favorite themes—the condemnation of bureaucrats—by citing "their inflated sense of importance" and condemned the Stalinist cult for poisoning the "atmosphere of the world revolutionary movement" as follows: "This cult, built on the bones of the best of the revolutionary generation that founded the Soviet Union and at the expense of the Soviet working class, finally became insupportable even for the bureaucracy which was its sole beneficiary." Lewit asserted that the defendants in the show trials confessed because they had reached a "breaking point." He also mentioned the Army purge and the purge of the Comintern in trying to reach a conclusion as to why Stalin was now being condemned by his accomplices. Lewit echoed a now familiar theme in accusing the new Kremlin leadership of being accomplices to Stalin's crimes and dismissed other theories about the denunciation of Stalin by writing that the bureaucracy that Trotsky had tirelessly condemned was pressured to denounce Stalinism by the force of the "Soviet working class," by the workers' revolt in East Germany and by the prisoners' strike in the Vorkuta forced-labor camp. Lewit also condemned the continued Soviet propaganda campaign against Trotsky.[142]

In the same issue it published a speech given by its editor Murry Weiss. In "The Vindication of Trotskyism," Weiss dissected Khrushchev's revelations of Stalin's "mass murder and terror," the mass deportations of nationalities, and Stalin's "crimes and blunders" during the Second World War. Not letting up, he cataloged Stalin's missteps in dealing with other communist states and denounced the cult of the individual and accused Stalin of being "absurdly ignorant" about agriculture. Weiss called Khrushchev to task for not revealing the persecution of Jewish leaders and continued the theme that Trotsky had revealed Stalin's crimes years earlier. Weiss also criticized the Department of State for using Khrushchev's speech as proof of the "inherent evil of communism." He referred to Trotsky's longtime criticism of the Soviet bureaucracy, stating that the bureaucracy was caused by the "weight of the Czarist past and the pressure of capitalist encirclement." Weiss extolled Trotsky and the Left Opposition and lambasted *Daily Worker* for belatedly making its public confession as to having "blindly and subserviently parroted all the lies of Stalin." He applauded the Trotskyists for being the only ones right from the beginning and predicted the "downfall of the Soviet bureaucratic caste," the victory of Russian Bolshevism and the triumph of the "world socialist revolution."[143]

The Trotskyists did not let up in 1957 when *International Socialist Review* used a review of Hershel D. Meyer's *The Khrushchev Report and the Crisis of the American Left* to condemn Stalin and Khrushchev.[144] Reviewer John Liang denigrated the author as a "Stalinist hack" and skewered his rationale for the purges being a "historical accident," due to Stalin's paranoia. Liang agreed that Stalin may have been paranoid, but he blamed the purges on a "reactional bureaucratic ruling class," one of Trotsky's main themes. Liang joined the chorus of blaming the current Kremlin leaders as "part and parcel of Stalin's terror machine."[145]

Trotskyists continued referring to the secret speech into the 1960s and 1970s. *International Socialist Review* published an article by Dick Roberts on the "Purge and Rehabilitation in the Soviet Union." Roberts concentrated on the purge of the military and the suspicious death of Soviet defector Walter Krivitsky. He skewered the Soviet history written by French leftist Louis Aragon. Roberts called him a "faithful disciple" of Stalin. Roberts praised Trotsky's exposure of Stalin's "lies and treacheries" and echoed the theme that Khrushchev did not "want to reveal his own complicity in the purges." Roberts charged that Stalin created a counter-revolution against the Old Bolsheviks that caused the degeneration of the "revolutionary Marxist movement."[146]

The Reactions of American Liberals

The reactions to the secret speech by anti-Stalinist liberals were exemplified by Sidney Hook, the chair of the Department of Philosophy at New York University and a former member of the American Committee for the Defense of Leon Trotsky. In a letter to the editor of the *New York Times*, he wrote that Khrushchev's condemnations of Stalin affirmed the findings of the Dewey Commission. He also slammed the show trials' defenders and the critics of the Dewey Commission and wrote that Stalinism was the "offspring of Leninism."[147]

In 1951 ex-communist Granville Hicks singled out *The Nation* as an "apologist for Soviet Russia" and for giving the Soviets the "benefit of almost every doubt" until the Nazi-Soviet non-aggression pact.[148] James Libbey examined the attitudes of the liberal weeklies *The Nation* and *New Republic* toward the Moscow show trials and their pro-Stalinist sentiments in his 1975 article "Liberal Journals and the Moscow Trials of 1936-38." He cited *New Republic's* dismissal of the findings of the Dewey Commission as an example. He concluded that "The Moscow trials raised controversies in the liberal journals because Stalin appeared similar to the very fascist dictators the Popular Front theoretically sought to destroy."[149]

Malcolm Cowley, a former editor of *New Republic*, published a recantation of his support of Stalin and of the Moscow show trials in 1984. He acknowledged that the show trials led to "bitterness and dissension in the intellectual world" and that all that he knew about Russia came "from written reports." He regretted his article on the second show trial, writing that it was a "painful document" for him to read in that he had accepted the confessions and had either been "deceived" or had "grossly deceived" himself. He also engaged in self-criticism of his review of the transcript of the third show trial, writing that he now "read those words with shame." He gave several reasons for his previous beliefs, including the secrecy around the extent of the purges and cited Robert Conquest's *The Great Terror* for opening his eyes. He apologized for his criticism of the Dewey Commission as he grudgingly acknowledged that the Trotskyists were "right about the trials." Perhaps Cowley was unaware of the irony that he was still following Moscow's line and engaging in *samokritika* (self-criticism), the public ritual that many Old Bolsheviks had to endure during the purges.[150]

The Reactions of American Intellectuals

Before the Second World War some left-wing intellectuals had joined the Communist Party and Communist-backed organizations. Years before the secret speech, pro-Soviet liberals and intellectuals had been blasted by anticommunist journalist Eugene Lyons. In 1941 he published *The Red Decade* on Stalinism in America in which he condemned the purges, the show trials, and American fellow travelers for their support of what he termed to be the "bloodletting" of the purges. He singled out the liberal weeklies *New Republic* and *The Nation* and *New York Times* correspondent Walter Duranty. Mincing no words, he concluded with the following: "There were no intellectual acrobatics which the fellow-travelers would not undertake to save their lovely faith in Russia. . . . They had accepted and explained away horror and super-horror."[151]

Lyons again excoriated the radical and liberal presses in 1946. He asserted that the Communist press had been in "goose-stepping formation" as it followed the Moscow line. He claimed that while *The Nation* and *New Republic* decried right-wing dictatorships, they rationalized such Communists' excesses as the use of forced labor.[152]

Even before the secret speech, some intellectuals had become disillusioned with Soviet communism, among them novelists Richard Wright and John Dos Passos and journalist Louis Fischer. The secret speech caused other intellectuals to recant their previous pro-Soviet stance. One of the most vocal renouncers was novelist Howard Fast who had won the first Stalin International Peace Prize in 1953, had been a Party member, and had written for Communist publications. He had been called before the House Un-American Activities Committee (HUAC), tried for contempt of Congress, and served three months in prison in 1950. The revelations in the secret speech led him to publish articles in *Daily Worker* and in other left-wing publications in which he described Khrushchev's speech as a record of "mistakes, large and small," and he made a strong declaration of his revulsion toward Stalin's crimes ("a record of barbarism and paranoiac bloodlust") while he still reiterated his faith in socialism, writing that "never again can I accept as a just practice under socialism that which I know to be unjust."[153] This public recantation led to a less-than-positive reaction from the mainstream press.[154] He was also criticized in the communist press.[155] Fast was again called before the House Un-American Activities Committee in 1957 where he invoked the Fifth Amendment against self-incrimination.[156]

He continued his criticism of American Communists through his memoirs *Naked God* and *Being Red* which chronicled his time in the Communist Party USA and reiterated his criticism of the American Party and its dictatorial leadership, including its arbitrary criticisms and expulsions of Party members who questioned or strayed from the official Party line.[157] Fast's high-profile defection has continued to be a subject of scholarly study.[158]

In contrast to Fast's defense of his defection from the Communist Party, well-known playwright Lillian Hellman took a more ho-hum approach to her pro-Soviet past. She had been called to testify before the House Un-American Activities Committee in 1952.[159] Later, in her memoir *Scoundrel Time*, she shrugged off her signing of the "Open Letter to American Liberals" in 1937 with this quote: "Whatever our mistakes, I do not believe that we did our country any harm."[160]

Khrushchev's Second Speech

At the Twenty-Second Party Congress in 1961 Khrushchev made a follow-up speech in which he again condemned Stalin and also condemned the aged former People's Commissar for Defense Klementi Voroshilov who had been in office during the purges. Voroshilov had also been part of a plot to oust Khrushchev in 1957. This led to more official acknowledgments of the use of torture to obtain confessions, Stalin's presumed paranoia and that the show trials were frame-ups.[161] Khrushchev was ousted from office in 1964. He died in 1971, and his memoir *Khrushchev Remembers* was published.[162] The *Bulletin* of the Workers League for a Revolutionary Party, the successor to the Leninist League, published a book review which skewered Khrushchev for his role in the purges in Ukraine; the reviewer also rejected the view that the purges and the show trials were caused by Stalin's personality.[163]

Now considered to be one of the most important speeches of the twentieth century, the secret speech was not officially published in the Soviet Union until 1989.[164] Understandably, it has been a continued subject of scholarly research to this day.[165]

The Discrediting of the Reporting of Walter Duranty

In the 1980s the reporting of *New York Times* foreign correspondent Walter Duranty was discredited. He had been the most famous journalist for the American press in Moscow during the 1920s and 1930s. He had won a Pulitzer Prize in 1932 for his reporting from the Soviet Union and was a prolific writer, publishing articles and memoirs on his time there. Criticism of Duranty gained momentum during a campaign spearheaded by North Americans of Ukrainian descent with calls to revoke Duranty's 1932 Pulitzer Prize for his deliberate understating of the extent of the devastating famine (*holodomor*) in Ukraine that was caused by the first Five Year Plan. Duranty was the subject of a critical biography in 1990 which took him to task for dismissing the reporting of other correspondents who accurately reported on the famine and for his following the Stalinist line on the show trials.[166] In a 1991 article Jacob Heilbrunn critiqued the reporting of both Duranty and Harold Denny, the other *New York Times* correspondent in Moscow. While not mentioning the censorship that the reporters had endured from the Soviet government, Heilbrunn termed their trial reporting to be the "first example of deliberate and systematic misreporting of a communist country."[167] In 1999 syndicated columnist John Leo ranked Duranty's reporting from Moscow as one of the biggest journalistic "Bloopers of the Century."[168] Criticism of Duranty resulted in the *New York Times* investigating his reporting and taking the unprecedented step of formally asking the Pulitzer Prize Board to rescind his prize.[169] The Board voted not to rescind.[170]

Echoes of Stalin's Rule

It may be tempting to think of the Moscow show trials and the purges as the excesses of a vanished system under a long-dead dictator, but such purges have continued to the present. Postwar Czechoslovakia, Hungary, the People's Republic of China, and the People's Democratic Republic of Korea (North Korea) have purged high officials and held show trials. In 1979 Stalin's admirer Saddam Hussein purged and executed members of the Ba'ath Party in Iraq.

Throughout the Cold War and during the Putin regime, American diplomats remained the targets of petty harassment, similar to the Soviets' anti-foreigner campaign in the 1930s.[171] During the Putin era dissidents have been jailed or killed. As Stalin used the rationale of being surrounded by capitalist countries during the purges, Vladimir Putin, the former KGB agent who became head of the post-Soviet Russian Federation in 1999, used the excuse of the encroachment of the North Atlantic Treaty Organization (NATO) as one of his reasons for invading Ukraine (the "special military operation") in 2022. The invasion of Ukraine is also reminiscent of Stalin's Winter War with Finland, another much smaller border country. To silence any criticism of this invasion and in employing Stalinist methods, the Russian government cracked down on dissidents and shut down all independent media.

Conclusion

In considering the Moscow show trials and the purges of the 1930s, there is the long-range geopolitical view that the Soviet period was another part of the perpetual rise-and-fall cycle of Russian history. The trials could also be considered as another in the string of manmade disasters that befell the Russian people in the first half of the twentieth century. They endured war, revolutions, a civil war, the Allied Expeditionary Forces, famines, and the imposition of a brutal, one-party dictatorship. Germany's invasion of the Soviet Union and its occupation of western border areas and Ukraine were final catastrophes in forty years of hardships. Yet the country has survived as being too big to fail.

During the 1930s there had been many explanations for the Moscow show trials, including Trotsky's comparison of them to the trials after the French Revolution when revolutionary factions turned on each other. There were also explanations that attributed the purges and the trials to unique aspects of the Russian national psyche and its Dostoievskian aspects, to Stalin's psychological makeup (including possible paranoia), his need to eliminate potential rivals, to keep close associates loyal and off-balance and his longstanding rivalry with Trotsky. During the first show trial, US Embassy staff members had a number of theories which included that the trial was to prevent expression of any dissatisfaction within the Party, to show that there would be no room for criticism under the new constitution, to eliminate the influence of former leaders, to blame Trotskyists and foreign agents for any economic failures, to kill Trotsky's influence in international circles, and to increase hatred for Germany. They also speculated that the defendants testified to escape torture, to get lesser sentences, to spare their families or to become martyrs for the good of the Party.

The fact that the Soviet Union was the world's only socialist country, encircled by capitalists, was exploited to fuel exaggerated threats of invasion, sabotage, and plots from the West, including plots from virulently anticommunist Nazi Germany and an increasingly militaristic and expansionist Japan. Stalin needed complete Party unity with accusers and victims playing their assigned roles, and the Soviet bureaucracy needed self-preservation. The swelling ranks of the Gulag provided massive amounts of free labor for economic development.

The purges were also opportunities for Stalin to rewrite the history of the Bolsheviks, the Russian Revolution, and the Civil War. With the elimination of the Old Bolsheviks, Stalin enhanced his own role, either by defaming the Old Bolsheviks or by completely erasing them from official history. Thus, he permanently silenced the colleagues of Lenin who could speak authoritatively on any deviations from Lenin's philosophy. More than one contemporary observer of Stalin's rule compared him to Ivan the Terrible, recalling the terror inflicted on the Russian people in the sixteenth century.

In the United States the Moscow show trials kept a focus on the Soviet Union and Stalin's regime. In spite of years of study and official reports, the US government had no coherent plan to deal with Stalin's death and was taken completely by surprise by Khrushchev's secret speech.

The obvious conclusions to be drawn from contemporaneous American reactions are that the censored accounts in the *New York Times* did not delve into the falsity of the charges and confessions but added firsthand color commentary on the demeanor of the judges, prosecutor, and defendants. The mainstream news weeklies were skeptical but were also no fans of Trotsky, and the anticommunist American press condemned the trials. On the political left there was the slavish devotion to Stalin by the leaders of the Communist Party USA and the continual opposition of the American Trotskyists with their accusations of the trials being frame-ups which ultimately proved to be correct. The trials became flashpoints for Communists and Trotskyists to take potshots at each other. There was also the slow awakening of the liberal weeklies and pro-Soviet intellectuals to the harsh realities of Stalin's regime.

Russians have viewed the purges from both points of view. There are the remembrances of the descendants of the purge victims. This is also the nostalgia for the days of Stalin's iron rule when the Soviet Union was powerful and feared.[172,173]

The Moscow show trials have also become a part of public political rhetoric in the United States. A reference to the trials occurred in 2018 when former FBI Deputy Assistant Director Peter Strzok was being grilled by members of the US House Committee on Oversight and Government Reform. Strzok had sent derogatory emails about then-candidate Donald Trump during the investigation of alleged Russian interference in the 2016 presidential election, and he was blasted by some Republican members of the Committee. Congressman Gerry Connolly (D-Virginia) came to Strzok's defense by comparing the hearing to a "Russian political show trial. It's got all the trappings—character assassination, demagoguery . . . cherry picking facts, sometimes fabricating facts."[174] Trump ally Roger Stone used the phrase "soviet-style show trial" to describe his trial for allegedly lying to US House of Representatives investigators.[175]

Since the breakup of the Soviet Union and the opening of government and Party archives, historians and Kremlinologists have published revelations on the inner workings of the government and the Party machinery during the 1930s. They have revised their theories on the causes and meaning of the purges and the Moscow show trials, debating Stalin's role as the sole instigator, the widespread nature of the purges, and any possible parallels in post-Soviet Russia. A letter resurfaced in 1987 that was a succinct indictment of Stalin's actions during the purges and the show trials. It was written in 1939 by Fedor Raskolnikov, a Soviet diplomat who listed Stalin's crimes, including destroying the People's Commissariat for Foreign Affairs and beheading the Army and Navy. Concerning the show trials, he wrote the following about Stalin: "With the help of dirty forgeries you staged false trials and made up accusations which are more ridiculous than the witch trials of the Middle Ages. . . . You have disgraced the people whom you have killed, and you have attributed their feats and merits to yourself."[176]

Even before the opening of the Soviet archives, American Embassy secretaries published their memoirs that included their eyewitness reporting, condemning everything about them. It is the present authors' opinion that during the trials these diplomats realized the horrors being inflicted on this vast nation at a time when other observers did not. George F. Kennan wrote in 1962 about Stalin's "shocking humiliation and degradation of old Party comrades," "merciless purging," and a "vast conflagration of mock justice, torture and brutality."[177] One official communiqué, sent under Ambassador Davies's name but undoubtedly bearing the stamp of the Embassy secretaries, summarized the devastation that other writers have taken hundreds of pages to document:

> The Terror here is a horrifying fact. . . . It is commonly alleged that the Secret Police of this Proletarian Dictatorship are as ruthless and as cruel as any during the old Tsarist regime. . . . This particular purge is undoubtedly political. . . . It is deliberately projected by the Party leaders, who themselves regretted the necessity for it, but in the performance of what they regard as their duty. . . . They recognize and regret that there must needs be many innocent who suffer in this situation, but they take the position that they must do this to save their cause, which is supreme and that the successful elevation of the condition of life of the proletariat will, in historical perspective, justify their present course. They wrap themselves about in the mantle of the angels to serve the devil. They are undoubtedly a strong, able group of ruthless idealists. But tyranny is tyranny, whatever be its government.[178]

Americans were fortunate to have such well-qualified and astute observers to this great upheaval as the three Embassy secretaries—Charles E. "Chip" Bohlen, Loy W. Henderson, and George F. Kennan. In spite of the limitations of the time, including the restrictions placed on foreigners and the relentless barrage of Soviet propaganda, they saw beyond ideology and official rhetoric to comprehend the harsh realities of the Moscow show trials that many of their contemporaries failed to see. They sent thoughtful, well-written reports to the Department of State, leaving a valuable legacy which is a credit to their knowledge and professionalism and is a credit to the country they served.

Notes

Introduction

1. J. Arch Getty, "*Samokritika* Rituals in the Stalinist Central Committee, 1933–38," *Russian Review* 58, no. 1 (January, 1999): 49–70.
2. J. Arch Getty and Oleg V. Naumov, *The Road to Terror: Stalin and the Self-Destruction of the Bolsheviks, 1932–1939* (New Haven, CT: Yale University Press, 1999), 588.
3. US Department of State, Foreign Relations Branch, *Foreign Relations of the United States: The Soviet Union, 1933–1939* (Washington, DC: Government Printing Office, 1952).
4. See Charles E. Bohlen, *Witness to History, 1929–1969* (New York: W. W. Norton, 1973), Loy W. Henderson, *A Question of Trust: The Origins of U.S.-Soviet Diplomatic Relations: The Memoirs of Loy W. Henderson*, ed. with an introd. by George W. Baer (Stanford, CA: Hoover Institution Press, 1986), George F. Kennan, *Memoirs, 1925–1950* (New York: Pantheon Books, 1967) and Joseph E. Davies, *Mission to Moscow: A Record of the Confidential Dispatches to the State Department, Official and Personal Correspondence, Current Diary and Journal Entries, Including Notes and Comment up to October, 1941* (New York: Simon and Schuster, 1941).
5. Robert Conquest, *The Great Terror: A Reassessment*, 40th anniversary ed. (New York: Oxford University Press, 2008), 67.
6. Roy A. Medvedev, *Let History Judge: The Origins and Consequences of Stalinism*, trans. Colleen Taylor, ed. David Joravsky and Georges Haupt (New York: Knopf, 1972), 566.
7. Stephen Kotkin, *Stalin: Waiting for Hitler, 1929–1941* (New York: Penguin Press, 2017), 552.
8. J. Arch Getty, *Origins of the Great Purges: The Soviet Communist Party Reconsidered, 1933–1938* (Cambridge: Cambridge University Press, 1987), 206.
9. Getty and Naumov, *The Road to Terror*, 583.
10. Robert C. Tucker, *Stalin in Power: The Revolution from Above, 1928–1941* (New York: W. W. Norton, 1990), 501; see also Joel Carmichael, *Stalin's Masterpiece: The Show Trials and the Purges of the Thirties, the Consolidation of the Bolshevik Dictatorship* (New York: St. Martin's Press, 1976) and Bernard Wolfe, "30 Years after Stalin's Great Purge," *New York Times Magazine*, September 18, 1966, SM66, SM122–40.

11 See Harvey Klehr, John Earl Anderson, and Fridrikh Igorevich Firsov, *The Soviet World of American Communism* (New Haven, CT: Yale University Press, 1995), 292, Harvey Klehr and John Earl Anderson, *The Secret World of Soviet Communism* (New Haven, CT: Yale University Press, 1998) and Harvey Klehr, *The Heyday of American Communism: The Depression Decade* (New York: Basic Books, 1984).

12 Theodore Draper, *The Roots of American Communism* (New York: Viking Press, 2003), xv; see also Sidney Hook, ed., "The Mystery of the Moscow Trials: A Logical Analysis," in *World Communism: Key Documentary Material* (Princeton, NJ: Van Nostrand, 1962), 100–17.

Chapter 1

1 *Bolshevik Propaganda: Hearings Before a Subcommittee of the Comm. on the Judiciary*, 65th Cong. 7 (1919) (statement of Thomas J. Tunney).

2 Robert Lansing, "The Secretary of State to the Ambassador in Great Britain (Davis)," in US Department of State, *Papers Relating to the Foreign Relations of the United States, 1920*, vol. 3 (Washington, DC: Government Printing Office, 1936), 445.

3 Leon Trotsky, "Letter from Leon Trotsky, Commissar of Foreign Affairs of the Newly Formed Soviet Government, to U. S. Ambassador David Francis, Received at the Embassy on November 21, 1917," accessed May 20, 1915, http://www.archives.gov.

4 US Department of State, Office of the Historian, "Milestones: 1921–1936: Recognition of the Soviet Union," accessed June 3, 2016, https://history.state.gov/milestones/1921-1936/ussr.

5 John Reed, *Ten Days that Shook the World* (New York: Boni and Liveright, 1919).

6 Dimitri von Mohrenschildt, "The Early American Observers of the Russian Revolution, 1917–1921," *Russian Review* 3, no. 1 (Autumn, 1943): 64–74.

7 Vladimir I. Lenin, "Letter to American Workers," in *Lenin's Collected Works*, vol. 28 (Moscow: Progress Publishers, 1965), 62–75.

8 Communist Party of America, *Constitution of the Communist Party of America: Adopted by the Founding Convention, Chicago, September 1–7, 1919*, in *Manifesto and Contitution* [sic]: *Report to the Communist International* (Chicago, IL: The Party, 1919), 1.

9 "Soviet and American Communist Parties," in *Revelations from the Russian Archives: Documents in English Translation*, ed. Diane P. Loenker and Ronald D. Bachman (Washington, DC: Library of Congress, 1997), accessed February 19, 2012, http://www.loc.gov/exhibits/archives/sova.html.

10 Ibid.
11 Winston James, "To the East Turn: The Russian Revolution and the Black Radical Imagination in the United States, 1917–1924," *American Historical Review* 126, no. 3 (September, 2021): 1001–45.
12 For an example, see "35,000 Jammed in Square," *New York Times*, March 7, 1930.
13 See House Comm. on Un-American Activities, H. R. Rep. No. 1694 (1953), Theodore Draper, *American Communism and Soviet Russia: The Formative Period* (New York: Viking Press, 1960), Theodore Draper, *The Roots of American Communism* (New York: Viking Press, 1957), Vivian Gornick, *The Romance of American Communism* (New York: Basic Books, 1977), Klehr, *The Heyday of American Communism* and Harvey Klehr, John Earl Haynes, and K. M. Anderson, "Orders from the Comintern," in *The Soviet World of American Communism* (New Haven, CT: Yale University Press, 1998), 14–106.
14 Bertram D. Wolfe, *The Trotsky Opposition: Its Significance for American Workers* (New York: Workers Library Publishers, 1928).
15 Communist International, Executive Committee, "Extracts from an ECCI Letter to the Sixth Convention of the CP of the USA," in *The Communist International, 1919–1943: Documents*, vol. 3, ed. Jane Degras (London: Royal Institute of International Affairs, 1971), 8–16.
16 For histories of American Trotskyism, see George Breitman, Paul Le Blanc, and Alan Wald, *Trotskyism in the United States: Historical Essays and Reconsiderations* (Atlantic Highlands, NJ: Humanities Press, 1996), James Patrick Cannon, *The History of American Trotskyism: Report of a Participant* (New York: Pioneer Publishers, 1944), Constance Ashton Meyers, *The Prophet's Army: The History of American Trotskyism, 1928–1941* (Westport, CT: Greenwood Press, 1977) and Tim Wohlforth, *The Struggle for Marxism in the United States: A History of American Trotskyism*. 2nd ed. (New York: Labor Publications, 1971).
17 "Hail the Socialist Workers Party!" *Socialist Appeal*, January 15, 1938.
18 Harvey Klehr and John E. Haynes, "Communists and the CIO: From the Soviet Archives," *Labor History* 35, no. 3 (1994): 444–5.
19 *Bolshevik Propaganda*, 114–62 (statement of Rev. Mr. George Simons); see also S. Doc No. 61 (1919).
20 "Jews from America in the Bolshevik Oligarchy," *Literary Digest*, March 1, 1919, 32.
21 See "Senate Orders Reds Here Investigated," *New York Times*, February 5, 1919, "Tells Senators of Mass Terror by Bolsheviks," *New York Times*, February 9, 1919, "Say Riffraff, Not the Toilers, Rule in Russia," *New York Times*, February 17, 1919, "Bolsheviki in the United States," *Literary Digest*, February 22, 1919, 11–13, "Francis Confirms All of the Horrors of Bolshevism," *New York Times*, March 9, 1919, "Extent of Bolshevik Infection Here," *Literary Digest*, January 17, 1929, 13–15, and "House Passes Bill to Curb Red Aliens," *New York Times*, December 21, 1919.

22 See *Communist and Anarchist Deportation Cases: Hearings Before the Subcommittee of the United States House Comm. on Immigration and Naturalization*, 66th Cong. (1920) (statement of W. A. Blackwood), *I. W. W. Deportation Cases: Hearings Before a Subcommittee of the United States House Comm. on Immigration and Naturalization*, 66th Cong. (1920) (statement of W. A. Blackwood), *Communist Labor Party Deportation Cases: Hearings Before a Subcommittee of the United States House Comm. on Immigration and Naturalization*, 66th Congress (1920) (statement of W. A. Blackwood) and "Deportation from the United States of Undesirable Russians," in US Department of State, *Papers Relating to the Foreign Relations of the United States, 1920*, vol. 3, 687–700.
23 "Communists' Trial Begins Tomorrow," *New York Times*, November 26, 1922.
24 Francis W. B. Coleman, "The Minister in Latvia (Coleman) to the Secretary of State," in US Department of State, *Papers Relating to the Foreign Relations of the United States, 1923*, vol. 2 (Washington, DC: Government Printing Office, 1938), 764–85.
25 "Appeal to President Harding on Behalf of Tikhon, Patriarch of the Russian Church, on Trial before a Soviet Tribunal," in US Department of State, *Papers Relating to the Foreign Relations of the United States, 1922*, vol. 2 (Washington, DC: Superintendent of Documents, 1938), 835–40.
26 US Department of State, "Displeasure Expressed by the United States at Sentences of Death Passed upon Roman Catholic Clergy in Russia," in US Department of State, *Papers Relating to the Foreign Relations of the United States, 1923*, vol. 2, 815–22.
27 See "The American Labor Alliance for Trade Relations with Russia," memorandum, n.d., Comintern Archives, file 515, 1.d., II, 1–18, and "Resumption of Trade with Russia," in US Department of State, *Papers Relating to the Foreign Relations of the United States, 1920*, vol. 3, 701–27, *Relations with Russia: Hearings on S. J. Res. 164, for the Reestablishment of Trade Relations with Russia*, 67th Cong. (1921) and Frank B. Kellogg, "Statement Concerning the Activities of the Department of State: Russia," in US Department of State, *Papers Relating to the Foreign Relations of the United States, 1928*, vol. 2 (Washington, DC: Government Printing Office, 1943), 825.
28 See Tim Tzouliadis, *The Forsaken: An American Tragedy in Stalin's Russia* (New York: Penguin Press, 2008).
29 See William Bassow, *The Moscow Correspondents* (New York: William Morrow, 1988).
30 See Walter Duranty, *Duranty Reports Russia* (New York: Viking Press, 1934) and Walter Duranty, *I Write as I Please* (New York: Simon and Schuster, 1935).
31 See Louis Fischer, *Man and Machines in Russia* (New York: H. Smith, 1932), Louis Fischer, *Soviet Journey* (New York: H. Smith and R. Haas, 1935), Louis Fischer, *The Soviets in World Affairs A History of the Relations Between the Soviet Union and the*

Rest of the World (London: J. Cape, 1930), Louis Fischer, *Why Recognize Russia? The Arguments for and Against the Recognition of the Soviet Government by the United States* (New York: Cape and Smith, 1931) and Louis Fischer, *Men and Politics: An Autobiography* (New York: Duell, Sloan & Pearce, 1941).

32 See William C. Bullitt, "The Ambassador in the Soviet Union (Bullitt)," in US Department of State, Foreign Relations Branch, *Foreign Relations of the United States: The Soviet Union, 1933-1939*, July 13, 2013, 359-60, and Loy W. Henderson, "The Chargé in the Soviet Union (Henderson) to the Secretary of State," in US Department of State, Foreign Relations Branch, *Foreign Relations of the United States: The Soviet Union, 1933-1939*, 389; see also James William Crowl, *Angels in Stalin's Paradise: Western Reporters in Soviet Russia, 1917-1937: A Case Study of Louis Fischer and Walter Duranty* (Washington, DC: University Press of America, 1982).

33 Anna Louise Strong, *I Change Worlds: The Re-Making of An American* (New York: Henry Holt, 1935).

34 See Eugene Lyons, *Moscow Carrousel* (New York: Knopf, 1935), Eugene Lyons, *Assignment in Utopia* (New York: Harcourt, Brace, 1937) and William Henry Chamberlin, *Soviet Russia: A Living History and a Record* (Boston, MA: Little, Brown, 1930).

35 See Daniel Aaron, *Writers on the Left: Episodes in American Literary Communism* (New York: Harcourt, Brace & World, 1961), David C. Engerman, *Modernization from the Other Shore: American Intellectuals and the Romance of Russian Development* (Cambridge, MA: Harvard University Press, 2003), James Burkhart Gilbert, *Writers and Partisans: A History of Literary Radicalism in America* (New York: Wiley, 1968), Richard H. Pells, *Radical Visions and American Dreams: Cultural and Social Thought in the Depression Years* (New York: Harper & Row, 1973), Alan M. Wald, *The New York Intellectuals: The Rise and Decline of the Anti-Stalinist Left from the 1930s to the 1980s* (Chapel Hill, NC: University of North Carolina Press, 1987), and Frank A. Warren, *Liberals and Communism: The Red Decade Revisited* (Bloomington, IN: Indiana University Press, 1966).

36 Judy Kutulas, "Becoming 'More Liberal': The League of American Writers, the Communist Party, and the Literary People's Front," *Journal of American Culture* 13, no. 1 (1990): 71-80.

37 For an example, see Waldo Frank, "The Writer's Part in Communism," *Partisan Review*, February, 1936, 14-17.

38 See George Novack, "American Intellectuals and the Crisis," *New International*, February, 1936, 23-7, "American Intellectuals and the Crisis," *New International*, June, 1936, 83-6; see also George Novack, "Radical Intellectuals in the 1930s," *International Socialist Review*, March-April, 1968, 21-34, James Burnham and Max Shachtman, "Intellectuals in Retreat," *New International*, January, 1939, 3-22, Granville Hicks, "Communism and the American Intellectuals," in Irving DeWitt

Talmadge, ed., *Whose Revolution? A Study of the Future Course of Liberalism in the United States* (New York: Howell, Soskin, 1941), 78–115, and James P. Cannon, "The Treason of the Intellectuals," *The Militant*, May 24, 1947.

39 See Joseph Barnes, "Cultural Recognition of Russia," *The Nation*, May 18, 1932, 565; see also Michael David-Fox, *Origins of the Stalinist Superiority Complex: Western Intellectuals inside the USSR* (Washington, DC: National Council for Eurasian and East European Research, 2004), accessed May 29, 2016, https://www.ucis.pitt.edu/nceeer/2004_819-05_David-Fox.pdf and Michael David-Fox, *Showcasing the Great Experiment: Cultural Diplomacy and Western Visitors to the Soviet Union, 1921–1941* (Oxford: Oxford University Press, 2012).

40 See Harpo Marx and Rowland Barber, "Exapno Mapcas Secret Agent," in *Harpo Speaks!* (New York: Limelight Editions, 1961), 299–337 and "Soviet Hails Harpo Marx," *New York Times*, December 19, 1933.

41 US Department of State, "Policy of the United States Toward the Soviet Government," in *Papers Relating to the Foreign Relations of the United States, 1920*, vol. 3, 436.

42 "Refusal by the Government of the United States to Recognize the Mission of L. Martens, Russian Soviet Agent in the United States," in US Department of State, *Papers Relating to the Foreign Relations of the United States, 1919, Russia* (Washington, DC: Government Printing Office, 1937), 133–9, see also Ludwig Martens, "Mr. L. Martens to the Secretary of State," in US Department of State, "Policy of the United States toward the Soviet Government," in *Papers Relating to the Foreign Relations of the United States, 1920*, vol. 3, 455–6, "Senators Denounce Martens," *New York Times*, December 21, 1919, *Russian Propaganda: Hearing Before a Subcommittee of the Committee on Foreign Relations*, 66th Cong. (1920), *Russian Propaganda*, S. Doc. 526 (1920), US Department of State, "Policy of the United States toward the Soviet Government," in *Papers Relating to the Foreign Relations of the United States, 1920*, vol. 3, 455–61, 478–80, U.S. Department of Labor, Bureau of Immigration, *In the Matter of L. C. A. K. Martens: Brief on Behalf of Mr. Martens* (n.p., 1920?) and "Where Is Martens?" *New York Times*, January 21, 1921.

43 See Georgi Vasilyevich Chicherin, "The Soviet Commissar for Foreign Affairs (Chicherin) to President Coolidge," in US Department of State, *Papers Relating to the Foreign Relations of the United States, 1923*, vol. 2, 787 and Georgi Vasilyevich Chicherin, "Soviet Diplomacy since the War," *Living Age*, March 22, 1924, 548–51.

44 William M. Feigenbaum, "Delegates Ask US Recognize Soviet Russia," *New York Call*, June 30, 1921, 1–2.

45 See Friends of the Soviet Union, *Recognize Soviet Russia: Demand Full Unconditional Diplomatic & Trade Relations with the Soviet Union* (New York: The Friends, 1932), microfilm and "Russian Recognition Up to Congress," *Daily Worker*, January 14, 1924.

46 See "The Question of Recognizing Russia," *New Republic*, March 8, 1922, 33, John Hanna, "Russia Unrecognized," *New Republic*, January 19, 1929, 116–19, and "Recognize Russia," *The Nation*, May 18, 1932, 558.

47 Charles Evans Hughes, "Continued Refusal by the United States to Recognize the Soviet Regime," in US Department of State, *Papers Relating to the Foreign Relations of the United States, 1923*, vol. 2, 755–8.

48 Samuel Gompers, "The President of the American Federation of Labor (Gompers) to the Secretary of State," in US Department of State, *Papers Relating to the Foreign Relations of the United States, 1923*, vol. 2 (Washington, DC: Government Printing Office, 1936), 758–60.

49 Edmund A. Walsh, "We Can't Recognize Soviet Russia Yet," *Nation's Business*, January, 1926, 20–3.

50 See *Recognition of Russia, Part 1: Hearing Before the Subcommittee on S. Res. 60 of the Senate Com. on Foreign Relations*, 68th Cong. (1924) and *Recognition of Russia, Part 2: Hearing Before the Subcommittee on S. Res. 60 of the Senate Comm. on Foreign Relations*, 68th Cong. (1924).

51 Frank B. Kellogg, "Statement Concerning the Activities of the Department of State: Russia," vol. 3, 822–5.

52 *Investigation of Communist Propaganda: Hearings Before a Special Comm. to Investigate Communist Activities in the United States*, 71st Cong. (1930).

53 William R. Castle, Jr., "The Acting Secretary of State to Diplomatic and Consular Officers," in US Department of State, *Papers Relating to the Foreign Relations of the United States, 1931*, vol. 2 (Washington, DC: Government Printing Office, 1946), 980–3.

54 *Congressional Digest*, October, 1933.

55 US Department of State, Office of the Historian, "Milestone: 1921–1936: Recognition of the Soviet Union," accessed July 13, 2013, https://history.state.gov/milestones/1921-1936/ussr.

56 "Recognition by the United States of the Soviet Union, November 16, 1933," in US Department of State, Foreign Relations Branch, *Foreign Relations of the United States: The Soviet Union, 1933–1939*, 1–62.

57 Franklin Delano Roosevelt, "President Roosevelt to the President of the Soviet All-Union Central Executive Committee (Kalinin)," in US Department of State, Foreign Relations Branch, *Foreign Relations of the United States: The Soviet Union, 1933–1939*, 17–18.

58 Franklin Delano Roosevelt, "President Roosevelt to the Soviet Commissar for Foreign Affairs (Litvinov)," in US Department of State, Foreign Relations Branch, *Foreign Relations of the United States: The Soviet Union, 1933–1939*, 27.

59 See "Recognition by the United States of the Soviet Union, November 16, 1933," in US Department of State, Foreign Relations Branch, *Foreign Relations of the United States: The Soviet Union, 1933–1939*, 28–36 and S. Doc. No. 90, at 11310 (1933); see

also "Text Accompanying Our Recognition of Russia," *New York Times*, November 18, 1933.

60 See Walter Duranty, "United States Recognizes Soviet, Exacting Pledge on Propaganda," *New York Times*, November, 18, 1933, "The United States and Russia Make Deal," *Literary Digest*, November, 25, 1933, 4, Louis Fischer, "Behind Russian Recognition," *The Nation*, January 3, 1934, 9–10; for a summary, see Chandler Anderson, "Recognition of Russia," *American Journal of International Law* 28, no. 1 (January, 1934): 90–8; for a comprehensive study, see Robert Paul Browder, *The Origins of Soviet-American Diplomacy* (Princeton, NJ: Princeton University Press, 1953).

61 For an example, see Max Shachtman, "The Price of Recognition: The Diplomacy of Stalin and the Diplomacy of Lenin: A Contrast," *The Militant*, November, 1933.

62 "Roosevelt Health Drunk in Moscow," *New York Times*, November 20, 1933.

63 *The Bullitt Mission to Russia: Testimony before the Comm. on Foreign Relations*, 66th Cong. (1919).

64 William C. Bullitt, Jr., "The Ambassador in the Soviet Union (Bullitt) to the Secretary of State," in US Department of State, Foreign Relations Branch, *Foreign Relations of the United States: The Soviet Union, 1933–1939*, 289.

65 William C. Bullitt, Jr., *The Great Globe Itself: A Preface to World Affairs* (New York: Scribner, 1946), 36–7.

66 See Davies, *Mission to Moscow*.

67 See Charles E. Bohlen, "To Be Shot, to Be Shot, to Be Shot," in *Witness to History 1929–1969* (New York: W. W. Norton, 1973), 37–55, Loy W. Henderson, "The Great Purge," in *A Question of Trust*, 424–61, and George F. Kennan, "Moscow and Washington, DC in the 1930s," in *Memoirs 1925–1950*, 58–86.

68 See George F. Kennan, "The Chargé in the Soviet Union (Kennan) to the Secretary of State," accessed October 9, 2015, http://nsarchive.gwu.edu/coldwar/documents/episode-1/kennan.htm; for the "X" article see George F. Kennan, "The Sources of Soviet Conduct," *Foreign Affairs* 25, no. 4 (July, 1947): 566–82; see also George F. Kennan, *Russia and the West under Lenin and Stalin* (Boston, MA: Little, Brown, 1961).

69 See Joseph E. Davies, "The Ambassador in Belgium (Davies) to President Roosevelt," in US Department of State, Foreign Relations Branch, *Foreign Relations of the United States: The Soviet Union, 1933–1939*, 600–1; see also Bohlen, *Witness to History, 1929–1969*, 45, Henderson, *A Question of Trust*, 313–16, and May E. Glantz, "Officer and Diplomat? The Ambiguous Position of Philip R. Faymonville and United States-Soviet Relations, 1941–1943," *Journal of Military History* 72, no. 1 (January, 2008): 141–77.

70 See US Department of State, Foreign Relations Branch, "Protest to the Soviet Union Against Activities of the Seventh Congress of the Communist International as a Violation of Pledge of Noninterference in the Internal Affairs of the United States," in

Foreign Relations of the United States: The Soviet Union, 1933–1939, 218–68, and "U. S. Protests to the Soviet over Reds' Activities Here," *New York Times*, August 26, 1935.

Chapter 2

1. See Herman Bernstein, "Russia after Lenin—Will Soviet Survive?" *New York Times*, January 27, 1924, "What Next in Russia?" *The Outlook*, February 7, 1924, 211–12, and "Stalin Emerges as the 'Dictator' of Russia," *New York Times*, August 9, 1926.
2. Norman Pereira, "Stalin and the Communist Party in the 1920s," *History Today* 42, no. 8 (August, 1991): 16–23.
3. "Rumors Say Trotsky Submits," *New York Times*, October 16, 1926.
4. "Trotsky Attacked by Stalin," *New York Times*, December 11, 1926.
5. "Russian Technicians," *New York Times*, November 23, 1930.
6. See "'Chitska' the Soviet Cleaner," *Literary Digest*, February 20, 1932, 15.
7. Eugene Lyons, "The 'Purging' of Russia's Communists," *Literary Digest*, March 17, 1934, 14, 30–1.
8. See "Stalin Tramples on His Enemies," *Literary Digest*, October 29, 1932, 12–13 and "Stalin as the New Lenin," *New Republic*, July 23, 1930, 275–7.
9. "Government," in *The Soviet Union: Facts, Descriptions, Statistics* (Washington, DC: Soviet Union Information Bureau, 1929), accessed September 11, 2021, https://www.marxists.org.
10. Ibid.
11. See Roman Gul, "Stalin's Bloodhound," *Living Age*, May, 1938, 226–9, Harold Denny, "Milder 'OGPU' Seen," *New York Times*, September 28, 1936, and "Beria for Yezhov," *Time*, December 19, 1938, 19.
12. See Walter Duranty, "Soviet Chiefs Stage Anti-Treason Show," *New York Times* June 22, 1922, "The Trial of the Russian Socialist Revolutionaries," *The Nation*, July 5, 1922, 24, Walter Duranty, "Death Sentence Sure in the Moscow Trial," *New York Times*, July 27, 1922, "The Moscow Trial," *New York Times*, August 11, 1922, Paxton Hibben, "Moscow's Treason Trial," *The Nation*, September 27, 1922, 299–300, and "The Moscow Sentence," *The Nation*, November 29, 1922, 588–9.
13. J. Louis Engdahl, "A Reply to Debs," *The Worker*, August 12, 1922.
14. Ibid.
15. Walter Duranty, "Stalin Denounces 'Technician's Plot,'" *New York Times*, April 19, 1928.
16. See Walter Duranty, "Score Plead Guilty in 'Engineers' Plot,'" *New York Times*, May 12, 1928, Walter Duranty, "Grim Soviet Court Opens Trial of 52," *New York Times*, May 19, 1928, Walter Duranty, "Capital Charge Thrills Don Trial," *New York Times*, May 25, 1928, Walter Duranty, "Ukrainian Fights Krylenko for Life," *New York*

Times, May 27, 1928, Walter Duranty, "Shakhta Trial Moves to Climax," *New York Times*, June 23, 1928, and Walter Duranty, "Last Pleas Heard in Shakta Tragedy," *New York Times*, July 4, 1928.
17 "Shahkta," *Time*, July 2, 1928, 17–18.
18 Editorial, *The Nation*, July 18, 1928, 53–4.
19 See Walter Duranty, "Plot to Start War Against the Soviet Charged in Moscow," *New York Times*, November 12, 1930, Walter Duranty, "Moscow Cries Death to Eight, 'Traitors,'" *New York Times*, November 26, 1930, Walter Duranty, "3 Plotters Confess at Moscow Trial," *New York Times*, November 27, 1930, Walter Duranty, "Soviet Engineers Deny 'Framing' Plot," *New York Times*, December 1, 1930, and Walter Duranty, "Say Emigrés Spoke of War on Soviet," *New York Times*, December 2, 1930.
20 See P. J. Philip, "Soviet Trial Scored as Fake by Emigres," *New York Times*, November 30, 1930.
21 See "Russia's Greatest Conspiracy Trial—Fact or Fake?" *Literary Digest*, December 20, 1930, 10, "Behind the Scenes in Moscow," *Literary Digest*, January 24, 1931, 13, and "Soviet Defense of the 'World-Infamous' Trial," *Literary Digest*, January 31, 1931, 13–14.
22 Eugene Lyons, "'Death to Wreckers?,'" in *Assignment in Utopia*, 370–80.
23 See W. W. Holmes, *The Wreckers Exposed in the Trial of the Counter-Revolutionary Industrial Party* (New York: Workers Library Publishers, 1931) and *Wreckers on Trial: A Record of the Trial of the Industrial Party Held in Moscow, Nov.-Dec., 1930*, ed. with a forward by Andrew Rothstein (New York: Workers Library, 1931).
24 A. G. Bosse, "The Background of the Moscow Espionage Trial," *Soviet Russia Today*, May, 1933, 7.
25 Jessie Rubin, "A Wrecker's Story," *Soviet Russia Today*, March, 1938, 20–1, 24.
26 Walter Duranty, "Wary Course Set for Soviet Trial," *New York Times*, March 3, 1931.
27 *The Case of N. P. Vitvitsky* (Moscow: State Law Publishing House, 1933).
28 See Walter Duranty, "Britons Guilty Says Soviet Press," *New York Times*, March 27, 1933, "See No End of Moscow Case," *New York Times*, March 28, 1933, "Say Soviet Quizzed Briton 21 Hours," *New York Times*, April 10, 1933, "Priznayu," *Time*, April 24, 1933, 20–2, and "Moscow's Red Drama of British Engineers," *Literary Digest*, April 29, 1933, 10–11.
29 Eugene Lyons, "Britishers on Trial," in *Assignment in Utopia*, 561–71.
30 See Liston M. Oak and Herbert Goldfrank, "What Is behind the British Embargo?" *Soviet Russia Today*, May, 1933, 3, 10 and Peter Bolm, "The World Political Background of the Engineers Trial," *The Communist*, May, 1933, 449–57.
31 *The Moscow Trial: New Light on the Case: Four Articles Reprinted from the Times of May 22, 23,24, and 25, 1933, Together with the Leading Article* (London: Times Publishing, 1933).
32 See Walter Duranty, "Trotsky Has Failed to Regain Power," *New York Times*, January 21, 1926, Walter Duranty, "Inner Opposition Preoccupies Reds," *New York Times*, July 13, 1927, and "Trotzky Out," *Time*, October 10, 1927, 20.

33 "Expulsion of Trotsky and Zinoviev: Statement of the Central Executive Committee of the Workers (Communist) Party of America, Nov. 20, 1927," *Daily Worker*, November 21, 1927.
34 See "Trotsky Banished as Menace to Soviet Union, Says High Russian Official Arriving at Berlin," *New York Times*, January 31, 1929, Elias Tobenkin, "Trotsky in Exile Cast His Shadow on Russia," *New York Times*, March 3, 1929, and "Exile Trotsky," *Time*, March 11, 1929, 31.
35 "Soviet Arrests 150 for Civil War Plot," *New York Times*, January 24, 1929.
36 See Leon Trotsky, "Trotsky Recounts the Inside Story of His Persecution," *New York Times*, February 26, 1929, Leon Trotsky, "Trotsky Describes Hardships of Exile," *New York Times*, February 27, 1929, and Leon Trotsky, "Trotsky Appraises His Enemy, Stalin," *New York Times*, February 29, 1929.
37 M. S. (Max Shachtman), "Trotsky's Deportation," *The Militant*, February 1, 1929.
38 Russian Soviet Federated Socialist Republic, *Penal Code*, Art. 58, Appendix, Special Section, ch. 1 (1950), accessed October 9, 2017, http://www.cyberussr.com/rus/uk58-e.html.
39 See Harold Denny, "Kiroff, High Soviet Leader, Slain," *New York Times*, December 2, 1934, Harold Denny, "Ex-Soviet Employe Is Kiroff Assassin," *New York Times*, December 3, 1934, and "Farewell, Dear Friend," *Time*, December 10, 1934, 24.
40 See Vern Smith, "Kirov's Death Stirs Masses," *Daily Worker*, December 3, 1934, and "Kirov, Tireless Fighter for Bolshevik Principles," *Daily Worker*, December 3, 1934.
41 See Harold Denny, "Soviet Arrests 71 in War on 'Terror,'" *New York Times*, December 4, 1934, and Harold Denny, "Counsel Barred in Soviet Trials," *New York Times*, December 5, 1934.
42 See Harold Denny, "66 Are Executed by Soviet, Accused of 'Terrorist' Plots," *New York Times*, December 6, 1934, Harold Denny, "12 More in Soviet Held as Plotters," *New York Times*, December 8, 1934, Harold Denny, "37 More Arrested in Russian 'Plots,'" *New York Times*, December 11, 1934, Harold Denny, "'Terror' Toll Is 75 as Soviet Shoots 9," *New York Times*, December 12, 1934, Harold Denny, "Russian Arrests Spreading Terror," *New York Times*, December 16, 1934, Harold Denny, "Red Rebel Group is Seized in Russia," *New York Times*, December 22, 1934, and Harold Denny, "Soviet Asks Hunt for Foes Continue," *New York Times*, December 31, 1934.
43 "Pure Terror," *Time*, December 17, 1934, 26–8; see also "They Always Confess," *Time*, February 4, 1935, 34.
44 "Killings in Russia Are Protested Here," *New York Times*, December 16, 1934.
45 See Harold Denny, "More Leaders Held as Foes of Soviet," *New York Times*, December 23, 1934, Harold Denny, "Plot to Kill Stalin with Foreign Help Linked to Assassin," *New York Times*, December 27, 1934, "14 More Executed for Kiroff Murder," *New York Times*, December 30, 1934, "Text of Court Statement,"

New York Times, December 30, 1934, and Harold Denny, and "Soviet Asks Hunt for Foes Continue," *New York Times*, December 31, 1934.

46 William Henry Chamberlin, "Behind the Events in Russia," *New York Times*, January 6, 1935.
47 Harold Denny, "Ex-Leaders Tried by Soviet in Plot," *New York Times*, January 6, 1935; see also Harold Denny, "Soviet Party Seen as Ruthless When Any of Its Members Rebel," *New York Times*, January 20, 1935, and Harold Denny, "Russia Presses 'Cleansing,'" *New York Times*, January 27, 1935.
48 "'Coward Scum!'" *Time*, December 31, 1934, 21.
49 "The Liberal Life," *Time*, January 28, 1935, 31.
50 Editorial, *The Nation*, December 26, 1934, 696.
51 See Oswald Garrison Villard, "The Russian 'Purging,'" *The Nation*, December 26, 1934, 729 and Oswald Garrison Villard, "The Russian Murders Again," *The Nation*, January 23, 1935, 91.
52 See Louis Fischer, "Behind the Kirov Executions—I," *The Nation*, May 8, 1935, 529–31 and Louis Fischer, "Behind the Kirov Executions—II," *The Nation*, May 15, 1935, 566–8.
53 The Week, *New Republic*, December 12, 1934, 115.
54 "The Russian Executions," *New Republic*, January 23, 1935, 292–3.
55 See "Telegram from the Comintern's Youth Organization to Gilbert Green, CPUSA, Regarding the Struggle Against Oppositionists," in *Enemies within the Gates: The Comintern and the Stalinist Repression, 1934–1939*, ed. William J. Chase, trans. Vadim A. Staklo (New Haven, CT: Yale University Press, 2001), 39, "Report of Comrade Heath on Kirov Assassination and Trotzky Counter Revolution," in Klehr, Haynes, and Anderson, *The Soviet World of American Communism*, 294–7, and "Telegram from the Political Commission of the ECCI Political Secretariat to the Communist Parties," in Chase, *Enemies within the Gates*, 40–1.
56 See "Zinoviev, Kamenev among Those Jailed in Kirov Murder," *Daily Worker*, December 24, 1934, "Kirov Killer Tells of Plot to Slay Stalin," *Daily Worker*, December 27, 1934, "Kirov Killer Aided by Latvian Envoy," *Daily Worker*, January 5, 1935, and "19 Confess Anti-Party Role Which Inspired the Murder of Kirov," *Daily Worker*, January 17, 1935.
57 Klemens Gottwald, "Trotzkyism—Agent of International Fascism," *Daily Worker*, January 30, 1935.
58 "Workers' Ire Mounts over Kirov Killing," *Daily Worker*, December 27, 1934.
59 See "The Executions in Soviet Russia," *New Masses*, December 25, 1934, 9–10, Herbert Goldfrank, "Significance of the Kirov Murder," *Soviet Russia Today*, March, 1935, 10, 19, Communist Party of the U.S.A., Central Committee, "Sergei Mironovitch Kirov," *The Communist*, January, 1935, 3, and Albert Radier, "The Historic Path of the Zinovievist Group," *The Communist*, March, 1935, 227–32.

60 M. Katz, *The Assassination of Kirov: Proletarian Justice versus White-Guard Terror* (New York: Workers Library Publishers, 1935).
61 Moissaye J. Olgin, *Trotskyism: Counter-Revolution in Disguise* (New York: Workers Library Publishers, 1935).
62 Will Herberg, "As to 'Red Terror,'" *Workers Age*, December 15, 1934.
63 Max Shachtman, "Behind the Kirov Assassination," *New International*, January, 1935, 4–6.
64 "Stalin Follows Hitler's Method," *Socialist Appeal*, February, 1935.
65 Leon Trotsky, *Leon Trotsky on the Kirov Assassination* (New York: Pioneer Publishers, 1935).
66 See Bohlen, *Witness to History, 1929–1969*, 42–3, Henderson, *A Question of Trust*, 426–32, and Kennan, *Memoirs, 1925–1950*, 64–5.
67 Duranty, *I Write as I Please*, 188.
68 See Robert Conquest, *Stalin and the Kirov Murder* (New York: Oxford University Press, 1989), Amy Knight, *Who Killed Kirov? The Kremlin's Greatest Mystery* (New York: Hill and Wang, 1999) and Matthew E. Lenoe, *The Kirov Murder and Soviet History* (New Haven, CT: Yale University Press, 2010).
69 Joseph E. Davies, "Moscow Notebook—An Ambassador's Report," *New York Times Magazine*, December 14, 1941, SM12-13, 24–6.
70 "List of Persons," in US Department of State, Foreign Relations Branch, *Foreign Relations of the United States: The Soviet Union, 1933–1939*, vii–xix.

Chapter 3

1 Union of Soviet Socialist Republics, People's Commissariat of Justice, *The Case of the Trotskyite-Zinovievite Terrorist Centre: Report of the Court Proceedings Heard before the Military Collegium of the Supreme Court of the U.S.S.R., Moscow, August 19–24, 1936* (Moscow: The Commissariat, 1936).
2 "Zinoviev the Thunderer," *Time*, July 21, 1924, 11.
3 "4 of 16 Won Soviet Fame," *New York Times*, August 25, 1936.
4 Harold Denny, "Russian Reds Oust 3 More Officials," *New York Times*, January 12, 1935.
5 Harold Denny, "Bolshevik Linked in Plot Ends Life," *New York Times*, August 23, 1936.
6 Union of Soviet Socialist Republics, People's Commissariat of Justice, *The Case of the Trotskyite-Zinovievite Terrorist Centre*, 164.
7 "Kameneff's Death in Jail Described," *New York Times*, October 21, 1936.
8 Joseph Stalin, "Answer of Comrade Stalin," in US Department of State, Foreign Relations Branch, *Foreign Relations of the United States: The Soviet Union, 1933–1939*, 523.

9. Loy W. Henderson, "The Chargé in the Soviet Union (Henderson) to the Secretary of State," In US Department of State, Foreign Relations Branch, *Foreign Relations of the United States: The Soviet Union, 1933–1939*, 520.
10. Ibid., 301.
11. Ibid., 301–2.
12. Ibid., 302–3.
13. Henderson, *A Question of Trust*, 433–40.
14. Harold Denny, "New Soviet Purge Nets 'Fascist Spy,'" *New York Times*, August 13, 1936.
15. "Soviet Indicts 16 as a Terror Band Guided by Trotsky," *New York Times*, August 15, 1936.
16. See Harold Denny, "Ex-Soviet Leaders Are Likely to Die for 'Terror Plot,'" *New York Times*, August 16, 1936, Harold Denny, "Soviet Plot Hunt Hits Trade Chiefs," *New York Times*, August 17, 1936, and Harold Denny, "'Trotskyists' Face Trial as Bandits," *New York Times*, August 18, 1936.
17. Walter Duranty, "Proof of a Plot Expected," *New York Times*, August 17, 1936.
18. Harold Denny, "16 in Soviet Admit 2 Plots to Kill Stalin and Others," *New York Times*, August 20, 1936.
19. Harold Denny, "Trotsky Is Called Real Conspirator in Anti-Soviet Plot," *New York Times*, August 21, 1936.
20. Harold Denny, "Trials Dramatize Soviet Struggles," *New York Times*, August 23, 1936.
21. Harold Denny, "Soviet Sentences 16 to Die in Plot to Kill Red Leaders," *New York Times*, August 24, 1936.
22. Harold Denny, "Workers Approve the Sentences," *New York Times*, August 25, 1936.
23. Harold Denny, "Russians Defend Executions," *New York Times*, August 30, 1936.
24. See "Confessions in Moscow," *New York Times*, August 23, 1936, and "The Stalin Purge," *New York Times*, August 26, 1936.
25. "Trial Diversion," *Time*, August 24, 1936, 29.
26. "Perfect Dictator," *Time*, August 31, 1936, 16–18.
27. "Soviet Police Uncover 'New Plot' Against Dictator," *Newsweek*, August 22, 1936, 16.
28. "'Mad Fascist Dogs' Meekly Admit Plot to Kill Stalin with Aid of Reich Secret Police," *Newsweek*, August 29, 1936, 10–11.
29. "World's Loneliest Man 'Protected' by Oslo Police," *Newsweek*, September 5, 1936, 16.
30. "Guilt and Doom: Sixteen Russians Hear Verdict after Fantastic Self-Vilification," *Literary Digest*, August 29, 1936, 15.
31. Eugene Lyons, "Moscow Demonstration Trial," *American Mercury*, January, 1937, 37–45.
32. "The Trial of the Trotskyites in Russia," *New Republic*, September 2, 1936, 88–9.

33 "'Old Bolsheviks' on Trial," *The Nation*, August 22, 1936, 201.
34 "The Shape of Things," editorial, *The Nation*, August 29, 1936, 226.
35 "The Moscow Trials," *The Nation*, October 10, 1936, 409.
36 See "Terrorist Plot by Trotskyists Bared in the USSR," *Daily Worker*, August 15, 1936, "Directed from Abroad by Trotsky to Kill Soviet Leaders," *Daily Worker*, August 15, 1936, "Trotskyist Tie with Nazis Revealed as Trials Near," *Daily Worker*, August 17, 1936, "Soviet Masses Ask No Mercy for Plotters," *Daily Worker*, August 17, 1936, "Trotsky-Nazi Lies," *Daily Worker*, August 17, 1936, "14 Accused Trotskyists Admit Guilt in Soviet Trial," *Daily Worker*, August 20, 1936, "Trotsky Gave Orders to Kill Stalin, Kirov, Say Plotters," *Daily Worker*, August 21, 1936, "Trotskyist Plotters Disclose Conspiracy to Assassinate Stalin, Red Army Chief," *Daily Worker*, August 21, 1936, "Trotsky Demanded Killing of Stalin in Plot for Power," *Daily Worker*, August 21, 1936, "Trotskyist Plotters Disclose Conspiracy to Assassinate Stalin, Red Army Chief," *Daily Worker*, August 22, 1936, and "People Hail Sentence of Plotters," *Daily Worker*, August 26, 1936.
37 "Trotskyism Plus Terrorism = Fascism" [editorial cartoon]. *Daily Worker*, August 22, 1936.
38 Khristian Rakovsy, "Soviet Press Asks Death for Plotters," *Daily Worker*, August 22, 1936.
39 See "Trotskyism, Spurned by Masses, Uses Nazi Aid Against USSR," *Daily Worker*, August 22, and "Socialists Should Repudiate Trotskyists in Their Ranks," *Daily Worker*, August 26, 1936.
40 "Careers of Kamenev, Zinoviev Spotted with Double Dealings Against Leadership of Soviets," *Daily Worker*, August 26, 1936.
41 See "The *Daily Worker* of CPUSA on the Trotsky-Zinovievist Terrorist Trial," in Klehr, Anderson, Anderson, *The Soviet World of American Communism*, 301–4.
42 See Klehr, Haynes, and Anderson, *The Soviet World of American Communism*, 312 and "Bare Trotsky Terror Plot," *Western Worker*, August 21, 1936. "Soviet Masses Ask No 'Clemency' for U.S.S.R. Enemies," *Western Worker*, August 24, 1936 and "Soviets Greet Plotters End," *Western Worker*, August 31, 1936.
43 See Joshua Kunitz, "The Moscow Trials," *New Masses*, October 20, 1936, 3–5, Joshua Kunitz, "Seeds of Counter-Revolution," *New Masses*, October 27, 1936, 11–13, and Joshua Kunitz, "Getting in Deeper," *New Masses*, November 3, 1936, 13–15.
44 Joshua Kunitz, "The End of the Road," *New Masses*, November 10, 1936, 18.
45 Sam Darcy, "Concerning the Press," in Klehr, Haynes, and Anderson, *The Soviet World of American Communism*, 314–17.
46 Communist International, Executive Committee, "Telegram from the ECCI to the CC of the CP of Czechoslovakia, Switzerland, Holland, France, Belgium, USA, Canada, Sweden, Norway, Denmark, and to Julius Regarding the Struggle Against Trotskyism," in *Enemies within the Gates? The Comintern and the Stalinist Repressions, 1934–1939*, ed. William J. Chase (New Haven, CT: Yale University Press, 2010), 191.

47 "The Trotsky Cesspool," *New Masses*, September 1, 1936, 4.
48 See "The *Nation* and Trotsky," *New Masses*, November 10, 1936, 11–13, and "Once More the '*Nation*,'" *New Masses*, December 22, 1936, 20.
49 Alexander Bittelman, "Review of the Month," *The Communist*, September, 1936, 813–15.
50 "A Summary Based on the Official Record of the Trial of the Trotsky-Zinoviev Terrorist Center," *Soviet Russia Today*, October, 1936, 11, 26.
51 Anna Louise Strong, "The Terrorists' Trial," *Soviet Russia Today*, October, 1936, accessed August 5, 2016, http://neworleans.media.indypgh.org/uploads/2007/02/the_terrorists_trial_15feb07.pdf.
52 See Communist International, Executive Committee, "Telegram from the ECCI to Earl Browder, CPUSA," in Chase, *Enemies within the Gates?* 150, M. Kreps, "Memorandum from M. Kreps to Dimitrov Regarding Publications about the 'Trotskyist-Zinovietite Terrorist Center,'" in *To Defend Assassins Is to Help Fascism*, ed. Georgi Dimitrov (New York: Workers Library Publishers, 1937), Andrei Y. Vyshinsky, *Trotskyism in the Service of Fascism Against Socialism and Peace* (New York: Workers Library Publishers, 1937) and D. N. Pritt, *At the Moscow Trial* (New York: International Publishers, 1937).
53 See Alexander Unger, "More Light on the Moscow Trial," *Soviet Russia Today*, February, 1937, 22, 30–1, and "D. N. Pritt on the Zinoviev Trial," *Soviet Russia Today*, February, 1937, 7.
54 "Soviets Doom Plotters," *Workers Age*, August 29, 1936.
55 "The Russian Events," *Workers Age*, September 5, 1936.
56 See A. Tarov, "Tarov Relates Torture of Real Bolsheviks in Stalin's Prisons," *New Militant*, October 19, 1935, A. Ciliga, "Jugoslav Communist Escapes from Siberia," *New Militant*, January 25, 1936, "Who Are the Exiled Revolutionists in Jails and Concentration Camps?" *New Militant*, January 25, 1936, "A Cry of Protest from a Siberian Exile Camp," *New Militant*, February 8, 1936, L. D. Trotsky, "'Tell the Workers the Truth about Stalin's Hounding of Revolutionists in the Soviet Union'— Trotsky Urges," *New Militant*, February 1, 1936, and "Our Voices Must Be Heard!" *New International*, June, 1936, inside front cover.
57 See "A Statement of Fact on Stalin's Terror, on Mr. H.earst and the Sunday Worker," *New Militant*, January 25, 1936, "Cablegram from Leon Trotsky Hits Hearst and Daily Worker Lies,'" *New Militant*, February 1, 1936, "Russian Fascists Hail the Anti-Bolshevik Terror in Soviet Union," *New Militant*, February 1, 1936, and "Pen Prostitute NO. 1," *New Militant*, February 1, 1936.
58 "Stalin's Terror Against Bolsheviks" [advertisement], *New Militant*, February 1, 1936.
59 See "Trotsky Says, 'Humbug,' of Moscow Trial," *New York Times*, August 20, 1936, and Joseph Shaplen, "Trotsky Accuses Stalin of Killings," *New York Times*, December 26, 1936.
60 Leon Trotsky, "Let Us Know the Facts," *Socialist Appeal*, September 1936.

61. "Editorial Statement on Stalinist Charges Against Leon Trotsky," *Socialist Appeal*, September 1936.
62. Leon Trotsky, "An Interview with Leon Trotsky on the Recent Moscow Trial," *Socialist Appeal*, October 1936.
63. Max Shachtman, "The Moscow Trial," *Socialist Appeal*, October 1936.
64. Max Shachtman, *Behind the Moscow Trial* (New York: Pioneer Publishers, 1936).
65. Nathan Frankel, "Review of *Behind the Moscow Trial* by Max Shachtman," *New Masses*, January 19, 1937, 23–4.
66. Theodore Dan, "The Trials and Executions in Moscow," *Socialist Appeal*, October, 1936.
67. "Stalin's Stooge?" *Time*, December 28, 1936, 17.
68. Walter Krivitsky, "Stalin's Third Degree Methods Are Revealed by Former GPU Agent," *Socialist Appeal*, July 9, 1938.
69. Lev Sedov, *The Red Book on the Moscow Trials: Documents* (London: New Park, 1980).
70. Leon Trotsky, "Zinoviev and Kamenev," *Fourth International* 2, no. 7 (August, 1941): 222–3.
71. James P. Cannon, "Early Years of the American Communist Movement," *International Socialist Review* 17, no. 4 (Fall, 1956): 127–30.
72. *Stalinism Betrays the Spanish Revolution: Behind the Murder of Zinoviev, Kamenev, Smirnov and the Frame-Up of Trotsky* (New York: Revolutionary Workers League of the U. S., 1936).
73. "The Moscow Trial," *Socialist Call*, September 5, 1936.
74. Friedrich Adler, "The Soviet Trial and Labor Unity," *Socialist Call*, November 21, 1936; see also Friedrich Adler, *The Witchcraft Trial in Moscow* (New York: Pioneer Publishers, 1937).
75. David P. Berenberg, "The Moscow Trial," *American Socialist Monthly*, December, 1936, 26–33.
76. Boris Nicolaevsky, *Letter of an Old Bolshevik* (New York: Rand School Press, 1937).
77. See Anna Larina, *This I Cannot Forget: The Memoirs of Nikolai Bukharin's Widow* (New York: W. W. Norton, 1993) and Robert C. Tucker, "On the 'Letter of an Old Bolshevik' as an Historical Document," Review of *Power and the Soviet Elite: "The Letter of an Old Bolshevik"* by Boris I. Nicolaevsky, *Slavic Review* 51, no. 4 (Winter, 1992): 782–5.

Chapter 4

1. See Harold Denny, "6 Soviet Leaders Now under Inquiry," *New York Times*, August 22, 1936, and "Pravda Paves Way for Trial of Radek," *New York Times*, October 8, 1936.

2 See Walter Duranty, "Soviet Tries Radek and 16 on Saturday as Trotsky's Aides," *New York Times*, January 20, 1937.
3 Union of Soviet Socialist Republics, People's Commissariat of Justice, *Report of the Court Proceedings in the Case of the Anti-Soviet Trotskyite Centre: Heard Before the Military Collegium of the Supreme Court of the U.S.S.R., Moscow, January 23–30, 1937* (Moscow: The Commissariat, 1937), 17.
4 Ibid., 5.
5 Ibid.
6 See Karl Radek, "Bertrand Russell's Sentimental Journey," *Living Age*, February 12, 1921, 390–3 and "Radek Assails Sinclair for Adopting Fascist Way," *New York Times*, October 7, 1934.
7 See Karl Radek, "Appeal for Trotsky," *The Militant*, January 1, 1929 and Walter Duranty, "Trotskyist Makes Bid for Return to Fold," *New York Times*, May 31, 1929.
8 Karl Radek, *Portraits and Pamphlets* (New York: R. M. McBride, 1935); for a mixed review, see Ludwig Lore, "Karl Radek," Review of *Portraits and Pamphlets* by Karl Radek, *The Nation*, October 23, 1935, 482–3.
9 See "Fate May Hang on Article," *New York Times*, October 8, 1936 and "Journalist Jailed," *Time*, October 19, 1936, 30.
10 "Radek Is Assailed as a Trotsky Aide," *New York Times*, January 5, 1937.
11 Louis Francis Budenz, "What Has Become of Karl Radek?" *American Mercury*, September, 1955, 143–8.
12 Conquest, *The Great Terror*, 31–2.
13 Karl Radek and Yuri Pyatakov, "Radek and Pyatakov Condemn Trotsky as Terrorist Plot Leader, Ally of Fascists and Principal Inspirer of Kirov Assassination," *Daily Worker*, August 24, 1936.
14 Communist International, Executive Committee, "Telegram from the ECCI Secretariat to Earl Browder," in *Enemies within the Gates: The Comintern and the Stalinist Repression, 1934–1939*, ed. William Chase (New Haven, CT: Yale University Press, 2001), 150.
15 Walter Duranty, "Radek Held Saved to Convict Others," *New York Times*, January 29, 1937.
16 George F. Kennan, "The Chargé in the Soviet Union (Kennan) to the Secretary of State," in US Department of State, Foreign Relations Branch, *Foreign Relations of the United States: The Soviet Union, 1933–1939* (Washington, DC: Government Printing Office, 1952), 362–5.
17 "Death of Sergo," *Time*, March [1], 1937, 22.
18 See "Ordjonikidze Dies Suddenly in Russia," *New York Times*, February 19, 1937, Walter Duranty, "Russians Grieving over Ordjonikidze," *New York Times*, February 20, 1937 and Walter Duranty, "750,000 in Parade at Soviet Funeral," *New York Times*, February 22, 1937.
19 Conquest, *The Great Terror*, 167–73.

20 Henderson, "The Chargé in the Soviet Union (Henderson) to the Secretary of State [Extract]," 304–5.
21 George F. Kennan, "Memorandum by the Second Secretary of Embassy in the Soviet Union (Kennan)," in US Department of State, Foreign Relations Branch, *Foreign Relations of the United States: The Soviet Union, 1933–1939*, 362–9.
22 Ibid., 363–4.
23 George F. Kennan, "Memorandum by the Second Secretary of Embassy in the Soviet Union (Kennan)," in US Department of State, Foreign Relations Branch, *Foreign Relations of the United States: The Soviet Union, 1933–1939*, 365.
24 George F. Kennan, "Kennan on the Cold War: An Interview with George Kennan," *CNN*, May–June, 1996, accessed March 15, 2015, http://www.johndclare.net/ cold_war7_Kennan_interview.htm.
25 Kennan, *Memoirs, 1925–1950*, 83.
26 Joseph E. Davies, "Behind the Moscow Trials," in *Mission to Moscow: A Record of Confidential Dispatches to the State Department, Official and Personal Correspondence, Current Diary and Journal Entries, Including Notes and Comments up to October, 1941* (London: V. Gollancz, 1942), 31–45.
27 Ibid., 34.
28 Ibid., 31–40.
29 Ibid.
30 Ibid., 45.
31 Kennan, *Memoirs, 1925–1950*, 83.
32 Henderson, "The Chargé in the Soviet Union (Henderson) to the Secretary of State," 381.
33 Cordell Hull, "Memorandum by the Secretary of State of a Conversation with the Ambassador of the Soviet Union (Troyanovsky)," in US Department of State, Foreign Relations Branch, *Foreign Relations of the United States: The Soviet Union, 1933–1939*, 396–7.
34 Dale Reynolds and Paul Kesaris, eds., "Soviet Russia," in *U. S. Military Intelligence Reports: Bi-Weekly Intelligence Summaries, 1928–1938* (Frederick, MD: University Publications of America, 1985), 16085–96. Microfilm.
35 Walter Duranty, "Plot with Reich and Japan Confessed at Soviet Trial," *New York Times*, January 24, 1937; see also "Plot to Spread Germs Charged," *New York Times*, January 24, 1937.
36 Walter Duranty, "Radek Wins Tilt of Wits at Trial," *New York Times*, January 25, 1937.
37 "Radek Bares Plot to Halt Railways," *New York Times*, January 25, 1937.
38 "Russian Plotters Say War on Soviet Was Fixed for 1937," *New York Times*, January 28, 1937.
39 "Japan Issues Denial," *New York Times*, January 28, 1937.
40 "Goering Denied Trotsky Link," *New York Times*, January 28, 1937.

41 Walter Duranty, "Death of 17 Asked at Moscow Trial," *New York Times*, January 29, 1937.
42 "Some of Accused Showed Fear," *New York Times*, January 29, 1937.
43 Walter Duranty, "Soviet Dooms 13," *New York Times*, January 30, 1937.
44 "Several of Convicted Wept," *New York Times*, January 30, 1937.
45 "Radek's Mother, 82, Near Death," *New York Times*, January 30, 1937.
46 "Denies Meeting in Norway," *New York Times*, January 30, 1937.
47 Walter Duranty, "Radek Held Saved to Convict Others," *New York Times*, January 31, 1937.
48 "13 Plotters' Pleas Futile in Moscow," *New York Times*, February 1, 1937.
49 Walter Duranty, "Verdict Widely Applauded," *New York Times*, February 1, 1937.
50 Walter Duranty, "Soviet Executes 13 as Trotskyists," *New York Times*, February 2, 1937.
51 "Manner of Execution Unstated," *New York Times*, February 2, 1937.
52 Walter Duranty, "All Russia Reacts to Treason Trial," *New York Times*, February 7, 1937.
53 Walter Duranty, "Why Stalin Wages Merciless War on Trotsky," *New York Times Magazine*, February 7, 1937, SM3, SM22.
54 "Soviet 'Purge' Jails Trotskyists," *New York Times*, February 7, 1937.
55 Walter Duranty, "Story of Russian 'Purge' Is Denied," *New York Times*, February 14, 1937.
56 "Topic of the Times," *New York Times*, January 28, 1937.
57 "Topic of the Times," *New York Times*, March 7, 1937.
58 Joseph Shaplen, "The Recent Moscow Trial," letter to the editor, *New York Times*, February 6, 1937.
59 Harold Denny, "Soviet to Send First Permanent Reporter," *New York Times*, June 2, 1934.
60 "Dictatorships Temporary, Says Soviet Who Sees Russians Turning to Democracy," *New York Times*, June 27, 1935.
61 Duranty, "Radek Wins Tilt of Wits at Trial."
62 See "American Writers Attempt to Save Romm," *New York Times*, January 24, 1937, "Friends Again Act in Romm's Behalf," *New York Times*, January 27, 1937, Paul W. Ward, "Vladimir Romm," *The Nation*, February 6, 1937 and "Trotskyist Plots Laid to Old Ideal," *New York Times*, March 3, 1937.
63 Joseph E. Davies, "Intercession for Vladimir Romm," in *Mission to Moscow*, 41–5.
64 Leon Trotsky, "Trotsky Denies Charges at Trial," *New York Times*, January 24, 1937.
65 "Trotsky's Defense," editorial, *New York Times*, February 17, 1937.
66 "Old & New Bolsheviks," *Time*, February [1], 1937, 20–4.
67 "Red Square Deal," *Time*, February 8, 1937, 25–6.

68 "Assorted Victims Fall under Stalin Steam Roller," *Newsweek*, April 24, 1937, 18–19.
69 "'Gangsters' Confess Conniving with Official Devil," *Newsweek*, January 30, 1937, 18.
70 "Soviet Trial: Ambassador Davies Arrives in Time to Hear Incredible Confession of Treason," *Literary Digest*, January 30, 1937, 12–13.
71 "Political Hostages," editorial, *Saturday Evening Post*, March 6, 1937, 24.
72 John D. Littlepage, *In Search of Soviet Gold* (New York: Harcourt, Brace, 1938).
73 See "New Light on Trotskyite Wrecking," *Soviet Russia Today*, February, 1938, 4–5.
74 Joseph Hansen, "Gold Is Where You Find It," *New International*, December, 1938, 382–3.
75 "Another Russian Trial," *New Republic*, February 3, 1937, 399–400.
76 "Russian Politics in America," *New Republic*, February 17, 1937, 33–4.
77 Malcolm Cowley, "The Record of a Trial," *New Republic*, April 7, 1937, 267–70.
78 "Agnosticism in the Moscow Trials," *New Republic*, May 19, 1937, 33–4.
79 Walter Duranty, "The Riddle of Russia: What Lies behind Recent Events in the USSR?" *New Republic*, July 14, 1937, 270–2.
80 John Stevens, "The Russian Purge, Seen from Below," *New Republic*, October 20, 1937, 295–6.
81 "Behind the Soviet Trials," *The Nation*, February 6, 1937, 143–5.
82 Max Radin, "The Moscow Trials: A Legal View," *Foreign Affairs*, October 16, 1937, 64–79.
83 William Renwick Riddell, "Recent Russian Trotskyite Centre Criminal Trial," *Journal of Criminal Law and Criminology* 28, no. 3 (September–October, 1937): 335–9.
84 For examples of Comintern directives on the second trial, see Communist International, Executive Committee, "Letter from the ECCI Secretariat to Leaders of Selected Communist Parties Regarding Propaganda Work during the Trial of Radek, Pyatakov and Others," in *Enemies within the Gates: The Comintern and the Stalinist Repression, 1934–1939*, ed. William J. Chase, trans. Vadim A. Staklo (New Haven, CT: Yale University Press, 2001), 192–3, and Communist International, Executive Committee, "On Carrying out the Campaign Against Trotskyism," in Chase, *Enemies within the Gates*, 202–3.
85 For examples of articles on the trial in *Daily Worker*, see "Trotzky Link to Plot War on Soviet Union," January 25, 1937, "War on USSR by Japan, Nazis Goal of Trotzkyists," January 25, 1937, Sender Garlin, " Martyrs of Socialist Construction Killed and Maimed by Trotskyite Murderers in the Soviet Union," January 25, 1937, Sender Garlin, "Trial Is Marked by Fairness of Procedure," January 26, 1937, "Trotzky Ordered Aides to 'Make Terms with Fascism' to Restore Capitalism in USSR," January 26, 1937, "Execute Them—Soviet Workers Ask," January, 26,

1937, "Witness Admits Trotzky Made Deals with Fascist Powers to Parcel USSR," January 27, 1937, "Japan Bought Spy Data from Trotskyites," January 28, 1937, "Accused Trotzkysits Never Were 'Old Bolsheviks,'" January 28, 1937, "Prosecutor Asks Death for All 17 Terrorists," January 29, 1937, "Piatakov, Spector Visits to Trotzky Confirmed in Norwegian Press," January 30, 1937, "Soviet Union Denies Appeals," February 1, 1937, and "Verdict of Court Is Voice of the People, Says Press of U.S.S.R.," February 1, 1937; see also "NY Workers Pledge Full Support of Stalin and USSR," *Daily Worker*, January 28, 1937.

86. For summations from the trial records in *Daily Worker*, see "Summary of Indictment," January 25, 1937, "Radek Testifies at Trial He Plotted with Fascist Powers to Defeat U.S.S.R. in War," January 26, 1937, "Trotzky's Own Report on Deal with Fascist Powers Is Detailed by Piatakov, Who Visited Him in Norway," January 30, 1937, and Andrei Vyshinsky, "Text of Final Summation Speech by Prosecutor Vyshinsky," January 30, 1937.

87. For examples of editorials in *Daily Worker*, see "Trotzky Plotted with Nazi Axmen to Behead the USSR," January 25, 1937, "Trotzky 'Theories' Lead into the Fascist Camp," January 26, 1937, "They Can't Answer Facts," January 27, 1937, and "The Common Enemy of Humanity," February 1, 1937.

88. See Alexander Troyanovksy, "USSR Envoy Assails Trotzkyist Plotters," *Daily Worker*, January 29, 1937 and Alexander Troyanovsky, "Trotzky's Own Words Confirm Trial Evidence, Says Troyanovsky," *Daily Worker*, February 4, 1937.

89. See Earl Browder, "Progressives: Rally to Halt World Conspiracy of Trotzkyism, Fascism," *Daily Worker*, January 30, 1937, "Browder Talks on Trotzky at Garden Friday," *Daily Worker*, February 3, 1937, "Thousands to Rally Against Trotzkyism Friday at Garden, *Daily Worker*, February 4, 1937, and "Browder Talks on Trotzkyism in Garden Tonight," *Daily Worker*, February 5, 1937.

90. See "18,000 in Garden Vow to Drive Trotzkyism Out of the Labor Movement," *Daily Worker*, February 6, 1937 and Earl Browder, "Trotzkysim and World Peace," *Daily Worker*, February 6, 1937; also published as *Trotskyism Against World Peace* (New York: Workers Library Publishers, 1937).

91. "Trotsky Assailed at Garden Rally," *New York Times*, February 6, 1937.

92. "Trotzky's Confession in the Hearst Press," *Daily Worker*, February 6, 1937.

93. Sherwood Eddy, review of *The Case of the Anti-Soviet Trotskyite Center: A Verbatim Report* by the Union of Soviet Socialist Republics, People's Commissariat of Justice, *Daily Worker*, June 4, 1937; reprint, "The Guilt of Leon Trotsky," *Soviet Russia Today*, June, 1937, 15, 25.

94. "Conning the News," *New Masses*, February 9, 1937, 12.

95. A. B. Magil, "Why Do They Confess?" *New Masses*, February 16, 1937, 3–5.

96. Dudley Collard, "What I Saw in Moscow," *New Masses*, February 23, 1937, 13; reprint, "A Lawyer Views the Radek Trial," *Soviet Russia Today*, March, 1937, 12.

97 See "The Moscow Trials: An Editorial," *New Masses*, February 9, 1937, 17–18, "Who Is Trotsky's Foe? An Editorial," *New Masses*, February 16, 1937, 18–20, and "Roundabout Roads to Trotskyism: An Editorial," *New Masses,* February 23, 1937, 19.

98 Charles Recht, "Descent to Hell," review of *The Case of the Anti-Soviet Trotskyite Center: A Verbatim Report* by the Union of Soviet Socialist Republics, People's Commissariat of Justice, *New Masses*, April 13, 1937, 24, 26.

99 Sam Darcy, "What's Going on in the Soviet Union?" *New Masses*, July 13, 1937, 3–6.

100 Joshua Kunitz, "'Guilty as Charged!'" *New Masses*, January 18, 1938, 8–9.

101 A. B. Magil, "Trotsky Admits It," *New Masses*, August 8, 1939, 15–16.

102 See Isidor Schneider, "Journalism in a New World," review of *Portraits and Pamphlets* by Karl Radek, *New Masses*, October 1, 1935, 38–9.

103 Karl Radek, "Germany's Strategic Plan," *New Masses*, May 5, 1936, 9–10.

104 Israel Amter, "The Trial of the Trotskyite Agents of Fascism," *The Communist*, March, 1937, 258–71.

105 Clarence A. Hathaway, "Trotskyism in the United States," *The Communist*, March, 1937, 271–8.

106 "The New Treason Trial," editorial, *Soviet Russia Today*, February, 1937, 7.

107 Leon Feuchtwanger, "Leon Feuchtwanger on This Trial," *Soviet Russia Today*, March, 1937, 12.

108 See Andrei Vyshinsky, "The Background of the Treason Trial," *Soviet Russia Today,* March, 1937, 24–30 and "Editor's Note," *Soviet Russia Today,* March, 1937, 30.

109 Theodore Bayer, "Your Questions Answered on the Moscow Trial," *Soviet Russia Today,* March, 1937, 32–3.

110 Newton D. Baker, "Newton D. Baker Reviews the Treason Trial Record," *Soviet Russia Today*, April, 1937, 8.

111 Sam Darcy, *An Eye-Witness at the Wreckers' Trial* (New York: Workers Library Publishers, 1937).

112 Alexander Bittelman, *Trotsky the Traitor* (New York: Workers Library Publishers, 1937).

113 William Z. Foster, *Questions and Answers on the Piatakov-Radek Trial* (New York: Workers Library Publishers, 1937). For an example of another anti-Trotsky pamphlet, see P. Lang, *Trotskyism and Fascism: The Anti-Communist Trial in Leipzig and the Trial of the Terrorists in Moscow* (New York: Workers Library Publishers, 1937).

114 *Traitors Accused: Indictment of the Piatakov-Trotskyite Group* (New York: Workers Library Publishers, 1937).

115 See Leon Trotsky, "Trotsky Derides Charges at Trial," *New York Times*, January 24, 1937, Leon Trotsky, "Trotsky Denies Charges," *New York Times*, January 24, 1937,

Leon Trotsky, "Trotsky Renews Denial," *New York Times*, January 25, 1937, and Leon Trotsky, "Trotsky Gives His Proof of Moscow Trial Falsity," *New York Times*, February 16, 1937.

116 "Trotsky Tells on Soviet Secret Police, Dispels Mystery of Moscow's Self-Accusing Patriots," *Newsweek*, February 13, 1937, 16.
117 Leon Trotsky, "The Real Soviet Russia," *American Mercury*, March, 1937, 355–68.
118 Leon Trotsky, *Truth about the Moscow Trials* (New York: Pioneer Publishers, 1937).
119 Albert Goldman, "Toward Socialist Clarity," *Socialist Appeal*, February, 1937, 26–7.
120 Socialist Appeal Institute, "Resolution Adopted on the Moscow Trials," *Socialist Appeal*, March, 1937, 44.
121 "Soviet Diplomats Expose Frame-Ups," *Socialist Appeal*, December 11, 1937.
122 *Why Did They "Confess"? A Study of the Radek-Piatakov Trial*, introd. by James Burnham (New York: Pioneer Publishers, 1937).
123 Max Eastman, *The End of Socialism in Russia* (London: Secker and Warburg, 1938).
124 See Jay Lovestone, "The Moscow Trial in Historical Perspective," *Workers Age*, February 6, 1937, 3 and Jay Lovestone, "The Moscow Trial in Historical Perspective," *Workers Age*, February 13, 1937, 3.
125 "The Moscow Trials: An Editorial Statement," *Workers Age*, February 20, 1937, 3–6.
126 M. Yomanowitz, "The Moscow Trials and the CI Crisis," *Workers Age*, May 8, 1937, 5.
127 "Radek and Bukharin Next," *Fighting Worker*, October 15, 1936.
128 "Trotskyists Set up a Paper International," *Fighting Worker*, October 15, 1936.
129 "More Moscow Trials," *Fourth International*, March, 1937, 1–8.
130 *The Truth about the Moscow Frame-Up Trials* (Chicago: Revolutionary Workers League U. S., 1937).
131 George Marlen (pseud.), "The Moscow Trials," in *Earl Browder: Communist or Tool of Wall Street: Stalin, Trotsky or Lenin* (New York: The Author, 1937), 409–10.
132 Francis Heisler, *The First Two Moscow Trials—Why?* pref. by Roy E. Burt (Chicago: Socialist Party USA, 1937).
133 See "Lenin Memorial, 1937" [cartoon] and "Digging the Grave of the Russian Revolution," *Labor Action*, January 30, 1937, "Why?" editorial, *Labor Action*, February 20, 1937, "Roster of Defendants in Latest Moscow Trial," *Labor Action*, February 20, 1937, and Charles Erskine Scott Wood, "Colonel Wood on Moscow Trial," *Labor Action*, February 20, 1937.

Chapter 5

1 For examples of articles on Trotsky's exile, see Anita Brenner, "Amid Mystery, Trotsky Moves on Again," *New York Times Magazine*, April 29, 1934, SM6-7, SM22,

Anita Brenner, "Stalin and Trotsky," *New York Times Magazine*, January 13, 1935, SM2, SM13, Harold Denny, "Moscow Asks Oslo to Expel Trotsky as a Conspirator," *New York Times*, August 30, 1936, "Mexico Harbors the Russian Exile Nobody Else Wants: Leon Trotsky," *Life*, February 22, 1937, 9–13, and "Trotsky, Stalin & Cárdenas," *Time*, January 25, 1937, 18–24.

2 See "Haven for Trotsky in Mexico Certain," *New York Times*, December 12, 1936, "Trotsky Committee Meets," *New York Times*, December 18, 1936, "Haven for Trotsky in Mexico Is Urged," *New York Times*, December 19, 1936, and Anita Brenner, "Trotsky Finds a Haven in Face of Stalin's Ire," *New York Times*, January 3, 1937.

3 American Committee for the Defense of Leon Trotsky, *World Voices on the Moscow Trials: A Compilation from the Labor and Liberal Press of the World* (New York: Pioneer Publishers, 1937), 1.

4 See Frank I. Kluckhohn, "Labor in Mexico Yields on Trotsky," *New York Times*, January 11, 1937, "Trotsky and Woe," *Time*, January 11, 1937, 24, Georgi Dimitrov and Mikhail Aleksandrovich Moskvin (pseud.), "Telegram from Dimitrov and Moskvin to Browder, CPUSA," in Chase, *Enemies within the Gates*, 197–8, "Trotsky and Kirov," *Soviet Russia Today*, January, 1937, 6–7, Vicente Lombardo Toledano, "Trotsky in Mexico," *New Masses*, February 2, 1937, 6–8, Alexander Bittelman, "Review of the Month," *The Communist*, February, 1937, 110–11, Joseph Freeman, "Trotsky in Coyoacán," *New Masses*, March 23, 1937, 14–16, and "Trotsky—Enemy of the People Everywhere," *Soviet Russia Today*, April, 1938, 4.

5 "Thomas Holds Trotsky Arrival in Mexico Will Spur an Inquiry into Moscow Trial," *New York Times*, December 17, 1936.

6 "Communist Party and Political Asylum," *Socialist Appeal*, January, 1937, 1–2.

7 See Frank I. Kluckhohn, "Trotsky in Mexico Asks Trial in Plot by Impartial Body," *New York Times*, January 10, 1937 and "Trotsky Telegram Repeats Challenge," *Labor Action*, February 13, 1937.

8 See "For an Impartial Commission of Inquiry!" *News Bulletin* (American Committee for the Defense of Leon Trotsky), January 27, 1937, 1 and "Trotsky Backers Act to Clear Him," *New York Times*, February 1, 1937.

9 Leon Trotsky, "For a Day in Court," *News Bulletin* (American Committee for the Defense of Leon Trotsky), January 27, 1937, 1.

10 See "The *Nation* and Trotsky: An Editorial," *New Masses*, November 10, 1936, 11–12, "Trotskyists Organize Anti-Soviet Campaign," *Soviet Russia Today*, January, 1937, 7, and "Aid and Comfort for the Fascists," *Soviet Russia Today*, March, 1937, 7.

11 See Mauritz A. Hallgren, "Hallgren Withdraws from American Trotzkyist 'Defense' Committee," *Daily Worker*, February 4, 1937 and Mauritz A. Hallgren, *Why I Resigned from the Trotsky Defense Committee* (New York: International Publishers, 1937); see also Mauritz A. Hallgren, "The Trotsky Controversy," letter to the editor, *New York Times*, February 5, 1937, "Gannett and Jaffe Resign from Trotzkyists

'Defense' Committee," *Daily Worker*, February 6, 1937, and "Readers' Forum," *New Masses*, February 16, 1937, 21.

12 Foster, *Questions and Answers on the Piatakov-Radek Trial*, 71–5.
13 "Group Here Seeking Hearing for Trotsky," *New York Times*, February 6, 1937.
14 Suzanne La Follette, "In Defense of Leon Trotsky," letter to the editor, *New York Times*, February 8, 1937.
15 "Committee Answers Counter-Campaign," *News Bulletin* (American Committee for the Defense of Leon Trotsky), February 19, 1937, 1, 3.
16 See "Hear Leon Trotsky" and "Mass Meetings on the Moscow Trials," [advertisements] *News Bulletin* (American Committee for the Defense of Leon Trotsky), February 3, 1937, 2 and "Police Will Guard Trotsky Rally Here," *New York Times*, February 8, 1937.
17 See "Trotsky to Talk by Phone to Audience Here," *New York Times*, February 3, 1937, "Trotsky's Speech Set for Tuesday," *New York Times*, February 4, 1937, "Group Here Seeking Hearing for Trotsky," *New York Times*, February 6, 1937, Conor Friedersdorf, "The Lawyer Who Told FDR He Couldn't Censor a Trotsky Speech," *The Atlantic*, July, 2013, accessed May 15, 2018, http://www.theatlantic.com, "Wire Break Balks Trotsky as 6,500 Await Speech Here," *New York Times*, February 10, 1937, and "2 Inquiries Start on Trotsky Fiasco," *New York Times*, February 11, 1937.
18 See "Mass Meeting Called by the American Committee for the Defense of Leon Trotsky," manuscript, February 9, 1937, accessed November 27, 2013, https://archive.org and Leon Trotsky, *I Stake My Life!* (New York: Pioneer Publishers, 1937).
19 See "Commission Demands Supported by 6,500," *News Bulletin* (American Committee for the Defense of Leon Trotsky), February 19, 1937, 1 and "Mass Meetings on Trials Held in Many Cities," *News Bulletin* (American Committee for the Defense of Leon Trotsky), February 19, 1937, 1.
20 Horace M. Kallen and John Dewey, "A Reaffirmation of Purpose," *News Bulletin* (American Committee for the Defense of Leon Trotsky), February 19, 1937, 3.
21 Sinclair Lewis, letter to the editor, *News Bulletin* (American Committee for the Defense of Leon Trotsky), March 16, 1937, 4.
22 See "Trotsky Inquiry Under Fire Here," *New York Times*, February 17, 1937 and "More Prominent Liberals Join Defense of Trotsky," *Labor Action*, February 27, 1937 and "Soviet Envoy Ridicules Bid to Trotsky Inquiry," *New York Times*, April 4, 1937.
23 "Whitewash Expedition Leaves U. S. to Visit Trotzky in Mexico," *Daily Worker*, April 3, 1937.
24 "Roundabout Roads to Trotskyism: An Editorial," *New Masses*, February 23, 1937, 19; see also Morris U. Schappes, letter to the editor, *New Masses*, March 2, 1937, 21.

25 "Trotsky Defense Seeks Personal Vindication," *Fighting Worker*, March 1, 1937, 2.
26 Sidney Hook, "My Running Debate with Einstein," *Commentary* 74, no. 1 (July, 1982): 37–52.
27 Harold Kirker and Burleigh Taylor Wilkins, "Beard, Becker and the Trotsky Inquiry," *American Quarterly* 13, no. 4 (Winter, 1961): 516–25.
28 Frank I. Kluckhohn, "Trotsky Explosively Wages His War of Words," *New York Times Magazine*, February 21, 1937, SM3-4, SM24.
29 See "Trial of Trotsky to Be All Trotsky," *New York Times*, April 5, 1937, Frank I. Kluckhohn, "Dewey 'Impartial' in Trotsky Inquiry," *New York Times*, April 7, 1937, and Frank I. Kluckhohn, "Trotsky Ready for Trial," *New York Times*, April 11, 1937.
30 See "Trotsky to Testify as 'Hostile Witness'," *New York Times*, April 6, 1937 and Albert Goldman, "Mr. Goldman's Position," letter to the editor, *New York Times*, April 10, 1937.
31 See Frank I. Kluckhohn, "Trotsky on 'Trial' Denies Reich Deal," *New York Times*, April 11, 1937, Frank I. Kluckhohn, "Plotters Meeting Denied by Trotsky," *New York Times*, April 13, 1937, Frank I. Kluckhohn, "Trotsky Says Paris Suppresses Proof," *New York Times*, April 14, 1937, Frank I. Kluckhohn, "Soviet Revolt Urged by Trotsky," *New York Times*, April 15, 1937, Frank I. Kluckhohn, "Trotsky Finishes His Side of Case," April 16, 1937, and Frank I. Kluckhohn, "Trotsky Opposes Mass Executions," *New York Times*, April 17, 1937.
32 John Dewey, "First Session," in *The Case of Leon Trotsky* (New York: Merit Publishers, 1968), accessed December 11, 2013, http://www.marxists.org.
33 Leon Trotsky, "Vladimir Romm—'Witness'," in *The Case of Leon Trotsky*, accessed December 11, 2013, http://www.marxists.org.
34 Leon Trotsky, *Stalin's Frame-Up System and the Moscow Trials* (New York: Pioneer Publishers, 1950); see also Paul Mattick, "Stalin's Frame-Up System and the Moscow Trials (Review)," review of *Stalin's Frame-Up System and the Moscow Trial*," by Leon Trotsky, *Western Socialist*, February, 1951.
35 See Frank I. Kluckhohn, "Beals Quits Group Hearing Trotsky," *New York Times*, April 18, 1937, Frank I. Kluckhohn, "'Trial' of Trotsky a Joke, Says Beals," *New York Times*, April 19, 1937, "'Pink Tea'," *Newsweek*, April 24, 1937, 19, Carlton Beals, "Mr. Beals Resigns from Trotsky Commission," *Soviet Russia Today*, May, 1937, 3, and Carleton Beals, "The Fewer Outsiders the Better," *Saturday Evening Post*, June 12, 1937, 23, 74, 76–8.
36 See "Trotsky Hints Beals Works for the Soviet," *New York Times*, May 26, 1937 and Leon Trotsky, letter to the editor, *Modern Monthly*, October, 1937, 5.
37 For an example, see "The Case of Ex-Commissioner Beals," *News Bulletin* (American Committee for the Defense of Leon Trotsky), May 3, 1937, 2.
38 "Trotsky on Trial," *New York Times*, April 11, 1937.
39 Lorine Pruette, "Trotsky 'Trial' Has Academic Air," *New York Times*, April 18, 1937.

40 "The Trotsky Commission," *The Nation*, May 1, 1937, 496–7.
41 *News Bulletin* (American Committee for the Defense of Leon Trotsky), May 3, 1937.
42 John Simkin, "John Dewey," *Spartacus Educational*, accessed July 24, 2021, https://spartacus-educational.com/USAdewey.htm.
43 "Trotsky Investigates Himself," *New Masses*, April 20, 1937, 28.
44 Marion Hammett and William Smith, "Inside the Trotsky 'Trial,'" *New Masses*, April 27, 1937, 6–11.
45 "Trotsky Trial Hit by Envoy as 'Flop,'" *New York Times*, April 23, 1937.
46 "The Farce in Mexico," *Soviet Russia Today*, May, 1937, 8–9.
47 Jack Ross, *The Socialist Party of America: A Complete History* (Lincoln, NB: University of Nebraska Press, 2015), 379–81.
48 "L. Trotsky Cross-Examined before Impartial Commission," *Labor Action*, April 17, 1937.
49 "Dewey Will Press Trotsky Inquiry," *New York Times*, May 8, 1937.
50 John Dewey, *'Truth Is on the March'* (New York: American Committee for the Defense of Leon Trotsky, 1937).
51 "Meddling Charged in Trotsky Inquiry," *New York Times*, May 10, 1937.
52 "2 Deny Accusation against Trotsky," *New York Times*, July 27, 1937.
53 "Trotsky's Trial," *Time*, May 17, 1937, 22.
54 "'Liberalism' in the Service of Fascism," *Soviet Russia Today*, June, 1937, 4–5.
55 "Socialist Acrobatics," *Soviet Russia Today*, June, 1937, 5.
56 Waldo Frank, "Moscow Trials," *New Republic*, May 12, 1937, 19–20; see also "Waldo Frank Proposes," *New Masses*, May 18, 1937, 10, "Committee Raps Substitute Inquiries," *News Bulletin* (American Committee for the Defense of Leon Trotsky), May 16, 1937, 1, "Mr. Stolberg Disposes," *New Masses*, May 18, 1938, 11, Waldo Frank, "Readers' Forum," letter to the editor, *New Masses*, May 25, 1937, 20 and Earl Browder, "Moscow Trials: Reply," *New Republic*, May 26, 1937, 76.
57 Commission of Inquiry into the Charges Made Against Leon Trotsky in the Moscow Trials, *The Case of Leon Trotsky: Report of Hearings on the Charges Made Against Him in the Moscow Trials* (New York: Harper and Brothers, 1937).
58 James T. Farrell, "Cause Célébre," review of *The Case of Leon Trotsky* by the Commission of Inquiry into the Charges Made Against Leon Trotsky in the Moscow Trials, *Saturday Review*, October 23, 1937, 22.
59 Edmund Wilson, "Stalin, Trotsky, and Willi Schlamm," review of *The Case of Leon Trotsky* by the Commission of Inquiry into the Charges Made Against Leon Trotsky in the Moscow Trials, *The Nation*, December 11, 1937, 648–52.
60 Bertram D. Wolfe, "Trotsky's Defense," review of *The Case of Leon Trotsky* by the Commission of Inquiry into the Charges Made Against Leon Trotsky in the Moscow Trials, *New Republic*, November 24, 1937, 79.

61 Leon Trotsky, "Bertram Wolfe on the Moscow Trials," *Socialist Appeal*, December 4, 1937.
62 "The Case of Leon Trotsky," *Socialist Appeal*, September 25, 1937 and "Committee Urges All Branches to Help in Sales Campaign of 'Case of Leon Trotsky'," *Socialist Appeal*, November 13, 1937.
63 See "Report on Trotsky to Be Heard Today," *New York Times*, December 12, 1937 and "Is Trotsky Innocent or Guilty?" [advertisement] *Socialist Appeal*, December 4, 1937.
64 "The Dewey Commission," *New Internationalist*, January, 1938, 6.
65 "Trotsky Cleared by Dewey Board," *New York Times*, December 13, 1937.
66 See "Trotsky," *New Republic*, December 22, 1937, 181–2 and Editorial, *The Nation*, December 25, 1937, 703.
67 Stanley Randolph, "Mr. Dewey Stakes His Reputation," *New Masses*, December 28, 1937, 9–10.
68 Robert Forsythe, "Is John Dewey Honest?" *New Masses*, January 4, 1938, 16.
69 Robert Forsythe, "The Disintegration of Mr. Stolberg," *New Masses*, February 1, 1938, 14.
70 Review of the Month, *The Communist*, January, 1938, 14–15.
71 "Trotsky Verdict Scored," *New York Times*, December 16, 1937.
72 *Socialist Appeal*, December 18, 1937; see also "Abstract of the Final Report of the Commission of Inquiry into Charges Made Against Leon Trotsky in the Moscow Trials," *Socialist Appeal*, December 18, 1937, 5–8.
73 Leon Trotsky, "Answers to Questions of Journalists on Verdict of Dewey Commission," *Socialist Appeal*, December 25, 1937.
74 See "Dr. Dewey Warns on Soviet Tactics," *New York Times*, December 14, 1937 and "Dewey Broadcasts on Trials," *Socialist Appeal*, December 18, 1937.
75 Corliss Lamont, "The Moscow Trials," *Soviet Russia Today*, January, 1938, 14, 36.
76 "Daily Worker Omits," Topics of the Times, *New York Times*, December 15, 1937.
77 Eugene Lyons, "'Friends of the G.P.U,'" in *The Red Decade: The Stalinist Penetration of America* (Indianapolis, IN: Bobbs-Merrill, 1941), 257–67.
78 John Dewey, "Significance of the Trotsky Trial," interview by Agnes E. Meyer, *International Conciliation*, no. 237 (February, 1938): 53–60.
79 Heywood Broun, "Shoot the Works," *New Republic*, January 12, 1938, 280.
80 Sidney Hook, "Broun v. Dewey," letter to the editor, *New Republic*, February 16, 1938, 48.
81 Commission of Inquiry into the Charges Made Against Leon Trotsky in the Moscow Trials, *Not Guilty: Report of the Commission of Inquiry into the Charges Made Against Leon Trotsky in the Moscow Trials* (New York: Harper and Brothers, 1938).
82 Reinhold Niebuhr, "Trials on Trial," review of *Not Guilty* by the Commission of Inquiry into the Charges Made Against Leon Trotsky in the Moscow Trials, *The Nation*, June 30, 1938, 112–13.

83 Frank Graves, "A Historic Document," review of *Not Guilty* by the Commission of Inquiry into the Charges Made Against Leon Trotsky in the Moscow Trials, *Socialist Appeal*, July 9, 1938.

84 See "New Soviet Trial Called 'Frame-Up,'" *New York Times*, March 1, 1938, and "Committee Asks Observers at New Moscow Trial," *News Bulletin* (American Committee for the Defense of Leon Trotsky), March 16, 1937, 1.

85 "Dewey Group Urges Troyanovsky to Accept Evidence to Disprove Soviet Trial Story," *New York Times*, March 7, 1938.

86 "Soviet Trial Denounced," *New York Times*, March 10, 1938.

87 Bertram D. Wolfe, untitled speech (Hotel Center, New York City, March 9, 1938). Manuscript.

88 "Trotzkyist Forgery Repudiated by Four Alleged 'Signers' of Letter for Investigation of Trial," *Daily Worker*, March 5, 1938.

89 "Accuses Dewey Group," *New York Times*, March 6, 1938.

90 Max Eastman, "A Letter to Corliss Lamont," *New International*, April, 1938, 122.

91 See Will Lissner, "Assassin Slays Tresca, Radical, in Fifth Avenue," *New York Times*, January 11, 1943, "Carlo Tresca Murdered!" *Labor Action*, January 18, 1943, "Tresca Slaying Still Unsolved," *Labor Action*, January 25, 1943, The Shape of Things, *The Nation*, January 16, 1943, 73–35, John Dos Passos, "Carlo Tresca," *The Nation*, January 23, 1943, "The Tresca Murder," *New Masses*, January 26, 1943, 11, and "Murdering Unity," *New Masses*, February 2, 1943, 7.

92 See David C. Engerman, "John Dewey and the Soviet Union: Pragmatism Meets Revolution," *Modern Intellectual History* 3, no. 1 (April, 2006): 33–63, Larry A. Hickman, "Dewey and Trotsky: Truth Is Not a Bourgeois Ideal," *Inter-American Journal of Philosophy* 3, no. 2 (December, 2012): 16–24, Arthur Jay Klinghoffer and Judith Apter Klinghoffer, "The Moscow Show Trials Case," in *International Citizens' Tribunals: Mobilizing Public Opinion to Advance Human Rights* (New York: Palgrave, 2007), 51–101, Jay Martin, "John Dewey and the Trial of Leon Trotsky," *Partisan Review* 68 (Fall, 2001): 519–35, Jay Martin, "Trial Days in Coyoacán," *Antioch Review* 59, no. 3 (Summer, 2001): 550–63, Alan B. Spitzer, "John Dewey, the 'Trial' of Leon Trotsky, and the Search for Historical Truth," *History and Theory* 29, no. 1 (February, 1990): 16–37; see also Alan Wald, "Memories of the John Dewey Commission: Forty Years Later," *Antioch Review* 35, no. 4 (Autumn, 1977): 438–51 and Xenia Zeldin, "John Dewey's Role on the 1937 Trotsky Commission," *Public Affairs Quarterly* 5, no. 4 (1990): 387–94.

93 Commission of Inquiry into the Charges Made Against Leon Trotsky in the Moscow Trials, *The Case of Leon Trotsky: Reports of Hearings on the Charges Made Against Him in the Moscow Trials* (New York: Merit Publishers, 1968).

94 George Novack, "Introduction to *The Case of Leon Trotsky*," *International Socialist Review*, July-August, 1968, 21–6.

95 See Sidney Hook, "Memories of the Moscow Trials," *Commentary*, March, 1984, 7–63, and Sidney Hook, "The Moscow Trials," letter to the editor, *Commentary*, August, 1984, 8, 10; see also James T. Farrell, "Dewey in Mexico," in *John Dewey: Philosophy of Science and Freedom*, ed. Sidney Hook (New York: Dial Press, 1950), 351–77.
96 John Chamberlain and James T. Farrell, "Trotsky: Friends and Enemies," letter to the editor, *New Republic*, February 24, 1937, 75.
97 "Trotsky: Friends and Enemies," letter to the editor, *New Republic*, February 24, 1937, 75–6.
98 Corliss Lamont, introduction to "An Open Letter to American Liberals," *Soviet Russia Today*, March, 1937, 14.
99 "An Open Letter to American Liberals," *Soviet Russia Today*, March, 1937, 14–15.
100 Sidney Howard, letter to Mary Van Kleeck, *News Bulletin* (American Committee for the Defense of Leon Trotsky), February 19, 1937, 3–4.
101 Earl Browder, "Testimony to the Communist International Executive Committee," in Klehr, Haynes, and Anderson, *The Soviet World of American Communism*, 304–6.
102 Eugene Lyons, "Hooray for Murder!" in *The Red Decade: The Stalinist Penetration of America*, 235–56.
103 Theodore Dreiser, "Is Leon Trotsky Guilty," in *Theodore Dreiser: Political Writings*, ed. Jude Davies (Urbana, IL: University of Illinois Press, 2011), 209–11.
104 Theodore Dreiser and John Dos Passos, "A Conversation: Theodore Dreiser and John Dos Passos," in *Theodore Dreiser: Political Writings*, 211–12.
105 Frederick L. Schuman, "Leon Trotsky: Martyr or Renegade?" *Southern Review* 3 (1937–1938): 51–74.
106 Correspondence, *Southern Review* 3 (1937–1938): 199–207.
107 Sidney Hook, "Liberalism and the Case of Leon Trotsky," *Southern Review* 3 (1937–1938): 267–82.
108 Correspondence, *Southern Review* 3 (1937–1938): 406–16.

Chapter 6

1 See Harold Denny, "Red Army Grows Swiftly in Strength and Prestige," *New York Times*, February 3, 1935, "Russia's Mighty Army," *Literary Digest*, February 9, 1935, 15, "Red Army Warns of Reich Military," *New York Times*, April 1, 1935, Walter Duranty, "Eyes Turn to the Vast Red Army," *New York Times Magazine*, April 28, 1935, SM1-2, SM21, and "'Strongest' of Armies: Russia Preparing to Defend Frontiers on East and West," *Literary Digest*, January 25, 1936, 13–14.
2 Karl Radek, "Marshals of the Soviet Union," in *U. S. Military Intelligence Reports: The Soviet Union, 1919–1941*, ed. Dale Reynolds (Bethesda, MD: University Publications of America, 1984), microfilm, reel 5, 200.

3 Untitled article, *New York Times*, August 27, 1936.
4 See "Red Army Orders Loyalty Stressed," *New York Times*, September 22, 1936, "Councils to Curb Soviet Generals," *New York Times*, May 18, 1937, and Walter Duranty, "Party Grip on the Red Army," *New York Times*, February 27, 1938; see also Edward F. Danowitz, "Party Control of the Soviet Army," *Marine Corps Gazette*, September, 1957, 19–22.
5 See "Soviet Murder Plot Laid to the 8 Generals," *New York Times*, June 13, 1937 and "Others Are Believed Held," *New York Times*, June 13, 1937.
6 Henderson, "The Chargé in the Soviet Union (Henderson) to the Secretary of State," 286–7 and "Tells Soviet Fliers to 'Keep Power Dry,'" *New York Times*, March 3, 1936.
7 Max Werner, "Mikhail Nikolaievich Tukhachevsky," *Living Age*, March 1, 1936, 234–6.
8 See "Chief of Soviet's Air Force Believed to Be under Arrest," *New York Times*, June 28, 1937 and "Soviet Air Force under New Leader," *New York Times*, February 15, 1938.
9 See "Bluecher's Arrest in Soviet Reported," *New York Times*, October 4, 1938 and "Bluecher Not Named among Soviet Heroes," *New York Times*, October 27, 1938; see also Reynolds, ed., *U. S. Military Intelligence Reports*, microfilm, reel 4, no. 102.
10 "3 Red Army Chiefs Seem in Difficulties," *New York Times*, May 1, 1938.
11 "Army Commander of the First Rank: I. P. Belov," in Reynolds, ed., *U. S. Military Intelligence Reports*, microfilm, reel 5, no. 206.
12 See "Marchal Vasili Konstantinovich, Bluecher," *American Quarterly on the Soviet Union* 1, no. 3 (October, 1938): 80–4 and "Marshal Semyon Mikhailovich Budyenny," *American Quarterly on the Soviet Union* 4, no. 3 (August, 1941): 54–6.
13 "Red Army Marshal, Accused, Ends Life," *New York Times*, June 1, 1937.
14 Conquest, *The Great Terror*, 200–1.
15 See Kotkin, *Stalin*, 422–5.
16 Joseph Stalin, "Report on the Work of the Central Committee to the Eighteen Congress of the C.P.S.U.(B.)," in *Works*, vol. 14 (London: Red Star Press, 1978), accessed August 13, 2021, https://www.marxists.org/reference/archive/stalin/works/1939/03/10.htm.
17 U. S. Central Intelligence Agency, *The Higher Military Council of the USSR* (Washington, DC: The Agency, 1964), 22.
18 See Welles Hangen, "9 Ex-Army Chiefs Cleared in Soviet," *New York Times*, April 14, 1956, Harrison E. Salisbury, "Purged Marshal Cleared in Soviet," *New York Times*, August 4, 1957, and "New Soviet Book Lists Red Victims," *New York Times*, October 26, 1958.
19 Khrushchev, Nikita S., "Report of the Central Committee of the CPSU: Delivered by N. S. Khrushchev, October 17, 1962," in *Documents of the 22nd Congress of the CPSU*, vol. 1 (New York: Crosscurrents Press, 1961), 219–35.

20 Henderson, "The Chargé in the Soviet Union (Henderson) to the Secretary of State," 376–8.
21 Ibid., 378–80.
22 Ibid., 383–5.
23 Ibid.
24 Ibid., 385–6.
25 Ibid., 519–20.
26 Loy W. Henderson, *A Question of Trust: The Origins of U. S.-Soviet Diplomatic Relations: The Memoirs of Loy W. Henderson* (Stanford, CA: Hoover Institution Press, 1983), 441–6, 455–6, and 459–60.
27 Joseph E. Davies, *Mission to Moscow: A Record of the Confidential Dispatches to the State Department, Official and Personal Correspondence, Current Diary and Journal Entries, Including Notes and Comment up to October, 1941* (London: Gallancz, 1942), 95–6; see also Henderson, *A Question of Trust*, 443–4, "Davies Entertains Red Army Leaders," *New York Times*, March 24, 1937, and "Davies & Bolshies," *Time*, April 5, 1937, 27–8.
28 Joseph E. Davies, "Killing of the Red Generals," in *Mission to Moscow*, 111.
29 Joseph E. Davies, "Life in Moscow," in *Mission to Moscow*, 112.
30 Joseph E. Davies, "Diary," in *Mission to Moscow*, 113.
31 Joseph E. Davies, "Effect of Purge on European Peace: Excerpt from a Letter to Stephen Early," in *Mission to Moscow*, 113–14.
32 Joseph E. Davies, "Why They Shot Tukhachevsky," in *Mission to Moscow*, 129–38; excerpts reprinted in Joseph E. Davies, "Moscow—An Ambassador's Report," *New York Times Magazine*, December 14, 1941, SM24.
33 Philip R. Faymonville, "Effect of Treason Trials on Army Morale," in *U. S. Military Intelligence Reports: The Soviet Union, 1919-1941*, ed. Dale Reynolds (Bethesda, MD: University Publications of America, 1984), reel 3, 339; see also David M. Glantz, "Attaché Assessments of the Impact of the 1930s Purges on the Red Army," *Journal of Slavic Military Studies* 2, no. 3 (1989): 417–38.
34 Philip R. Faymonville, "Treason Trials, Red Army" in Reynolds, ed., *U. S. Military Intelligence Reports*, reel 3, 341.
35 E. R. W. McCabe, "Red Army Executions," in Reynolds, ed., *U. S. Military Intelligence Reports*, reel 3, 358.
36 "Two High Officials Suspect in Soviet," *New York Times*, February 17, 1937.
37 Harold Denny, "Marshal Demoted in Red Army Shift," *New York Times*, May 17, 1937.
38 Harold Denny, "Soviet Hunts Foes in All Directions," *New York Times*, June 4, 1937.
39 See Harold Denny, "Red Army Plotting Leads to New War on Soviet 'Enemies,'" *New York Times*, June 6, 1937, and Harold Denny, "Soviet Production Hit by Spy Scare," *New York Times*, June 7, 1937.

40 Harold Denny, "Purge of Red Army Hinted in Removal of Four Generals," *New York Times*, June 10, 1937; see also Harold Denny, "Soviet to Try 8 Generals in Secret Today as Spies," *New York Times*, June 11, 1937, and Harold Denny, "8 Soviet Generals Doomed as Spies Aiding Alien Foes," *New York Times*, June 12, 1937.

41 "8 Generals Killed as Spies by Soviet," *New York Times*, June 13, 1937.

42 Frederick T. Birchall, "Rumors Flood Europe," *New York Times*, June 13, 1937.

43 Elias Tobenkin, "Stalin's Rule Here at Gravest Crisis," *New York Times*, June 13, 1937.

44 "The Red Army," editorial, *New York Times*, June 17, 1937.

45 "Russians Support Trials, Envoy Says," *New York Times*, June 17, 1937.

46 Frederick T. Birchall, "New Theory 'Explains' the Drama in Russia," *New York Times*, June 20, 1937.

47 Harold Denny, "Defense League Purged in Soviet," *New York Times*, June 23, 1937.

48 Harold Denny, "Fear and Anxiety in Russia Make Crisis Worst in Years," *New York Times*, June 24, 1937.

49 Harold Denny, "Many Doubts Rise in Russia on Guilt of Eight Generals," *New York Times*, June 26, 1937.

50 See "Red Purge," *New York Times*, June 27, 1937 and "Topics of the Times," June 27, 1937.

51 Pertinax (pseud.), "8 Slain Generals Linked with Reich," *New York Times*, August 1, 1937.

52 Harold Denny, "Soviet Orders Political Officers to Tighten Hold on the Red Army," *New York Times*, April 12, 1938.

53 See "Soviet Marshal Is Reported in Disgrace," *New York Times*, February 27, 1938, "New Army Purge Disclosed by Paper," *New York Times*, June 21, 1938, "Purge Takes Half Soviet's Officers," *New York Times*, June 23, 1938, and Harold Denny, "Russian General among 80 in Purge," *New York Times*, July 28, 1939.

54 Untitled article, *New York Times*, February 27, 1938.

55 Harold Denny, "Soviet 'Cleansing' Sweeps Through All Strata of Life," *New York Times*, September 13, 1937.

56 "Reprimands & Death," *Time*, June 14, 1937, 24.

57 "Eight Dead Dogs," *Time*, June 21, 1937, 23–4.

58 "Stalin's Secrets," *Time*, July 5, 1937, 21–2.

59 "Mystery: Who Killed Young Stalin—Or Is He Alive?" *Newsweek*, June 12, 1937, 11–12.

60 "Monster Kills Its Frankenstein: Critics Again Deride Bear with Clay Feet," *Newsweek*, June 19, 1937, 14–15.

61 "Kremlin, Nazis Combine to Deride Communist Inefficiency," *Newsweek*, June 26, 1937, 10–11.

62 "Even Reporters Jitter at Alice-in-Wonderland Purges," *Newsweek*, July 3, 1937, 15–16.

63 "Red Baton: Mystery Marshal Takes Command of Russia's Army in New Stalinist Shake-Up," *Literary Digest*, May 29, 1937, 15.
64 "'Soso' Strikes: Stalin, Mourning Mother, Has Eight 'Traitor' Generals Shot," *Literary Digest*, June 19, 1937, 10–11.
65 "Behind Russia's Veil," *Literary Digest*, July 13, 1937, 12.
66 Bernard Pares, "Crisis in the Kremlin," *Living Age*, August, 1937, 478–81.
67 Eugene Lyons, "Stalin's Purge: A War Measure," *Current History*, July, 1937, 55–9; see also "Purge and the Red Army," *Current History*, November, 1938, 58.
68 "Ten Years of Soviet Terror," *American Mercury*, November, 1937, 298–306.
69 Oswald Garrison Villard, Issues and Men, *The Nation*, June 10, 1937, 176–7.
70 "Soviet Chills and Fever," *New Republic*, June 23, 1937, 174.
71 H. N. Brailsford, "What Has Happened in the USSR?" *New Republic*, July 28, 1937, 323–5.
72 Balticus (pseud.), "The Russian Mystery: Behind the Tukhachevsky Plot," *Foreign Affairs* (October, 1937): 44–59.
73 George Fielding Eliot, "The Russian Army," *American Quarterly on the Soviet Union* 1, no. 3 (October, 1938): 19–24; see also Hanson W. Baldwin, "Mighty Army of Russia Guards Two Frontiers," *New York Times Magazine*, February 20, 1938, SM3-5, SM17-24, Virginia Cowles, "Russia Discounted as Military Power," *New York Times*, April 9, 1939, Walter Duranty, "Red Army's Morale Tested," *New York Times*, August 21, 1938, and Erich Wollenberg, "How Strong Is Russia?" *American Mercury*, August, 1939, 410–17.
74 Walter Krivitsky, "Why Stalin Shot His Generals," *Saturday Evening Post*, April 22, 1939, 16–17, 71–5, 77; see also Walter Krivitsky, *In Stalin's Secret Service* (New York: Harper and Brothers, 1939), 211–43.
75 Milton Howard, "Newspaper Falsefication [sic] of Cleansings in the Soviet Union," *Daily Worker*, June 25, 1937.
76 "Harpies over Russia," *New Masses*, June 22, 1936, 3.
77 "More on Tukhachevsky," *New Masses*, July 20, 1937, 9–10.
78 "The Strength of the People's Red Army," *Soviet Russia Today*, February, 1938, 6; see also "The Eight Generals," *Soviet Russia Today*, July, 1937, 5.
79 Jay Lovestone, "The Meaning of the Soviet 'Purges,'" *Workers Age*, July 3, 1937, 5–6.
80 Leon Trotsky, "Trotsky Sees Army Opposed to Stalin," *New York Times*, March 7, 1938.
81 John G. Wright (pseud.), "Stalin Intensifies Purge," Soviet Union Notes, *Socialist Appeal*, April 2, 1938.
82 John G. Wright (pseud.), "Crisis in the Soviet Armed Forces," Soviet Union Notes, *Socialist Appeal*, April 16, 1938.
83 "Krivitsky Reveals Stalin Attempts to Woo Hitler," *Socialist Appeal*, April 25, 1938.
84 "Orloff Is Removed as Soviet Navy Head," *New York Times*, October 1, 1937.
85 "Admiral Victoroff in Disfavor," *New York Times*, January 12, 1938.

86 See "Says Admiral Was Traitor," *New York Times*, February 23, 1938 and "Secret Execution of Two Soviet Admirals as 'Fascist Spies' Disclosed by Voroshiloff," *New York Times*, February 24, 1938.

87 See "Soviet Navy Denuded of High Officers of '37," *New York Times* August 31, 1938, and Untitled article, *New York Times* August 31, 1938.

88 Harold Denny, "Red Army Inducts Men with Fanfare," *New York Times*, August 29, 1938 and "Would Purge Naval Strategy," *New York Times*, August 29, 1938.

89 "Russian General among 80 in Purge," *New York Times*, July 28, 1939.

90 John G. Wright (pseud.), "Admirals Given Liquidation Order," Soviet Union Notes, *Socialist Appeal*, April 16, 1938.

91 G. B. Guenther, "High Officers Removed from the Red Navy," in Reynolds, ed., *U. S. Military Intelligence Reports: The Soviet Union, 1919–1941*, reel 3, 373.

92 U. S. Navy, Division of Naval Intelligence, Eastern European Division, *Intelligence Report* (Washington, DC: Office of Chief of Naval Operations, Intelligence Division, 1943), accessed January 9, 2017, http://www.allworldwars.com/USSR-Navy-1943-Part-I.html.

93 Vladimir Spartakovich Milbakh, "Political Repression of the Pacific Ocean Fleet Commanders and Chiefs in 1936–1939," *Journal of Slavic Military Studies* 21 (2008): 53–112.

94 Alexander Kirk, "Chargé in the Soviet Union (Kirk) to the Secretary of State," in US Department of State, Foreign Relations Branch, *Foreign Relations of the United States: The Soviet Union, 1933–1939*, 745–6.

95 See Victor Alexandrov, *The Tukhachevsky Affair* (Englewood Cliffs, NJ: Prentice-Hall, 1964), Paul W. Blackstock, "The Tukhachevsky Affair," *Russian Review* 28, no. 2 (April, 1969): 171–90, Thomas G. Butson, *The Tsar's Lieutenant: The Soviet Marshal* (New York: Praeger, 1984), Steven J. Main, "The Arrest and 'Testimony' of Marshal of the Soviet Union M. N. Tukhachevsky (May-June 1937)," *Journal of Slavic Military Studies* 10, no. 1 (1997): 151–95, William J. McGranahan, "The Fall and Rise of Marshal Tukhachevsky," *Parameters: Journal of the US Army War College* 7, no. 4 (1978): 62–72, Frank Schauff, "Company Choir of Terror: The Military Council of the 1930s: The Red Army Between the XVII and XVIII Party Congresses," *Journal of Slavic Military Studies* 12, no. 2 (1999): 123–63, and Sally W. Stoecker, *Forging Stalin's Army: Marshal Tukhachevsky and the Politics of Military Innovation* (Boulder, CO: Westview Press, 1998).

96 Christopher Paul McPadden, *Mikhail Nikolayevich Tukhachevsky (1893–1937): Practitioner and Theorist of War* (Arlington, VA: Institute of Land Warfare, Association of the United States Army, 2006), accessed May 4, 2015, http://www.ausa.org; see also Stephen Budiansky, "The Bolshevik Who Believed in Tanks," *World War II*, May–June, 2011, 25.

97 Donald Rayfield, *Stalin's Hangmen: An Authoritative Portrait of a Tyrant and Those Who Served Him* (London: Viking Press, 2004), 322.

98 Kotkin, *Stalin*, 378.
99 See Derek Mixon, "Purge of the Red Army: Limiting Military Innovation," *Armor Journal*, September–October, 2011, 26-7, Donald Cameron Watt, "Who Plotted Against Whom? Stalin's Purge of the Soviet High Command Revisited," *Journal of Slavic Military Studies* 3, no. 1 (1990): 46-65, Peter Whitewood, "The Purge of the Red Army and Soviet Mass Operations, 1937-38," *Slavonic and East European Review* 93, no. 2 (April, 2015): 286-314, Peter Whitewood, *The Red Army and the Great Terror: Stalin's Purge of the Soviet Military* (Lawrence, KS: University Press of Kansas, 2016), Peter Whitewood, "Subversion in the Red Army and the Military Purge of 1937-1938," *Europe-Asia Studies* 67, no. 1 (January, 2015): 102-22, and Peter Whitewood, "Towards a New History of the Purge of the Military, 1937-1938," *Journal of Slavic Military Studies* 24 (2011): 605-20.
100 R. Walton Moore, "Memorandum by the Acting Secretary of State," in US Department of State, Foreign Relations Branch, *Foreign Relations of the United States: The Soviet Union, 1933-1939*, 319-20.
101 Henderson, "The Chargé in the Soviet Union (Henderson) to the Secretary of State," 388-90.
102 Ibid., 391-4.
103 Henderson, "The Chargé in the Soviet Union (Henderson) to the Secretary of State [Extracts]," 398-400.
104 Harold Denny, "'Personal Liberty' in Russia," *New York Times*, May 5, 1935.
105 See Harold Denny, "Russians Ordered to Halt Sabotage," *New York Times*, April 22, 1937, Harold Denny, "Soviet Gives Rules for Foiling Spies," *New York Times*, May 6, 1937, Harold Denny, "Fear of Saboteurs Dominant in Russia," *New York Times*, May 23, 1937, "Many Aliens Leave Country," *New York Times*, June 6, 1937, Leonid Zakovsky, "Alien Firms Held Anti-Soviet Bases," *New York Times*, August 8, 1937, William F. McDermott, "Tension and Strain Apparent in Russia," *New York Times*, August 22, 1937, and "Soviet Increases Its Hunt for Spies," *New York Times*, February 26, 1938.
106 Harold Denny, "Fury of Soviet Spokesmen Points to Vast Discontent," *New York Times*, June 25, 1937.
107 Moore, "Memorandum by the Acting Secretary of State," 319-20.
108 Henderson, "The Chargé in the Soviet Union (Henderson) to the Secretary of State," 374-6.
109 Tzouliadis, *The Forsaken*.
110 See Henderson, "The Chargé in the Soviet Union (Henderson) to the Secretary of State," 391-4, 635-8.
111 Joseph E. Davies, "Memorandum by the Ambassador in the Soviet Union (Davies) of a Conversation with the Soviet People's Commissar for Foreign Affairs (Litvinov)," in US Department of State, Foreign Relations Branch, *Foreign Relations of the United States: The Soviet Union, 1933-1939*, 534-6.

112 Kirk, "The Chargé in the Soviet Union (Kirk) to the Secretary of State," 663.
113 See Henderson, "The Chargé in the Soviet Union (Henderson) to the Secretary of State," 441–2 and Joseph E. Davies, "The Ambassador in the Soviet Union (Davies) to the Secretary of State," in US Department of State, Foreign Relations Branch, *Foreign Relations of the United States: The Soviet Union, 1933–1939*, 445–6.
114 George F. Kennan, "Memorandum by Mr. George F. Kennan of the Division of European Affairs [extracts]," in US Department of State, Foreign Relations Branch, *Foreign Relations of the United States: The Soviet Union, 1933–1939*, 398–400, 446–7.
115 Loy W. Henderson, "The Chargé in the Soviet Union (Henderson) to the Secretary of State," 400–1.
116 Ibid., 633–5.
117 Ibid., 514–18.
118 See "Soviet Executes 8 Leaders," *New York Times*, December 20, 1937, "Karakhan Noted as Expert on East," *New York Times*, December 20, 1937, and "Secret Police Hit in Soviet Purge," *New York Times*, December 21, 1937.
119 "Soviet Purge List Includes 3 Envoys," *New York Times*, November 12, 1937.
120 "The Grim Summons," Topics of the Times, *New York Times*, November 13, 1937.
121 See "'Pressing and Desperate,'" *Time*, December 13, 1937, 23.
122 See Alexandre Barmine, "Stalin a Betrayer, Ex-Envoy Asserts," *New York Times*, December 23, 1937, Alexandre Barmine, "Russian Disunity Is Laid to Stalin," *New York Times*, December 25, 1937, Alexandre Barmine, "2 Executions Held a Sop to Cossacks," *New York Times*, December 26, 1937, Alexandre Barmine, "Bukharin Believed Already Executed," *New York Times*, December 29, 1937; see also "Envoy Assails Barmine," *New York Times*, December 29, 1937.
123 "Death and Diplomacy," *Newsweek*, January 3, 1938, 22–3.
124 "Purge Goes on," *New Republic*, January 5, 1938, 240–1.
125 John G. Wright (pseud.), "Diplomats in Grip of Purge," International Notes, *Socialist Appeal*, December 4, 1937.
126 Max Shachtman, "New G.P.U. Frame-Ups Exposed," *Socialist Appeal*, December 25, 1937.
127 Victor Serge, "Stalin's Terror Continues with Envoy's Recall," *Socialist Appeal*, October, 1938.
128 Kirk, "The Chargé in the Soviet Union (Kirk) to the Secretary of State," 758–9.
129 Joseph E. Davies, "The Ambassador in Belgium (Davies) to the Secretary of State," in US Department of State, Foreign Relations Branch, *Foreign Relations of the United States: The Soviet Union, 1933–1939*, 760–1.
130 Kotkin, *Stalin*, 448.
131 John G. Wright (pseud.), "Litvinov's Removal Certain," Soviet Union Notes, *Socialist* Appeal, February 5, 1938.

132 Stuart Grummon, "The Chargé in the Soviet Union (Grummon) to the Secretary of State," in US Department of State, Foreign Relations Branch, *Foreign Relations of the United States: The Soviet Union, 1933-1939*, 770-3.
133 Harold Denny, "Ill Health Is Cited," *New York Times*, May 4, 1939.
134 "Resignation of Litvinov Upsets Alliance with French and British," *Social Justice*, May 15, 1939, 3.
135 Harold Roberts, "Litvinov Ouster Bid to Hitler," *Socialist Appeal*, May 9, 1939.
136 Hugh Phillips, *Maxim M. Litvinov and Soviet-American Relations, 1918-1946* (Washington, DC: Woodrow Wilson International Center for Scholars, 1996), 10, https://www.wilsoncenter.org; see also Geoffrey Roberts, "The Fall of Litvinov: A Revisionist View," *Journal of Contemporary History* 27, no. 4 (October, 1992): 639-57.
137 Louis Fischer, *Russia's Road from Peace to War: Soviet Foreign Relations, 1917-1941* (New York: Harper & Row, 1960), 285-90.
138 Teddy J. Uldricks, "The Impact of the Great Purges on the People's Commissariat of Foreign Affairs," *Slavic Review* 36, no. 2 (June, 1977): 167-204.
139 Kotkin, *Stalin*, 628.
140 Alastair Kocho-Williams, "The Soviet Diplomatic Corps and Stalin's Purges," *Slavonic and East European Review* 86, no. 1 (January, 2008): 90-110.
141 Loy W. Henderson, "Problems in Connection with the Protection of U. S. Citizens in the Soviet Union," in *A Question of Trust: The Origins of U.S.-Soviet Diplomatic Relations: The Memoirs of Loy W. Henderson* (Stanford, CA: Hoover Institution Press, 1986), 366-70.
142 "Text of the Communication Accompanying Our Recognition of Russia," *New York Times*, November 18, 1933.
143 "Arrest and Detention of American Citizens by the Soviet Government in Contravention of the Undertaking of November 16, 1933," in US Department of State, Foreign Relations Branch, *Foreign Relations of the United States: The Soviet Union, 1933-1939*, 491-503.
144 Cordell Hull, "The Secretary of State to the Chargé in the Soviet Union (Henderson)," in US Department of State, Foreign Relations Branch, *Foreign Relations of the United States: The Soviet Union, 1933-1939*, 497.
145 See Henderson, "The Chargé in the Soviet Union (Henderson) to the Secretary of State," 497-8, 500-2, Hull, "Memorandum by the Secretary of State of a Conversation with the Ambassador of the Soviet Union (Troyanovsky)," 498-500, 627, Davies, "The Ambassador in the Soviet Union (Davies) to the Secretary of State," 562-3.
146 See "American Couple Vanish Mysteriously in Moscow," *New York Times*, December 10, 1937, "Soviet Is Pressed to Find Robinsons," *New York Times*, December 11, 1937, "Hull Asks Moscow for Urgent Action to Find Robinsons," *New York Times*, December 12, 1937, "Moscow Still Hunts Missing Robinsons,"

New York Times, December 13, 1937, "'Robinsons' Got Passports by Fraud to Enter Russia," *New York Times*, December 15, 1937, Harold Denny, "Soviet Takes Steps to Hold 'Robinsons,'" *New York Times*, December 17, 1937, "Mrs. Rubens Found to Be Mrs. Robinson," *New York Times*, January 6, 1938, "U. S. Note Demands to Know If Soviet Holds Mrs. Rubens," *New York Times*, January 8, 1938, "Mrs. Rubens Held in Soviet Prison," *New York Times*, January 19, 1938, "U. S. Officials Fail to See Mrs. Rubens," *New York Times*, January 23, 1938, "U. S. Presses Right to See Mrs. Rubens," *New York Times*, January 26, 1938, "U. S. Aides See Mrs. Rubens," *New York Times*, February 11, 1938, "Mrs. Rubens Rejects Any Help From U. S." *New York Times*, February 12, 1938, Walter Duranty, "Mrs. Rubens Meek in Russians' Spell," *New York Times*, February 14, 1938, Ellery C. Stowell, "The Robinson Case," *American Journal of International* Law 32, no. 2 (April, 1938): 320–4, Harold Denny, "Rubens Mystery Takes a New Turn," *New York Times*, June 11, 1939, Harold Denny, "Mrs. Rubens Tried," *New York Times*, June 10, 1939, Harold Denny, "Jailers Were Kind, Says Mrs. Rubens," *New York Times*, June 23, 1939, and Harold Denny, "Mrs. Rubens Visits Moscow Embassy," *New York Times*, June 30, 1939.

147 See "Marinelli Office in 'Robinson' Case," *New York Times*, December 16, 1937, "2 Inquiries Center on 'Robinsons' Case," *New York Times*, December 22, 1937, "Link Rubens Name in 'Robinson' Case," *New York Times*, December 28, 1937, "Marinelli Linked to Robinson Case," *New York Times*, December 29, 1937, "Passports Issued as Political Favor in Robinson Case," *New York Times*, December 31, 1937, "Finding of 'Agent' in Robinson Case Brings Lepke Clue," *New York Times*, January 7, 1938, "Hearings Continue in Robinson Mystery," *New York Times*, January 13, 1938, "Jury Hears Tresca in Rubens Inquiry," *New York Times*, February 22, 1938, "Rubens Witness Seized as Member of Passport Ring," *New York Times*, March 29, 1938, "Marinelli Offers Data on Robinsons," *New York Times*, March 29, 1938, "Jailed as Witness in Passport Fraud," *New York Times*, March 30, 1938, "Rubenses Are Spies, Red Paper Charges," *New York Times*, November 15, 1938, "Witnesses Indicted in Passport Fraud," *New York Times*, April 5, 1939, "Spy Tale Unfolds in Passport Trial," *New York Times*, April 13, 1939, "Marinelli in Dark on Passport Power," *New York Times*, April 14, 1939, "Lawyer's Kinsman Links Him to Spy," *New York Times*, April 20, 1939, "Red Link Revealed in Passport Trial," *New York Times*, April 21, 1939, "Rubens Paid $550 to Pose as Editor," *New York Times*, April 22, 1939, "Hasty Departure of Rubens Related," *New York Times*, April 25, 1939, "U. S. May Unravel Red Spy Mystery," *New York Times*, April 26, 1939, "Spy's Data Clue in Passport Trial," *New York Times*, April 27, 1939, "Ex-Envoy Testifies in Passport Trial," *New York Times*, April 29, 1939, "Both Sides Sum up in Passport Trial," *New York Times*, May 2,

1939, "3 Are Found Guilty in Passport Fraud," *New York Times*, May 3, 1939, "3 Get 2 Years Each in Passport Fraud," *New York Times*, May 10, 1939, and "Rubens' Case Led to Trial of 3 Here," *New York Times*, June 10, 1939.
148 Herbert Solow, "'Stalin's American Passport Mill," *American Mercury*, July, 1939, 302-9.
149 Nat Levine, "Krivitsky Reveals Rubens Identity," *Socialist Appeal*, May 12, 1939.
150 See James P. Cannon, "Cannon Exposes Attempt to Use the 'Robinson' Case Against U. S. Trotskyists," *Socialist Appeal*, December 25, 1937, James P. Cannon, "'Robinson-Rubens' Frameup Prepared for U.S. Spy Scare," *Socialist Appeal*, January 1, 1938, Junius (pseud.), "View Confirmed in 'Robinson'-GPU Mystery," *Socialist Appeal*, January 8, 1938, Junius (pseud.), "All Trails Lead to Stalinist Camp in the Robinson-Rubens Case," *Socialist Appeal*, January 15, 1938, "Moscow Admits 'Robinsons' Held for 'Espionage,'" *Socialist Appeal*, January 22, 1938, Junius (pseud.), "Moscow in Difficulty with Robinson Case," *Socialist Appeal*, January 29, 1938, Junius (pseud.), "Real Plan behind Rubens Case Now Becoming Clearer," *Socialist Appeal*, February 5, 1938, Tony Chapman, "Mrs. Rubens 'Freed,' Spins New Plot on Kremlin Order," *Socialist Appeal*, July 4, 1939, Junius (pseud.), "Jury to Get New Facts in Rubens Case," *Socialist Appeal*, February 19, 1938, Junius (pseud.), "Arrested Photographer a Stalinist Sympathizer," *Socialist Appeal*, April 2, 1938, and Junius (pseud.), "Grand Jury Indicts Two in Rubens Mystery Case," *Socialist Appeal*, April 9, 1938.
151 See Henderson, "The Chargé in the Soviet Union (Henderson) to the Secretary of State," 389-90 and Edward Page, Jr., "Memorandum by Mr. Edward Page, Jr., of the Division of European Affairs," in US Department of State, Foreign Relations Branch, *Foreign Relations of the United States: The Soviet Union, 1933-1939*, 590-1.
152 See Henderson, "The Chargé in the Soviet Union (Henderson) to the Secretary of State," 394-6 and Davies, "The Ambassador in the Soviet Union (Davies) to the Secretary of State," 397-8.
153 "Difficulties from Soviet Authorities Interfering with the Proper Functioning of the American Embassy in Moscow," in US Department of State, Foreign Relations Branch, *Foreign Relations of the United States: The Soviet Union, 1933-1939*, 624-69.
154 Hull, "Memorandum by the Secretary of State of a Conversation with the Ambassador of the Soviet Union (Troyanovsky)," 624-7.
155 George F. Kennan and Edward Page, Jr., "Memorandum by Messrs. George F. Kennan and Edward Page, Jr., of the Division of European Affairs," in US Department of State, Foreign Relations Branch, *Foreign Relations of the United States: The Soviet Union, 1933-1939*, 657-60.

Chapter 7

1. Harold Denny, "Purge Aids Stalin Bar Foes at Polls," *New York Times*, September 15, 1937; see also "Primer by Denny," *Time*, September 27, 1937, 18.
2. "Report on Russia," editorial, *New York Times*, September 14, 1937.
3. William Henry Chamberlin, "Stalin: Portrait of a Degenerate," *American Mercury*, February, 1938, 206–18.
4. William Henry Chamberlin, "Stalin Is Russia's Worst Czar," *American Mercury*, September, 1938, 1–10.
5. "Purge of Purgers," *Time*, January 31, 1938, 18.
6. "Purge in Russia," *Literary Digest*, November 20, 1937, 10.
7. Maxwell S. Stewart, "Twenty Years of Progress," *The Nation*, November 3, 1937, 523–6.
8. "Russia and the World," *The Nation*, November 3, 1937, 521.
9. Henderson, "The Chargé in the Soviet Union (Henderson) to the Secretary of State," 508.
10. Harold Denny, "Soviet Ends Purge in Ranks of Party," *New York Times*, January 18, 1938.
11. Union of Soviet Socialist Republics, People's Commissariat of Justice, *Report of the Court Proceedings in the Case of the Anti-Soviet "Bloc of Rights and Trotskyites"* (Moscow: The Commissariat, 1938); see also A. I. Rykov, Genrikh Iagoda, Robert C. Tucker, and Stephen F. Cohen, *The Great Purge Trial* (New York: Grosset & Dunlap, 1965).
12. Rupert Collley, "Nikolai Buhkarin—A Brief Summary," March 15, 2016, accessed August 19, 2021, https://www.rubertcolley.com.
13. Nikolai I. Bukharin, "To the Presidium of the Supreme Soviet of the USSR," in *Revelations from the Russian Archives*, ed. Loenker and Bachman, 109–10.
14. Kotkin, *Stalin*, 560.
15. See "Bucharin Formally Ousted," *The Militant*, August 15, 1929, Walter Duranty, "Hints Suppression of 'Rebel' Bukharin," *New York Times*, October 30, 1929, Walter Duranty, "Soviet Sees Heresy among Reds Ended," *New York Times*, November 27, 1929, "Bukharin Falls," *Time*, December 2, 1929, 28, "Bukharin Returns to Party Conclaves," *New York Times*, February 4, 1932, Harold Denny, "High Soviet Editor Again in Disfavor," *New York Times*, February 11, 1936, "Bukharin Rejects Views Laid to Him," *New York Times*, February 15, 1936, "Bukharin Rebuke No Rift," *New York Times*, February 16, 1936, "Crack! Crack!" *Time*, February 24, 1936, 27, and "Soviet Exonerates Bukharin and Rykoff," *New York Times*, September 10, 1936.
16. See Harold Denny, "Bukharin and Rykoff Resist Confessing to the Charges Against Them in Russia," *New York Times*, March 25, 1937 and "Bukharin Accused by Soviet Academy," *New York Times*, May 22, 1937.

17 See Ken Coates, *The Case of Nikolai Bukharin* (Nottingham: Spokesman Books, 1978), Stephen F. Cohen, *Bukharin and the Bolshevik Revolution: A Political Biography, 1888–1938* (New York: Knopf, 1977), Stephen F. Cohen, "Bukharin's Fate," *Dissent* 45, no. 2 (Spring, 1988): 58–68, George Katkov, *Trial of Bukharin* (New York: Stein & Day, 1969) and Roy Medvedev, *Nikolai Bukharin: The Last Years* (New York: W. W. Norton, 1980).

18 See Walter Duranty, "Russian Reds Call Rykof Two-Faced," *New York Times*, November 3, 1930, Edwin L. James, "Stalin Dismisses Rykoff as Soviet Prime Minister," *New York Times*, December 20, 1930, "Rykoff Is Expelled from Last Office," *New York Times*, December 22, 1930, "Rykoff Out," *Outlook and Independent*, December 31, 1930, 685–6, "Communist Dictator Fires Last of Old Bolsheviks," *Newsweek*, October 30, 1936, 18, Harold Denny, "9 More Executed in Russian Plots," *New York Times*, August 25, 1937, and Harold Denny, "Soviet Accuses 7 of Rightist Plot," *New York Times*, August 26, 1937.

19 Alexei Rykov, "Letter from Rykov," in *Revelations from the Russian Archives*, ed. Loenker and Bachman, 111.

20 See "Stalin Persecutes Rakovsky," *The Militant*, March 8, 1930, "Rakovsky in Exile in Northern Siberia," *New York Times*, March 25, 1933, "Rakovsky, Exiled Soviet Envoy, Capitulates," *New York Times*, February 20, 1934, and "Rakovsky Is Assailed," *New York Times*, April 3, 1937.

21 Khristian Rakovsky, "Soviet Press Asks Death for Plotters," *Daily Worker*, August 22, 1936,

22 See Denny "Milder 'OGPU' Seen," *New York Times*, September 28, 1936, "Superspy Moves: Head of Dreaded Russian Ogpu Quits Terrifying Prison Building," *Literary Digest*, October 10, 1936, 15–16, Harold Denny, "Ex-Chief of OGPU, Yagoda, to Be Tried," *New York Times*, April 4, 1937, Harold Denny, "Moscow Shocked by Yagoda's Case," *New York Times*, April 5, 1937, Topics of the Times, "Ogpu Chief Falls," *New York Times*, April 6, 1937, and Harold Denny, "Russians Rejoice at Yagoda Ousting," *New York Times,* April 11, 1937.

23 See "Farm Commissar Removed by Soviet," *New York Times*, October 30, 1937, Harold Denny, "2 Ex-Commissars Linked in Spying," *New York Times*, January 12, 1938. "Vice Commissar of Foreign Trade Accuses Own Office of Wrecking Soviet's Interest," *New York Times*, July 25, 1937, and "28 Trade Officials Dropped in Soviet," *New York Times*, February 13, 1938.

24 A. Timofeyev, "Vyshinski, Soviet Prosecutor," *Living Age*, January, 1938, 418–29.

25 Harold Denny, "Confession False, Soviet Aide Says," *New York Times*, March 3, 1938.

26 "'Lined with Despair,'" *Time*, March 14, 1938, 25–8.

27 Harold Denny, "Soviet Aide Asserts Guilt, Again Reversing Himself," *New York Times*, March 4, 1938.
28 See Otto D. Tolischus, "German Executed as Soviet Plotter," *New York Times*, March 5, 1938 and Conquest, *The Great Terror*, 352.
29 Andrei Vyshinsky, "Morning Session, March 11, 1938," in Union of Soviet Socialist Republics, People's Commissariat of Justice, *Report of the Court Proceedings in the Case of the Anti-Soviet "Bloc of Rights and Trotskyites,"* 697.
30 Davies, "The Ambassador in the Soviet Union (Davies) to the Secretary of State," 369.
31 Ibid., 527.
32 Ibid., 528.
33 Ibid., 532–3.
34 Ibid., 544–5.
35 Davies, "Diary," in *Mission to Moscow*, 116–17.
36 Ibid., 175.
37 Ibid., "Purge Conditions in Moscow," 176.
38 Davies, "Bukharin Treason Trial," in *Mission to Moscow*, 177.
39 Ibid., 178.
40 Davies, "So-Called Bukharin Mass Treason Trial," in *Mission to Moscow*, 178–9.
41 Davies, "Fifth Columnists in Russia: A Study in Hindsight—1941," in *Mission to Moscow*, 179–84.
42 Bohlen, "To Be Shot, to Be Shot, to Be Shot," 51.
43 Ibid., 37–51.
44 Walter Duranty, "21 Soviet Ex-Leaders Face Trial," *New York Times*, February 28, 1938.
45 Walter Duranty, "Russians Approve Trial of Ex-Chiefs," *New York Times*, March 1, 1938.
46 "Moscow's New Purge," editorial, *New York Times*, March 1, 1938.
47 "Text of the Indictment Accusing 21 Defendants of Treason to the Soviet Union," *New York Times*, March 3, 1938.
48 Topics of the Times, "Twenty Years After," *New York Times*, March 4, 1938.
49 Harold Denny, "Soviet Court Told of Trotsky Funds," *New York Times*, March 5, 1938.
50 Harold Denny, "Trial in Moscow a Strange Picture," *New York Times*, March 6, 1938; see also "Moscow Trial," *New York Times*, March 6, 1938.
51 Harold Denny, "Bukharin Says He Led Coup Plot, Aiming to Set up Fascist Regime," *New York Times*, March 6, 1938.
52 "Briton Contradicts Zelensky," *New York Times*, March 6, 1938.
53 Harold Denny, "Trial of Russians at Halfway Point," *New York Times*, March 7, 1938.
54 Harold Denny, "Bukharin Fighting to Save His Record," *New York Times*, March 8, 1938.

55 Harold Denny, "Russians Confess Murders by Poison," *New York Times*, March 9, 1938.
56 Harold Denny, "Soviet Deaths Laid to Yagoda's Threats," *New York Times*, March 10, 1938.
57 Harold Denny, "Death for 19 Asked at Russian Trial," *New York Times*, March 12, 1938,
58 Harold Denny, "18 Russians to Die for Treason Plot," *New York Times*, March 13, 1938.
59 "Rykov Weeps at Sentence," *New York Times*, March 13, 1938.
60 Harold Denny, "Wide Plot Shown by Moscow Trial," *New York Times*, March 14, 1938.
61 Elias Tobenkin, "Troyanovsky Firm on Moscow Trial," *New York Times*, March 20, 1938.
62 "Foreigners in Moscow," editorial, *New York Times*, March 22, 1938,
63 Joseph Davies, "The Case of the Arrests of Soviet Employees of the American Correspondents," in US Department of State, Foreign Relations Branch, *Foreign Relations of the United States: The Soviet Union, 1933–1939*, 535–6.
64 Alexander Kerensky, letter to the editor, *New York Times*, April 24, 1938.
65 "Revelations," *Time*, March 7, 1938, 24.
66 "'Thank God!'" *Time*, March 21, 1938, 26–7.
67 "Most Bizarre of Purges Bursts on Red Army's 20th Birthday," *Newsweek*, March 7, 1938, 17–18.
68 "Pattern Stands out in Series of Purge Trials," *Newsweek*, March 14, 1938, 16–17.
69 "Justice in Wonderland," *Newsweek*, March 21, 1938, 19.
70 Walter G. Krivitsky, "Why Did They Confess?" *Saturday Evening Post*, June 17, 1939, 5–6, 96–8, 100–3; see also Krivitsky, *In Stalin's Secret Service*, 126–45.
71 "The Fourth Moscow Trial," *New Republic*, March 9, 1938, 117.
72 "Moscow Loses Caste," *New Republic*, March 16, 1938, 151–2; see also "On the Moscow Trials," Correspondence, *New Republic*, April 13, 1938, 306–7.
73 Bruce Bliven, "A Letter to Stalin," *New Republic*, March 30, 1938, 216.
74 "Bruce Bliven," *New Republic*, February 3, 2014, 2.
75 "From a Moscow Observer," *New Republic*, May 4, 1938, 383–4.
76 Malcolm Cowley, "Moscow Trial: 1938," review of Union of Soviet Socialist Republics, People's Commissariat of Justice, *The Case of the Anti-Soviet Bloc of Rights and Trotskyists: A Verbatim Report*, *New Republic*, May 18, 1938, 50–1.
77 Malcolm Cowley, "Moscow Trial: II," review of Union of Soviet Socialist Republics, People's Commissariat of Justice, *The Case of the Anti-Soviet Bloc of Rights and Trotskyists: A Verbatim Report*, *New Republic*, May 25, 1938, 79–80.
78 John Patrick Diggins, "The *New Republic* and Its Times: Seventy Years of Enlightened Mistakes, Principles Compromises, and Unconventional Wisdom." *New Republic*, December 10, 1984, 43.

79 Oswald Garrison Villard, "The Latest Batch of Victims Now on the Rack," *The Nation*, March 12, 1938, 302.
80 Oswald Garrison Villard, "Issues and Men," *The Nation*, March 19, 1938, 322.
81 Paul Scheffer, "From Lenin to Stalin," *Foreign Affairs*, April, 1938, 445–53.
82 Harvey T. Mann, "Totalitarian Justice: Trial of Bukharin, Rykov, Yagoda, et al," *American Bar Association Journal* 24, no. 12 (December, 1938): 970–6, 1029–30.
83 Mary Van Kleeck, "The Moscow Trials," Comments and Correspondence, *Pacific Affairs* 11, no. 2 (June, 1938): 233–7.
84 William Henry Chamberlin, "The Moscow Trials," letter to the editor, *Pacific Affairs* 11, no. 3 (September, 1938): 367–70.
85 Owen Lattimore, Comments and Correspondence, *Pacific Affairs* 11, no. 3 (September, 1938): 370–2.
86 John N. Hazard, review of *The Case of the Anti-Soviet Bloc of Rights and Trotskyists: A Verbatim Report*, *Pacific Affairs* 11, no. 3 (September 1938): 401–4.
87 Walter Duranty, "The Bukharin-Yagoda Trial," in *The Kremlin and the People* (New York: Reynal and Hitchcock, 1941), 70–115.
88 Louis Fischer, "The Moscow Trials and Confessions," in *Men and Politics: An Autobiography*, 502–31.
89 Communist International, Executive Committee, "On Carrying Out a Campaign of Enlightenment in Connections with the Trial of the Bloc of Rights and Trotskyites," in William J. Chase and Vadim A. Staklo, *Enemies within the Gates? The Comintern and the Stalinist Repression, 1934–1939* (New Haven, CT: Yale University Press, 2002), 295–8.
90 See "21 Trotzkyists Face Trial for Murder of Gorky, Others," *Daily Worker*, February 28, 1938, and "Unmasking a Monstrous Plot," editorial, *Daily Worker*, March 1, 1938.
91 "Millions of Workers, Peasants and Intellectuals Shudder with Revulsion on Learning of Monstrous Right-Trotzkyist Plot," *Daily Worker*, March 1, 1938.
92 "20 Trotzkyists Plead Guilty as Moscow Treason Trial Opens," *Daily Worker*, March 3, 1938.
93 "Text of Indictment of 21 Bukharin-Trotzkyist Spies, Assassins," *Daily Worker*, March 3, 1938.
94 "Moscow Trial Proofs Mount," *Daily Worker*, March 4, 1938.
95 "Reich Paid $1,000,000 to Trotzky for Spying," *Daily Worker*, March 5, 1938.
96 "Bukharin's Co-Plotters Link Him to 1918 Plot to Kill Lenin and Stalin," *Daily Worker*, March 8, 1938; see also Harry Gannes, "USSR Foes Go Dizzy Seeking Answers to Trial Confessions," *Daily Worker*, March 8, 1938.
97 For examples of the defendants' testimonies, see "Documentary Proof Produced in Court Compels Krestinsky to Admit Guilt," *Daily Worker*, March 3, 1938, "Bessonov Testifies to Krestinsky's Orders for Trotzky-Nazi Spying-Wrecking Activities," *Daily Worker*, March 4, 1938, "Grinko Tells of Deals with Fascist

States to Separate the Ukraine from the U.S.S.R.," *Daily Worker*, March 5, 1938, "Chernov Testifies How He Became German Spy," *Daily Worker*, March 5, 1938, "Rakovsky Testifies to Trotzky's Orders to Help Japan Organize War on China," *Daily Worker*, March 7, 1938, "Bukharin-Trotzky Clique Plotted with Tukhachevsky for Military Coup in '37," *Daily Worker*, March 7, 1938, "Bukharin Testimony Shows His Plotting Meant Victory of Fascism in U. S. S. R," *Daily Worker*, March 8, 1938, "Bukharin, under Vishinsky Questioning, Testifies Sanctioning Pact with Nazis," *Daily Worker*, March 9, 1938 and "Witness Yakovleva Tells of Bukharin's Order in 1918 to Kill Lenin and Stalin," *Daily Worker*, March 9, 1938.

98 See "Vyshinsky Summary Nails Trotskyist-Bukharin Traitors of Fascist Plot Against Soviet Union," *Daily Worker*, March 12, 1938, "Last Statements of Accused Bukharin-Trotskyist Traitors," (part 1) *Daily Worker*, March 15, 1938, "Last Statements of Accused Bukharin-Trotskyist Traitors," (part 2) *Daily Worker*, March 15, 1938, "Text of Verdict on Bukharin-Trotzkyist Traitors," *Daily Worker*, March 15, 1938, "Soviet People Hail Verdict Against Traitors as Victory," *Daily Worker*, March 15, 1938 and Sander Garlin, "The Criminals Failed to Halt Life in USSR," *Daily Worker*, March 15, 1938.

99 See "Court Hears Doctors Tell of Drugging Gorky, USSR Leaders to Death in Plot," *Daily Worker*, March 10, 1938, "Disgraced Doctors under Vyshinsky Questioning Describe the Fiendish Murder of Maxim Gorky," *Daily Worker*, March 10, 1938, "Bulanov Tells How 'Isolation from Party Life' Made Him Servile Agent of Yagoda's Murder Plots," *Daily Worker*, March 11, 1938. "Yagoda Tells That His Murders of Soviet Leaders Were Trotzky Plot to Restore Capitalism in U.S.S.R," *Daily Worker*, March 11, 1938, "Disgraced Doctors Describe the Fiendish Murder of Gorky," *Daily Worker*, March 11, 1938, "Pletnev with Tainted Medical Record Tells of His Criminal Participation in Murder of Soviet Leaders," *Daily Worker*, March 12, 1938, and "Yagoda Confesses to Fiendish Murders of Soviet Leaders," *Daily Worker*, March 12, 1938.

100 Sender Garlin, "Yezhov Looms as Leading Figure in Exposure of Trotzkyist Spies," *Daily Worker*, March 8, 1938.

101 Mikhail Koltsov, "Bloodhound Yagoda," *Daily Worker*, March 10, 1938.

102 R. Page Arnot, "'Old Guard' or Rogues Gallery," *Daily Worker*, March 8, 1938.

103 Harry Gannes, "Capitalist Press Falls Back on 'Queries' When Evidence Piles up of Guilt of 21," *Daily Worker*, March 10, 1938.

104 Earl Browder, "Lessons of the Moscow Trials," *Daily Worker*, March 19, 1938; reprints, *The Communist*, April, 1938, 306–21, and *Traitors in American History: Lessons of the Moscow Trials* (New York: Workers Library Publishers, 1938).

105 Upton Sinclair, "A Letter to Eugene Lyons," *Daily Worker*, March 4, 1938; reprints, *New Masses*, March 8, 1938, 5–6 and *Upton Sinclair on the Soviet Union* (New York: New Masses, 1938).

106 Upton Sinclair and Eugene Lyons, *The Terror in Russia? Two Views* (New York: R. R. Smith, 1938; see also review of "*Terror in Russia? Two Views* by Upton Sinclair and Eugene Lyons, *Saturday Review*, July 9, 1938, 21; for a review in a Trotskyist newspaper, see Frank Graves, "Lyons versus Sinclair," review of *Terror in Russia* by Upton Sinclair and Eugene Lyons, *Socialist Appeal*, July 9, 1938.
107 Sender Garlin, "Eastman Is Revealed as British Agent by Rakovsky at Trial," *Daily Worker*, March 7, 1938.
108 "Max Eastman Sues," *New York Times*, May 11, 1938.
109 See "Soviet Justice and Its Foes," "Pitfalls for Prophets," and "A Service for Peace," *New Masses*, March 8, 1938, 11–12.
110 Joshua Kunitz, "The Moscow Trial," *New Masses*, March 15, 1938, 3–6.
111 Joshua Kunitz, "The Moscow Trial—II," *New Masses*, March 23, 1938, 13–16.
112 John Sutton, "Wreckers in High Places," *New Masses*, May 24, 1938, 7–9.
113 Nikolai Bukharin, "Crisis of Capitalist Culture," *New Masses*, December 4, 1934, 16–19.
114 Alexander Bittelman, "Destruction of Bloc of 'Rights and Trotskyites' Renders Great Service to Anti-Fascist Camp,'" *The Communist*, April, 1938, 291–6.
115 V. J. Jerome, "Bukharin—The Path of a Traitor," *The Communist*, June, 1938, 526–33.
116 V. J. Jerome, "Bukharin—The Path of a Traitor," *The Communist*, July, 1938, 642–51.
117 Joseph Starobin, "The Moscow Trial: Its Meaning and Importance," *Young Communist Review*, April, 1938, 16–19.
118 "Americans Also Confess," *Soviet Russia Today*, April, 1938, 5.
119 "A Word on Mr. Lyons and Mr. Villard," *Soviet Russia Today*, April, 1938, 5.
120 John Garnett, "A Trial of Traitors," *Soviet Russia Today*, April, 1938, 6–10.
121 Andrei Vyshinsky, "The Treason Case Summed Up," *Soviet Russia Today*, April, 1938, 22–5.
122 Theodore Bayer, "Your Questions Answered," *Soviet Russia Today*, April, 1938, 26, 32.
123 John Garnett, "The Moscow Trial Record," review of *The Case of the Anti-Soviet Bloc of Rights and Trotskyites: A Verbatim Report*, *Soviet Russia Today*, June, 1938, 20–1.
124 "To the Editors of the *New Republic*—and Others," *Soviet Russia Today*, July, 1938, 5–6.
125 "Trotskyist Allies of Franco," *Soviet Russia Today*, July, 1938, 6.
126 B. N. Ponomarev, *The Plot Against the Soviet Union and World Peace: Facts and Documents Compiled from the Verbatim Report of the Court Proceedings in the Case of the Anti-Soviet "Bloc of Rights and Trotskyites"'* (New York: Workers Library Publishers, 1938).
127 Emilion Yaroslavsky, *The Meaning of the Soviet Trials: Including the Official Text of the Indictment of the Bukharin-Trotskyist Bloc*, introd. by William Z. Foster (New York: Workers Library Publishers, 1938).

128 Victor Serge, "The End of Henry Yagoda," *Socialist Appeal*, August 28, 1937,
129 See Jack Weber, "The Wave of Trials in the U.S.S.R.," *Socialist Appeal*, September, 1937, and John G. Wright (pseud.), "Stalin's Purge Extends into the Youth and Penetrates the 'Politburo,'" *Socialist Appeal*, November 27, 1937.
130 See Leon Trotsky, "Trotsky Sees Trial as Reply to Dewey," *New York Times*, March 3, 1938, "Trotsky Suggests 4 Knew Too Much," *New York Times*, March 4, 1938, "Trotsky Forecasts Vishinsky Tactic," *New York Times*, March 5, 1938, "Trotsky Sees Army Opposed to Stalin," Leon Trotsky, "Trotsky Accuses Stalin in Murder," *New York Times*, March 8, 1938, and "Trotsky Sees Plots Dictated by Policy," *New York Times*, March 9, 1938.
131 See "Stalin Stages New Frame-Up," *Socialist Appeal*, March 5, 1938, John C. Wright (pseud.), "Last of Lenin's Colleagues Face Doom," *Socialist Appeal*, March 5, 1938, and "New Trial Is Climax of Two-Year Purge," *Socialist Appeal*, March 5, 1938.
132 "Stalin Regime Desperate," *Socialist Appeal*, March 12, 1938.
133 "Shachtman Talks on Trial to 800," *Socialist Appeal*, March 12, 1938.
134 "New York Soviet Consulate Picketed to Protest Trial," *Socialist Appeal*, March 12, 1938.
135 "Soviet Consulate Picketed in Frisco," *Socialist Appeal*, March 19, 1938.
136 "Moscow Trial Special Supplement," *Socialist Appeal*, March 12, 1938.
137 See "Lenin's Aides Shot," *Socialist Appeal*, March 19, 1938.
138 "An Open Letter to Members of the Communist Party," *Socialist Appeal*, March 19, 1938.
139 See "Trial Causes New Fissures in C. P. Ranks," *Socialist Appeal*, March 26, 1938, and "Unit Quits Communist Party Denounces Moscow Frameups," *Socialist Appeal*, April 23, 1938.
140 James Burnham, "Aftermath of the Trials," *Socialist Appeal*, March 26, 1938.
141 For examples, see John G. Wright (pseud.), Soviet Union Notes, *Socialist Appeal*, March 26, 1938, and John G. Wright (pseud.), Soviet Union Notes, *Socialist Appeal*, April 2, 1938.
142 Leon Trotsky, "Hitler's Austria Coup Aided by Moscow Trial," *Socialist Appeal*, March 26, 1938.
143 Alfred Rosmer, "Enough of Mud! Enough of Blood!" *Socialist Appeal*, April 23, 1938.
144 Leon Trotsky, "Stalin's Trial as a Terrorist Demanded of League by Trotsky," *Socialist Appeal*, April 23, 1938.
145 Li Fu-Jen, "Stalin Saves Rakovsky for New Frame-Up Trial," *Socialist Appeal*, March 19, 1938.
146 "Lyons versus Sinclair," review of *Terror in Russia? Two Views* by Upton Sinclair and Eugene Lyons, *Socialist* Appeal, July 9, 1938.
147 Max Eastman, "A Letter to Corliss Lamont," 122.
148 "The Trial of the 21," editorial, *New International*, April, 1938.

149 George Novack, "History to Order," review of *Traitors in American History: Lessons of the Moscow Trials* by Earl Browder, *New International*, May, 1938, 156–7.
150 Leon Trotsky, "Their Morals and Ours," *New International*, June, 1938, 163–73.
151 "Moscow Frame-Up Aids Reaction," *The Fighting Worker*, April 1, 1938.
152 "Around the Blody [sic] Purge," *In Defense of Bolshevism*, April 5, 1938.
153 See "Soviet Trial Delay Urged by U. S. Group," *New York Times*, March 1, 1938 and "Liberals Ask Stay of New Moscow Frameup," *Socialist Appeal*, March 5, 1938.
154 See Corliss Lamont, "Lamont Assails Dewey for Attack on Trials," *Daily Worker*, March 7, 1938 and "Accuses Dewey Group," *New York Times*, March 6, 1938.
155 "8,000 Meet to Denounce Trial," *Socialist Appeal*, March 19, 1938.
156 Bertram D. Wolfe, "Speech on the Moscow Purge Trials," in *Breaking with Communism: The Intellectual Odyssey of Bertram D. Wolfe*, ed. Robert Hessen (Stanford, CA: Hoover Institution Press, 1990), 37–40.
157 Bertram D. Wolfe, "Records of the Moscow Trials," Autumn, 1938. Manuscript.
158 Norman Thomas, "The Moscow Trials," *Modern Monthly*, March, 1938, 4, 13.
159 Norman Thomas and Joel Seidman, *Russia—Democracy or Dictatorship?* (New York: League for Industrial Democracy, 1939).
160 Robert Forsythe, "Norman Thomas on the Sidelines," *New Masses*, December 7, 1938, 12.
161 "The Moscow Trials: A Statement by American Progressives," *New Masses*, May 5, 1938, 19; reprint, "American Progressives on the Moscow Trials," *Soviet Russia Today*, May, 1938, 5.
162 "A Reply to Malcolm Cowley," *Soviet Russia Today*, August–September, 1938, 28, 31.
163 "Street-Walkers of the G.P.U.," *Socialist Appeal*, April 23, 1938.
164 Corliss Lamont, letter to the editor, *Free Inquiry* 1, no. 4 (Fall, 1981): 3.
165 Philip Rahv, "Trials of the Mind," *Partisan Review* 4, no. 5 (April, 1938): 3–11.
166 Lyons, "Hooray for Murder!," 246–56.
167 Bohlen, *Witness to History, 1929–1969*, 53.
168 Loy W. Henderson, *A Question of Trust: The Origins of U.S.-Soviet Diplomatic Relations: The Memoirs of Loy W. Henderson*, ed. with an introd. by George W. Baer (Stanford CA: Hoover Institution Press, 1986), 461.
169 Kennan, *Memoirs, 1925–1950*, 525.

Chapter 8

1 Stalin, "Report on the Work of the Central Committee to the Eighteenth Congress of the C.P.S.U.(B.)." March 10, 1939, in *Works*, vol. 14 (London: Red Star Press, 1978), accessed March 19, 2023, https://marxists.org.
2 Harold Denny, "Stalin Says Purge Didn't Hurt Soviet," *New York Times*, March 12, 1939.

3 "'Purified Soviet,'" *Newsweek*, April 9, 1939, 22.
4 R. O. G. Urch, "A 'New Era' in Russia," *Barrons's*, May 8, 1939, 3.
5 Harold Denny, "Russia Combats Fear by 'Purge of Purgers,'" *New York Times*, January 15, 1939.
6 "Moscow Frameups Exposed by Trial of Ukraine GPU," *Socialist Appeal*, January 7, 1939.
7 Joseph Barnes, "The Great Bolshevik Cleansing," *Foreign Affairs* 17, no. 3 (April, 1939): 556–68.
8 *History of the Communist Party of the Soviet Union (Bolsheviks): Short Course* (New York: International Publishers, 1939), 246–352.
9 Henderson, "The Chargé in the Soviet Union (Henderson) to the Secretary of State," 381.
10 Kirk, "The Chargé in the Soviet Union (Kirk) to the Secretary of State," 753–6.
11 Harold Denny, "Stalin's Russia: World Enigma," *New York Times Magazine*, October 8, 1939, SM1–2, SM23.
12 M. N. (pseud.), "Towards the Drawing of a Balance Sheet on the Kremlin's Purges," *Socialist Appeal*, June 30, 1939.
13 Bohlen, *Witness to History, 1929–1969*, 49–50.
14 Franklin D. Roosevelt, radio address to the American Youth Congress, February 10, 1940, http://www.fdrlibrary.marist.edu/_resources/images/msf/.
15 See Arnaldo Cortesi, "Trotsky Dies of His Wounds," *New York Times*, August 22, 1940, "Trotsky's Career a Rebellious One," *New York Times*, August 22, 1940, and "Bloody Murder in Mexico Ends Great Revolutionary Career of Leon Trotsky," *Life*, September 2, 1940, 17–21.
16 See "Leon Trotsky," editorial, *The Nation*, August 31, 1940, 165, Louis Fischer, "Trotsky and Stalin," *The Nation*, September 7, 1940, 191–2, and "The Old Man," *New Republic*, September 2, 1940, 292.
17 See Dwight Macdonald, "Trotsky Is Dead," *Partisan Review*, September–October, 1940, 339–53.
18 Victor Serge, "In Memoriam: L. D. Trotsky," *Partisan Review*, September, 1942, 388–91.
19 Paul Goodman, "The Death of Leon Trotsky," *Partisan Review*, September–October, 1940, 425–9.
20 See "Trotzky Dies after Attack by Follower," *Daily Worker*, August 22, 1940, and "Follower of Trotzky Tells Motives in Assassination," *Daily Worker*, August 23, 1940.
21 "As He Sowed," editorial, *New Masses*, September 2, 1940, 16.
22 See James P. Cannon, "To the Memory of the Old Man," *Socialist Appeal*, September 7, 1940, J. R. Johnson, "A Tribute to Our Fallen Leader, Leon Trotsky," *Labor Action*, September 2, 1940, Max Shachtman, "The Murder of Leon Trotsky," *Labor Action*, September 16, 1940, Max Shachtman, "The Murder of Leon

Trotsky," *Labor Action*, September 23, 1940, Max Shachtman, "Leon Trotsky: His Heritage," *New International*, September, 1940, Joseph Hansen, "With Trotsky to the End," *Fourth International*, October, 1940, 115–23, and Albert Goldman, *The Assassination of Leon Trotsky: The Proofs of Stalin's Guilt* (New York: Pioneer Publishers, 1940).

23 See "Trotsky Memorial Number," *Fourth International*, August, 1941, R. Craine, "We Pay Tribute to Our Many Martyrs in the Cause of Liberty," *Labor Action*, April 26, 1943, "Stalin's Guilt in Trotsky Murder Bared by Ex-Daily Worker Editor," *The Militant*, March 8, 1947, Joseph Hansen, "Stalin's Frame-Up System," *Fourth International*, July–August, 1950, 105–11, "New Evidence on Trotsky's Murder," *International Socialist Review*, Summer, 1957, 75–9, and Ted Grant, "The Impact of Trotsky's Death," *The Militant*, August 17, 1990.

24 Max Eastman, "The Character and Fate of Leon Trotsky," *Foreign Affairs*, January, 1941, 332–42.

25 "Protest the Stalinist Murder of Leon Trotsky," *Fighting Worker*, September 1, 1940.

26 U. S. Federal Bureau of Investigation, "Leon Trotsky," in *FBI Records: The Vault* (Washington, DC: The Bureau, 1934–1966), accessed August 5, 2022, https://vault.fbi.gov.

27 *American Aspects of Assassination of Leon Trotsky: Hearings Before the United States House Comm. on Un-American Activities*, 81st Cong. (1950).

28 *Hearing Before the Subcommittee to Investigate the Administration of the Internal Security Act and Other Internal Security Laws, Committee on the Judiciary*, 87th Cong. (1955) (testimony of Alexander Orlov).

29 See Rita T. Kronenbitter, *Leon Trotsky: Dupe of the NKVD* (Washington, DC: U. S. Central Intelligence Agency, 1994).

30 "Mme. Trotsky Asks Soviet Review," *New York Times*, November 5, 1961.

31 See Don Isaac Levine, *The Mind of an Assassin* (Westport, CT: Greenwood Press, 1979), Nicholas Mosby, *The Assassination of Trotsky* (London: Sphere Books, 1972), and Bertrand M. Patenaude, *Trotsky: Downfall of a Revolutionary* (New York: Harper Perennial, 2010).

32 See "Gen. Krivitsky Found Dead," *New York Times*, February 11, 1941, "Finding Is Delayed in Krivitsky's Death," *New York Times*, February 12, 1941, "Case of Krivitsky Closed as Suicide," *New York Times*, February 13, 1941; see also "'General Krivitsky' Exposes Himself," *New Masses*, July 4, 1939, 8–10, "The Murder of Krivitsky," *Fourth International*, February, 1941, 35–6, U. S. Federal Bureau of Investigation, "Walter G. Krivitsky," in *FBI Records: The Vault* (Washington, DC: The Bureau, 1999) and Gary Kern, *A Death in Washington: Walter G. Krivitsky and the Stalin Terror* (New York: Enigma, 2003).

33 Arthur Koestler, *Darkness at Noon*, trans. by Daphne Hardy (New York: Macmillan, 1941).

34 For book reviews, see Ralph Thompson, "Books of the Times," *New York Times*, May 20, 1941, Harold Strauss, "The Riddle of Moscow's Trials," *New York Times Book Review*, May 25, 1941, 1, 18, N. L. Rothman, "Three Stages of the Soviet Mind," *Saturday Review*, May 24, 1941, 7, "Brightest in Dungeons," *Time*, May 26, 1941, 100–2, Louis B. Salomon, "Moscow Purge," *The Nation*, May 24, 1941, 620, and Malcolm Cowley, "Punishment and Crime," Books in Review, *New Republic*, June 6, 1941, 766–7.

35 Albert Goldman, "False Light on the Moscow Trials," *Fourth International*, November, 1941, 280–2.

36 Joseph E. Davies, *Mission to Moscow: A Record of Confidential Dispatches to the State Department, Official and Personal Correspondence, Current Diary and Journal Entries, Including Notes and Comment up to October, 1941* (New York: Simon and Schuster, 1941); excerpts reprinted as "Moscow Notebook: An Ambassador's Report," *New York Times Magazine*, December 14, 1941, SM12–13, SM24–6.

37 For book reviews, see William Henry Chamberlin, "Mr. Davies Reports on Russia," *New York Times Book Review*, January 4, 1942, BR1, BR18, Ralph Thompson, review of *Mission to Moscow* by Joseph E. Davies, Books of the Times, *New York Times*, December 29, 1941, Henry C. Wolfe, "Millionaire in Moscow," *Saturday Review*, January 10, 1942, 5, Michael Karpovich, "Mission to Moscow," *Journal of Modern History* 14, no. 3 (September, 1942): 397–8, Walter Duranty, "A Daniel Come to Judgment," *New Republic*, January 12, 1942, 60–1, Margaret Marshall, "Mr. Davies's Revelations," *The Nation*, January 1, 1942, 118–19, Eugene Lyons, "The Purification of Stalin," *American Mercury*, January, 1942, 112–14, and Eugene Lyons, "Note on a Best-Seller," The State of the Union, *American Mercury*, April, 1942, 461–4.

38 See Joseph Starobin, "Moscow Diary," review of *Mission to Moscow* by Joseph E. Davies, *New Masses*, January 11, 1942, 20–2, William Lindsay, "Soviet-American Friendship: The Contribution of 'Mission to Moscow,'" review of *Mission to Moscow* by Joseph E. Davies, *The Communist*, March, 1942, 179–94, and Ernest J. Simmons, "Mission to Moscow," review of *Mission to Moscow* by Joseph E. Davies, *Science & Society* 6, no. 2 (Spring, 1942): 164–9.

39 Leon Colbert, "The Moscow Trials, 1942 Version," *Partisan Review*, March, 1942, 160–4.

40 Max Shachtman, "Ambassador Davies' War Mission: The New Revelations of Ex-Ambassador Davies," review of *Mission to Moscow* by Joseph E. Davies, *New International* February, 1942, 9–13.

41 See John Dewey, "Russia's Position," letter to the editor, *New York Times*, January 11, 1942, and Arthur Upham Pope, "Dewey Is Disputed," letter to the editor, *New York Times*, January 18, 1942.

42 Joseph E. Davies, "How Russia Blasted Hitler's Spy Machine," *American Magazine*, December, 1941, 80, 110–12.

43 Grandizo Munis, "Who Are Hitler's Agents in Russia? An Answer to Ex-Ambassador Davies," *Fourth International*, December, 1941, accessed March 19, 2023, https://marxists.org.

44 Michael Curtiz, *Mission to Moscow* (Burbank, CA: Warner Brothers, 1943).

45 For reviews of the film, see James Agee, Films, *The Nation*, May 22, 1943, 749–50, N. C. (Norman Cousins), "'Mission to Moscow,'" *Saturday Review*, June 5, 1943, 12–13, Bosley Crowther, review of *Mission to Moscow*, *New York Times*, April 30, 1943, Bosley Crowther, "Missionary Zeal," *New York Times*, May 9, 1943, Manny Farber, "Mishmash," *New Republic*, May 10, 1943, 636, "Hollywood Goes to Moscow," *Time*, May 10, 1943, 25, Eugene Lyons, "'Mission to Moscow,'" letter to the editor, *Saturday Review*, May 15, 1943, 17, Eugene Lyons, "Memo. on Movie Reviewers," *American Mercury*, July, 1943, 80–2, "Mission II—and I," *Time*, May 17, 1943, 25, "'Mission to Moscow,'" *Life*, May 10, 1943, 39–42 and "Successful Mission," *Newsweek*, May 10, 1943, 74.

46 Joy Davidman, "Journey into Truth," review of *Mission to Moscow*, *New Masses*, May 11, 1943, 28, 30.

47 See John Bates, "Frameup Movie Nears Completion," *Militant*, January 9, 1943, 1, 2, Reva Craine, "How the Film Falsifies the Record," *Labor Action*, May 24, 1943, R. Fahan, "Hollywood Face-Lifters Make a Lend-Lease Offering to Stalin," *Labor Action*, May 10, 1943, 3, A. G. (Albert Gates), "A Mission in Fraud," *Labor Action*, May 24, 1943, 3, Susan Green, "Mr. Davies—Lawyer and Whitewasher," *Labor Action*, May 24, 1943 and "'New Leader' Hits Davies' Movie," *The Militant*, January 9, 1943.

48 See John Dewey and Suzanne La Follette, "Several Faults Are Found in 'Mission to Moscow' Film," letter to the editor, *New York Times*, May 9, 1943, Arthur Upham Pope, "'Mission to Moscow' Film Viewed as Historical Realism," letter to the editor, *New York Times*, May 16, 1943, John Dewey and Suzanne La Follette, "Moscow Film Again Attacked," letter to the editor, *New York Times*, May 24, 1943, and John Dewey and Suzanne La Follette, "More on 'Mission to Moscow,'" letter to the editor, *New York Times*, June 19, 1943.

49 Joy Davidman, "Mission of Sabotage," *New Masses*, May 25, 1943, 29.

50 Howard Koch, "A Dramatist's Viewpoint on 'Mission to Moscow,'" *New York Times*, June 13, 1943.

51 Bohlen, *Witness to History, 1929–1969*, 123.

52 See *Hearing Regarding the Communist Infiltration of the Motion Picture Industry*, 80th Cong., 10 (1947) (statement of Jack L. Warner).

53 Todd Bennett, "Culture, Power, and *Mission to Moscow*: Film and Soviet-American Relations during World War II," *Journal of American History* 88, no. 2 (September,

2001): 489–502, Steve Boisson, "Mission to Moscow," *American History* 48, no. 6 (February, 2014): 60–4, David Culbert, ed., *Mission to Moscow* (Madison, WI: University of Wisconsin Press, 1980), Phillip L. Gianos, "The Movies and World War II," in *Politics and Politicians in American Film* (Westport, CT: Praeger, 1998), 123–7, Robert Fyne, "From Hollywood to Moscow," *Literature/Film Quarterly* 13, no. 3 (1985): 194–9, and Ronald Radosh and Allis Radosh, "A Great Historic Mistake: The Making of *Mission to Moscow*," *Film History* 16 (2004): 358–77; reprint in Ronald Radosh and Allis Radosh, *Red Star over Hollywood: The Film Colony's Long Romance with the Left* (San Francisco, CA: Encounter Books, 2005), 93–108.

54 See *FBI Records: The Vault* (Washington, DC: The Bureau, 1934–1966), accessed April 18, 2020, https://vault.fbi.gov.

55 Arthur Koestler and R. H. S. Crossman, *The God that Failed* (New York: Harper, 1949).

56 Sidney Hook, "The Problems of the Ex-Communist," *New York Times Magazine*, July 11, 1954, M7, M24–7.

57 See US Department of State, *Foreign Relations of the United States: 1952–1954, Volume VIII: Eastern Europe; Soviet Union; Eastern Mediterranean* (Washington, DC: Government Printing Office, 1988), 1048–58; see also Harrison E. Salisbury, "*Pravda*'s Attack on Kennan Vexes U. S.," *New York Times*, September 27, 1952, Walter H. Waggoner, "Kremlin Demands U. S. Recall Kennan, Charging Slander," *New York Times*, October 4, 1952, "A Kremlin Blunder," *New York Times*, October 4, 1952, "Kennan Is Not Surprised," *New York Times*, October 5, 1952, Harrison E. Salisbury, "Quick Soviet Reply on Kennan Is Due," *New York Times*, October 11, 1952, and George F. Kennan, "Persona Non Grata," in *Memoirs, 1950–1963* (New York: Pantheon Books, 1972), 145–67.

58 "Vicious Spies and Killers under the Mask of Academic Physicians," *Pravda*, January 13, 1953, accessed May 8, 2012, http://www.cyberussr.com/rus/vrach-ubijca-e.html.

59 Jacob D. Beam, "The Chargé in the Soviet Union (Beam) to the Department of State," in US Department of State, *Foreign Relations of the United States, 1952–1954, Volume VIII*, 1069–70.

60 John Foster Dulles, "The Secretary of State to the Embassy in the Soviet Union," US Department of State, *Foreign Relations of the United States, 1952–1954: Volume VIII*, 1073–5.

61 See "Moscow Arrests 9, Lays Murder Plot to Jewish Doctors," *New York Times*, January 13, 1953, "Further Arrests Expected in 'Plot' of Soviet Doctors," *New York Times*, January 14, 1953, Harry Schwartz, "Moscow's Charges Held Purge Omen," *New York Times*, January 14, 1953, Harrison E. Salisbury, "Soviet Uses 'Plot' as Anti-West Goad," *New York Times*, January 15, 1953, Harry Schwartz, "9 Soviet Doctors Treated Top Reds," *New York Times*, January 15, 1953, Harry Schwartz,

"Moscow's Moves Hint at Another Big Purge," *New York Times*, January 18, 1953, "New Purge," *New York Times*, January 18, 1953, and Harrison Salisbury, "Soviet Widens Vigilance," *New York Times*, January 19, 1953.

62 "Behind Russia's New Anti-Semitism Are the Real Assassins," *Labor Action*, January 26, 1953.

63 Beam, "The Chargé in the Soviet Union (Beam) to the Department of State," 1140–3.

64 See "*Pravda*'s Editorial on Abuses in the Doctor's Case," *New York Times*, April 7, 1953, reprint, "The Case of the Soviet Doctors," *New World Review*, May, 1953, 58–60.

65 See "Skepticism Confirmed," *New York Times*, April 4, 1953, Harrison E. Salisbury, "Whole Case 'False,'" *New York Times*, April 4, 1953, Harry Schwartz, "Moscow Betrays an Inner Struggle for Power," *New York Times*, April 5, 1953, Walter H. Waggoner, "Soviet Strain Seen in Doctor Reversal," *New York Times*, April 5, 1953, "The Purge Begins," *New York Times*, April 7, 1953, and Harry Schwartz, "The Fantastic 'Doctors' Plot'—A Drama of Soviet Political Intrigue," *New York Times*, April 12, 1957; see also Franz Borkenau, "Was Malenkov behind the Anti-Semitic Plot?" *Commentary*, January–June, 1953, 439–46.

66 U. S. Central Intelligence Agency, Office of Current Intelligence, "*The Doctors' Plot*" (Washington, DC: The Agency, 1953).

67 See David Remnick, "Soviet Paper Publishes Testimony about Stalin's 'Doctors' Plot,'" *Washington Post*, February 6, 1988 and Felicity Barringer, "Soviet Survivor Relives 'Doctors' Plot,'" *New York Times*, May 13, 1988.

68 See Jonathan Brent and Vladimir P. Naumon, *Stalin's Last Crime: The Plot Against the Jewish Doctors, 1948–1953* (New York: HarperCollins, 2003), I. A. Rapoport, *The Doctors' Plot of 1953* (Cambridge, MA: Harvard University Press, 1991), Louis Rapaport, *Stalin's War Against the Jews: The Doctors' Plot and the Soviet Solution* (New York: Free Press, 1990) and A. Mark Clarfield, "The Soviet 'Doctors' Plot'—50 Years on," *BMJ* 325 (December 21-28, 2002): 1487–9.

69 Beam, "The Chargé in the Soviet Union (Beam) to the Department of State," 1083–5.

70 "Stalin's Illness Similar to Paralysis That Brought on Death of Lenin," *New York Times*, March 4, 1953.

71 "Communists of U. S. Voice Their Grief," *New York Times*, March 5, 1953.

72 Ibid.

73 Communist Party of the U. S. S. R., Central Committee, "The Death of Premier Stalin," *Current History*, April 1953, 247–8.

74 George Morgan, "Program of Psychological Preparation for Stalin's Passing from Power," in US Department of State, *Foreign Relations of the United States, 1952–1954, Volume VIII*, 1059–60.

75 See Francis B. Stevens, "Memorandum by Francis B. Stevens of the Office of Eastern European Affairs to the Deputy Director of the Psychological Strategy Board (Morgan)," in US Department of State, *Foreign Relations of the United States, 1952–1954, Volume VIII*, 1071–3, and W. Park Armstrong, "Department of State Intelligence Estimate: Implications of Stalin's Collapse," in US Department of State, *Foreign Relations of the United States, 1952–1954, Volume VIII*, 1086–90, and S. Everett Gleason, "Memorandum of Discussion at the 135th Meeting of the National Security Council, Washington," in US Department of State, *Foreign Relations of the United States, 1952–1954, Volume VIII*, 1091–4.

76 "Editorial Note," in US Department of State, *Foreign Relations of the United States, 1952–1954, Volume VIII*, 1098; see also Anthony Leviero, "'Cold War' Set-Up in U.S. Unprepared," *New York Times*, March 6, 1953.

77 See Paul H. Nitze, "Memorandum by the Director of the Policy Planning Staff (Nitze) to the Secretary of State," in US Department of State, *Foreign Relations of the United States, 1952–1954, Volume VIII*, 1107–8, Walter Bedell Smith, "Memorandum by the Under Secretary of State (Smith) to the Acting Director of the Psychological Strategy Board (Morgan)," in US Department of State, *Foreign Relations of the United States, 1952–1954, Volume VIII*, 1111–13, Emmet J. Hughes, "Memorandum by the Administrative Assistant to the President (Hughes) to the President," in US Department of State, *Foreign Relations of the United States, 1952–1954, Volume VIII*, 1113–15, James Cowles Hart Bonbright, "Memorandum by the Deputy Assistant Secretary of State for European Affairs (Bonbright) to the Under Secretary of State (Smith)," in US Department of State, *Foreign Relations of the United States, 1952–1954, Volume VIII*, 1133–4.

78 See Charles E. Bohlen, "Memorandum by the Counsel of the Department of State (Bohlen)," in US Department of State, *Foreign Relations of the United States, 1952–1954, Volume VIII*, 1100–2, 1108–11.

79 See Beam, "The Chargé in the Soviet Union (Beam) to the Department of State," 1099, 1100, 1102–6.

80 S. Everett Gleason, "Memorandum of Discussion at the 136th Meeting of the National Security Council, Washington, March 11, 1953," in US Department of State, *Foreign Relations of the United States, 1952–1954, Volume VIII*, 1117–29.

81 "Probable Consequences of the Death of Stalin and of the Elevation of Malenkov to Leadership in the USSR," in US Department of State, *Foreign Relations of the United States, 1952–1954, Volume VIII*, 1125–9; reprint, U. S. Central Intelligence Agency, *Probable Consequences of the Death of Stalin and of the Elevation of Malenkov to Leadership in the USSR* (Washington, DC: The Agency, 1953), https://www.cia.gov/library/readingroom/docs/DOC_0000269303.pdf.

82 W. A. Ryser, "VOA Says Stalin's Death Brings No Relief from Communism," *UPIs 20th Century Top Stories*, March 6, 1953, ProQuest Central.

83 *Committee on Foreign Relations Selected Executive Sessions*, vol. 14, 83rd Cong., 459–90 (1953) (briefing on impact of Stalin's death on Soviet foreign and domestic policies).

84 U. S. Central Intelligence Agency, Office of Current Intelligence, *Death of Stalin* (Washington, DC: The Agency, 1953).

85 For examples, "Crisis in Moscow," *New York Times*, March 5, 1953, "Stalin Rose from Czarist Oppression to Transform Russia into Mighty Socialist State," *New York Times*, March 5, 1953, and Richard Cavendish, "Death of Stalin," *History Today*, March, 2003, 55.

86 See Alexander Orlov, "The Ghastly Secrets of Stalin's Power," *Life*, April 6, 1953, 110–23, and "The Man Himself," *Life*, April 27, 1953, 145–58; see also Alexander Orlov, *The Secret History of Stalin's Crimes* (New York: Random House, 1953), Edward P. Gazur, *The FBI's KGB General* (New York: Carroll and Graf, 2001) and Boris Volodarsky, *Stalin's Agent: The Life and Death of Alexander Orlov* (New York: Oxford University Press, 2015).

87 Samuel L. Sharp, "Stalin's Place in History," *New Republic*, March 16, 1953, accessed November 8, 2016, https://newrepublic.com/article/131051/stalins-place-history.

88 Isaac Deutscher, "The Legacies and Heirs of J. V. Stalin," *The Reporter*, April 14, 1953, 10–16.

89 Bertram D. Wolfe, "The Struggle for the Soviet Succession," *Foreign Affairs*, July, 1953, 548–65.

90 Jessica Smith, "Stalin and His Heritage," *New World Review*, May, 1953, 3–10.

91 George Clarke, "Stalin's Role—Stalinism's Future," *Fourth International*, January-February, 1953, 5–13.

92 Albert Gates (pseud.), "Stalin's Place in History: Assessing the Social Role of the Great Assassin," *New International*, May-June, 1953, accessed March 19, 2023, https://marxists.org.

93 Charles E. Bohlen, "The Ambassador in the Soviet Union (Bohlen) to the Secretary of State," in US Department of State, *Foreign Relations of the United States, 1952-1954, Volume VIII*, 1193–6.

94 Armando Ianucci, *The Death of Stalin* (Hollywood, CA: Paramount Home Entertainment, 2018, 2017). DVD.

95 See Walter Bedell Smith, "My Three Years in Moscow," *New York Times*, November 9, 1949, Edward Crankshaw, "Beria, Russia's Mystery of Mysteries," *New York Times Magazine*, April 2, 1950, SM9, 28–9, Harry Schwartz, "Beria's Demotion in Soviet Is Seen," *New York Times*, January 3, 1953, Drew Middleton, "Beria Called a Key to Soviet Enigma," *New York Times*, January 19, 1953, Boris I. Nicolaevsky, "Soviet Struggle for Power," *New York Times*, April 17, 1953, "Beria Strikes Again," *New York Times*, April 19, 1953, and Harry Schwartz, "'Purger of the Purgers' Adds to His Power," *New York Times Magazine*, April 19, 1953, SM32–3.

96 "The Ouster of Lavrenti P. Beria," *Current History*, August, 1953, 122–4.
97 "Editorial Note," in US Department of State, *Foreign Relations of the United States, 1952–1954, Volume VIII*, 1206.
98 Charles E. Bohlen, "The Ambassador to the Soviet Union (Bohlen) to the Department of State," in US Department of State, *Foreign Relations of the United States, 1952–1954, Volume VIII*, 1207.
99 John Foster Dulles, "Statement by Secretary Dulles," *Department of State Bulletin*, July 20, 1953, 72; see also W. H. Lawrence, "Ouster Acclaimed," *New York Times*, July 11, 1953.
100 Bohlen, *Witness to History, 1929–1969*, 354–8.
101 See C. L. Sulzberger, "Beria's Downfall Opens Host of New Questions," *New York Times*, July 12, 1953; see also "Beria's Fall in Kremlin Clash," *New York Times*, July 12, 1953, Harry Schwartz, "Rise and Fall of Beria," *New York Times*, July 19, 1953 and "Moscow Mysteries," editorial, *New York Times*, July 24, 1953; see also Bertram D. Wolfe, "Stalin's Ghost at the Party Congress," *Foreign Affairs*, July, 1956, 548–65.
102 "Purge of the Purger," *Time*, July 20, 1953, 23–9.
103 Alexander Orlov, "The Beria I Knew," *Life*, July 20, 1953, 33, 35–6.
104 Letter from Washington, *New Yorker*, July 25, 1953, 48–55.
105 Isaac Deutscher, "The Kremlin Triumvirs: One Down, Two to Go," *The Reporter*, September 1, 1953, 15–19.
106 Alexander Werth, "The Beria Case," *The Nation*, July 18, 1953, 44.
107 "Mr. Dulles Thinks Twice," editorial, *The Nation*, July 25, 1953, 62–4.
108 "Beria Loses: Can Freedom Gain?" editorial, *New Republic*, July 20, 1953, 7.
109 "Who Arrested Beria—and Why?" *New Republic*, July 20, 1953, 5.
110 Bertram D. Wolfe, "The Struggle for the Soviet Succession," 561.
111 "*Daily Worker* Assays Effect of Beria's Fall," *New York Times*, July 13, 1953.
112 Jessica Smith, "The Beria Case," *New World Review*, August, 1953, 15–18.
113 Abe Stein, "The Downfall of Beria: Exploding the Myth of Kremlin Democratization," *New International*, May–June, 1953, 111–29.
114 Bohlen, "The Ambassador to the Soviet Union (Bohlen) to the Department of State," 1222–3.
115 U. S. Central Intelligence Agency, Office of Current Intelligence, *Purge of L. P. Beria* (Washington, DC: The Agency, 1954).
116 W. H. Lawrence, "Why Do They Confess?—A Communist Enigma," *New York Times Magazine*, May 8, 1949, SM7, SM26, SM28–9 and Drew Middleton, "Beria Confesses and Awaits Trial, Soviet Announces," *New York Times*, December 17, 1953.
117 Godfrey Blunden, "Moscow Trial: A Dark Drama," *New York Times Magazine*, August 16, 1953, SM11–12, SM32–3.

118 See "Soviet Indictment of Beria and Aides," *New York Times*, December 17, 1953 and "Soviet Text on Trial of Beria and 6 Aides," *New York Times*, December 24, 1953.
119 Middleton, "Beria Confesses and Awaits Trial, Soviet Announces," *New York Times*, December 17, 1953.
120 "Now Beria," *New York Times*, December 20, 1953.
121 See Harrison E. Salisbury, "Great Loss of Life Is Laid to Beria," *New York Times*, February 28, 1954, Clifton Daniel, "4 Security Aides Executed by Soviet as Beria Plotters," *New York Times*, December 24, 1954, Harrison E. Salisbury, "Soviet Army Role Stressed in Purge," *New York Times*, December 26, 1954, "New Group of Beria Aides Executed in Soviet Georgia," *New York Times*, November 23, 1955, and Harry Schwartz, "Beria Case Is Still a Mystery," *New York Times*, November 27, 1955.
122 Harrison E. Salisbury, "Beria's Troops Held Moscow, But He Hesitated and Lost," *New York Times*, September 21, 1954.
123 "Some Unanswered Questions in the Beria Case," *I. F. Stone's Weekly*, January 2, 1954, 2.
124 Isaac Deutscher, "Beria's Trial—The Old Show?" *The Reporter*, February 2, 1954, 22–3, 26–7.
125 "Who Killed Beria?" *New Republic*, January 4, 1954, 4.
126 See "Indictment Traces Beria Conspiracy Back to 1920," *Daily Worker*, December 18, 1953, "Beria Convicted, Executed as Traitor," *Daily Worker*, December 24, 1953, "Wide Spy Links Cited in Beria Death Sentence," *Daily Worker*, December 25, 1953, and "Soviet Supreme Court's Finding in the Case of Beria and Six Aides," *Daily Worker*, December 28, 1953.
127 Bertram D. Wolfe, "How Beria Died," in *Khrushchev and Stalin's Ghost: Text, Background and Meaning of Khrushchev's Secret Report to the XXth Congress on the Night of February 24–25, 1956* (New York: Praeger, 1957), 316–17.
128 See Sergo Lavrenevich Beria, *Beria, My Father: Inside Stalin's Kremlin* (London: Duckworth, 2001), James H. Hansen, "The Kremlin Follies of '53 . . . The Demise of Lavrenti Beria," *International Journal of Intelligence and Counterintelligence* 4, no. 1 (1990): 101–14, Amy W. Knight, *Beria: Stalin's First Lieutenant* (Princeton, NJ: Princeton University Press, 1993), D. M. Strickland and Jeanne Farrow, *The Beria Affair: The Secret Transcripts of the Meeting Signalling the End of Stalinism* (Commack, NY: Nova Science Publishers, 1992), and Tadeusz Wittlin, *Commissar: The Life and Death of Lavrenty Pavlovich Beria* (New York: Macmillan, 1972).

Chapter 9

1 US Department of State, Foreign Relations Branch, *Foreign Relations of the United States: The Soviet Union, 1933–1939*, xii.

2 US Central Intelligence Agency, Office of Current Intelligence, *Death of Stalin* 23.
3 See Welles Hangan, "Mikoyan Attacks Stalin's Policies," *New York Times*, February 18, 1956, Anastas I. Mikoyan, "Excerpts from Mikoyan Speech on Stalin" *New York Times*, February 19, 1956, Harrison E. Salisbury, "End of the Stalin Cult," *New York Times*, February 24, 1956, Harrison E. Salisbury, "The Decline of Stalin," *New York Times*, February 26, 1956; see also "Russia's New Face," *Newsweek*, March 5, 1956, 34–5, Leon Volkov, "How Long Can Khrushchev Keep His Fellow Reds . . . In Line?" *Newsweek*, March 5, 1956, 34–5, and Issac Deutscher, "Communist Party Congress: The Break with Stalinism," *The Reporter*, March 22, 1956, 31–5.
4 Nikita S. Khrushchev, "On the Cult of Personality" (speech, Twentieth Communist Party Congress, Moscow, February 25, 1956), 84 Cong. Rec. 9389-9403 (1956); reprints, "Text of Speech on Stalin by Khrushchev as Released by the State Department," *New York Times*, June 5, 1956; see also *Speech of Nikita Khrushchev before a Closed Session of the 20th Congress of the Communist Party of the Soviet Union on February 25, 1956*, Subcomm. to Investigate Administration of Internal Security Act and Other Internal Security Laws, 85th Cong. (1957), Nikita S. Khrushchev and Boris I. Nikolaevsky, *The Crimes of the Stalin Era: Special Report to the 20th Congress of the Communist Party of the Soviet Union* (New York: New Leader, 1956) and Nikita Sergeevich Khrushchev, *The Anatomy of Terror: Khrushchev's Revelations about Stalin's Regime*, introd. by Nathaniel Weyl (Washington, DC: Public Affairs Press, 1956).
5 *On Overcoming the Cult of the Individual and Its Consequences: Resolution of the Central Committee of the Communist Party of the Soviet Union* (London: Soviet News, 1956); reprint, "Text of the Soviet Communist Party Announcement on the Anti-Stalin Campaign," *New York Times*, July 2, 1956.
6 US Information Agency, "Policy Information Statement for the United States Information Agency," in US Department of State, *Foreign Relations of the United States, 1955–1957: Soviet Union and Eastern Mediterranean*, vol. 24 (Washington, DC: Government Printing Office, 1989), 56–8.
7 US Department of State, Office of Intelligence Research, Division of Research for USSR and Eastern Europe, "The Twentieth Congress of the Communist Party of the Soviet Union," in US Department of State, *Foreign Relations of the United States, 1955–1957: Soviet Union and Eastern Mediterranean*, 63.
8 "Editorial Note," in US Department of State, *Foreign Relations of the United States, 1955–1957: Soviet Union and Eastern Mediterranean*, 72.
9 US Department of State, Office of the Historian, "Milestones: 1953–1960: Khrushchev and the Twentieth Congress of the Communist Party, 1956," accessed May 7, 2018, https://history.state.gov/milestones/1953-1960/khrushchev-20th-congress; see also Abraham Rabinovich, "Got Secret Speech, Israeli Ex-Spy Says,"

Globe and Mail, February 8, 1982 and Malitiaha Mayzel, "Israeli Intelligence and the Leakage of Khruschev's 'Secret Speech,'" *Journal of Israeli History* 32, no. 2 (2013): 257–83.

10 David Binder, "'56 East Europe Plan of C.I.A. Is Described,'" *New York Times*, November 30, 1976.

11 See Charles E. Bohlen, "Telegram from the Embassy in the Soviet Union to the Department of State," in US Department of State, *Foreign Relations of the United States, 1955–1957: Soviet Union and Eastern Mediterranean*, 82–4, 103–4, 111–13, Herbert E. Hoover, Jr., "Telegram from the Department of State to the Embassy in the Soviet Union," in US Department of State, *Foreign Relations of the United States, 1955–1957: Soviet Union and Eastern Mediterranean*, 107–8, Herbert E. Hoover, Jr., "Circular Telegram from the Department of State to Certain Diplomatic Missions," in US Department of State, *Foreign Relations of the United States, 1955–1957: Soviet Union and Eastern Mediterranean*, 109–10, Charles E. Bohlen, "Notes of the Secretary of State's Staff Meeting, Washington, June 25, 1956, 9:15 a.m.," in US Department of State, *Foreign Relations of the United States, 1955–1957: Soviet Union and Eastern Mediterranean*, 117–18.

12 S. Everett Gleason, "Memorandum of Discussion at the 280th Meeting of the National Security Council, Washington, March 22, 1956," in US Department of State, *Foreign Relations of the United States, 1955–1957: Soviet Union and Eastern Mediterranean*, 72–5.

13 US Department of State, Office of Intelligence Research, "The Desecration of Stalin: Intelligence Brief Prepared by the Office of Intelligence Research," in US Department of State, *Foreign Relations of the United States, 1955–1957: Soviet Union and Eastern Mediterranean*, 75–82.

14 Jacob E. Beam, "Memorandum from the Deputy Assistant Secretary of State for European Affairs (Beam) to the Deputy Under Secretary of State for Political Affairs (Murphy)," in US Department of State, *Foreign Relations of the United States, 1955–1957: Soviet Union and Eastern Mediterranean*, 85–7.

15 Walter Newbold Walmsley, Jr., "Telegram from the Embassy in the Soviet Union to the Department of State," in US Department of State, *Foreign Relations of the United States, 1955–1957: Soviet Union and Eastern Mediterranean*, 88–91.

16 Ibid., 91–3.

17 Richard H. Davis, "Memorandum from Richard H. Davis of the Policy Planning Staff to the Director of the Staff (Bowie)," in US Department of State, *Foreign Relations of the United States, 1955–1957: Soviet Union and Eastern Mediterranean*, 93–5.

18 Robert Daniel Murphy, "A Crucial Contest with the Communist World," *Department of State Bulletin*, April 2, 1956, 556–9.

19 John Foster Dulles, "Significance of New Soviet Line Concerning Stalin Era," *Department of State Bulletin*, April 16, 1956, 637–8.

20 Allen W. Dulles, "The Purge of Stalinism," *Department of State Bulletin*, May 7, 1956, 758–65.
21 Robert Daniel Murphy, "The Soviet Reappraisal of Stalin," *Department of State Bulletin*, April 30, 1956, 719–22.
22 Frank C. Wisner, "Memorandum from the Deputy Director (Plans) of Central Intelligence (Wisner) to the Director (Dulles)," in US Department of State, *Foreign Relations of the United States, 1955–1957: Soviet Union and Eastern Mediterranean*, 96–8.
23 See Harrison E. Salisbury, "Was Stalin Put to Death to Avert Blood Purge?" *New York Times*, September 20, 1954, "Was Stalin Killed by His Own Comrades?" *I. F. Stone's Weekly*, March 26, 1956, 1, G. F. Hudson, "Why Did Khrushchev Do It? De-Stalinization and the Manner of Stalin's Death," *Commentary*, May, 1957, 439–46, and Zhores A. Medvedev, "The Puzzle of Stalin's Death," *Russian Social Science Review* 45, no. 1 (January–February, 2004): 83–97.
24 US Department of State, Operations Coordinating Board, Special Working Group on Stalinism, "Summary of US Policy Guidance and Actions Taken to Exploit the Campaign: Report by the Operations Coordinating Board's Special Working Group on Stalinism," in US Department of State, *Foreign Relations of the United States, 1955–1957: Soviet Union and Eastern Mediterranean*, 99–103.
25 Bohlen, "Telegram from the Embassy in the Soviet Union to the Department of State," 113–15.
26 Charles E. Bohlen, "Khrushchev's Secret Speech," in *Witness to History* (New York: Norton, 1973), 393–404.
27 See US Department of State, Office of the Historian, "Milestones: 1953-1960"; Khrushchev, "Text of Speech on Stalin by Khrushchev as Released by the State Department"; for a reprint of the speech, see Khruschev, *The Anatomy of Terror: Khruschev's Revelations about Stalin's Regime*, (Washington, DC: Public Affairs Press, 1956).
28 John Foster Dulles, "The Contest Between Freedom and Despotism," *Department of State Bulletin*, July 2, 1956, 3–7; reprint, "Freedom versus Despotism: Constant Dedication to Liberal Principles of Peaceful Change," *Vital Speeches of the Day*, July 15, 1956, 578–81.
29 S. Everett Gleason, "Memorandum of Discussion at the 289th Meeting of the National Security Council, Washington, June 28, 1956," in US Department of State, *Foreign Relations of the United States, 1955–1957: Soviet Union and Eastern Mediterranean*, 118–23.
30 US Department of State, Office of Special Assistant for Intelligence "Soviet Resolution on Cult of Personality: Memorandum Prepared in the Office of Special Assistant for Intelligence," in US Department of State, *Foreign Relations of the United States, 1955–1957: Soviet Union and Eastern Mediterranean*, 124–5.

31 Frank G. Wisner, "Memorandum from the Deputy Director (Plans) of Central Intelligence (Wisner) to the Deputy Under Secretary for Political Affairs (Murphy)," in US Department of State, *Foreign Relations of the United States, 1955–1957: Soviet Union and Eastern Mediterranean*, 125–7.

32 John Foster Dulles, "State Department Transcript of Remarks by Secretary Dulles at News Conference," *Department of State Bulletin*, July 23, 1956, 145–50; reprint, "State Department Transcript of Remarks by Secretary Dulles at News Conference," *New York Times*, July 12, 1956.

33 US Central Intelligence Agency, Senior Research Staff on International Communism, "The Present Communist Controversy: Its Ramifications and Possible Repercussions: Paper Prepared by the Senior Research Staff on International Communism in the Central Intelligence Agency," in US Department of State, *Foreign Relations of the United States, 1955–1957: Soviet Union and Eastern Mediterranean*, 128–37.

34 US Central Intelligence Agency, Senior Research Staff on International Communism, *The Twentieth CPSU Congress in Retrospect: Its Principal Issues and Possible Effects on International Communism* (Washington, DC: The Agency, 1956), accessed April 12, 2017, http://www.faqs.org/cia/index_102.html.

35 Comm. on Un-American Activities, H.R. Rep. No. 2189 (1956); see also "Experts to Assay New Moscow Line," *New York Times*, March 26, 1956, and Allen Drury, "Stalinism Drive Leads to Warning," *New York Times*, May 20, 1956.

36 Ibid., 169.

37 A. B. (Abraham Brumberg), "Iconoclasm in Moscow," *Problems of Communism*, March, 1956, 1–2.

38 J. D. (pseud.), "Anatomy of Tyranny: Mr. Khrushchev's Attack on Stalin," *Problems of Communism*, July, 1956, 1–8.

39 Hugo Dewar, *The Modern Inquisition* (London: Wingate, 1953).

40 Hugo Dewar, "The Moscow Trials 'Revised'," *Problems of Communism*, January, 1957, 46–9.

41 Wolfgang Leonhard, "Terror in the Soviet System: Trends and Portents," *Problems of Communism*, November, 1958, 1–7.

42 Leopold Labedz, "Resurrection—and Perdition," *Problems of Communism*, March–April, 1963, 48–9.

43 Harrison E. Salisbury, "Secret Khrushchev Talk on Stalin 'Phobia' Related," *New York Times*, March 16, 1956.

44 See Welles Hangan, "9 Ex-Army Chiefs Cleared in Soviet," *New York Times*, April 14, 1956, Harry Schwartz, "Soviet May Scan Old Purge Trials," *New York Times*, April 23, 1956, "New Soviet Book Lists Red Victims," *New York Times*, October 28, 1956, "Ex-Red Army Aide is Rehabilitated," *New York Times*, August 26, 1957, Harrison E. Salisbury, "Purged Marshal Cleared in Soviet," *New York Times*, August 14, 1957, and "Victim of Stalin Purge Gets New Soviet Praise," *New York Times*, March 27, 1958.

45 "Vishinsky Overruled," editorial, *New York Times*, April 29, 1956.
46 "Murder Will Out," *Time*, March 26, 1956, 30–1.
47 "'The Truth of Today,'" *Time*, April 9, 1956, 40.
48 "Death & Deviation," *Time*, April 16, 1956, 30–1.
49 "'The Real Story . . . Kremlin's Secrets . . . Twelve Days That Shook Communism," *Newsweek*, March 26, 1956, 46–7.
50 Leon Volkov, "Myth-Killer and the March toward a New Stalin," *Newsweek*, April 2, 1956, 44.
51 "Why Top Reds Turn on Stalin," *U.S. News & World Report*, March 30, 1956, 21–5.
52 "'Kremlin Has Opened Pandora's Box,'" *U.S. News & World Report*, March 30, 1956, 36–8, 40, 42.0.
53 "In the Muddy Wake of the Moscow Melodrama," *I. F. Stone's Weekly*, March 26, 1956, 1, 44.
54 Alexander Orlov, "Sensational Secret behind Damnation of Stalin," *Life*, April 23, 1956, 34–8.
55 Isaac Don Levine, "Document on Stalin as Czarist Spy," *Life*, April 23, 1956, 47–8, 50–1.
56 "Several Important 'Crimes of Stalinism' Haven't Been Solved," *Saturday Evening Post*, May 19, 1956, 10.
57 "Stalin's Former Friends," *New Republic*, March 26, 1956, 5.
58 Mark Gayn, "Purge of Stalin's Ghost: Inquiry into an Inquest," *The Nation*, April 28, 1956, 354–6.
59 John Simkin, "Mark Gayn," in *Spartacus Educational*, accessed October 2, 2021, http://www.spartacus-educational.com.
60 "The Renunciation of Infallibility," *The Nation*, June 16, 1956, accessed November 4, 2015, https://www.thenation.com.
61 Richard Lowenthal, "The Repudiation of Stalinism: Can the Party Co-Exist with the People?" *Encounter*, May, 1956, 59–68; reprint, *Dissent*, Summer, 1956, 314–26.
62 Dwight Macdonald, "'A Worthy Pioneer!'" *Encounter*, June, 1956, 41–3.
63 Harrison E. Salisbury, "Khrushchev Talk on Stalin Bares Details of Rule Based on Terror," *New York Times*, June 5, 1956.
64 James Reston, "U. S. Exploiting Material from Khrushchev Speech," *New York Times*, June 5, 1956.
65 Harry Schwartz, "Record Disputes Khrushchev Line," *New York Times*, June 6, 1956.
66 "Khrushchev's Revelations," editorial, *New York Times*, June 10, 1956.
67 "Excerpts from the Historical Secret Speech," *Time*, June 11, 1956, 36–9.
68 "Echoes of the Terror," *Time*, June 18, 1956, 31–2.
69 "Big Story and a Leak," *Newsweek*, June 19, 1956, 76.
70 George F. Kennan and William C. Bullitt, Jr., "'What Should We Do about Russia,'" *U.S. News and World Report*, June 29, 1956, 68–77.

71. "Khrushchev's Crimes Exposed," *U. S. News & World Report*, September 7, 1956, 128–42; reprint, Chester S. Williams, *Soviet Crimes and Khrushchev's Confessions: A Factual Report with a Chronology of 72 Citations in the 38 Year Criminal Record* (New York: Freedom House, 1956).
72. "The Mess in Moscow Deepens: Confession Khrushchev Had to Make Means Danger—and Opportunity," editorial, *Life*, June 25, 1956, 31.
73. "'Khrush' and 'Bulge' Got the Affability Act from 'Old Joe,'" editorial, *Saturday Evening Post*, August 25, 1956, 10.
74. Paul Wohl, "Purge of Stalin: It Points up the Struggle among His Successors," *Barron's*, March 26, 1956, 5–8.
75. Alexander Dallin, "More Rewriting of History," *New Republic*, June 11, 1956, 26–30.
76. Isaac Deutscher, "The Stalinists' Case Against Stalin," *The Reporter*, July 12, 1956, 22–6.
77. Philip R. Mosely, "Soviet Foreign Policy: New Goals or New Manners?" *Foreign Affairs*, July, 1956, 541–53.
78. Lewis Coser, "The New Turn in Russia," *Dissent*, Spring, 1956, 124–8.
79. Irving Howe, "Notes on the Russian Turn," *Dissent*, Summer, 1956, accessed March 4, 2022, https://www.dissentmagazine.org/article/new-turn-russia.
80. Julian Towster, "Changing Russian Politics," *Current History*, January, 1958, 1–6.
81. William Henry Chamberlin, "Khrushchev's War with Stalin's Ghost," *Russian Review* 21, no. 1 (January, 1962): 2–10.
82. Kennan, *Russia and the West under Lenin and Stalin*, 256–8.
83. See Aleksandr I. Solzhenitsyn, "Solzhenitsyn on Soviet Penal System," *New York Times*, December 29, 1973, Aleksandr I. Solzhenitsyn, "Solzhenitsyn on Purge Trials of the 30's," *New York Times*, December 31, 1973; see also Aleksandr I. Solzhenitsyn, *The Gulag Archipelago, 1918–1956* (New York: Harper & Row, 1974–1978).
84. See Yuri Larin, "Up from History's 'Dustbin,'" *New York Times*, July 7, 1978, Stephen F. Cohen, "Why Bukharin's Ghost Still Haunts Moscow," *New York Times Magazine*, December 10, 1978, SM74–84, "Rehabilitate Bukharin, Widow Asks Moscow," *New York Times*, November 30, 1987, Philip Taubman, "50 Years after His Execution, Soviet Panel Clears Bukharin," *New York Times*, February 6, 1988, Felicity Barringer, "Widow of Bukharin Fulfills Her Mission 50 Years Later," *New York Times*, February 8, 1988, Stephen F. Cohen, "Bukharin Redux," *The Nation*, February 20, 1988, 222, and Philip Taubman, "Bukharin's Status in Party Restored," *New York Times*, July 10, 1988; see also Anna Larina, *This I Cannot Forget: The Memoirs of Nikolai Bukharin's Widow* (New York: W. W. Norton, 1993), and Gregory Paul, *Politics, Murder and Love in Stalin's Kremlin: The Story of Nikolai Bukharin and Anna Larina* (Stanford, CA: Stanford University Press, 2010).

85 Wendy Goldman, *The Mass Dissemination of Terror: Workers and the First Moscow Show Trial* (Seattle, WA: National Center for Eurasian and East European Research, 2008), 11, accessed June 5, 2021, https://www.ucis.pitt.edu/nceeer/2008_819-12g_Goldman.pdf.
86 For a CIA analysis of the effect of the secret speech on foreign Communist parties, see US Central Intelligence Agency, Senior Research Staff on International Communism, "The Present Communist Controversy: Its Ramifications and Possible Repercussions," in US Department of State, *Foreign Relations of the United States, 1955–1957: Soviet Union and Eastern Mediterranean*, vol. 24 (Washington, DC: US Government Printing Office, 1957). 128–36; for collection of documents from international Communist parties, including the American Party, see Henry L. Roberts, ed., *The Anti-Stalin Campaign and International Communism: A Selection of Documents* (New York: Columbia University Press, 1956).
87 See Eugene Dennis (pseud.), "Dennis Comments on Soviet Communist Party Statement," *Daily Worker*, March 20, 1956 and William Z. Foster, "Lessons from the Stalin Question," *Daily Worker*, March 28, 1956.
88 Max Weiss, *The Meaning of the XXth Congress of the Communist Party of the Soviet Union* (New York: International Publishers, 1956), 21.
89 Ibid., 24.
90 Dorothy Healey, *Dorothy Healey Remembers: A Life in the American Communist Party* (New York: Oxford University Press, 1990), 152–7.
91 See *Appendix IV: On the Report of the Central Committee of the Communist Party of the Soviet Union Delivered by Comrade Khrushchev to the Twentieth Party Congress* (Chicago, IL: Revolutionary Union, 1956).
92 See "Proletarian Revolution and Renegade Khrushchev (In Defense of Stalin)," *Turning Point*, April–May, 1956, "Khrushchev's Un-Secret Speech," *Turning Point*, August, 1956, and "First Aid for Communists Suffering from Shock," *Turning Point*, January–February, 1957.
93 Nikita S. Khrushchev, "Stalin's Repressions Spelled out in Khrushchev's Speech Made Public Here," *Daily Worker*, June 5, 1956.
94 "The Khrushchev Speech," editorial, *Daily Worker*, June 6, 1956.
95 "The Daily Worker and the Khrushchev Speech," editorial, *Daily Worker*, June 7, 1956.
96 Eugene Dennis (pseud.), "The U.S.A. and Khrushchev's Special Report," *Daily Worker*, June 18, 1956.
97 Communist Party of the United States, "Statement of the National Committee of the Communist Party of the United States, June 24, 1956," *Daily Worker*, June 25, 1956; reprint, "Text of Statement by Communist Party," *New York Times*, June 25, 1956.

98 "An Historic Statement," editorial, *Daily Worker*, June 26, 1956.
99 Wayne Phillips, "U. S. Reds Demand Russia Tell More on Stalin Terror," *New York Times*, June 25, 1956.
100 "Reevaluation and Correction," *New World Review*, May, 1956, 50–8.
101 "More on Corrections of Stalin Era," *New World Review*, June, 1956, 42–5.
102 Jessica Smith, "The Khrushchev Report," *New World Review*, June, 1956, 49–53.
103 "On Overcoming the Stalin Cult," *New World Review*, August, 1956, 55–60.
104 "A Note to Our Readers," editorial, *New World Review*, August, 1956, 54–5.
105 Ralph Parker, "Russia's Changing Scene," *New World Review*, August, 1956, 3–6.
106 Communist Party of the United States of America, National Committee, *Draft Resolution for the 16th National Convention of the Communist Party, U.S.A.* (New York: New Century Publishers, 1956); for differing eyewitness accounts of the convention, see Healey, *Dorothy Healey Remembers: A Life in the American Communist Party*, 163–4, and Bernard Rosenberg, "The Communist Party Convention," *Dissent*, Spring, 1957, 152–6.
107 Lucy S. Dawidowicz, *The Communist Party, U.S.A., in Crisis* (New York: American Jewish Committee, Library of Information, n.d.).
108 See US Federal Bureau of Investigation, "Communist Party, U.S.A. Summary—Activities, July-December" (February, 1956), "Communist Party, U.S.A. Summary—Activities," January-June (August 16) and "The Communist Party Line, May-September" (October 12) in *The Communist Party USA and Radical Organizations, 1953–1960: FBI Reports from the Eisenhower Library* (Bethesda, MD: University Publications of America, 1990). Microfilm.
109 See *The 16th Convention of the Communist Party, U.S.A.: Interim Report of the Subcommittee to Investigate the Administration of the Internal Security Act and Other Internal Security Laws*, 85th Cong. (1957) and J. Edgar Hoover, *An Analysis of the 16th Annual Convention of the Communist Party of the U. S.*, 85th Cong. (1957) (statement of J. Edgar Hoover, Director, Federal Bureau of Investigation).
110 J. Edgar Hoover, "Communist 'New Look': A Study in Duplicity," *Elks Magazine*, August, 1956, 4–5, 45–8.
111 Ralph Parker, "A Year of Great Changes," *New World Review*, November, 1956, 8–11.
112 G. D. H. Cole, "The USSR after 39 Years," *New World Review*, December, 1956, 13–17.
113 Corliss Lamont, "A Message from Corliss Lamont," *New World Review*, November, 1956, 23.
114 Bertram D. Wolfe, "The Crimes of the Stalin Era," in *Khrushchev and Stalin's Ghost*, 88–258.
115 Dorothy Healey, "On the Status of the Party," *Political Affairs*, March, 1958, 48.
116 Boris N. Ponomarev and Andrew Rothstein, *History of the Communist Party of the Soviet Union* (Moscow: Foreign Languages Publishing House, 1960).

117 Bertram D. Wolfe, "The New Gospel According to Khrushchev," *Foreign Affairs*, July, 1960, 576–87.
118 Joseph Starobin, "1956—A Memoir," *Problems of Communism*, November, 1956, 1, 64–70.
119 Harry Haywood, *Black Bolshevik: Autobiography of an Afro-American Communist*, (Chicago: Liberator Press, 1978), 606.
120 Vivian Gornick, "They Were True Believers," *New York Times*, April 30, 2017.
121 Sergio A. Rossi, "Western Communists on the Defensive," *Foreign Affairs* 35, no. 2 (January, 1957): 201–12.
122 Jerry Harris, "First Reaction: U. S. Communist Leaders Confront the Khrushchev Revelations," *Science & Society* 61, no. 4 (Winter, 1997/1998): 502–12.
123 See *Investigation of Un-American Propaganda Activities in the United States: Hearings Before the Comm. on Un-American Activities*, 79th Cong. (1946) (testimony of Louis F. Budenz), *Trotskyite Terrorist International: Hearing Before the Senate Subcommittee to Investigate the Administration of the Internal Security Act and Other Internal Security Laws*, 94th Cong. (1976) and Donna T. Haverty-Stacke, *Trotskyists on Trial: Free Speech and Political Persecution since the Age of FDR* (New York: New York University Press, 2016).
124 Joseph Hansen, "Soviet Law Journal Assails Stalin 'Confession' System," *The Militant*, April 30, 1956.
125 Myra Tanner Weiss, "Marxism v. Stalinism," *The Militant*, April 30, 1956.
126 See "The Stalin Frame-Up System and the Moscow Trials," advertisement, *The Militant*, April 30, 1956 and "Public Meetings," advertisements, *The Militant*, June 11, 1956.
127 See "Myra Tanner Weiss Opens Tour in L. A." *The Militant*, May 28, 1956, "Key '56 Issues Discussed at Dobbs, Weiss Meetings," *The Militant*, June 4, 1956 and "Myra Weiss on Tour Explains Soviet Events," *The Militant*, June 11, 1956.
128 See Leon Trotsky, "Trotsky's Speech to the Dewey Commission," *The Militant*, April 30, 1956, Leon Trotsky, "Facts of Trotsky's Life Refuted Vyshinsky," *The Militant*, May 7, 1956, Leon Trotsky, "The Three Crucial Points of the Soviet Trials," *The Militant*, May 14, 1956, Leon Trotsky, "Trotsky Explains Marxist View of Terrorism," *The Militant*, May 28, 1956, Leon Trotsky, "Underlying Reasons for the Charge of Sabotage," *The Militant*, May 28, 1956, Leon Trotsky, "The Marxist Position on War and Revolution," *The Militant*, June 4, 1956, Leon Trotsky, "The Whys and Wherefores of the Trials," *The Militant*, June 11, 1956, Leon Trotsky, "Is Leninism Responsible for Stalin Cult?" *The Militant*, June 18, 1956, and Leon Trotsky, "Bolshevik Traditions and Fourth International," *The Militant*, June 25, 1956.
129 Socialist Workers Party, National Committee, "SWP Resolution Evaluates Crisis of Stalinism," *The Militant*, May 7, 1956.
130 Daniel Roberts, "Kremlin Steps up Campaign Against 'Rotten Elements,'" *The Militant*, May 7, 1956.

131 See Daniel Roberts, "Soviet Revokes Stalin's Confession Trial Laws," *The Militant*, May 14, 1956, and "The Stalinist 'New Look,'" editorial, *The Militant*, June 18, 1956.

132 "Where Is Khrushchev's Speech?" editorial, *The Militant*, May 14, 1956.

133 Tom Kerry, "CP National Committee Spurs Right Swing," *The Militant*, May 21, 1956, Daniel Roberts, "A Belated Stalinist Correction," *The Militant*, May 21, 1956, "*Daily Worker*'s First Mention of Lenin Testament," *The Militant*, May 28, 1956, Daniel Roberts, "How CP Members React to End of Stalin Cult," *The Militant*, June 4, 1956, Daniel Roberts, and "Communist Party is Rocked by Khrushchev Confessions," *The Militant*, June 18, 1956.

134 Nikita S. Khrushchev, "Text of Khrushchev Speech on Stalin Crimes," *The Militant*, June 11, 1956.

135 "Trotskyism Vindicated!" editorial, *The Militant*, June 11, 1956.

136 George Lavan, "Moscow Trials Frame-Ups, Kremlin Leader Now Admits," *The Militant*, June 11, 1956.

137 Murry Weiss, "A Letter to My Parents," *The Militant*, June 18, 1956.

138 William Bundy, "Stalin a Felon—But Right! Says Strong," *The Militant*, June 18, 1956.

139 "1. The World Crisis of Stalinism," *The Militant*, June 25, 1956.

140 James P. Cannon, "Khrushchev's Report on Stalin's Crimes," *The Militant*, July 2, 1956.

141 John Thayer, "Trotskyist Leaders Challenge CP Heads to Public Debate," *The Militant*, July 2, 1956.

142 Morris Stein (pseud.), "The End of the Stalin Cult: The Meaning of the 20th Congress," *Fourth International*, Spring, 1956, 39–44, 70–1.

143 Murry Weiss, "The Vindication of Trotskyism: Khrushchev's Report on Stalin's Crimes," *International Socialist Review*, Summer, 1956, 79–83; see also Joseph Hansen, "'But Why Did They Confess?'" *International Socialist Review*, Summer, 1956, 102–5.

144 Hershel D. Meyer, *The Khrushchev Report and the Crisis in the American Left* (New York: Independence Publishers, 1956).

145 John Liang, "Paranoic, Yes; But Still a Genius," *International Socialist Review*, Summer, 1957, 100–1.

146 Dick Roberts, "Purge and Rehabilitation in the Soviet Union," *International Socialist Review*, Fall, 1964, 125–6.

147 Sidney Hook, "Exposing Soviet Purges," letter to the editor, *New York Times*, April 1, 1956; see also Sidney Hook, "The Problem of the Ex-Communist," *New York Times Magazine*, July 11, 1954, SM7, 24–7.

148 Granville Hicks, "The Liberals Who Haven't Learned: Why the Soviet Illusion Still Lingers," *Commentary*, April, 1951, 319–29.

149 James K. Libbey, "Liberal Journals and the Moscow Trials of 1936–38," *Journalism Quarterly* 52, no. 1 (Spring, 1975): 85–92, 137.
150 Malcolm Cowley, "Echoes from Moscow: 1937–1938," *Southern Review* 20 (1984): 1–11.
151 Eugene Lyons, "Russian Purges and American Liberals," in *The Red Decade: The Stalinist Penetration of America*, 235–45.
152 Eugene Lyons, "A Tour of the Leftist Press," *Nation's Business*, August, 1946, 47–51.
153 See Howard Fast, "The Soviet Union," *Daily Worker*, May 17, 1956, Howard Fast, "I Shall Apologize No More," *Daily Worker*, June 12, 1956, Howard Fast, "I. My Decision," and "II. A Comment: The Editors," *Mainstream*, March, 1957, 29–47, and Harry Schwartz, "Fast Condemns Soviet Leaders," *New York Times*, March 2, 1957.
154 See "Never Again?" *Time*, June 25, 1956, 17, Eugene Lyons, "Open Letter to Howard Fast," *New Leader*, July 9, 1956, 6–8 and Howard Fast, "Reply to Eugene Lyons," *Masses & Mainstream*, August, 1956, 54–9, Harry Schwartz, "Reds Renounced by Howard Fast," *New York Times*, February 1, 1957, and "Red Twilight in America," editorial, *New York Times*, February 11, 1957.
155 See Harry Schwartz, "Reds Here Chide 'Liberal' Faction," *New York Times*, March 23, 1957, "Foster Says Fast 'Slanders' Soviet," *New York Times*, June 18, 1957, "Howard Fast Assailed by Soviet as a 'Deserter' and Slanderer," *New York Times*, August 25, 1957, Harry Schwartz, "Novelist Replies to Soviet Charge," *New York Times*, August 26, 1957, and Harry Schwartz, "Editor of *Worker* Assails Fast," *New York Times*, August 30, 1957.
156 "Howard Fast Balks at Queries on Reds," *New York Times*, February 22, 1957.
157 See Howard Fast, *The Naked God: The Writer and the Communist Party* (New York: Praeger, 1957), Howard Fast, *Being Red: A Memoir* (Boston, MA: Houghton Mifflin, 1990) and Harry Schwartz, "Fast Denounces Rich Reds in U. S.," *New York Times*, August 29, 1957.
158 See Hershel D. Meyer, *History and Conscience: The Case of Howard Fast* (New York: Anvil-Atlas, 1958), Phillip Deery, "Finding His Kronstadt: Howard Fast, 1956 and American Communism," *Australian Journal of Politics and History* 58, no. 2 (June, 2012): 181–202, Andrew MacDonald, *Howard Fast: A Critical Companion* (Westport, CT: Greenwood Press, 1996), and Gerald Sorin, *Howard Fast: Life and Literature in the Left Lane* (Bloomington, IN: Indiana University Press, 2012); for other prominent writers, see Koestler and Crossman, ed., *The God that Failed*.
159 See U. S. Congress, Committee on Un-American Activities, *Hearings Regarding Communist Infiltration of the Hollywood Motion-Picture Industry*, 82nd Congress, May 31, 1952, v. 8, 3541–9 (statement of Lillian Hellman).
160 Lillian Hellman, *Scoundrel Time* (Boston, MA: Little, Brown, 1976), 154–5.
161 Nikita S. Khrushchev, "Condensed Version of Khrushchev's Speech to Soviet Communist Party Congress," *New York Times*, October 18, 1961; see also Theodore

Shabad, "Voroshilov Is Denounced as a Leader in 1957 Plot," *New York Times*, October, 18, 1961, Harry Schwartz, "Tortures in '30s Linked to Stalin," *New York Times*, November 11, 1961, Harry Schwartz, "The Stalin Years—As Rewritten," *New York Times*, November 19, 1961, and Harry Schwartz, "Soviet Press Hints Frame-Up in Purge Trials of the 1930's," *New York Times*, March 21, 1963.

162 Nikita S. Khrushchev, Edward Crankshaw, and Strobe Talbott, *Khrushchev Remembers* (Boston, MA: Little, Brown, 1971).

163 Robert Black, "Khrushchev Remembers," *Bulletin* (Workers League for a Revolutionary Party), August 9, 1971, 7–10.

164 Michael Dobbs, "Khrushchev's 'Secret Speech' Printed," *Washington Post*, April 6, 1989, A28.

165 For examples, see Kathleen E. Smith, *Moscow 1956: The Silenced Spring* (Cambridge, MA: Harvard University Press, 2017), John Etty, "Khrushchev's 'Secret Speech,'" *History Review*, no. 56 (December, 2006): 10–15, Edward Crankshaw, "The Secret Speech and the World Stage," in *Khrushchev: A Career* (New York: Viking Press, 1966), 27–44, and Boris I. Nicolaevsky "Khrushchev's 'Secret Speech,'" in Boris I. Nicolaevsky and Janet D. Zagaria, *Power and the Soviet Elite: The "Letter of an Old Bolshevik" and Other Essays* (New York: Praeger, 1965), 201–8; for a Russian perspective, see Karl E. Loewenstein, "Re-Emergence of Public Opinion in the Soviet Union: Khrushchev and Responses to the Secret Speech," *Europe-Asia Studies* 58, no. 8 (December, 2006): 1329–45.

166 S. J. Taylor, *Stalin's Apologist: Walter Duranty, The New York Times's Man in Moscow* (New York: Oxford University Press, 1990); see also Harrison E. Salisbury, "'The Paris Workings,'" in *Without Fear or Favor: The New York Times and Its Times* (New York: Times Books, 1980), 458–66.

167 See Jacob Heilbrunn, "The *New York Times* and the Moscow Show Trials," *World Affairs* 153, no. 3 (Winter, 1991): 87–101, and Jacob Heilbrunn, "Bad Trip," *New Republic*, May 13, 1996, 10.

168 John Leo, "Bloopers of the Century," *Columbia Journalism Review* 17, no. 5 (January–February, 1999): 38–40.

169 Jacques Steinberg, "Times Should Lose Pulitzer from 30's, Consultant Says," *New York Times*, October 23, 2003.

170 See Neil Conan, "Pulitzer Prize Committee Reviews Award Given to *New York Times* Journalist Walter Duranty 70 Years Ago," *Talk of the Nation*, NPR, June 11, 2003, Pulitzer Prize Board, "Statement on Walter Duranty," *News*, November 21, 2003, accessed February 9, 2015, http://www.pulitzer.org/news/statement-walter-duranty and David Kirkpatrick, "Pulitzer Board Won't Void '32 Award to *Times* Writer," *New York Times*, November 22, 2003.

171 See Josh Rogin, "Russia Is Harassing U.S. Diplomats All over Europe," *Washington Post*, June 27, 2016, Elise Labott, "US Accuses Russia of Harassing Diplomats,"

CNN Wire Service, June 27, 2016, ProQuest Central, and "Moscow Dismisses U.S. Department of State's Allegations on Harassment of American Diplomats in Russia," *Interfax*, October 4, 2016, ProQuest Central.

172 See Bagila Bukharvayeva, "Stalin's Purge 1937 Remembered in Russia," *Washington Post*, July 25, 2007.

173 See Alec Luhn, "Stalin, Russia's New Hero," *New York Times*, March 11, 2016, and Lawrence Martin, "Indictment of Stalin Airs an Old Taboo," *Globe and Mail*, July 1, 1987.

174 *Hearing before the Comm. on Oversight and Government Reform*, 118th Cong. (2018) (statement of Rep. Gerry Connolly).

175 Roger Stone, "Roger Stone Tells Fans His Court Hearing Was a 'soviet-style show trial,'" posted January 6, 2021, accessed December 6, 2021, https://www.bing.com/videos.

176 Fedor F. Raskolnikov, "Raskolnikov's Open Letter to Stalin," August 17, 1939, *Matiè et Revolution*, accessed March 4, 2018, https://matierevolution.fr/spip.php?article3344.

177 Kennan, *Russia and the West under Lenin and Stalin*, 306–7.

178 Davies, "The Ambassador in the Soviet Union (Davies) to the Secretary of State," 545–6.

Selected Bibliography

American Committee for the Defense of Leon Trotsky. *News Bulletin*. New York: The Committee, 1937.

American Committee for the Defense of Leon Trotsky. *World Voices on the Moscow Trials: A Compilation from the Labor and Liberal Press of the World*. New York: Pioneer Publishers, 1937.

Barnes, Joseph. "The Great Bolshevik Cleansing," *Foreign Affairs* 17, no. 3 (April, 1939): 556–68.

Bittelman, Alexander. "Destruction of Bloc of 'Rights and Trotskyites' Renders Great Service to Anti-Fascist Camp," *The Communist*, April, 1938, 291–6.

Bittelman, Alexander. *Trotsky the Traitor*. New York: Workers Library Publishers, 1937.

Bliven, Bruce. "A Letter to Stalin," *New Republic*, March 30, 1938, 216–17.

Bohlen, Charles E. "To Be Shot, to Be Shot, to Be Shot," in *Witness to History, 1929–1969*, 37–55. New York: Norton, 1973.

Browder, Earl. *Traitors in American History: Lessons of the Moscow Trials*. New York: Workers Library Publishers, 1938.

Browder, Earl. *Trotskyism Against World Peace*. New York: Workers Library Publishers, 1937.

Cannon, Joseph P. "Khrushchev's Report on Stalin's Crimes," *The Militant*, July 2, 1956.

Chamberlin, William Henry. "Khrushchev's War with Stalin's Ghost," *Russian Review* 21, no. 1 (January, 1962): 3–10.

Chamberlin, William Henry. "Stalin: Portrait of a Degenerate," *American Mercury*, February, 1938, 206–18.

Commission of Inquiry into the Charges Made Against Leon Trotsky in the Moscow Trials. *Not Guilty: Report of the Commission of Inquiry into the Charges Made Against Leon Trotsky in the Moscow Trials*. New York: Harper and Brothers, 1938.

Communist Party of the United States of America. *Draft Resolution for the 16th National Convention of the Communist Party, U.S.A.* New York: New Century Publishers, 1956.

Communist Party of the United States of America. National Committee. "Statement," *New York Times*, June 25, 1956.

Conquest, Robert. *The Great Terror: A Reassessment*. 40th anniversary ed. New York: Oxford University Press, 2008.

Correspondence. *Southern Review* 3 (1937–1938): 199–207, 406–16.

Cowley, Malcolm. "Echoes from Moscow: 1937-1938," *Southern Review* 20 (1984): 1–11.

Cowley, Malcolm. "Moscow Trial: 1938," review of *The Case of the Anti-Soviet Bloc of Rights and Trotskyists: A Verbatim Report*, *New Republic*, May 18, 1938, 50–1.
Cowley, Malcolm. "Moscow Trial: II," *New Republic*, May 25, 1938, 79–80.
Cowley, Malcolm. "Record of a Trial," *New Republic*, April 7, 1937, 267–70.
Darcy, Sam. *An Eye-Witness at the Wreckers' Trial*. New York: Workers Library Publishers, 1937.
Davies, Joseph E. *Mission to Moscow: A Record of Confidential Dispatches to the State Department, Official Personal Correspondence, Current Diary and Journal Entries, Including Notes and Comment up to October, 1941*. New York: Simon and Schuster, 1941.
Dennis, Eugene (pseud.) "The U.S.A. and Khrushchev's Special Report," *Daily Worker*, June 18, 1956.
Denny, Harold. "Fear and Anxiety in Russia Make Crisis Worst in Years," *New York Times*, June 24, 1937.
Denny, Harold. "Fury of Soviet Spokesmen Points to Vast Discontent," *New York Times*, June 26, 1937.
Denny, Harold. "Many Doubts Rise in Russia on Guilt of Eight Generals," *New York Times*, June 26, 1937.
Denny, Harold. "Purge Aids Stalin Bar Foes at Polls," *New York Times*, September 15, 1937.
Denny, Harold. "Soviet 'Cleansing' Sweeps Through All Strata of Life," *New York Times*, September 13, 1937.
Denny, Harold. "Stalin's Russia: World Enigma," *New York Times Magazine*, October 8, 1939, SM1–2, SM23.
Dewey, John. *'Truth Is on the March'!* New York: American Committee for the Defense of Leon Trotsky, 1937.
Dulles, Allen W. "The Purge of Stalinism," *Department of State Bulletin*, May 7, 1956, 758–65.
Dulles, John Foster. "The Contest Between Freedom and Despotism," *Department of State Bulletin*, July 2, 1956, 3–7.
Duranty, Walter. "The Riddle of Russia: What Lies Behind Recent Events in the USSR?" *New Republic*, July 14, 1937, 270–2.
Duranty, Walter. "What Next in Russia's Stirring Drama?" *New York Times*, June 27, 1937.
"Editorial Statement on Stalinist Charges Against Leon Trotsky," *Socialist Appeal*, September, 1936, 10–11.
Fast, Howard. *Being Red: A Memoir*. Boston: Houghton Mifflin, 1990.
Fast, Howard. "Man's Hope," *Daily Worker*, June 12, 1956.
Fast, Howard. *The Naked God: The Writer and the Communist Party*. New York: Praeger, 1957.
Fast, Howard. "The Soviet Union," *Daily Worker*, May 17, 1956.
Fischer, Louis. "The Moscow Trials and Confessions," in *Men and Politics: An Autobiography*, 502–31. New York: Duell, Sloan & Pearce, 1941.

Foster, William Z. *Questions and Answers on the Piatakov-Radek Trial.* New York: Workers Library Publishers, 1937.

Gayn, Mark, "Purge of Stalin's Ghost: Inquiry into an Inquest," *The Nation*, April 28, 1956, 354–6.

Getty, J. Arch and Oleg V. Naumov, *The Road to Terror: Stalin and the Self-Destruction of the Bolsheviks, 1932–1939.* New Haven, CT: Yale University Press, 1999.

Hallgren, Mauritz A. *Why I Resigned from the Trotsky Defense Committee.* New York: International Publishers, 1937.

Hammett, Marion and William Smith, "Inside the Trotsky 'Trial,'" *New Masses*, April 27, 1937, 6–11.

Hansen, Joseph. "Stalin's Frame-Up System," *International Socialist Review*, July–August, 1956, 105–11.

Heisler, Francis. *The First Two Moscow Trials—Why?* Pref. by Roy E. Burt. Chicago: Socialist Party USA, 1937.

Henderson, Loy W. *A Question of Trust: The Origins of U.S.-Soviet Diplomatic Relations: The Memoirs of Loy W. Henderson.* Stanford, CA: Hoover Institution Press, 1986.

Hook, Sidney, ed. "Khrushchev on Stalin's Crimes," in *World Communism*, 110–17. Princeton, NJ: Van Nostrand, 1962.

Hook, Sidney. "Liberalism and the Case of Leon Trotsky," *Southern Review* 3 (1937–1938): 267–82.

Hook, Sidney. "Memories of the Moscow Trials," *Commentary* 77, no. 3 (March, 1984): 57–63.

Jerome, V. J. "Bukharin—The Path of a Traitor," *The Communist*, June, 1938, 526–33, 642–51.

Kennan, George F. *Memoirs, 1925–1950.* New York: Pantheon Books, 1967.

Kennan, George F. and William C. Bullitt, Jr., "What Should We Do about Russia," *U.S. News and World Report*, June 29, 1956, 68–77.

Khrushchev, Nikita S. *Report of the Central Committee of the CPSU to the 22nd Congress of the Communist Party of the Soviet Union*, 226–8. New York: Crosscurrent Press, 1956.

Klehr, Harvey, John Earl Haynes, and F. I. Firsov, *The Secret World of American Communism.* New Haven, CT: Yale University Press, 1995.

Klehr, Harvey, John Earl Haynes, and K. M. Anderson, *The Soviet World of American Communism.* New Haven, CT: Yale University Press, 1998.

Kunitz, Joshua. "The End of the Road," *New Masses*, November 10, 1936, 18.

Kunitz, Joshua. "The Moscow Trial," *New Masses*, March 15, 1938, 3–6.

Kunitz, Joshua. "The Moscow Trial—II," *New Masses*, March 23, 1938, 13–16.

Lamont, Corliss "A Message from Corliss Lamont," *New World Review*, November, 1956, 23.

Libbey, James K. "Liberal Journals and the Moscow Trials of 1936–38," *Journalism Quarterly* 52, no. 1 (Spring, 1975): 85–92, 137.

Lyons, Eugene. "Moscow Demonstration Trial," *American Mercury*, January, 1937, 37–45.

Lyons, Eugene. *The Red Decade: The Stalinist Penetration of America*. Indianapolis, IN: Bobbs-Merrill, 1941.

Marxist Internet Archive, https://www.marxists.org.

"Mass Meeting Called by the American Committee for the Defense of Leon Trotsky," manuscript, February 9, 1937.

Meyer, Agnes E. "Significance of the Trotsky Trial," *International Conciliation* 237 (February, 1938): 53–60.

"Moscow Trial Special Supplement," *Socialist Appeal*, December 18, 1937.

"Moscow Trial Special Supplement," *Socialist Appeal*, March 12, 1938.

"The Moscow Trials: A Statement by American Progressives," *New Masses*, May 5, 1938, 19.

"An Open Letter to American Liberals," *Soviet Russia Today*, March, 1937, 14–15.

Preliminary Commission of Inquiry into the Charges Made Against Leon Trotsky in the Moscow Trials. *The Case of Leon Trotsky: Report of Hearings on the Charges Made Against Him in the Moscow Trials*. New York: Merit Publishers, 1968.

"The Purge Goes on," *New Republic*, January 5, 1938, 240–1.

"Reevaluation and Correction," *New World Review*, May, 1956, 50–8.

Reynolds, Dale and Paul Kesaris, eds., *U. S. Military Intelligence Reports: Bi-Weekly Intelligence Summaries, 1928-1938*. Frederick, MD: University Publications of America, 1985. Microfilm.

Salisbury, Harrison E. "Khrushchev Talk on Stalin Bares Details of Rule Based on Terror," *New York Times*, June 5, 1956.

Schuman, Frederick L. "Leon Trotsky: Martyr or Renegade?" *Southern Review* 3 (1937–1938): 51–74.

Shachtman, Max. *Behind the Moscow Trial*. New York: Pioneer Publishers, 1936.

Sinclair, Upton and Eugene Lyons. *The Terror in Russia? Two Views*. New York: Smith, 1938.

Smith, Jessica. "The Khrushchev Report," *New World Review*, June, 1956, 49–53.

Socialist Appeal Institute. "Resolution Adopted on the Moscow Trials," *Socialist Appeal*, March, 1937.

Starobin, Joseph. "1956—A Memoir," *Problems of Communism*, November, 1956, 1, 64–70.

Starobin, Joseph. "The Moscow Trial: Its Meaning and Importance," *Young Communist Review*, April, 1938, 16–19.

Stein, Morris (pseud.). "The End of the Stalin Cult: The Meaning of the 20th Congress," *Fourth International*, Spring, 1956, 39–44, 70–1.

Taylor, S. J. *Stalin's Apologist: The New York Times's Man in Moscow*. New York: Oxford University Press, 1990.

"Ten Years of Soviet Terror," *American Mercury*, November, 1937, 298–306.

"Text of Statement by Communist Party," *New York Times*, June 25, 1956.

Thomas, Norman and Joel Seidman. *Russia—Democracy or Dictatorship?* New York: League for Industrial Democracy, 1939.
U. S. Congress. House. Committee on Un-American Activities. *The Great Pretense: A Symposium on Anti-Stalinism and the 20th Congress of the Soviet Communist Party.* Washington, DC: Government Printing Office, 1956.
U. S. Department of State. *Foreign Relations of the United States: Eastern Europe; Soviet Union; Eastern Mediterranean, 1952-1954, Volume VIII.* Washington, DC: Government Printing Office, 1988, 1048-58.
U. S. Department of State. *Foreign Relations of the United States, 1955-1957: Soviet Union and Eastern Mediterranean.* Washington, DC: Government Printing Office.
U. S. Department of State. Foreign Relations Branch. *Foreign Relations of the United States: Soviet Union, 1933-1939.* Washington, DC: Government Printing Office, 1952.
Weiss, Max. *The Meaning of the XVIth Congress of the Communist Party of the Soviet Union: Report to the National Committee of the Communist Party, USA.* New York: New Century, 1956.
Why Did They "Confess?" A Study of the Radek-Piatakov Trial, introd. by James Burnham. New York: Pioneer Publishers, 1937.
Wolfe, Bertram D. *Khrushchev and Stalin's Ghost.* New York: Praeger, 1956.
Wolfe, Bertram D. "The New Gospel According to Khrushchev," *Foreign Affairs*, July, 1960, 576-87.
Wolfe, Bertram D. "Speech on the Moscow Purge Trials," in *Breaking with Communism: The Intellectual Odyssey of Bertram D. Wolfe*, edited by Robert Hessen, 37-40. Stanford, CA: Hoover Institution Press, 1990.
Wolfe, Bertram D. "The Struggle for the Soviet Succession," *Foreign Affairs*, July, 1953, 548-65.

Index

Adler, Friedrich 46
aftermath of Moscow show trials 131–47, 149–83
   American intellectuals reactions 177–8
   American journalists reactions 159–65
   American liberals reactions 176–7
   American radicals reactions 165–76
   Beria, fall of 142–6
   "Doctors' Plot" 138–9
   Duranty's reporting, discrediting of 179
   Eighteenth Communist Party Congress 131–3
   Khrushchev's second speech 178–9
   Khrushchev's secret speech/destalinization 149–50
   official US reactions 150–9
   radical political parties in United States 137–8
   Stalin's death 140–2
   Stalin's rule, echoes of 179–80
   Trotsky, assassination of 134–7
   Yezhov, purge of 133–4
Algren, Nelson 126
Alknis, Yakov Ivanovich 85
Allied Expeditionary Forces 8
All-Union Society for Cultural Ties Abroad (VOKS) 14, 101
Alsop, Joseph 160
Alsop, Stewart 160
ambassadors 17–18
   Bullitt, William C. 16–18
   Davies, Joseph E. 18
   Troyanovsky, Alexander Antonovich 18
American Committee for the Defense of Leon Trotsky 3, 67, 69–72, 74–8, 125–6
   Commission of Inquiry 71–8
   Hallgren's resignation, responses to 70–1
   mass meetings 71
American communism 8–10. *See also* Communist Party USA
American Jewish Committee 169
American media 13
American Mercury 41, 65, 94, 109
American-Russian Chamber of Commerce 13, 102
American Socialist Party 8, 15, 42, 45–6, 66, 67, 74
American Trotskyists 3, 30, 33, 106, 127, 135, 137–8, 172–6, 182
American Workers Party 10
Amter, Israel 63
Angleton, James 151
Anglo-Saxon judicial system 60
anti-Bolshevik advertisement 6
anti-foreigner campaign 100–6, 117
anti-Semitism 87, 104, 139
anti-trial pamphlets 45–6, 65, 73
anti-Trotsky cartoons 122
Antonov-Ovseyenko, Vladimir 104
Army Trial 83–99
   American journalists reactions 90–6
   American radicals reactions 96–7
   articles on 90–6
   critics of 96–7
   Davies opinions on 88–9
   defendants of 84–5
   Denny's opinion 90–4
   Embassy's interest in 87–90
   Faymonville on 89–90
   judges 85
   official US reactions 86–90
   purge of military 84–6
Arnold, Benedict 64
Arnold, Valentin Volfridovich 51
Article 58, Penal Code of Russian SFSR (1927) 27–8, 35, 111, 144–5
assassinations
   of Kirov, Sergei 27–39, 42, 44, 59, 64
   of Trotsky, Leon 134–7

Assignment in Utopia (Lyons)   25

Bakayev, Ivan Petrovich   35
Baker, Newton D.   64–5
Baldwin, Roger   14
Balticus (pseud.)   95
Barmine, Alexandre   65, 103, 121
Barnes, Joseph   117, 132–3
Basseches, Nicholas   94
Bayer, Theodore   122–3
Beals, Carleton   72–3, 81
Beam, Jacob D.   138–41
Beard, Charles   72
Becker, Carl   72
Being Red (Fast)   178
Belov, I. P.   85
Berenberg, David P.   46
Beria, Lavrenti Pavlovich   24, 131, 139, 141–6
Berman-Yurin, Konon Borisovich   36–7
Bessanov, Sergei Alexeyevich   112
Birchall, Frederick T.   91
Bittelman, Alexander   43, 64, 122
Blanch, Arnold   127
Blitzstein, Marc   126–7
Bliven, Bruce   118
Bloc of Rightists and Trotskyites (1938)   109–28
   American journalists, reactions of   115–20
   American liberals, reactions of   125–7
   American radicals, reactions of   120–5
   charge of medical murder   112
   conduct of trial   110–13
   defendants   111–12
   official US reactions   113–15
Blunden, Godfrey   145
Blyukher, Vasily Konstantinovich   85–6, 95
Boguslavsky, Mikhail Solomonovich   51
Bohlen, Charles E. "Chip"   2, 18, 31, 113, 115, 127–8, 134, 137, 139, 143, 145, 151, 153, 155–6, 183
Bolshevism   12
Booth, John Wilkes   64
Borah, William   15–16
Brailsford, H. N.   95
Bridges, Harry   10–11

Broun, Heywood   77, 79
Browder, Earl   9, 58, 61, 70–2, 75, 80, 121, 125, 138
Budenz, Louis   50, 127, 157
Budyonny, Semyon Mikhailovich   85–6
Bukharin, Nikolai   22, 24, 38, 46, 49, 63, 65, 111, 115–17, 121–2, 136, 165
Bulanov, Pavel Petrovich   112
Bulganin, Nikolai   163
Bullitt, William C.   17–18, 100, 157, 162–3
Burnham, James   65, 124
Burr, Aaron   64, 123

Cannon, James P.   44–5, 67, 74
Cárdenas, Lázaro   61, 69
Carnovksy, Morris   126
"Case of the Anti-Soviet Trotskyite Centre, The" (1937)   49–67
   American Committee for Defense of Leon Trotsky   69–72, 74–9
   American journalists, reactions of   55–60
   American radicals, reactions of   60–7
   conduct of trial   49–52
   defendants   50–1
   Dewey Commission and   72–8
   Duranty on   55–7, 59–60
   official US reactions   52–5
   "Open Letter to American Liberals" on   79–81
   other American reactions to   69–81
   Radek on   55
"Case of the Trotskyite-Zinovievite Terrorist Centre, The" (1936)   35–47
   American journalists, reactions of   39–41
   American radicals, reactions of   42–6
   conduct of trial   35–8
   defendants   36–7, 39–40
   official US reactions   38–9
Caspary, Vera   126
Castle, William R., Jr.   16
Central Intelligence Agency (CIA)   135, 139, 141, 145, 151–2, 155–6
Chamberlin, William Henry   13, 29, 79, 109, 119, 135, 164
Chambers, Whitaker   157

Chase, William J.   51
Chernov, Mikhail Alexandrovich   111
Chicago Daily News   96
Chubar, Vlas   111–12
Clarke, George   142
Cole, G. D. G.   170
Collard, Dudley   62
Comintern   2, 12, 43, 51
Commission of Inquiry. *See* Dewey Commission
Communist, The   10, 43, 63, 76, 122
Communist League of America   10
Communist Party of the Soviet Union   12, 131–3, 143, 149–50, 166
Communist Party USA   3, 8–11, 26–7, 30, 33, 42, 58, 64–5, 69–70, 80, 96, 120, 137–8, 160, 172, 180
  Communist, The   10
  Daily Worker   9–10
  New Masses   9–10
Congressional Digest   16
Congress of Industrial Organizations (CIO)   10
Conquest, Robert   3, 177
contacts between the United States and the Soviet Union   11–14
Coughlin, Charles E.   104
Cowley, Malcolm   59, 74, 79, 81, 118–19, 127, 176–7
Current History   94, 164

Daily Worker   9–10, 15, 29–30, 42, 51, 60–2, 71, 73, 96, 120–1, 125, 134, 137–8, 140, 145–6, 173, 175, 178
Dan, Theodore   45
Darcy, Sam   62–3
Darkness at Noon (Koestler)   131, 136, 165–7, 182–3
David, Fritz   36–7
Davidovna, Olga   36
Davies, Joseph E.   2, 18, 32–3, 52–4, 88–9, 102, 113–14, 117, 136–7, 165–7, 182–3
Death of Stalin (film)   142
Death of Stalin (U. S. Central Intelligence Agency)   141–2
Debs, Eugene V.   8, 24

Denny, Harold   24, 28–9, 33, 39–40, 49, 90–4, 96, 101, 104, 109–10, 116–17, 132–3
destalinization   150
Deutscher, Isaac   141, 145–6, 163
Dewar, Hugo   158
Dewey, John   72, 74–6, 78, 81, 136, 137
Dewey Commission   72–8
Dimitrov, Georgi   43
diplomatic recognition   15–17
diplomatic relations   1–2, 7–8, 19
Dissent   161, 164
"Doctors' Plot"   138–9
Dos Passos, John   14, 80
Draper, Theodore   4
Dreiser, Theodore   14, 79–80
Dreitzer, Ephim Alexandrovich   36
Drobnis, Yakov Naumovich   51
Dulles, Allen   143, 151–2, 155–6
Dulles, John Foster   139, 153
Duncan, Isadora   14
Duranty, Walter   13, 16, 25, 31, 33, 40, 51, 55–9, 109, 115–16, 120, 125, 136, 177–9
Dybenko, Pavel Efimovich   85

Earl Browder, Communist or Tool of Wall Street: Stalin, Trotsky or Lenin (Marlen)   67
Early, Stephen   89
Eastman, Max   65–6, 78, 124, 135
Eddy, Sherwood   62
Eideman, Robert Petrovich   84
Eighteenth Communist Party Congress   131–3
Einstein, Albert   72
Eisenhower, Dwivht D.   140, 160
Ekdokimov, Grigori E.   35–6
Eliot, George Fielding   95
Embassy personnel   18–19
Embassy secretaries   18
Encounter   161
Estonia   11

Farrell, James T.   14, 75, 79, 81
Fast, Howard   177
Faymonville, Philip R.   19, 89–90, 115
Federal Bureau of Investigation (FBI)   135

Feldman, B. M.   85, 87–8
Feuchtwanger, Leon   64
Fighting Worker   66, 71–2, 125
Finerty, John F.   72
first Moscow show trial   35–47
First Two Moscow Trials-Why, The? (Heisler)   67
Fischer, Louis   13, 29, 79, 104, 120, 125, 177
Five Year Plan   22–3, 62–3
Foreign Affairs   60, 95, 132, 135, 141, 144, 165
Foreign Relations of the United States (FRUS)   2
Foreign Relations of the United States: Soviet Union, 1933-1939   32, 106
Forsaken: An American Tragedy in Stalin's Russia, The (Tzouliadis)   102
Forsythe, Robert   76, 126
Foster, William Z.   10, 64, 70, 123, 165
Fourth International   45, 136, 142
Francis, David   7–8
Frank, Waldo   75
Friends of Soviet Russia   10
Friends of the Soviet Union   10
Frunze Red Naval Academy   98

Galler, L. M.   98
Gamarnik, I. B.   86–7, 92–3
Garnett, John   122–3
Gayn, Mark   161
Géraud, André   92
Germany   86, 94, 97, 114, 134
Getty, J. Arch   1, 4
Glavlit, Soviet censorship agency   2, 13
Glotzer, Albert   142
God that Failed, The (Koestler and Crossman)   138
Goldman, Albert   65, 72, 136
Gompers, Samuel   15
Goodman, Paul   134
Gorky, Maxim   112, 114, 116
Gornick, Vivian   171
Goryachev, E. I.   85
Government Political Administration (GPU)   23
Great Depression   14
Great Globe Itself, The (Bullitt)   18

Great Pretense, The (House Un-American Activities Committee)   156
Great Soviet Encyclopedia   86, 159
Great Terror, The (Conquest)   3, 177
Grinko, Grigori Fedorovich   111–12
Grummon, Stuart   104
Gulag   13, 23–4, 150, 158, 165, 181
Gulag Archiipelago, The (Solzhenitzyn)   165

Hallgren, Mauritz A.   70, 79
Hammett, Dashiell   126
Hansen, Joseph   172
Harding, Warren G.   12
Hathaway, Clarence   63–4
Haywood, Harry   171
Hazard, John N.   119–20
Healey, Dorothy   166, 170
Heisler, Francis   67
Hellman, Lillian   79, 126
Henderson, Loy W.   2, 18, 31–3, 37–9, 52, 54, 86–8, 100–3, 105–6, 110, 128, 133, 183
Hicks, Granville   176
History of the Communist Party of the Soviet Union (Bolshevik)   132–3, 170–1
Hitler, Adolph   137–8
Holtzman, Edouard Solomonovich   36
Hook, Sidney   81, 138, 176
Hoover, J. Edgar   54, 69–70, 157, 169
House Un-American Activities Committee (HUAC)   81, 131, 135, 137, 156–7, 178
Howard, Sidney   80
Howe, Irwin   164
Hrasche, Ivan Yosifovich   51
Hughes, Charles Evans   12, 15
Hughes, Langston   14, 126
Hull, Cordell   54, 105–6
Hurst, Fanny   14

Ikramov, Akmal   112
In Defense of Bolshevism   125
Independent Labor League of America   126
Industrial Party (Prompartiya) trial (1930)   25–6
In Search of Soviet Gold (Littlepage)   58

In Stalin's Secret Service (Krivitsky) 96
intellectuals 13–14, 177–8
International Council of Trade and Industrial Unions 10
International Socialist Review 45, 174–6
Intourist 101
I Stake My Life (Trotsky) 71
Ivanov, Vladimir Ivanovich 112
Izvestia 111

Journal of Slavic Military Studies 98

Kaganovich, Lazar 29, 35
Kalinin, Mikhail 16–17
Kamenev, Lev Borisovich 21–2, 29–30, 35–7
Karakhan, Leo 103
Kasharin, I. D. 85
Kazakov, Ignaty Nikolayevich 112
Kellogg, Frank B. 15–16
Kennan, George F. 2, 18, 31–3, 51–4, 102, 106, 128, 138, 154, 156, 162, 182
Kent, Rockwell 79
Kerensky, Alexander 25, 117
Khodjayev, Faizulla 112
Khrushchev, Nikita 3, 31, 86, 146, 155, 159
  Khrushchev and Stalin's Ghost (Wolfe) 170
  Khrushchev Remembers (Khrushchev) 178–9
  second speech 178–9
  secret speech/destalinization 149–50
Khrushchev Report and the Crisis of the American Left (The) (Meyer) 175–6
Kirchwey, Freda 124
Kirk, Alexander, C. 104, 133
Kirov, Sergei Mironovich 27–31, 35–6
Van Kleeck, Mary 79, 119
Klehr, Harvey 4
Kluckhohn, Frank L. 72
Knickerbocker, Hubert R. 93
Knyazev, Ivan Alexandrovich 51
Koch, Howard 137
Kocho-Williams, Alastair 105
Koestler, Arthur 131, 136, 159
Kork, August Ivanovich 85

Kossior, Stanislav 35
Kotkin, Stephen 4, 86, 99, 104–5, 111
Krestinsky, Nikolai 12, 104, 111–13, 120–1
Krivitsky, Walter 45, 95–6, 105, 117–18, 125, 135
Krylenko, Nikolai 24
Kryuchkov, Pyotr P. 112
Kunitz, Joshua 42, 63, 121–2, 127

Labedz, Leopold 158–9
Labor Action 67, 74, 139
Labor Appeal 10
La Follette, Suzanne 70–2, 77, 137
Lamont, Corliss 76–7, 79, 124–5, 127, 170
Lansing, Robert 7
Lardner, Ring, Jr. 79
Larina, Anna 46, 165
Lattimore, Owen 119
Latvia 11–12
League of American Writers 13
Lenin, Vladimir 7–8, 21, 111, 150
Leningrad Centre 29
Leninist League 125
Leonhard, Wolfgang 158
Leon Trotsky: Dupe of the NKVD (Kronenbitter) 135
Lerner, Max 79
Let History Judge (Medvedev) 3–4
Letter of an Old Bolshevik (Nicolaevsky) 46
"Letter to American Workers" 8
Levin, Lev Grigorievich 112
Lewis, Sinclair 14, 71
Lewit, Morris 174–5
Liang, John 175–6
Life 141, 160, 163
Literary Digest 41, 94, 110
Lithuania 12
Littlepage, John. D. 58, 63
Litvinov, Ivy Low 58, 89
Litvinov, Maxim 89, 102, 104
Litvinov Conversations 16
Living Age 94
Livshits, Yakov Abramovich 51
Lovestone, Jay 9, 66, 96–7, 125
Lowenthal, Richard 161
Lurye, Moissei Ilyich 36

Lurye, Nathan Lazarevich 36–7
Lynd, Robert S. 79
Lyons, Eugene 13, 22, 25, 58, 77, 80, 94, 121, 124, 127, 177

McCabe, E. W. R. 90
Macdonald, Dwight 134
McWilliams, Carey 79
Magil, A. B. 62
Malenkov, Georgi 141–4, 149, 154, 159, 162
Mann, Harvey T. 119
Marlen, George 67
Martens, Ludwig C. A. K. 15
Marx, Harpo 14
Marxism 14
Matulevich, I. O. 51, 112
Maximov-Dikovsky, Venyamin Adamovich 112
Medvedev, Roy 3–4
Men and Politics (Fischer) 120
Menshevik trial 26
Mercader, Ramón 134
Metropolitan-Vickers trial (1930) 26
Meyer, Hershel D. 175
Mikoyan, Anastas I. 149–50
Milestone, Lewis 79
Militant, The 172–5
Military political commissars 84, 87, 92
Mission to Moscow (Davies) 18, 32, 114, 131, 136–7
Mission to Moscow (film) 136–7
Modern Inquisition, The (Dewar) 158
Molotov, Vyacheslav 29, 104
Moore, R. Walton 100–1
Morgen Freiheit 42
Moscow Collegium of Defence 49
Moscow Reserve Centre 29
Moscow show trials (1922–35) 24–6
Moscow show trials (1936–38)
  aftermath of 131–47, 149–83
  conduct of 31–2
  errors/excesses relating to 152
  first 35–47
  foundations 26–31
  "Moscow Trials: Statement of Progressives" 3, 126–7
Mosely, Philip E. 164

prelude to 21–33
previous show trials 24–6
second 49–67, 69–81
secret police, role of 23–4
Stalin, rise of 21–3
third 109–28
US reporting on 32–3
Mrachkovsky, Sergei Vitalevich 36
Muralov, Nikolai Ivanovich 51
Murphy, Robert Daniel 153–6
Muste, A. J. 44

Naked God, The (Fast) 178
Nation, The 2, 13, 15, 29, 41, 60, 73, 76, 79, 94, 110, 119, 122–3, 144, 160–1, 176
National Security Council 141, 155
Naumov, Oleg V. 1, 4
Nazi aid 42
Nazi-Soviet Nonaggression Pact (1939) 9, 134
New International 10, 14, 71, 74, 124–5, 145
New Masses 9–10, 14, 42–3, 62–3, 73–4, 76, 96, 121–2, 126, 134–5, 137
New Militant 43–4
New Republic 13, 15, 29, 41, 59, 76, 79, 94–5, 103, 118–19, 123, 125, 141, 145–6, 160–1, 176
Newsweek 58, 65, 93, 103, 117–18
New York Herald-American 61
New York Times 2, 13, 16, 24–5, 28, 36–7, 40, 55–7, 61, 65, 70–3, 77, 84–6, 90–2, 98, 101, 103–5, 109, 115–17, 132–3, 136–8, 140, 143, 145–7, 154–5, 159, 161, 167, 181
Nicolaevsky, Boris 46, 157
Nikolaev, Leonid Vasilievich 27
NKVD (People's Commissariat for Internal Affairs) 23–4, 84
Norkin, Boris Osipovich 51
Not Guilty (American Committee for the Defense of Leon Trotsky) 77
Novack, George 14, 70–1, 78

Official Gazette 98
Olberg, Valentin Pavlovich 36–7
Old Bolsheviks 1, 4, 95, 117, 119, 128, 145

"Open Letter to American Liberals" 79–81
Origins of the Great Purges (Getty)   4
Orjonikidze, Grigori Konstantinovich   35, 52
Orlov, Alexander   141, 143, 160
Orlov, Vladimir   98

Pacific Affairs   119
Page, Edward, Jr.   106
"Parallel Centre" trial. *See* "Case of the Anti-Soviet Trotskyite Centre, The" (1937)
Pares, Bernard   94
Parker, Dorothy   79, 126
Parker, Ralph   168–70
Partisan Review   14, 127, 134, 136
People's Commissariat for Agriculture   111
People's Commissariat for Finance   111
People's Commissariat for Foreign Affairs   101–3
People's Commissariat for Foreign Trade   111
Pickel, Richard Vitoldovich   36
Pletnev, Dmitri Dmitrievich   112, 114
Political Affairs   170
political police   109, 132
Ponomorev, Boris Nikolayevich   123
Pope, Arthur Upham   136
Portraits and Pamphlets (Radek)   50
Post, Marjorie Merriweather   88
Postyshev, Pavel P.   35
Pravda   87, 93, 111, 120, 138, 143, 167
Primakov, V. M.   85
Pritt, D. N.   43
Problems of Communism   157–9, 171
Pruette, Lorine   73
purges   1–5
Pushin, Gavril Yefremovich   51
Putin, Vladimir   180
Putna, Vitovka Kazimirovich   84
Pyatakov, Georgi ("Yuri")   24, 38, 50–1, 55–7

Question of Trust, A (Henderson)   39, 88

Radek, Karl   17, 24, 38, 49–50, 52–3, 55, 58, 62–3, 73

radical political parties in United States   8–11, 137–8
Radin, Max   60
Rahv, Philip   127
Rakovsky, Khristian   42, 65, 111, 121
Rataichak, Stanislav Antonovich   51
Rayfield, Donald   99
Recht, Charles   62
Red Army   83–99
Red Decade, The (Lyons)   77, 127
Red International of Labor Unions (Profintern)   10
Red International of Trade Unions   12
Red Scare   11
Reed, John   8
Reingold, Isak I.   36
Religion   12
Reston, James   162
Reuther, Walter   10
Revolutionary Workers League   45
Riddell, William Renwick   60
Riga   12
Riutin, Martemian   22
Riutin Platform (1932)   22–3
Rivera, Diego   69–70
Road, The (Spiro)   67
Road to Terror, The (Getty and Naumov)   4
Roberts, Dick   176
Robeson, Paul   14
Robinson-Rubens case   105–6
Rodell, Fred   59
Romm, Vladimir   55, 57–8, 65, 73
Roosevelt, Franklin D.   2, 16–17, 134
Roots of American Communism, The (Draper)   4
Rosenberg, Ethel   138
Rosenberg, Julius   138
Rosengoltz, Arkady P.   105, 111
Rossi, Sergio A.   171–2
Ruehle, Otto   72
Russian Progressive Political Committee   28
Russian Review   164–5
Russian Revolution   8
Rychkov, N. M.   51
Rykov, Alexei   23, 38, 56, 65, 111, 116–17, 121, 172

Salisbury, Harrison E.   145, 149–51, 154, 159, 161
samokritika (public self-criticism)   1, 22, 32, 36, 167, 177
Saturday Evening Post   58, 95–6, 117–18, 160, 163
Saturday Review   121
Scheffer, Paul   94, 119
Scherbukov, Alexander   138
Schuman, Frederick L.   80
Schwartz, Harry   162
secret police, Stalin's   23–4
secret speech   149–50
Sedov, Lev   3, 37, 51–2, 134
Serebryakov, Leonid Petrovich   51, 58
Serge, Victor   104, 134
Shachtman, Max   44–5, 71, 123, 126, 136
Shakhty trial for economic crimes (1928)   25
Shaplen, Joseph   57
Shaposhnikov, Boris Mikhailovich   85
Sharangovich, Vasily Fomich   112
Shaw, Irwin   126
Shcherbakov, Alexander   138–9
Shestov, Alexei Alexandrovich   51
Sinclair, Upton   121, 124
Sivkov, A. K.   98
skepticism   37–40
Smirnov, Ivan Nikitich   36–8
Smith, Jessica   168
Smith Act (1943)   137–8
Socialist Appeal   10, 44–5, 65, 75–6, 97–8, 103–5, 123–7, 132, 134
Socialist Appeal Institute   65
Socialist Call   45–6
Socialist Labor Party   8
Socialist Revolutionaries   24
Socialist Workers Party (SWP)   3, 10, 123–4, 126, 138, 172
Sokolnikov, Grigori   50
Solzhenitsyn, Alexander   165
Southern Review   80–1
Soviet Crimes and Khrushchev's Confessions   163
Soviet Navy purges   97–9
Soviet Russia Pictorial   10, 15
Soviet Russia Today   26, 43, 64, 75, 79, 96, 122–3, 126–7
Soviet Union
  recognition of   15–17
  US ambassadors to   17–18
Soviet Union: Facts, Descriptions, Statistics, The   23
Spiro, George   67
Staklo, Vadim A.   51
Stalin, Joseph   3–4, 12, 35–7, 50, 84, 86, 88, 93–6, 99, 109, 111, 125, 131–3, 136, 141, 150, 160, 165–6, 168
  American press on   22–3
  anti-German stance   92
  anti-Semitism   55, 87, 104, 139
  death   140–2
  Five Year Plan   22–3
  Party rolls, purging of   22–3
  rise of   21–3
  rule, echoes of   179–80
  secret police   23–4
  state institutions, purging of   22–3
  versus Trotsky philosophies   21–2
Stalin in Power (Tucker)   4
Stalinism Betrays the Spanish Revolution   45
Stalin's Frame-Up System and the Moscow Trials   73
Stalin's Hangmen (Rayfield)   99
Starobin, Joseph   122
Stewart, David Ogden   79
Stewart, Maxwell   79, 110
Stolberg, Benjamin   72, 76
Stroilov, Mikhail Stepanovich   51
Strong, Anna Louise   13, 43, 79, 127, 136
Sulzberger, C. I.   143
Sutton, John   122

Tallinn   12
Ten Days That Shook the World (Reed)   8
Ter-Vaganyan, Vagarshak Arutyunovich   36
third Moscow show trial. *See* Bloc of Rightists and Trotskyites (1938)
Thomas, Norman   30, 69, 79, 126
Thompson, Dorothy   14
Time magazine   29, 40, 45, 58, 93, 103, 117–18, 159, 162
Tobenkin, Elias   91

Tomsky, Mikhail Pavlovich   3, 52
Towster, Julian   164
trade   13
Trade Union Education League   10
Tresca, Carlo   72, 78
Trotsky, Leon   2–3, 7, 21–2, 24, 27, 30,
    36–7, 42–4, 49–67, 80, 83,
    123–5, 134–7, 160
  American Committee for the Defense
    of   69–72
  assassination of   134–7
  asylum   69–72
  CIA analysis of   135
  Dewey Commission and   72–8
  as disloyal to Lenin   133
  FBI investigation on   135
  life in Mexico   72
Trotskyism   10–11, 18, 27, 30,
    42–4, 56–7, 61, 74, 77, 79,
    91, 109, 122–3, 125, 142,
    162, 173
Trotskyist Fourth International   10
Trotsky Opposition, The   9
Troyanovsky, Alexander Antonovich
    18, 54, 57, 61, 71, 74, 76–8,
    91–3, 100–1, 103, 106, 117,
    119, 125
*Truth about the Moscow Frame-Up Trials,
    The*   66–7
Truth about the Moscow Trials, The   65
Tucker, Robert C.   4
Tukhachevsky, Mikhail   83–4, 86,
    88, 91, 94–5, 114, 154
Turok, Yosif Dmitrievich   51
Twentieth Communist Party
    Congress   149–50, 166
Tzouliadis, Tim   102

Uborevich, Jeronim Petrovich   85
Uldricks, Terry J.   104
Ulrikh, Vasily Vasilyevich   31, 51, 83,
    112, 115
Unger, Alexander   43
United States. Congress   16, 141, 169
United States. Information Agency   151
*United States Military Intelligence
    Reports*   49–50
United States. Office of Naval
    Intelligence   98

United States–Soviet Union relations
    (1917–33)   1, 7–19
  ambassadors   17–18
  American communism   8–11
  American Trotskyism   8–11
  contacts   11–14
  diplomatic recognition   15–17
  diplomatic relations   1–2, 7–8, 19
  embassy personnel   18–19
  "Red Scare"   11
U. S. News and World Report   160, 162–3

Vansler, Joseph   97, 103–4, 124
Viktorov, M. V.   98
Villard, Oswald Garrison   29, 75, 94–5,
    119, 122
VOKS   14, 101
Voroshilov, Klementi   35, 83–4, 93, 98–9,
    162, 178
Vyshinsky, Andrey   25–6, 37, 49–50,
    52–6, 112–13, 115–16, 122, 141,
    159, 172

Walmsley, Walter Newbold, Jr.   153, 155
Walsh, Edmund   15
Warner, Jack L.   137
Weisner, Frank C.   154
Weiss, Murray   175
Weiss, Myra Tanner   172–3
Welles, Sumner   88–9
Werth, Alexander   145
West, Nathaniel   79
Western Worker   42
Why Did They Confess?   65
"Why They Shot Tukhachevsky"
    (Davies)   89
Williams, William Carlos   14
Wilson, Edmund   75
Wilson, Woodrow   8, 64
Wisner, Frank C.   154
Witchcraft Trial in Moscow, The   46
Wohl, Paul   163
Wolfe, Bertram D.   75, 126, 141
Workers Age   43, 66
Workers League for a Revolutionary
    Party   178–9
Workers Party of the United States   10
Wright, Frank Lloyd   14
Wright, John G. (pseud.)   97, 103–4, 124

Wright, Richard 177

Yagoda, Genrikh Grigorievich 24, 38, 111–12, 115–17, 120, 145–6, 167–8
Yakir, Iona Emanuilovich 85, 87–8
Yaroslavsky, Emilian 123
Yegorov, Alexander 85, 94
Yevlev, B. I. 112
Yezhov, Nikolai Ivanovich 24, 38, 49, 84, 93–4, 121
    ill health 134
    purge of 131–4
Yezhovshchena 49
Young Communist Review 122

Zelensky, Isaac Abramovich 112
Zhdanov, Andrei A. 35, 138–9
Zhukov, Georgi 164
Zinoviev, Grigori (Yuri) 21–2, 24, 29–30, 35–8, 84
Zubarev, Prokopy Timofeyevich 112

www.ingramcontent.com/pod-product-compliance
Lightning Source LLC
Chambersburg PA
CBHW071810300426
44116CB00009B/1267